Pir-o-Murshid Inayat Khan

1882-1927

COMPLETE WORKS

OF

PIR-O-MURSHID

HAZRAT INAYAT KHAN

ORIGINAL TEXTS: LECTURES ON SUFISM

1922 II: September-December

Source Edition

OMEGA PUBLICATIONS
NEW LEBANON

Previous volumes in this series:

Biography of Pir-o-Murshid Inayat Khan (1979)

Complete Works of Pir-o-Murshid Hazrat Inayat Khan, Original Texts:

Sayings, Part I (*Gayan, Vadan, Nirtan*, 1982, revised edition 1989)

Sayings, Part II (*Bowl of Saki*, *Aphorisms*, unpublished sayings, etc., 1982, rev. ed. 1989)

Lectures on Sufism:

1922 I: January-August (1990)

1923 I: January-June (1989)

1923 II: July-December (1988)

Edited by Mrs. Munira van Voorst van Beest and Prof. Sharif Graham; published by Omega Publications, 256 Darrow Road, New Lebanon NY 12125-2615, USA, in collaboration with the Nekbakht Foundation.

ISBN 0-930872-63-0

DEDICATION

This volume is dedicated to

Munira van Voorst van Beest

the founding editor of these *Complete Works*

of Pir-o-Murshid Hazrat Inayat Khan.

In fulfilling her commission from Sakina Furnée,

the original Keeper of the Biographical Department,

she designed the way of working on and presenting

these teachings of Pir-o-Murshid Inayat Khan.

Her overwhelming, untiring dedication to her task

serves as an inspiration to all of us who continue her work.

Before her passing in September of 1990, she completed

a substantial part of the basic work on the present volume.

Table of Contents

SUPPLEMENT: 1923

ACKNOWLEDGEMENTS

This volume has been produced by a collaborative effort extending across several years. Much of the most basic work, including all the transcribing from Sakina Furnée's shorthand into regular written English, was done by Munira van Voorst van Beest before she passed away in September of 1990. She also did a great deal of the comparison work with the manuscripts, and so many, perhaps most, of the footnotes in this volume were prepared by her. Please see the Dedication on the page iii for some indication of the debt which all users of these *Complete Works* owe to the founding editor.

Another valued collaborator, Dr. M. C. Rubab Monna, has also passed on during the preparation of this volume. She was part of the Editorial Committee for these volumes, and it was at her suggestion that a full listing and description of the documents appears with each lecture. She also often helped with the various terms appearing in the lectures, a special interest of hers (she prepared the *Short Dictionary of the Foreign Words in Hazrat Inayat Khan's Teaching*, Alkmaar, The Netherlands, 1991). Her visits to Suresnes and her lively interest in all aspects of the work will be sorely missed.

Shaikh-al-Mashaikh Mahmood Mahboob Khan, also of the Editorial Committee, has continued to offer most valuable advice and to check many linguistic and factual matters. He has especially contributed to the accuracy of the Preface, Glossary and List. His wife Harunnisa kindly checked the Indian words.

J. M. Kore Salvato has been involved with this volume from the outset, performing all the various editorial functions. Her tasks have ranged from the actual preparation of the texts to repeated proofreadings. Her expertise and care have greatly enhanced the presentation and saved us from many errors.

A few other Sufi friends have proven most helpful in the proofreading, a very exacting task for a book of this kind. The Board of the Nekbakht Stichting has provided the staff members with the necessary financial support to carry on this work, and also with the equally necessary moral support.

PREFACE

This volume continues the publication of the lectures of Pir-o-Murshid Inayat Khan (1882-1927), a renowned musician and Sufi teacher from India who came to the West in 1910. The first two volumes in this series, both published in 1982, and republished in revised editions in 1989, presented the sayings of Pir-o-Murshid Inayat Khan. The next two volumes, published in 1988 and 1989, contained the lectures from 1923. The most recently published volume (1990) presented the lectures from the first part of 1922, from January through August. The present volume begins in September of 1922 and continues through the end of the year. It also presents several lectures from 1923 which were not included in the volumes for that year because the dates of the lectures were not yet known when those volumes were published.

Background Information on Lectures

The period from September to December of 1922 divides itself into four distinct periods based on the geographical location of the lectures: the Netherlands, England, Switzerland, and Paris. The dates and locations are summarized below and are also indicated with each lecture:

Itinerary, September to December 1922

1-13 September	Lectures in Katwijk, the Netherlands
5-16 October	Lectures in London, Brighton, and Southampton, England
16-25 November	Lectures in Basel, Zürich, Lausanne, Montreux, Clarens, Vevey, and Morges, Switzerland
1-18 December	Lectures in Paris, France

Late in August of 1922, Pir-o-Murshid Inayat Khan completed the first Summer School held around his new family home in Suresnes, France, a near western suburb of Paris (but still in those days, unlike today, clearly outside the city). Among those in attendance at the Summer School were a number of Dutch *mureeds*, including the Baron and Baroness van Tuyll van Serooskerken (known by their Sufi names, Sirdar and Saida), who had also been among the very small group present the previous summer in Wissous, southwest of Paris. The van Tuylls especially wanted Pir-o-Murshid Inayat Khan to offer a series of lectures in the Netherlands, and to that end put their seaside villa in Katwijk-aan-Zee at his disposal. Therefore, after a week with his family in Suresnes, Pir-o-Murshid Inayat Khan began a lecture series in Katwijk on Friday, September 1.

In the December issue of *Sufism*, the English Sufi journal of that time, Sophia Saintsbury Green, the editor, gave an account of the Dutch Summer School, and especially described the atmosphere which pervaded the long twilight sessions at which the series of lectures on "The Inner Life" was given. Each lecture was preceded by a silence of half an hour. Exceptionally, Pir-o-Murshid Inayat Khan did not entertain questions after these lectures.

In actuality, there were two series of lectures. Every afternoon Pir-o-Murshid Inayat Khan would speak on "The Problem of the Day", and every evening he would speak on "The Inner Life". Sirdar van Tuyll had arranged for two *mureeds* who knew shorthand to come from England to take down the lectures: Marya Khushi Cushing, originally from New York, and Edgar Shabaz Mitchell from Southampton, England. According to Saida van Tuyll's recollection many years later[1] it was Mrs. Cushing who took down the series "The Inner Life" and Mr. Mitchell who took down "The Problem of the Day" (but not beginning until September 4). Earlier records only indicate "a professional stenographer" taking down "The Inner Life".

The records for "The Inner Life" as taken down, probably in shorthand, seem not to have been preserved at all. Very quickly after the lectures, transcriptions were made and work must have begun at once on preparing a book, since *The Inner Life* appeared for sale in December of the same year. The book was issued from the Sufi Book Depot, which was actually in Southampton, although London is listed as the place of publication. It must, therefore, have been some of the English *mureeds*, under the supervision of Nargis Dowland, who prepared the book for publication. The shorthand manuscripts and transcriptions were probably used in the preparation of the book, and afterwards no one thought to preserve them or deposit them with the Biographical

1. Two letters to this effect from Saida van Tuyll, dated 20 January and 1 September 1964 respectively, are cited in Wil van Beek, *Hazrat Inayat Khan* (New York, 1983), 241.

Department archive. In any case, we have here the very exceptional instance where the first publication is the oldest and best manuscript, and our few footnotes point only to annotations made in copies of the book.

The lectures on "The Problem of the Day", on the other hand, have never been published or even privately circulated. Pir-o-Murshid Inayat Khan used that phrase as a lecture title quite often, so that a number of talks called "The Problem of the Day" have been published in various places; however, none of those is from the present series, which has remained in manuscript all these years. Knowing that Pir-o-Murshid Inayat Khan often gave different lectures with the same title, people naturally imagine that they must have much the same content. However, a careful comparison reveals that often there is very little overlap in material, even when two lectures with the same title are given in different places only a few days apart. The present series on "The Problem of the Day" is by far the most extensive ever given by Pir-o-Murshid Inayat Khan. It seems curious that "The Inner Life" was published so quickly, while "The Problem of the Day" has never before been published at all.

When the two weeks in the Netherlands were completed, Pir-o-Murshid Inayat Khan may have first returned to France for a period, or he may have gone directly to England, where he had lived from 1914 to 1919, and where the largest number of his followers still remained. He received, as always, a most warm welcome from the English *mureeds*, who were still hardly able to accept that he had moved to the Continent. Early in October he began a series of lectures in London, gave a special class to *mureeds* in Brighton, and perhaps gave a lecture in Southampton as well. He then returned to France, to his home, and during this time (mid-October to early November), as far as we know, no lectures were given.

His next journey was to the recently established Headquarters of the Sufi activities in Geneva. He remained in Geneva during the first half of the month, undoubtedly discussing the administration of the organization with its officers, the Executive Supervisor (Mr. E. de Cruzat Zanetti) and the General Secretary (Talewar Dussaq), assisted by his sister, the Countess Pieri, who the next year was appointed the General Treasurer. It was probably during this period that Pir-o-Murshid Inayat Khan continued his dictation of Indian musical lessons to Lakmé van Hogendorp, the daughter of the Baroness Mahtab van Hogendorp, who lived in Switzerland and was helping to organize the Headquarters. Perhaps Lakmé, still in her teens at this time, was practising her skills at writing from dictation, but she must have had some special interest in Indian music to be chosen for this task. Her English was excellent; however, for the many musical terms in various Eastern languages mentioned by Pir-o-Murshid Inayat Khan, she could only make a phonetic approximation, leaving a considerable puzzle to the present editors to decipher the terms and identify them for the Glossary.

In the second half of November, Pir-o-Murshid Inayat Khan made a lecture tour of Switzerland, beginning in Basel and Zürich. When lectures were given in places where English was not the common language, the practice was to translate the lecture sentence by sentence into the local language, in this case German. Probably the translation was done by Sherifa Goodenough, whose mother was Austrian and who was entirely fluent in German (and several other languages as well). It is in her typescript that the first lecture has come down to us. For both of these lectures we have the simultaneous German translation, but we have no report of the words as spoken in English. The established policy in such cases for this series is to give the original in whatever language it has come down to us, and not to make a new translation. When a contemporaneous retranslation back into English exists, as with one of these lectures, we present that also.

After the lectures in Switzerland's two largest cities, Pir-o-Murshid Inayat Khan made a tour of several places along the shore of Lake Geneva. A professional stenographer was hired to take these lectures down, and they exist in the archive files in carefully typed versions on fine paper. Unfortunately, the stenographer was not accustomed to Pir-o-Murshid Inayat Khan's Indian accent in English (although it was less pronounced by this time) and therefore took some things down incorrectly. For example, Pir-o-Murshid Inayat Khan almost always began his lectures by addressing his audience "Beloved Ones of God", and then giving the subject of the lecture. The stenographer (who may not have been a native speaker of English) thought he heard "In the reverence of God" and wrote that. This phrase having established itself in his mind, he wrote it also at the beginning of the other three lectures he reported. Sherifa Goodenough, seeing this error and perhaps others when she received the typed transcripts, wrote in her bold hand across the top of each lecture "Very Incomplete". Since she was the person commissioned by Pir-o-Murshid Inayat Khan to prepare his lectures for distribution to Sufi Centres or for publication in book form, her authority in these matters was very considerable. In fact, her designation of the transcripts as "Very Incomplete" and her own decision not to use them has resulted in their remaining unpublished until now. However, a careful reading and comparison to other lectures on similar topics indicates that the reports are in fact substantially accurate and complete, though not so reliable as those taken down by those more familiar with Pir-o-Murshid Inayat Khan's way of speaking. Fortunately, for the last lecture in the series, given in Morges on November 25th, Sakina Furnée was present to take down the lecture accurately in shorthand.

A few days later Pir-o-Murshid Inayat Khan returned to Suresnes, and during the first three weeks of December he gave an unusually large number of public lectures and special classes for *mureeds*. Many of these concern art, poetry, and music, perhaps subjects of special interest to the French audience.

At the end of the sequence for 1922 we have also included several talks which we believe to have been given in that year, but for which no specific date is known. Generally, Pir-o-Murshid Inayat Khan's lectures can be quite accurately dated. In many cases the date is included in the shorthand record itself, but even when it is not, a precise date often appears on one or more of the typed versions of the lecture. Very rarely these dates are inaccurate, but for the most part they correspond with all other known information about the lecture. Even when there is no date on any version, a fairly accurate date can sometimes be determined from where the lecture is recorded in the shorthand notebooks of Sakina Furnée, the most extensive source for our basic texts. If dates are known for the preceding and following lectures, we clearly have a range of possible dates. This can also sometimes be corroborated with what is known about Pir-o-Murshid Inayat Khan's whereabouts on a particular date, as his travel itinerary has been preserved for some periods.

Finally, in a supplement at the end of the lectures, we have included nine lectures from 1923. The two volumes for 1923 were published in 1989. Since that time, intensive work on the short lectures which were made into the *Gatha* series (please see Preface to 1922 I, pp. xvi-xx), many of which were given in 1922, has revealed that eight previously undated lessons were actually given in 1923, three in February and five in September. In addition, a long lecture given in Florence on the last day of October in 1923 had for many years been erroneously placed in a file for 1922, which was discovered only in the course of the work on the present volume. In the future, when the volumes for 1923 require reprinting, these lectures will be placed in their proper chronological order; for the moment, they appear in this supplement and are indexed along with the material for 1922.

Notes to Lectures

For each lecture, the basic printed text is the one closest to the actual words of Pir-o-Murshid Inayat Khan. Its origin is indicated in the upper right-hand corner. All differences from this earliest text in other early documents, up to and including first publication (if any), are indicated in the notes. An abbreviated title is assigned to each document. A complete list of the documents compared, along with specific information about each document for that particular lecture, appears before the beginning of the notes. Where one or more of the listed documents is not cited in the notes, this indicates a text identical to the basic text.

Over the course of years, different typewritten copies and stencils were prepared at International Headquarters in Geneva for distribution among *mureed*s. In many cases, the earliest Headquarters' stencils (in earlier years called "cyclostyled copies") show very extensive editing, and often, therefore, were considered by Sakina Furnée to be incorrect; at the same time, however, chronologically these old stencils were nearer to the original than later Headquarters' stencils, and sometimes they show originally spoken words which were lost in later edited copies of the lecture. However, on the whole, later stencils show a return to something closer to the original reporting, apparently reflecting an editorial decision by Sherifa Goodenough, who was primarily responsible for these documents. Many Headquarters' stencils are found in the archives, on which Sakina Furnée noted the differences as compared to her shorthand reporting, writing the original words in the margin. In certain cases, however, she did not write the original word(s) in the margin, apparently indicating that she accepted the change.

There exists an extensive *errata* list on which Sirdar van Tuyll and Sakina Furnée exchanged comments as to the revisions which had been made in the texts, dating from the 1950s. Although this list does not cover all the lectures, it is mentioned in the notes, since the work they were doing then is so similar to, and therefore entirely relevant to, the work of comparison done in the preparation of these books. In many instances Sirdar suggested accepting editorial changes made by Sherifa Goodenough, while Sakina's choices in the revision of the text always inclined toward what was said by the Pir-o-Murshid, which to her was more important than the correctness or refinement of the English, in keeping with Pir-o-Murshid Inayat Khan's often expressed wish that his words be preserved as exactly as possible (please see Preface to 1922 I, pp. xiv-xv).

The footnote numbers in the text have been repeated in the following instances:

1. When the note refers to a lengthy set of words rather than just a few, the note number appears both at the beginning and the end;
2. When the same information applies to more than one place.

Table of Contents

In the Table of Contents the lectures have been listed under the title which appears on the basic text. Many lectures bear the same title; in some cases, in order to distinguish them, the first few words have been added in quotation marks following the title. In the absence of any title, a selection from the first few words of the lecture appears in quotation marks.

When lectures were given without any title, one was usually added later by those using the lecture in their Sufi Centres. In several cases the title was changed at International Headquarters in documents prepared for use in the Centres, and the chapter headings in the books in which the lectures were published also show changes.

As far as books and classified series of lectures are concerned, these later titles can be found by consulting Appendix A.

Appendix A

Appendix A is designed to show what a particular lecture may have become later on. One use, of course, was as a chapter for a book. Another very common use was as a lesson to be distributed to Sufi Centres, which included several different series for different purposes. The *Gatha*s and the *Githa*s were texts for *mureed*s of particular levels of initiation. The various *Gatheka* series were for a more general use. Those in possession of the books or copies of the lessons will be able to use this appendix to discover the source of the material, and then to compare the edited versions with the original lectures.

Explanation of Abbreviations

This list, which follows this preface, offers the general meaning of each abbreviation. The list of documents preceding the notes for each lecture indicates a more specific meaning of the abbreviation for that particular lecture. For information about the *mureeds* who took down or later edited the lectures, please refer to the List of Persons, etc.

Glossary

Even though explanations of foreign terms are generally given only in the glossary, in some instances an immediate understanding of a term is so essential to understanding the statement that a brief explanation has been included in the notes. The spelling of Indian words in the series of lessons on Indian music published in this volume does not always correspond to that in Lakmé van Hogendorp's handwritten copy—taken down from dictation as she heard the words, which often were terms unknown to her—but had to be corrected in order to make sense. This was done with the help of some standard works on Indian music: *The Music and Musical Instruments of Southern India and the Deccan* by C. R. Day (1891); *The Music of Hindostan* by A. H. Fox Strangways (1914); *The Music of India* by H. A. Popley (1966); *A Treatise on Ancient Hindu Music* by Arun Bhattacharya (1978); *Music in India: The Classical Traditions* by Bonnie C. Wade (1979); *The Life of Music in North India* by Daniel M. Neuman (1980); *Dhrupada* by Indurama Srivastava (1980); and *Hindustani Music in the 20th Century* by Wim van der Meer (1980). Most of the problematic terms were submitted to an expert on the matter, Prof. R.C. Mehta, editor of the *Journal of the Indian Musicological Society*, published in Baroda, India, who was found willing to check these terms and to give an explanation of each term or to correct the explanation already given. Further helpful suggestions were offered by Prof. Richard Eaton and Mr. Brian Silver. In this way it has been possible to reconstruct from apparently incomprehensible words what was most likely said by Pir-o-Murshid Inayat Khan.

List of Persons, Places and Works

Of the names of deities, persons, peoples, geographical locations, works, etc., mentioned in the lectures in this volume, a short explanation has been given following the Glossary. In many cases, these might appear to be so well known or readily available in reference works that no explanation is required. However, these *Complete Works* are intended for wide distribution to preserve the precise contents of the teachings of Pir-o-Murshid Inayat Khan wherever there may be an interest in them. In some cases this may be far from seemingly readily available reference works, so an attempt has been made to make these volumes as complete in themselves as reasonably possible.

Index

The extensive analytical index at the end of the book may prove useful for private study, for preparing lectures, as well as for scholarly purposes in general. The intent has been to be inclusive and to provide some idea of the content in the reference.

The Illustration of Documents which has appeared as an appendix in each of the previously published volumes in this series has been omitted in the present volume because all the relevant documents have already been illustrated in other volumes.

In conclusion, the objects of this book, and indeed of the whole series, may be summed up as threefold:

— to safeguard for posterity the teachings of Pir-o-Murshid Inayat Khan gathered in the Biographical Department;
— to serve as the basis of future publications and translations;
— to make the earliest source materials of Pir-o-Murshid Inayat Khan's words available to scholars, researchers, students, and the many persons interested today in finding authentic texts of Sufi spiritual teachings.

Donald A. Sharif Graham
Staff Member of the Foundation
Nekbakht Stichting

34, rue de la Tuilerie
92150 Suresnes, France

1995

EXPLANATION OF ABBREVIATIONS

Note: For further information about the persons mentioned here, please see the List of Persons, Places, and Works, p. 391

bk. - book, first edition of the works of Pir-o-Murshid Inayat Khan as edited by Sherifa Goodenough or others.

c. - copied text, copy

corr. - corrected, correction(s).

e.t. - an early typewritten copy made from Sakina Furnée's shorthand transcription, not typewritten by her, and showing some alterations and inaccuracies. Sometimes these copies were corrected by Sakina after comparison with her shorthand reporting. In some cases such an early typewritten copy was used by Sherifa Goodenough for an initial preparation of the text to be used for multiplication and/or publication.

Fm. - Mrs. Fazal Mai Egeling, a Dutch mureed, or an annotation in her handwriting.

Gd. - Miss Sherifa Goodenough, an early English mureed and secretary and editor to Pir-o-Murshid Inayat Khan, or a document prepared by her.

Gr. - Miss Sophia Saintsbury Green, an early English mureed, or a document in her handwriting.

Gru. - Dr. O. C. Gruner, an English mureed and early editor for Pir-o-Murshid Inayat Khan, or a document prepared by him.

h. - handwritten, or a document in handwriting.

Hl. - Mlle C. Hulot, a French mureed living in Paris, or her reporting of a simultaneous French translation, sentence by sentence, while the lecture was being given.

Hq. - International Headquarters, Geneva, Switzerland, which was the administrative and coordinative centre for the different sections of the Sufi Order, renamed "Sufi Movement" in October 1923.

hwr. - handwriting, handwritten.

Kf. - Kefayat Gladys I. LLoyd, an English mureed, or a document prepared by her..

Kr. - Miss A. Kafia Kerdijk, an early Dutch mureed, or a document prepared by her.

l. - later, especially applying to typescripts (l.tp.) from the period after 1940.

Lf. - Mlle H. Lefèbvre, an early French mureed living in Paris, or her reporting of a simultaneous French translation, sentence by sentence, while the lecture was given, or a handwritten copy made by her from this text.

lh. - longhand.

Lm. - Lakmé van Hogendorp. Pir-o-Murshid Inayat Khan dictated two series of lessons on Indian music to her in Switzerland.

L.M. - *Le Message*, a French bulletin published in the 1930s.

Mc. - Mrs. Marya Khushi Cushing, an American mureed from New York who took down some lectures of Pir-o-Murshid Inayat Khan in shorthand, or a document prepared by her.

Ng. - Miss Nargis Dowland, an early mureed from Southampton, England, or a document prepared by her.

o.t. - an old typescript, probably made from the original reporting during Pir-o-Murshid Inayat Khan's lifetime.

p. - preparation, referring to manuscripts made as part of the editing process in preparation for private distribution or printing in a book.

q.a. - the question(s) and answer(s) after a lecture, or on another occasion, or, in a few instances, as a special "question class".

r. - report, or reporting, a word used here to mean an exact record of what Pir-o-Murshid Inayat Khan said on a particular occasion.

S. - *The Sufi*, a journal printed in England beginning in 1934.

Sf. - *Sufism*, a quarterly journal published in England from 1921 through 1924, edited by Miss Sophia E. M. Saintsbury Green

sh. - shorthand, shorthand reporting.

Sk. - Sakina Furnée, one of Pir-o-Murshid Inayat Khan's secretaries, who from 1922 on took down most of his lectures in shorthand, or a document prepared by her.

S.Q. - *The Sufi Quarterly*, a journal published in Geneva from 1925 through 1933, edited by Ronald A. L. Mumtaz Armstrong.

Sr. - Sirdar van Tuyll van Serooskerken, a Dutch mureed; or, Sirdar's reportings and copied texts made from annotations taken down by him in longhand during the lectures.

Sr.Sk. - an extensive errata list on which in later years Sakina Furnée and Sirdar van Tuyll exchanged comments in the 1950s and '60s on revisions made in the texts.

st. - stencil, a cyclostyled copy prepared at Headquarters, Geneva, for distribution to Sufi Centres.

S.W. - Miss Salima Wiseman, an English mureed from Southampton, England, or a document in her handwriting.

Sz. - Mr. Edgar Shabaz Mitchell, an English mureed, who took down some lectures in shorthand, or the documents prepared by him.

t., tp.	-	typewritten, typewritten copy, typescript.
tr.	-	transcription; translation.

A typewritten copy made by Mrs. Cushing from her own shorthand reporting of the lecture.

Katwijk, Holland, September 1st, 1922
Afternoon lecture.

The Problem of the Day[1]

The Sufi message has as its main mission to consider the problems of the day and then to direct our activity to do what is necessary in order to bring about better conditions, in which is the fulfillment of our mission.

The life in the world can be divided into five different aspects: the[2] spiritual progress[3], the[2] moral progress[3], the[2] social progress[3], mental[4] progress[3] and physical progress.[3]

[5] Therefore we have to consider the five aspects of life in order to understand the problem of the day clearly. During the periods of the ancient

---

Documents:

Mc. = a typewritten copy made by Mrs. Marya Cushing from her own shorthand reporting:
(Mc.)Gr.: some later editing by Miss Sophia Green
(Mc.)Sr.: some corr. by Sirdar van Tuyll

Sk.tp. = a typewritten copy made in later years from "Mc." under Sakina Furnée's direction, with most of the corr., add., etc. incorporated.

This is the first in a series of lectures given at Katwijk, a seaside village in the Netherlands near Leiden, from 1 to 12 September 1922 in the afternoon, during a Summer School held at the house where Sirdar and Saida van Tuyll, then newly married, were living at that time.

Notes:

1. (Mc.)Gr.: later added the number "1";
Sk.tp.: added "(1)"
2. (Mc.)Gr.: "the" crossed out;
Sk.tp.: "the" omitted
3. (Mc.)Gr.: "progress" crossed out; (Mc.)Sr.: "progress" restored
4. (Mc.)Gr.: "mental" replaced with "intellectual"; (Mc.)Sr.: "intellectual" crossed out and "mental" restored
5. (Mc.)Gr.: added in the margin beside this paragraph: "Introduction"; (Mc.)Sr.: "Introduction" crossed out

civilizations the[6] progress has been made in one direction and,[7] lacking in other directions[8,9] [10]the progress fell down by the lack of balance[10]. But as man has evolved, so his progress has been all-around[11]. No doubt, in the[2] recent times the world has again lost its balance by being too much engrossed in materialism and by becoming too much absorbed in commercialism, and the consequences of this have been the war and the world unrest, which is still existing after what is called peace.

In order to bring about better conditions in the world ~~in order~~ that humanity may progress and have balance, the best thing would be to consider every one of the above-said[12] five subjects[13] pertaining to the[2] life in general.

The Sufi Order[14] is a nucleus formed of brotherhood, not of a Sufi brotherhood, but a human brotherhood. The members of this Order have joined in a group to serve the cause of the world revival for God and humanity. Every member of the Order must therefore realize that their own spiritual development is not sufficient; that it is necessary for everyone in the Order that a part of their time, their activity, their thought and their energy must be devoted to the service of humanity, especially in this direction, of considering the problems of the day.

---

6. (Mc.)Gr.: "the" crossed out;
   Sk.tp.: "the" restored
7. (Mc.)Sr.: the comma replaced with "has been";
   Sk.tp.: "has been" instead of a comma
8. (Mc.)Gr.: "others" instead of "other directions"; (Mc.)Sr.: "other directions" restored
9. (Mc.)Sr.: "therefore" added;
   Sk.tp.: "therefore" added
10. (Mc.)Gr.: rewritten to read: "it failed from want of balance";
    (Mc.)Sr.: restored to the original words and added "real": "the real progress fell down by the lack of balance";
    Sk.tp.: "the real progress fell down by the lack of balance"
11. (Mc.)Gr.: "all-around" changed into "all-round";
    Sk.tp.: "all-round"
12. (Mc.)Gr.: "said" crossed out; (Mc.)Sr.: "said" restored;
    Sk.tp.: "above-said"
13. (Mc.)Sr.: "as" added;
    Sk.tp.: "as" added
14. "Sufi Order" in 1922 was still the general name for all different branches of Sufi activities. In October 1923 this name was officially replaced with "Sufi Movement".

Copied from the book The Inner Life, 1st edition.

1

I

The Preparation for the Journey

The inner life is a journey, and before starting to take it there is a certain preparation necessary. If one is not prepared there is always the risk of having to return before one has arrived at one's destination. When a person goes on a journey and when he has to accomplish something, he must know what is necessary on the path, and what he must take with him in order that his journey may become easy and that he may accomplish what he has started to accomplish. The journey one takes in the inner life is as long as the distance between life and death, it being the longest journey one ever takes throughout life; and one must have everything prepared, so that after reaching a certain distance one may not have to turn back.

The first thing that is necessary is to see that there is no debt to be paid. Every soul has a certain debt to pay in life; it may be to his mother or father, his brother or sister, to his husband or wife or friend, or to his children, his race or to humanity; and if he has not paid what is due, then there are cords with which

---

Documents:

Bk. = the first edition of the book *The Inner Life*, published by the Sufi Order (Society in England), Southampton, England, in December 1922. It contains ten lectures, given in September 1922 at Katwijk, the Netherlands, during a Summer School, which were taken down by a professional stenographer. No book-preparation of this text or other earlier document has been found to date.

Sk.corr. = some corrections made by Sakina Furnée in a copy of the book *The Inner Life*, 1st ed.

Gd.corr. = some corrections made by Sherifa Goodenough in a copy of the book *The Inner Life*, 1st ed.

Notes:

1. From the "Quarterly Magazine for Seekers after Truth": *Sufism*, edited by Sophia Saintsbury Green, of December 1922, and a hwr. annotation by Sirdar van Tuyll, it is known that this lecture was given at Katwijk, the Netherlands, on Friday, Ist September 1922, in the evening (v. Preface).

he is inwardly tied, and they pull him back. Life in the world is fair trade,—if one could only understand it, if one knew how many souls there are in this world with whom one is connected or related in some way. Or those we meet freshly every day, to everyone there is something due, and if one has not paid one's obligations, the result is that afterwards one has to pay with interest. There is the inner justice which is working beyond the worldly justice, and when man does not observe that inner law of justice, it is because at that time he is intoxicated, his eyes are closed, and he really does not know the law of life. But that intoxication will not last,—there will come a day when the eyes of every soul will be opened, and it is a pity if the eyes open when it is too late. It is better that the eyes are opened while the purse is full, for it will be very difficult if the eyes open at the time when the purse is empty. To some consideration is due, to some respect, to some service, to some tolerance, to some forgiveness, to some help,—in some way or other, in every relation, in every connection there is something to pay, and one must know before starting the journey that one has paid it, and be sure that one has paid it in full, so there is nothing more to be paid. Besides this it is necessary that man realizes before starting his journey that he has fulfilled his duties,—his duty to those around him and his duty to God. But the one who considers his duty to those around him sacredly does his duty to God.

Man must also consider before starting on his journey whether he has learned all he desired to learn from this world. If there is anything he has not learned, he must finish it before starting the journey. For if he thinks "I will start the journey, although I had the desire to learn something before starting," in that case he will not be able to reach his goal. That desire to learn something will draw him back. Every desire, every ambition, every aspiration that he has in life must be gratified. Not only this,—man must have no remorse of any kind when starting on this journey and no repentance afterwards. If there is any repentance or remorse it must be finished before starting. There must be no grudge against anybody, and no complaining of anyone having done him harm, for all these things which belong to this world, if man took them along, would become a burden on the spiritual path. The journey is difficult enough, and it becomes more difficult if there is a burden to be carried. If a person is lifting a burden of displeasure, dissatisfaction, discomfort, it is difficult to bear it on that path. It is a path to freedom, and to start on this path to freedom man must free himself,—no attachment should pull him back, no pleasure should lure him back.

Besides this preparation one needs a vehicle, a vehicle in which he journeys. That vehicle has two wheels, and they are balance in all things. A man who is one-sided, however great his power of clairvoyance or clairaudience, whatever be his knowledge, yet he is limited, he cannot go very far, for it requires two wheels for the vehicle to run. There must be a balance,—the balance of the head and the heart, the balance of power and wisdom, the balance of activity and repose. It is the balance which enables man to stand the strain of this journey and permits him to go forward, making his path easy. Never imagine for one moment that those who show lack of balance can ever proceed further on the spiritual journey, however greatly in appearance they may seem to be spiritually inclined. It is only the balanced ones who are capable of experiencing the external life as fully as the inner life; to enjoy thought as much as feeling, to rest as well as to act. The centre of life is rhythm, and rhythm causes balance.

On this journey certain coins are necessary also, to spend on the way. And what are these coins? They are thoughtful expressions in word and in action. On this journey man must take provision to eat and drink, and that provision is life and light. And on this journey man has to take something in which to clothe himself against wind and storm and heat and cold, and that garment is the vow of secrecy, the tendency to silence. On this journey man has to bid farewell to others when starting, and that farewell is loving detachment; before starting on this journey he has to leave something behind with his friends, and that is happy memories of the past.

Friends, we are all on the journey; life itself is a journey. No one is settled here, we are all passing onward, and therefore it is not true to say that if we are taking a spiritual journey we have to break our settled life; there is no one living a settled life here; all are unsettled, are all on their way. Only, by taking the spiritual journey you are taking another way, one which is easier, better and more pleasant. Those who do not take this way, they also will come in the end; the difference is in the way. One way is easier, smoother, better; the other way is full of difficulties, and as life has no end of difficulties from the time one has opened one's eyes on this earth, so one may just as well choose the smoother way to arrive at the destination at which all souls will some time arrive.

By Inner Life[2] is meant a life directed toward Perfection[3], which may be called the Perfection[3] of Love, Harmony, and Beauty; in the words of the orthodox, toward God.

The inner life is not necessarily in an opposite direction to the worldly life, but the inner life is a fuller life; the worldly life means the limitedness of life; the inner life means a complete life. The ascetics who have taken a direction

---

2. Sk.corr.: "inner life"
3. Ibid.: "perfection"

quite opposite to the worldly life, have done so in order to have the facility to search into the depth of life, but by going in one direction alone, it does not make a complete life. Therefore the inner life means the fullness of life.

In brief one may say that the inner life consists of two things; action with knowledge, and repose with passivity of mind. By accomplishing these two contrary motions, and by keeping balanced in these two directions, one comes to the fullness of life. A person who lives the inner life is as innocent as a child; even more innocent than a child, but at the same time more wise[4] than many clever people put together. This shows as a development in two contrary directions. The innocence of Jesus is known to the ages. In his every movement, in his every action, he showed to be as a child. All the great saints and sages,—the Great Ones who have liberated humanity, have been as innocent as children, and at the same time wiser, much more so than the worldly wise. And what makes it so? What gives them this balance? It is repose with passiveness. When they stand before God they stand with their heart as an empty cup; when they stand before God to learn they unlearn all things that the world has taught them; when they stand before God, their ego, their self, their life, is no more before them. They do not think of themselves in that moment with any desire to be fulfilled, with any motive to be accomplished, with any expression of their own, but as empty cups that God may fill their being, that they may lose the false self.

Therefore the same thing helps them in their everyday life to show a glimpse of the quiet moment of repose they had with God. They show in their everyday life innocence, and yet not ignorance; they know things, and they do not know. They know if somebody is telling a lie, but do they accuse that person, do they say, "You are telling a lie"? They are above it. They know all the plays of the world, and they look at them all passively; they rise above things of this world which make no impression on them. They take people quite simply. Some may think that they are ignorant in their world-lives, that they take no notice of things that are of no importance. Activity with wisdom makes them more wise, because it is not everybody in this world who directs his every action with wisdom. There are many who never consult wisdom in their action; there are others who seek refuge under wisdom after their action, and very often it is then too late. But the ones who live the inner life, all direct their activity with wisdom; every moment[5], every action, every thought, every word is first thought out, is first weighed and measured and analyzed before it is expressed. Therefore

---

4. Gd.corr., Sk.corr.: "wiser" instead of "more wise"
5. Gd.corr., Sk.corr.: "movement" instead of "moment"

in the world everything they do is with wisdom, but before God they stand with innocence, there they do not take worldly wisdom.

Man often makes mistakes, either by taking one way or the other, and therefore he lacks balance and he does not come to touch perfection. For an[6] instance, when he takes the way of activity in the path of God, he also wishes to use his wisdom there; in the path of God also he wishes to be active where he does not need action. It is just like swimming against the tide; where you must be innocent, if you use your wisdom there it is the greatest error. Then there are others who are accustomed to take passivity as a principle with which they stand before God in their innocence; and they wish to use the same principle in all directions of life, which would not be right.

---

6. Gd.corr.: "an" crossed out

A typewritten copy made by Mrs. Marya Cushing
from her own shorthand reporting of the lecture.

Katwijk, Holland, Saturday afternoon,
September 2nd, 1922

1

The Problem of the Day [2]

The first aspect of the problem of the day is the physical life. This can be divided into three aspects: food, cleanliness and living.[3]

No doubt the[4] science is considering the subject very much, but at the same time,[5] that life is complicated as it is today, makes things[6] difficult to live a natural life in every respect. In ancient times when the[7] agriculture was the main occupation of the human race, and for that reason the lands of all countries

---

Documents:

Mc. = a typewritten copy made by Mrs. Marya Cushing from her own shorthand reporting
(Mc.)Gr.: some editing by Miss Sophia Green
(Mc.)Sr.: some corr. by Sirdar van Tuyll
(Mc.)Sk.: some add. and changes by Sakina Furnée

Sk.tp. = a typewritten copy made in later years from "Mc." under the direction of Sakina Furnée, with most of the corr. and add. incorporated

Notes:

1. (Mc.)Gr.: "Physical" written above, then crossed out
2. (Mc.)Sk.: "The Problem of the Day" replaced with "Physical Development";
   (Mc.)Sr.: "The Problem of the Day" restored;
   (Mc.)Gr.: later "II" added after "The Problem of the Day", to indicate that it was the second lecture in this series;
   Sk.tp.: "The Problem of the Day" as a title, "Physical Development" as a subtitle, and "(2)" instead of "II" after "Physical Development"
3. (Mc.)Gr.: "living" first replaced with "way of life", then with "life in the world" instead;
   (Mc.)Sr.: "life in the world" crossed out and "living" restored
4. (Mc.)Gr.: "the" crossed out;
   Sk.tp.: "the" omitted
5. (Mc.)Gr.: "the fact" added instead of a comma;
   Sk.tp.: "the fact" instead of a comma
6. (Mc.)Gr.: "things" replaced with "it";
   Sk.tp.: "it" instead of "things"
7. (Mc.)Gr.: "when the" crossed out;
   Sk.tp.: "when the" omitted

were fertile and there was ample to eat. At the present time the lands which have been used in former times for cultivation are now[8] occupied by factories and [9]industrial purposes; and there are many countries in Europe just now which have to depend for their food on other countries, having allowed the whole land to be used for industrial purposes. The consequence is that the principal need of human life, which is food, is not independently produced in one's own land. The way of living as it is just[10] now, gathering together in cities and towns, does not give that facility that people had in the ancient times. They were happy, having a little ancient cottage on [11]their piece of land, but a larger piece[11] of land attached to it; whether rich or poor, they would grow their own vegetables and cultivate that ground for their use, so that everyone thought at the[12] time that he is[13] the king of a little piece of ground. I myself have seen some[14] parts near the Himalayas today having the same custom. Instead of paying the soldiers a regular payment in money they are given a piece of land to cultivate themselves, and they are the happiest people, everyone thinking he has a piece of land, where he can grow whatever he likes; and think what joy it is for a person to say, this is my ground, and on this piece of land I can grow [15]potatoes or tomatoes or[15] whatever I like. His magnetism[16], his work, his labour has been given to it, and from that something has grown, which he eats and[17] fruits that he has so carefully reared. The magnetism itself brings him a satisfaction, and in this way the

---

8. (Mc.)Gr.: "now" crossed out;
   Sk.tp.: "now" omitted
9. (Mc.)Gr.: "for" added;
   Sk.tp.: "for" added
10. (Mc.)Gr.: "just" crossed out;
    (Mc.)Sr.: "just" restored
11. (Mc.)Gr.: rewritten to read, "with a piece";
    Sk.tp.: "with a piece" instead of "on their piece of land, but a larger piece"
12. (Mc.)Gr.: "the" changed into "that";
    Sk.tp.: "that" instead of "the"
13. (Mc.)Gr.: "is" changed into "was";
    Sk.tp.: "was" instead of "is"
14. Sk.tp.: "some" omitted
15. (Mc.)Gr.: this part of the sentence crossed out;
    (Mc.)Sk.: "potatoes or tomatoes or" restored
16. (Mc.)Gr.: "magnetism" replaced with "thought";
    (Mc.)Sk.: "magnetism" restored;
    (Mc.)Sr.: "thought, his magnetism," instead of "magnetism";
    Sk.tp.: "thought, his magnetism,"
17. (Mc.)Gr.: "which he eats and" replaced with "that takes shape";
    (Mc.)Sr.: "that takes shape" crossed out, "which" and "eats" restored, "and" replaced with a comma;
    Sk.tp.: "which he eats", instead of "which he eats and"

country keeps rich. What does one do with metal, with gold and silver if there is not sufficient food? The riches that one sees in modern towns, where people live in luxury, do you think it is a natural life? Are they very healthy? No, because health comes from a natural life; that natural occupation of cultivating the ground in agriculture and gardening, that[18] seems to have been lost.

On one side the[4] science is making a great headway in finding out the various diseases and perhaps their remedies. But at the same time the diseases are increasing because of the life lived in towns and crowded places, and the food stored in tins and in barrels; the meat perhaps sent from one country to another, and after so many months it arrives. By this unnatural[19] food people become ill, and that illness spreads. On the one side science is improving, on the other side the[4] life is going down. There have not been so many diseases in the ancient times as one finds today. A man may think that perhaps the ancient physicians did not find out[20] so many diseases, but that is not true. The life was more natural.

[21]It is a great question whether meat is a desirable thing to be allowed to be eaten as a food every day,[22] and the answer is that there are many sides to that question. There are places, such as the deserts of Sahara, of Arabia and Syria, where vegetables are not to be found, where man cannot live without meat. Many have asked why the Prophet Mahommed[23] did not prohibit his followers from eating meat, and the same answer may be given. And not only that; the animals that are used by mankind for meat, if they were not used by mankind, they[24] would be used[25] by lions and tigers, and there would be many more lions

---

18. (Mc.)Gr. or (Mc.)Sr.: "that" crossed out;
    Sk.tp.: "that" omitted
19. (Mc.)Gr.: "unnatural" replaced with "unwholesome";
    (Mc.)Sr.: "unnatural" restored
20. (Mc.)Sr.: "find out" replaced with "recognise";
    Sk.tp.: "recognise" instead of "find out"
21. (Mc.)Gr.: a hwr. annotation in the margin beside this paragraph (ending with "that illness comes");
    (Mc.)Sr.: the annotation crossed out, after which only the last word: "omit" is still legible; therefore the reason for wanting to omit this paragraph is not known. It may have been Miss Sophia Green's intention to use this lecture, in a somewhat abbreviated form, for publication in a Sufi magazine. Or perhaps she intended to add this part on vegetarian diet to another lecture on the same subject.
22. (Mc.)Gr.: "a daily food" instead of "a food every day";
    (Mc.)Sk., (Mc.)Sr.: restored to "as a food every day"
23. Sk.tp.: "Mohammed"
24. (Mc.)Gr.: "by mankind, they" crossed out;
    (Mc.)Sk., (Mc.)Sr.: "by mankind" restored;
    Sk.tp.: "they" omitted

and tigers in the world. But at the same time[26] vegetable food is by every means[27] advisable and desirable for the health in every way, if only the vegetable food is fresh and clean. If decayed, if the vegetables are bad[28], it is worse than meat, because there again life begins to show itself in the form of insects, [29]and it is just the same, or perhaps worse, when the vegetables are not fresh enough to eat[29]. Very often by eating vegetables people get illnesses, many different insects become born[30] in vegetables, and the consequence is that illness comes.[21]

Besides this, [31] the outdoor life, which may be called the restaurant life, is becoming more fashionable for the rich and for the well-to-do, and home life, which is the ideal life, is ~~becoming~~ being neglected. Today there seems to be an increasing tendency toward restaurant life, which is now turning into what ~~is~~ they call [32] . [33]This is quite contrary to what at one time the Brahmins did. The Brahmins believed in keeping their kitchens so pure and clean, that no outsider could enter into their kitchens[34]; they considered food something so sacred, a symbol of spiritual food[35] on the earth, that no outsider should touch it, for they did not know what he was[36] doing before[37], where he was coming from,

---

25. (Mc.)Gr.: "used" replaced with "eaten";
    (Mc.)Sr.: "used" restored
26. (Mc.)Gr.: "at the same time" crossed out;
    (Mc.)Sr.: "at the same time" restored
27. (Mc.)Gr.: "by every means" crossed out;
    (Mc.)Sk.: "by every means" restored;
    Sk.tp.: "by every means" omitted
28. (Mc.)Gr.: "bad" replaced with "not fresh";
    Sk.tp.: "not fresh" instead of "bad"
29. (Mc.)Gr.: this part of the sentence crossed out;
    (Mc.)Sk., (Mc.)Sr.: this part of the sentence restored
30. (Mc.)Gr.: "are bred" instead of "become born";
    (Mc.)Sr.: "become born" restored
31. (Mc.)Gr.: "Besides this," and one indecipherable word crossed out;
    (Mc.)Sk., (Mc.)Sr.: "Besides this," restored
32. (Mc.)Gr.: "club life" filled in;
    Sk.tp.: "club life" added
33. (Mc.)Gr.: "Omit" written beside this part of the paragraph (From "This is quite contrary" to the end of the paragraph: "at the time he cooked.";
    (Mc.)Sr.: "Omit" crossed out. See under note 21.
34. (Mc.)Gr.: "into their kitchens" changed into "them";
    Sk.tp.: "them" instead of "into their kitchens"
35. (Mc.)Gr.: "of spiritual food" moved to after "on the earth";
    (Mc.)Sr.: put back "of spiritual food" before "on the earth"
36. (Mc.)Gr.: "was" changed into "had been";
    Sk.tp.: "had been" instead of "was"

or what influence he was bringing. And the one who cooked the food must be a Brahmin also, which means, he must be of the same thought; he must not be a person of inferior thought. An inferior person must not cook for a superior person, as the latter's stage of evolution demands a person of his own stage to cook for him, or he himself will cook it[38]. And then[39] they ate on leaves and they[40] sat on little boards, not on carpets or things which could have the germs of those who come and go, but clean boards, washed every day, on which they sat separately, not touching each other; and[41] they were helped with their own hands, and the dinner was served on leaves; in the bowls made of leaves[42] the liquid food was served, no spoons or forks to be washed in the same thing[43], perhaps having been eaten with, by[44] a hundred or a thousand people in the same restaurant, and wiped by the same towel, and who knows! cooked by whom, [45]what evolution that person was, [46]in what attitude he was at the time he cooked.[33]

[47]Now, when life was meant to be a most joyful life . . . .

---

37. (Mc.)Gr.: "before" crossed out;
    (Mc.)Sk.: "before" restored;
    Sk.tp.: "before" omitted
38. (Mc.)Gr.: "it" crossed out;
    Sk.tp.: "it" omitted
39. (Mc.)Gr.: "then" crossed out;
    Sk.tp.: "then" omitted, but later reinserted by Sakina
40. (Mc.)Gr.: "they" crossed out;
    (Mc.)Sk., (Mc.)Sr.: "they" restored
41. (Mc.)Gr.: "and" crossed out;
    Sk.tp.: "and" omitted
42. (Mc.)Gr.: "in the bowls made of leaves" moved to after "the liquid food was served";
    (Mc.)Sr.: "in the bowls made of leaves" put back before "the liquid food was served"
43. (Mc.)Gr.: "thing" replaced with "place";
    (Mc.)Sk., (Mc.)Sr.: "thing" restored
44. (Mc.)Gr.: "eaten with, by" replaced with "used by";
    (Mc.)Sk.: "eaten with, by" restored;
    Sk.tp.: "used by" instead of "eaten with, by"
45. (Mc.)Gr.: "or of" added;
    Sk.tp.: "or of" added
46. (Mc.)Gr.: "or" added;
    Sk.tp.: "or" added
47. (Mc.)Gr.: this passage, ending with "restaurants" crossed out;
    (Mc.)Sk.: the first part of this passage restored (up to "joyful life");
    (Mc.)Sr.: this incomplete passage replaced with, "Now, when man is looking for . . . for the life in the restaurants";
    Sk.tp.: "Now, man is looking for the life in the restaurants"

the life in the restaurants[47]. . . . . ,[48] a person thinks that it is a great deal of trouble to arrange food at home,--that it is much better to go out; even if they have[49] a home, they want[50] to go out to dine, or dining[51] at a club, which is a miniature restaurant again. All these things bring about a tendency to a life far removed from hygienic principles, although there is so much talk going on about hygienic food and what one should eat. The conventionalities of the day are becoming greater. For one meal there are so many things that are to be washed and cleaned afterwards, that life becomes burdensome. [52]If there are ten people living in a family, they [53] a boy, a laundryman to clean the table linen[52,54]. If one only knew how life could be made simple, it would not only be less work and trouble, but more hygienic, less expense and less trouble,[55] less responsibility[56]. How many people there are in the world today, who owing to the greater complexity of food, do not wish to establish a home; they wish to eat outside such as students and travellers[56]. [57]There was a time in the East when students and travellers would consider it the greatest joy if they had to cook for themselves. Even the Princes were taught, as one of their occupations in life, to cook for themselves. Whom can you trust more than yourself, and who can

---

48. (Mc.)Gr.: added "Today" before "a person";
(Mc.)Sr.: crossed out "Today a person" and filled in "and he";
Sk.tp.: "and he" instead of "a person"
49. (Mc.)Gr.: "they have" changed into "he has";
Sk.tp.: "he has"
50. (Mc.)Gr.: "they want" changed into "he wants";
Sk.tp.: "he wants"
51. (Mc.)Gr.: "dining" replaced with "to dine";
(Mc.)Sr.: "have dinner" instead of "dining";
Sk.tp.: "have dinner" instead of "dining"
52. (Mc.)Gr.: this sentence ("If there . . . table linen") crossed out;
(Mc.)Sk.: this sentence restored;
Sk.tp.: this sentence omitted
53. (Mc.)Gr.: one or two illegible words, forming part of the sentence under note 52, also crossed out
54. (Mc.)Gr.: added, "besides the need of waiters", then crossed out
55. (Mc.)Gr.: "less trouble" crossed out;
Sk.tp.: "less trouble" omitted
56. (Mc.)Gr.: rewritten to read, continuing the sentence ending with "responsibility" and replacing the next one ("How many people . . . and travellers"): "all of which things as often prevent the desire to marry and make a home; they wish to eat outside, as do also students and travellers." In the margin, in Gr.'s hwr.: "end here";
(Mc.)Sr.: crossed out the sentence as rewritten in "(Mc.)Gr." and also crossed out "end here";
Sk.tp.: the sentence was restored to the one in "Mc."
57. (Mc.)Gr.: beside the following sentences ("There was a time . . .') to the end of the paragraph (". . . why not make it?") is written in Gr.'s hwr. "Omit". See note 21.
(Mc.)Sr.: this passage restored and "Omit" crossed out

know properly[58] what you want? When a person is master of his choice he may cook every day what he wants. Nobody else knows what he wishes. When a person is always dependent upon others for his food, which is the principal thing in[59] life, he does not live a life. In this direction he lives mechanically; he does not know life. He must have his free choice to cook what he wants, or whether he wishes to eat or not, it must be his choice. One day, if he wishes to go without food, he can go[60]. One day if he wishes to eat something with people that day,[61] he can do so, or to make a concoction of certain things, why not make it?[57]

Another thing is that life must have[62] its full expression; in eating, in drinking, we must have a choice; one[63] must have the[64] taste developed, it is one of the five senses; if this sense is not satisfied, the principal thing in life is not satisfied. The little infant, as soon as he comes, the first thing he wants is food. And do not think that food is in the material world alone, but also in the spiritual world what you need is food. From the beginning to the end there is appetite and there is food. Besides this, the life today forces upon man appointed hours, fixed hours even for food; that thing which is allowable at every moment of the day has been so [65] nowadays that mothers teach their children also to be timely in asking for their food, and they deprive of[66] freedom, from the beginning, the natural appetite which has its moments just like a wave. It is a wave which comes as an appetite asking for food. But the child must know[67] that it is not

---

58. (Mc.)Sr.: "properly" changed into "better";
(Mc.)Sk.: "properly" restored;
Sk.tp.: "better" instead of "properly"
59. (Mc.)Gr.: "physical" added;
(Mc.)Sr.: "physical" crossed out
60. (Mc.)Gr.: "go" changed into "do so";
Sk.tp.: "do so" instead of "go"
61. (Mc.)Gr.: "with people that day" replaced with "which people say is prohib";
(Mc.)Sr.: "with people that day" restored
62. (Mc.)Gr.: "life must have" changed into "life is to have";
(Mc.)Sr.: "if life is to have";
Sk.tp.: "if life is to have"
63. (Mc.)Sr.: "one" changed into "we";
Sk.tp.: "we" instead of "one"
64. (Mc.)Sr.: "the" changed into "our";
Sk.tp.: "our" instead of "the"
65. (Mc.)Gr.: filled in "regulated";
Sk.tp.: "regulated" instead of an open space
66. (Mc.)Gr.: "of" crossed out
67. (Mc.)Gr.: "must know" changed into "is told";
Sk.tp.: "is told" instead of "must know"

dinner time. From[68] childhood, when he is a king of life, he comes with that[69] natural appetite and thirst, [70]when he wishes to eat and drink, but we with our conventionalities in the world and rules and regulations, we say, "No, this is not the time; at the proper time you will be given food."

It is all these things that limit life. Why do people have short lives? In the ancient times people lived longer because they lived a natural life. Now they live for a short time because their lives are divided by man-made laws. The birds and animals in the forests do not know physicians and doctors and do not know prescriptions. Why? They eat when they are hungry, sleep when they desire to sleep, and they drink when they feel thirsty. They do not eat when they do not like to eat. When a person is not eating when the hour has come, then everybody in the family will ask: "Why do you not eat, what is the matter with you, what has gone wrong?" From all sides they will come and ask you: "Do you not want to eat, it is not good for you not to eat." And then there is grandmother coaxing that you must eat when you are not feeling like it. Or you must eat this or that; and the doctor tells you that you must not eat much of this, and you must eat much of that.[71] The only thing to consider is that what you like, that it is the best thing for you to eat[72]; your love for it, your liking for it makes it a medicine for you.

Now they talk about analysis, that certain elements are in you and to harmonize with those elements you must eat certain other elements. It is very good for science, one must read it with interest. But do you think that such analysis will give us satisfaction in living? No! Nature is perfect, and that perfection is reflected in your own heart. At every moment you are inspired by that nature; your every inclination in life is inspired by that nature, and if those outside laws tell you you must not have it, what does that mean? It means that man is standing as an obstacle in the path of God. God inspires from within, and man says, "No, that must not be."

What we want in life today is simplicity; less complexity in life, less conventionality, and what is most desirable just now is to keep close to the laws

---

68. (Mc.)Gr.: "From" changed into "In";
Sk.tp.: "In" instead of "From"
69. (Mc.)Gr.: "that" changed into "a";
Sk.tp.: "a" instead of "that"
70. (Mc.)Gr.: "and knows" added;
Sk.tp.: "and knows" before "when he wishes"
71. (Mc.)Gr.: added, "In this way a person not inclined to eat becomes ill";
(Mc.)Sr.: the added sentence was crossed out
72. (Mc.)Gr.: added, "and when you want it, is the right time for you to eat";
(Mc.)Sr.: the added sentence was crossed out

of nature and to allow life to experience life.[73]

---

73. (Mc.)Gr.: "experience life" changed into "fully express itself";
(Mc.)Sr.: "fully express itself" replaced with "its own want of freedom, its own rhythm," then "its own want of freedom" crossed out;
Sk.tp.: "its own rhythm" instead of "to experience life"

Copied from the book The Inner Life, 1st ed.

[1]

II

The Object of the Journey

The first and principal thing in the inner life is to establish a relation with God, making God the object with which we relate ourselves, such as Creator, Sustainer, Forgiver, Judge, Friend, Father, Mother and Beloved. In every relation we must place God before us and become conscious of that relation so that it will no more remain an imagination; because the first thing a believer does is to imagine. He imagines that God is the Creator and tries to believe that God is the Sustainer; and he makes an effort to think that God is a Friend, and an attempt to feel that he loves God. But when this imagination would become a reality then exactly as one feels for one's earthly beloved sympathy, love and attachment, so one must feel the same with God. However greatly a person may be pious, good or righteous, yet without this his piety or his goodness are not a reality to him.

The work of the inner life is to make God a reality, so that He is no more

---

Documents:

Bk. = the first edition of the book The Inner Life, published by the Sufi Order (Society in England), Southampton, England, in December 1922. It contains ten lectures, given in September 1922 at Katwijk, the Netherlands, during a Summer School, which were taken down by a professional stenographer. No book-preparation of this text or other earlier document has been found to date.

Fm.corr. = a corr. made by Fazal Mai Egeling in a copy of the book The Inner Life presented to her by Sophia Green on January 24, 1923

Sk.corr. = some corrections made by Sakina Furnée in a copy of the book The Inner Life, 1st ed.

Gd.corr. = some corrections made by Sherifa Goodenough in a copy of the book The Inner Life, 1st ed.

Notes:

1. From the "Quarterly Magazine for Seekers after Truth": Sufism, edited by Sophia Saintsbury Green, of December 1922, and a hwr. annotation by Sirdar van Tuyll, it is known that this lecture was given at Katwijk, the Netherlands, on Saturday, 2nd September 1922, in the evening (v. Preface).

an imagination; that this relation that man has with God may seem to him more real than any other relation in this world, and when this happens then all relations, however near and dear, become less binding. But at the same time by that a person does not become cold; he becomes more loving. It is the godless man who is cold, impressed by the selfishness and lovelessness of this world, because he partakes of those conditions in which he lives. But the one who is in love with God, the one who has established his relation with God, his love becomes living; he is no more cold; he fulfills his duties to those related to him in this world much more than does the godless man.

Now, as to the way in which man establishes this relation, and[2] which relation is the most desirable to establish with God, what should he imagine? God as Father, as Creator, as Judge, as Forgiver, as Friend, or as Beloved?[3]

The answer is, that in every capacity of life we must give God the place that is demanded by the moment. When crushed by the injustice, the coldness of the world, when man looks at God, the perfection of Justice, he no more remains agitated, his heart is no more disturbed, he consoles himself with the justice of God. He places the just God before him, and by this he learns justice. The sense of justice awakens in his heart, and he sees things in quite a different light. When man finds in this world the motherless or fatherless, then he thinks that there is the mother and father in God; and even if he was in the presence of the mother and father, that these are only related on the earth. The Motherhood and Fatherhood of God is the only real relation. The mother and father of the earth only[4] reflect a spark of that motherly and fatherly love which God has in fulness and perfection. Then man finds that God can forgive, as the parents can forgive the child if he was in error. Then man feels the goodness, kindness, protection, support, sympathy coming from every side, he learns to feel that it comes from God, the Father-mother[5] through all. When man pictures God as Forgiver he finds that there is not only in this world a strict justice, but there is love developed also, there is mercy and compassion, there is that sense of forgiveness, that God is not the servant of law, as is the Judge in this world. He is Master of law; He judges when He judges, when He forgives He forgives; He has both powers, He has the power to judge and He has the power to forgive. He is Judge because He does not close his eyes to all man does; He knows, He weighs and measures and He returns what is due to man; and He is Forgiver

---

2. Sk.corr.: "as to" added
3. Ibid.: instead of beginning a new paragraph, "The answer is" follows after "Beloved?"
4. Ibid.: "only" moved to after "reflect"
5. Ibid.: "Mother" instead of "mother"

because beyond and above His power of justice there is His great power of Love and Compassion which is His very being, which is His own nature, and therefore it is more and in greater proportion and working with a greater activity than His power of justice. We, the human beings in this world, if there is a spark of goodness or kindness in our hearts, avoid judging people. We prefer forgiving to judging. Forgiving gives us naturally a greater happiness than taking revenge; unless a man is on quite a different path.

The man who realizes God as a friend is never lonely in the world, neither in this world nor in the hereafter. There is always a friend, a friend in the crowd, a friend in the solitude, or while he is asleep unconscious of this outer world, and when he is awake and conscious of it; in both cases the friend is there in his thought, in his imagination, in his heart, in his soul. And the man who makes God his Beloved, what more does he want? His heart becomes awakened to all the beauty there is within and without. To him all things appeal, everything unfolds itself, and it is beauty to his eyes, because God is all-pervading, in all Names and all Forms; therefore his Beloved is never absent. How happy therefore is the one whose Beloved is never absent, because the whole tragedy of life is the absence of the beloved, and one whose beloved is always there, when he has closed his eyes the Beloved is within, when he has opened his eyes the Beloved is without. His every sense perceives the Beloved; his eyes see Him, his ears hear His voice. When a person arrives at this realization then he, so to speak, lives in the presence of God; then to him the different forms and beliefs, faiths and communities do not count. To him God is all in all; to him God is everywhere. If he goes to the Christian Church or to the Synagogue, to the Buddhist temple, to the Hindu shrine, or to the mosque of the Muslim[6], there is God. In the wilderness, in the forest, in the crowd, everywhere he sees God.

This shows that the inner life does not consist in closing the eyes and looking inward. The inner life is to look outwardly <u>and</u> inwardly and to find one's belief[7] everywhere. But God cannot be made a Beloved unless the love element is awakened sufficiently. The one who hates his enemy and loves his friend, he cannot call God his Beloved, for he does not know God. When love comes to its fulness, then one looks at the friend with affection, on the enemy with forgiveness, on the stranger with sympathy. There is love in all its aspects expressed when love rises to its fulness, and it is the fulness of love which is

---

6. Ibid.: "Moslim"
7. Fm.corr.: "belief" changed into "Beloved"; Gd.corr.: "beloved"

worth offering to God. It is[8] that time when[9] man recognizes in God one's[10] Beloved, one's [10] Ideal, and by that, although he rises above the narrow affection of this world, in reality he is the one who knows how to love even his friend. It is the lover of God who knows love, when he rises to that stage of the fulness of love.

The whole imagery of the Sufi literature in the Persian language, written by great poets, such as Rumi, Hafiz, and Jami, is the relation between man as the lover and God as Beloved, and when one reads [11]understanding that, and developed in that affection, [11] then one sees what pictures the mystics have made and to what note their heart has been tuned. It is not easy to develop in the heart the love of God, because when one does not see or realize the object of love one cannot love. God must become tangible in order that one may love Him, but once a person has attained to love God he has really entered[12] the journey of the spiritual path.

---

8. Sk.corr.: "at" added
9. Gd.corr., Sk.corr.: "when" changed into "that"
10. Ibid.: "his" instead of "one's"
11. Sk.corr.: "--understanding that, and developed in that affection--"; however, appparently a word is still missing
12. Ibid.: "upon" added

A typewritten copy made by Marya Cushing, probably from her own shorthand reporting of the address.[1]

Church of All, Sunday, 3 September.

Beloved ones of God,

I would like to speak a few words introducing or explaining about the service which has been so ably performed by our worthy[2] Cheraga, Miss Green.

The Sufi Order[3] constitutes three aspects in its mission: The main aspect is the development of individuals, the unfoldment of souls, which is the object of every soul in the world, whatever be the grade of its advancement. The second side of the activities is brotherhood, which is most necessary at this time in the world, when humanity has been divided into so many sections, and although there are many different ways by which brotherhood can be brought about, there are many questions that might be discussed and many problems on that subject could be solved. But, in short, one can say, that wisdom is the best medium of uniting mankind, whatever be his nation or whatever be his race. For all this division, all separateness, all prejudice and hatred that exists among the nations and races, is unnatural,

---

Document:

Mc. = a typewritten copy made by Mrs. Marya Cushing from her own shorthand reporting of the lecture, which is not in the archives
(Mc.)Gr.: some editing by Miss Sophia Green on "Mc."

Notes:

1. This address by Pir-o-Murshid was given after the performance in English by Miss Sophia Green of what later became known as the Universal Worship; this was the first service in Holland, in Pir-o-Murshid Inayat Khan's presence, on 3rd September 1922, at Sirdar and Saida van Tuyll's house at Katwijk, during the first Summer School held in the Netherlands. (From a "Historical Note" by Saida van Tuyll, carefully kept in the archives of the Biographical Department by Sakina Furnée; in the margin, besides this information, Saida wrote her name, thereby confirming the correctness of this statement. The previous year the Service of Universal Worship in the Church of All had been established in London.)
2. (Mc.)Gr.: "worthy" changed into "first"
3. In 1922 the different activities of the workers in the Sufi cause were still known as "The Sufi Order"; in October 1923 the name was officially changed to 'Sufi Movement".

for the natural man is inclined to unite;[4] the natural man is[4] inclined to have no barriers between them, and it is the unnatural state of affairs which has divided humanity so that today man is blood-thirsty of[5] his fellowman.

Therefore, it is the Sufi message, it is the divine message, which is working through this activity, and the workers in this activity united together are called the Sufi Order, which is not a community, which is not at all a desire on our part that the whole humanity should become members of the Sufi Order. No, never. Our only desire is that we who realize the importance and value of the Cause and the divine hand in the Cause, might unite together, might have the facility of meeting together, of thinking in what way we could serve God and humanity by establishing brotherhood in ourselves, that the call of harmony and love be awakened and we be the first to show ourselves as examples of that brotherhood in the Cause of which we are prepared to work and devote our lives.

There is another side to it, which is the devotional side, which in every way is a most important side, upon which the unfoldment of the soul depends. There are many ways to progress in spirituality, but devotion is the ideal and best way. The Church of All therefore provides a religion to those who have none, who wish to have one, for human nature is made so that the soul yearns constantly[6], and many souls[7] there are in this world, who have been discontented with the faith and beliefs which have been enforced upon them by their parents and guardians, or in which they are compelled to live by the force of their community or race. They lose the faith in that belief, and at the same time constantly yearn to find something in their life which can take the place of that innate yearning which wants a belief.

But at the same time it is a school for those who already have a religion given by their parents or teachers. They come to learn in this school of the Church of All that tolerance which is[8] the spirit of the religion of these days, the desire to respect and to recognize and appreciate wisdom in all forms where it is given; in the Buddhist scripture or in the Zoroastrian scripture, in Hinduism, in Christianity, or in the scriptures of Islam. It teaches to respect not only the scriptures of the past, but the wisdom in whatever religion it is given. Therefore the Church of All is all churches. You may call it a church because we offer prayers, but I call it a school

4. (Mc.)Gr.: rewritten to read, "naturally men are"
5. Ibid.: "of" changed into "towards"
6. Ibid.: added, "for religion"
7. Ibid.: "many souls" moved to after "there are"
8. Ibid.: "is" changed into "must be"

where we learn ~~to listen~~ the lesson of all religions, an assembly gathered in devotion, whatever religion a person may belong to, he has his scripture on that table; his scripture revered, read and listened to by everyone with the same respect as the other scriptures. In this way wisdom is recognized and respected in all forms, wisdom which alone is the essence of religion, and[9] ~~of~~ the various religions are only its different expressions, which in the Church of All are all united and made one.

Really speaking, this side of the Sufi activity is perhaps more important than any other side, for the reason that today the more we study life, the more we study the condition of the world, the more we find that what the world wants is religion. But what religion? Not a sectarian religion, not a religion which fixes its dogmas, forms and ceremonies upon every other religion, as different from it, but a religion which accepts all religions. A member of the Church of All is open to go to his own church, whatever be his class of[10] religion. He is free to observe all the customs, the manners of his race, of his nation. He is free to adhere to his scriptures or the Master in whom he has devotion. He is not told, "Now, forget that particular Master, this Master is better." No! What he is asked is to become tolerant to others, to become respectful to others' beliefs[11] and to recognize wisdom which comes in different forms, and in that way to enrich his belief, his faith, in the religion to which he himself belongs.

Therefore every member of the Church of All who is deeply impressed by the ideal with which this activity has been working, must consider himself not only a member of the Church of All, but a worker of this movement, a worker with wisdom, with gentleness, not such a worker as the religious missionary of many different religions, who annoy[12] another person by attacking his religion, by showing what is wrong in this belief, in this religion, by wanting to take him away from his faith. No! Not a worker of that sort. A worker who is impressed by the motherhood and fatherhood[13] of God and who sees in all human beings his brother and his sister; and[14] who feels interest in them, and who sees in all the channels that the souls are working in, that they are only the channels, whatever be their faith, their belief, to let him have that, and only to erase from their hearts the doubts and

---

9. Ibid.: "and" replaced with "for"
10. Ibid.: "class of" crossed out
11. Ibid.: "to others' beliefs" changed into "of the belief of others".
12. Ibid.: "annoy" changed into "angers"
13. Ibid.: "Motherhood and Fatherhood"
14. Ibid.: "and" crossed out

spots of intolerance, of prejudice, and those discords of inharmonious feeling toward one another. That this worker must tune them as a musician tunes his instrument; do not force upon them that they must join this Church of All; if they are willing to join, it is their privilege, if they are not willing to join, let them stay away. The message is working through all channels, directly or indirectly. As long as a person is willing to . . . [15] we need not pull him in . . . [16]. By attacking a person for going in the wrong way we push him still further on the wrong way.

Therefore the work of the member of the Church of All is of a very delicate and very gentle character. But at the same time, it is a hope that [17] the members of our blessed Order, who are blessed by wisdom, who are blessed by all the Teachers of humanity, who are blessed by all the scriptures and wisdom in all its forms, of whatever period, and who have accepted it in all scriptures, [18]in all the names and religions, in the names of all the Teachers, they are blessed a thousand-fold, and when they sincerely wish to serve God and humanity in this direction, they will surely be guided and blessed.

---

15. Mc.: an open space
    (Mc.)Gr.: filled in, "believe in anything sincerely"
16. Mc.: an open space
17. (Mc.)Gr.: "that" changed into "for"
18. Ibid.: "and" added

A typescript made by Shabaz Mitchell from his own shorthand reporting of the lecture.

[1] [2]

The Problem of the Day [3]

When speaking of the question of the mental development of humanity, I should like to say that what is mostly needed in these critical times in the world, is the right mentality. Every kind of the generation[4] follows the wrong mentality means the attitude of mind.[5] Wrong mentality is the wrong attitude of mind.

It is upon [6]attitude of mind that the whole life of men[7] depends--his rise, his fall, his success, his failure, his happiness, or unhappiness, all are mostly

---

Documents:

Sz. = a typewritten copy, made by Shabaz Mitchell from his own shorthand reporting of the lecture
(Sz.)Gr.: some editing by Miss Sophia Green
(Sz.)Sz.: some add. by Shabaz Mitchell to his own typescript
(Sz.)Sr.: some add. and corr. by Sirdar van Tuyll
(Sz.)Sk.: some corr. and alterations by Sakina Furnée

Sk.tp. = a typewritten copy made in later years from "Sz." under Sakina Furnée's direction, with most of the corr., add., etc. incorporated

Notes:

1. (Sz.)Sr.: "Monday 4 September" added;
Sk.tp.: "Monday, September 4th, 1922" added
2. (Sz.)Sz.: "No. 3. Shabaz" added above;
(Sz.)Sr.: "Shabaz" crossed out
3. (Sz.)Sz.: afterwards Shabaz Mitchell replaced "The Problem of the Day" with "Mental Development";
(Sz.)Sk.: "The Problem of the Day" restored before "Mental Development";
(Sz.)Gr.: added "III" after "The Problem of the Day", thereby indicating that it was the third lecture in this series;
Sk.tp.: "Mental Development" added as a subtitle after "The Problem of the Day" and "(3)" written at the end of the line
4. (Sz.)Gr.: "the generation" corr. into "degeneration";
Sk.tp.: "degeneration"
5. (Sz.)Gr.: "means the attitude of mind" crossed out;
Sk.tp.: "means the attitude of mind" omitted
6. (Sz.)Gr.: "the" added;
Sk.tp.: "the" added
7. (Sz.)Sr.: "men" changed into "man";
Sk.tp.: "man"

caused by the mentality. In these times when commercialism is reigning over the world and when competition has become the central theme, when[8] one is desirous of getting the best of another, then man sees nothing else but his own benefit for which he struggles along through life.

At such a time for the law of evolution what is most necessary is the right attitude of mind. Going astray,[9] the orthodox phrase, means wrong attitude, and once the mind has taken a wrong attitude, the mentality is wrong. To that person everything seems wrong because his mentality has become wrong and all reflected in a wrong mentality becomes wrong. For an instance, when a thief travels in the train, he looks with suspicion at the person who travels by his side, suspecting him to be a thief. A selfish person can never understand that there can be such a thing as unselfishness. Just like [10] a person who has suffered all through life, he [11] cannot say that there exists happiness in the world. And the person who knows what is joy, to him the whole life becomes beautiful. It shows that the whole world becomes favourable, unfavourable, agreeable or disagreeable, pleasant or unpleasant according to one's mentality. All manner of the generation [4] such as not honour [12] of [13] one's word, no care of keeping one's promise, no desire for self-respect, no wish to maintain the [14] dignity, all such things come from the wrong mentality.

Now the question is what causes the [14] wrong mentality? The wrong mentality is like an obsession, which is caused by a certain [15] absorption in [16]certain direction of this dense earth. If one is entirely absorbed in collecting

---

8. (Sz.)Gr.: "each" added before "one";
   (Sz.)Sr.: "each or everyone" instead of "one";
   Sk.tp.: "everyone"
9. (Sz.)Gr.: "Going astray" put in quotation marks and moved to after "the orthodox phrase,";
   Sk.tp.: "The orthodox phrase 'going astray,' "
10. (Sz.)Gr.: "like" changed into "as";
    (Sz.)Sk.: "as" crossed out;
    Sk.tp.: "as" instead of "like"
11. (Sz.)Gr.: "he" crossed out;
    Sk.tp.: "he" omitted
12. (Sz.)Gr.: "honouring" instead of "honour";
    Sk.tp.: "honouring"
13. (Sz.)Gr.: "of" crossed out;
    Sk.tp.: "of" omitted
14. (Sz.)Sr.: "the" crossed out;
    Sk.tp.: "the" omitted
15. (Sz.)Gr.: "a certain" replaced with "an";
    Sk.tp.: "a certain" omitted
16. (Sz.)Gr.: "a" added;
    Sk.tp.: "a" added

wealth, he does not think for one moment of anything else in life. His whole mind, this [17] thought is concentrated upon it, his every effort is directed to it. Then he knows nothing else but this [17] object which blinds him, making him regardless of all virtues of love and beauty [18] to his fellowmen, of righteousness, of his obligation to his dear ones, those who are near him, and his relation and duty to God.

Not only one thing; there are many such things--love of power, of rank, of position, fighting for all things of this world. When a man is fully absorbed he loses his balance. But by this it does not mean that wealth [19] is not for a man, that [19] position or rank [20] is [21] not for a [22] man. [23] It does not mean that earthly comfort, convenience or advantage is not for a man. [23] It is all for man if he does not lose his poise over it, if he does not allow himself to be wholly [24] absorbed in it. If he only keeps his balance and sees that there is something else also in life . . . [25] To have a right mentality, it [26] does not mean that a person should leave the life of this world. [27] If he left it, it would not be the right mentality. Right mentality is to have a direction through life which leads to the object of one's mind, of one's heart, of one's soul. By having the right attitude of mind one

---

17. (Sz.)Sr.: "this" changed into "his";
Sk.tp.: "his" instead of "this"
18. (Sz.)Sr.: "beauty" changed into "duty";
Sk.tp.: "duty" instead of "beauty"
19. (Sz.)Gr.: crossed out "is not for a man, that";
(Sz.)Sk.: "is not for man, that" restored;
Sk.tp.: "is not for man, that"
20. (Sz.)Gr.: "or earthly comfort" added;
(Sz.)Sr.: "or earthly comfort" crossed out
21. (Sz.)Gr.: "is" changed into "are";
Sk.tp.: "are"
22. (Sz.)Gr.: "a" crossed out;
Sk.tp.: "a" omitted
23. (Sz.)Gr.: this sentence was crossed out;
(Sz.)Sk.: the sentence restored, but omitting "a" before "man";
Sk.tp.: "It does not mean that earthly comfort, convenience or advantage is not for man."
24. (Sz.)Gr.: "wholly" changed into "totally";
Sk.tp.: "totally" instead of "wholly"
25. (Sz.)Gr.: Five words, forming a separate sentence, crossed out and thereby becoming illegible (it might say, "Then man has got it.");
Sk.tp.: this sentence omitted
26. (Sz.)Gr.: "it" crossed out;
Sk.tp.: "it" omitted
27. Sz.: one word crossed out when the typescript was made

strikes a path in life which is the path. Life becomes easy, one's working [28] life becomes easy and [29] pleasant, all needs of the world, wealth or power, or position [30], they all lead one to a higher life, for all help him instead of hindering his path, if he would only strike the right road.

Now the question is how can one attain [31] to   to [31] it. By right thinking, by right feeling, by right speaking, by right activity. And what is right in this matter? The answer is: that which causes pleasure to begin, which is easy to do, which causes happiness in its accomplishments. And what is wrong? When [32] one begins with fear, when [33] one continues with doubt, and when [33] one finishes with remorse. Then [34] sometimes one does not see in the beginning what is right and what is wrong. In the end one sees. But why is it? It is because of negligence; it is not because one [35] has not got the sense to realize it. If there was no sense of discerning right or wrong [36] man [37] would never have been made responsible for his action, neither by man nor by God. How can one learn it? One can learn it by consulting with oneself, by consulting with one's innermost being before one takes a step in any direction. And be sure that the one who lives aright will be guided in the right path and his life will be easy and safe.

But one who does not care, intoxicated by the momentary intoxication of life, it is he who slides on to [38] the wrong track. . . . [39] one experience, . . . [40]

---

28. (Sz.)Sr.: "working" changed into "work in";
Sk.tp.: "work in"
29. (Sz.)Gr.: "easy and" crossed out;
Sk.tp.: "easy and" omitted
30. (Sz.)Gr.: three words added, then crossed out, thereby becoming illegible
31. (Sz.)Gr.: "to", one illegible word (perhaps "keep"), "to" crossed out;
Sk.tp.: "to ... to" omitted
32. (Sz.)Sr.: "When" changed into "What";
Sk.tp.: "What"
33. (Sz.)Gr.: "when" changed into "what";
Sk.tp.: "what"
34. (Sz.)Gr.: "Then" replaced with "Now";
Sk.tp.: "Now" instead of "Then"
35. (Sz.)Gr.: "one" changed into "man";
Sk.tp.: "man" instead of "one"
36. (Sz.)Gr.: "in" added;
Sk.tp.: "in" added
37. (Sz.)Gr.: "he" added;
Sk.tp.: "he" added
38. (Sz.)Gr.: one illegible word changed into "onto";
Sk.tp.: "out of" instead of the illegible word, later changed into "onto" by Sk.
39. (Sz.)Gr.: this part of the sentence was replaced with, "One man may realize this after" whereby the originally tp. words became illegible;
Sk.tp.: "One may realize this after"

A man who does not learn his lesson from one experience, is slow. A person who does not learn his lesson after two experiences, he is to be pitied. And the one who does not learn his lesson after three experiences is [41] hopeless. To act rightly he [42] needs love, love for doing what is right. In little things one can practise this in keeping one's room tidy, in dressing, in writing a letter. In every little thing one does in life, if he has the desire to do it rightly, that makes right mentality. And when man neglects in small things, in everyday life, to finish as nicely as he ought to have finished, by his carelessness, his negligence, in big things it is the same. In the things which are of great importance, great value in life, there also he shows his negligence. When there is a little hole in the cloth, it becomes a larger and larger hole in time. When it is little it does not come to his notice. He does not think anything of it ~~and~~. He thinks it does not matter; and so he maintains it. He nourishes it, and there will come one day when it will become so large that he will be frightened at its sight. In the schools today there [43] is education given of geography, of grammar, of history, and many more things, and the most important education which must be given from childhood to the children, to the youths, is of cultivating their hearts, the love of right-doing, of right-thinking, which would make out of them both ideal men and women, the lack of which humanity is feeling more and more. If only in the world we were right thinking people, if there was a majority of it, [44] the right mentality, humanity would not have suffered such tests of late. All diseases and catastrophes and misfortune are mostly brought about by wrong mentality. In the life of individuals and in the life of multitudes people do not know at the moment, because every thing takes time to work out its results, and as man does not [45] the answer to his right doing and wrong doing at the same moment, he thinks, "There is not such a thing as result, there is only action." There is an action which

---

40. (Sz.)Gr.: this sentence was replaced with, "and another does not do so after a thousand", whereby the originally tp. sentence, the last part of which was crossed out, became illegible (the last four words are: "not make him realize.");
    Sk.tp.: "and another does not do so after a thousand."
41. (Sz.)Gr.: "indeed" added;
    (Sz.)Sr.: "indeed" crossed out
42. (Sz.)Gr.: "he" crossed out;
    (Sz.)Sk.: "he" restored;
    Sk.tp.: "he" omitted
43. Sk.tp.: "there" omitted
44. Ibid.: "it," omitted
45. (Sz.)Gr.: "get" added;
    Sk.tp.: "get" added

results immediately, and the other action in [46] a long time, as [47] in a year's time, in ten years, in twenty years. But there is no action which has no result. There is no voice which has no echo. And when the time of results comes, the person is surprised. He has forgotten; he does not know what has been the cause of this result. The right thought leads to all that is right, from one right thing to the other right thing. It attracts benefit, [48]one benefit and then a greater benefit [49]. And the wrong attitude has its wrong results; as the time passes, it becomes worse and worse and worse. Then a person becomes so perplexed that he cannot see good in any thing, he cannot see right anywhere, it is all wrong, until the life becomes so burdensome that even God the Creator seems wrong. [50]Why did He create the soul? The whole affair of life seems to him to be wrong because it is [51] himself who has become all wrong; it [52] has turned all wrong. It is never too late in life to change that [53] attitude.

Man has a spark of divine light in him. Constantly there is the voice of the divine guidance in him, and it is not true that now it is too late to change it [54] attitude. To change the attitude for a man is as easy as changing [55]of the side [56]. All that is necessary [57] to study life and to cultivate that sense of discernment between right and wrong; and to grow to learn to appreciate the beauty of what is called right; and by constantly doing this, man strikes the right path which will result in attaining the desired goal.

---

46. (Sz.)Sr.: "in" changed into "after";
Sk.tp.: "after" instead of "in"
47. (Sz.)Sr.: "as" crossed out;
Sk.tp.: "as" omitted
48. (Sz.)Gr.: "first" added;
Sk.tp.: "first" added
49. (Sz.)Gr.: "benefit" crossed out;
(Sz.)Sr.: "benefit" restored
50. (Sz.)Gr.: added, "He asks";
Sk.tp.: "He asks" added
51. (Sz.)Gr.: "he" added;
Sk.tp.: "he" added
52. (Sz.)Gr.: "it" replaced with "and";
Sk.tp.: "and" instead of "it"
53. (Sz.)Sr.: "that" changed into "one's";
Sk.tp.: "one's" instead of "that"
54. (Sz.)Sr.: "it" first changed into "its", then crossed out and "one's" added;
Sk.tp.: "one's"
55. (Sz.)Gr.: "of" crossed out
56. (Sz.)Sr.: "sides" instead of "the side";
(Sk.tp.: "sides"
57. (Sz.)Gr.: "is" added;
Sk.tp.: "is" added

Copied from the book The Inner Life, 1st ed.

1

III

Fulfilment of the Obligations of Human Life

The position of the person living the inner life becomes like that of a grown-up person living among many children. At the same time, outwardly there seems no such difference as is apparent in the age of the children and the grown person, the difference lying in the size of his outlook, which is not always apparent. One who lives the inner life becomes much older than those around him, and yet outwardly he is the same as every other person. Therefore the man who has arrived at the fulness of the inner life adopts quite a different policy to[2] the one who is just beginning to tread that path, and also a different one to[3] that of the man who knows intellectually something about the inner life, but who really does not live it. The action again is different in the world, for the latter will criticize others who do not know what he thinks he knows, and will look upon them with pride and conceit, or with contempt, to think that they have not

---

Documents:

Bk. = the first edition of the book The Inner Life, published by the Sufi Order (Society in England), Southampton, England, in December 1922. It contains ten lectures, given in September 1922 at Katwijk, the Netherlands, during a Summer School, which were taken down by a professional stenographer. No book-preparation of this text or other earlier document has been found to date.

Sk.corr. = some corrections made by Sakina Furnée in a copy of the book The Inner Life, 1st ed.

Gd.corr. = some corrections made by Sherifa Goodenough in a copy of the book The Inner Life, 1st ed.

Notes:

1. From the "Quarterly Magazine for Seekers after Truth": Sufism, edited by Sophia Saintsbury Green, of December 1922, and a hwr. annotation by Sirdar van Tuyll, it is known that this lecture was given at Katwijk, the Netherlands, on Monday, 4th September 1922, in the evening (v. Preface).
2. Sk.corr.: "to" changed into "from"
3. Gd.corr.: "to" changed into "from"

risen to the mystery, to the height to which he has risen, and which he understands. He wishes to disconnect himself with people, saying that they are backward in their evolution, and that he cannot go with them. He says: "I am more advanced; I cannot join them in anything; they are different, I am different." He laughs at the petty ideas of those who surround him, and looks upon them as human beings with whom he must not associate, with whom he must not join in all things they do because he is much more advanced than they are.

But for the one who comes to the fulness of the inner life it is a great joy to mingle with his fellowman, just as it is for parents to play with their little children; the best moments of their lives are when they feel as a child with their children and when they can join in the play of the children. The parents who are kind and loving, if a child brings to them a doll's cup will pretend that they are drinking tea, and that they are enjoying it; they do not let the child think that they are superior, or that this is something in which they must not join. They play with the child, and they are happy with it, because the happiness of the children is theirs also.

This is the action of the man who lives the inner life, and it is for this reason that he agrees and harmonizes with people of all grades of evolution, whatever be their ideas, their thoughts, their belief, or their faith; in whatever form they worship or show their religious enthusiasm. He does not say: "I am much more advanced than you are, and to join you would be going backwards." The one who has gone so far forward can never go backwards, but by joining them he takes them along with him, onward. If he went on alone he would consider that he avoided his duty towards his fellowman, which he should perform. It is the empty pitcher that makes the noise when you knock upon it, but the pitcher which is full of water does not make any sound, it is silent, speechless.

So the wise live among all the people of this world, and they are not unhappy. The one who loves all is not unhappy. Unhappy is he who looks with contempt at the world, who hates human beings, and thinks he is superior to them; the one who loves them thinks only that they are going through the same process that he has gone through. It is from the darkness that he has to come into the light. It is just a difference of moments, and he with great patience passes those moments while his fellowmen are still in darkness, not making them know that they are in darkness, not letting them feel hurt about it, not looking upon them with contempt, only thinking that for every soul there is childhood, there is youth and maturity. So it is natural for every human being to go through this process. I have seen with my own eyes souls who have attained saintliness, and who have reached to great perfection; and yet such a soul would stand before the idol of stone with another[4] fellowman and worship, not letting him know that he was in any way more advanced than other men, keeping himself in a humble guise, not making any pretence that he had gone further in his spiritual evolution.

The further such souls go, the more humble they become; the greater the mystery they have realized, the less they speak about it. You would scarcely believe it if I were to tell you that during four years of the presence of my Murshid I have hardly more than once or twice had a conversation on spiritual matters. Usually the conversation was on worldly things, like[5] everybody else; nobody would perceive that here was a God-realized man, who was always absorbed in God. His conversation was like the conversation of every other person, he spoke on everything belonging to this world, never a spiritual conversation, not any special show of piety, or spirituality, and yet his atmosphere, [6]voice of his soul, and his presence revealed all that was hidden in his heart. Those who are God-realized and those who have touched wisdom speak very little of the subject. It is those who do not know who try to discuss it, not because they know, but because they themselves have doubts. When there is knowledge there is satisfaction, there is no tendency towards dispute. When one disputes it is because there is something not satisfied. Friends, there is nothing in this world, wealth or rank, position, power, or learning that can give such conceit as the slightest little amount of spiritual knowledge, and once a person has that conceit then he cannot take a further step; he is nailed down to that place where he stands, because the very idea of spiritual realization is in selflessness. Man has either to realize himself as something, or as nothing. In this realization of nothingness there is spirituality. If one has any little knowledge of the inner laws of nature, or if one has any sense of thinking, "How good I am, how kind I am, how generous, how good[7]-mannered, how influential, or how attractive," the slightest idea of anything of this kind coming into the mind, [8]closes the doors which lead into[9] the spiritual world. It is such an easy path to tread and yet so difficult. Pride is so natural to a human being; man may deny a virtue a thousand times in words, but he cannot help admitting it with his feelings, for the ego itself is pride. Pride <u>is</u> the ego, man cannot live without it. In order to attain to spiritual knowledge, in order to become conscious of the inner life, one does not need to learn very much, because here he has to know what he already knows,

---

4. Sk.corr.: "another" replaced with "a"
5. Gd.corr.: added "that of"
6. Ibid.: "the" added
7. Ibid.: "well" instead of "good"
8. Sk.corr.: "it" added
9. Ibid.: "to" instead of "into"

only he has to discover it himself. For his understanding of spiritual knowledge he does not need the knowledge of anything except himself. He acquires the knowledge of the self, which is himself, so near and yet so far.

Another thing the lover of God shows, is the same tendency as the human lover. He does not talk about his love to anybody. He cannot talk about it. Man cannot say how much he loves his beloved, no words can express it, and besides, he does not feel like talking about it to anybody. Even if he could, in the presence of his beloved he would close his lips. How then could the lover of God make a profession, "I love God!" The true lover of God keeps his love silently hidden in his heart, like a seed sown in the ground, and if the seedling grows, it grows in his actions towards his fellowman. He cannot act except with kindness, he cannot feel anything but forgiveness; every movement he makes, everything he does, speaks of his love, but not his lips.

That shows that in the inner life the greatest principle that one should observe is to be unassuming, quiet, without any show of wisdom, without any manifestation of learning, without any desire to let anyone know how far one had advanced, not even letting oneself know how far one has gone. The task to be accomplished is the entire forgetting of oneself and harmonizing with one's fellowman; acting in agreement with all, meeting everyone on his own plane, speaking to everyone in his own tongue, answering the laughter of one's friends with a smile, and the pain of another with tears, standing by one's friends in their joy and their sorrow, whatever be one's own grade of evolution. If a man through his life became like an angel he would accomplish very little. The accomplishment which is most desirable for man is to fulfil the obligations of human life.

Tuesday afternoon, September 5th[1]

The Problem of the Day [2]

Moral Question [3]

Those today in the world who observe any particular moral concept[4] have their peculiar ideas about them, which are either derived from their religion, race, community or family. And there are many others who do not observe the laws of religion or of the community. Many among them do not give any attention to this subject whatever. In this present age of materialism this idea is ever on the increase, that we are here in this world for some time, we don't know why, and the only thing that seems to them easy and convenient is to eat, drink and make merry. It is for this reason that humanity is going from bad to worse, having no regard for the soul, God, or the hereafter. It seems [5] those simple ones who make their life contented in their home, family or community, [6] they only seem[7] to observe principles, religious or social. But many in this world, just now, with all

---

Documents:

Sz. = a reporting by Shabaz Mitchell, mainly in longhand, but with several passages taken down in shorthand; a transliteration of these passages was made afterwards in the same document.
(Sz.)Sz.: some corr., etc. made by Shabaz Mitchell in his own reporting,
(Sz.)Gr.: one add. to "Sz." by Miss Sophia Green,
(Sz.)Sr.: one word changed in "Sz." by Sirdar van Tuyll

Sk.tp. = a typescript made from "Sz." in later years under Sakina Furnée's direction, with corr., add., etc. incorporated

Notes:

1. Sk.tp.: "afternoon" omitted, "1922" added
2. (Sz.)Gr.: added "IV" after the title, thereby indicating that it was the fourth lecture in this series; Sk.tp.: "(4)" added
3. (Sz.)Sr.: "Question" changed into "development"; Sk.tp.: "Moral Development" added after the title
4. (Sz.)Sz.: "concept" changed into "conceptions"; Sk.tp.: "conceptions" instead of "concept"
5. (Sz.)Sz.: "to" added; Sk.tp.: "to" added
6. (Sz.)Sz.: "that" added; Sk.tp.: "that" added
7. (Sz.)Sz.: "seem" replaced with "have"; Sk.tp.: "have" instead of "seem"

their education and advanced activity in the affairs of life, in commerce, politics and education, seem to have no regard for what may be called the moral principle. It does not mean that humanity does not need it. Every soul needs it. It only means that the souls need it and yet cannot find it—firstly, for the reason of various religions having their own moral precepts, and in many things differing from one another. And at the present moment having less voice in the state, besides, every country having its own moral ideas, peculiar to itself, each considering one's own to be the right[8] one and ignoring the truth of the other. Therefore, the Sufi Message brings to humanity the moral of the time, the moral which does not limit itself in principles, fixed in words; but in this age, the Sufi Order[9] strikes the note of the age. All of the morals are fountain drops, falling after having arisen, but this moral which the Sufi brings is that stream which rises and falls into many drops. The Sufi Message therefore points out the foundation of moral, the spring of moral, instead of limiting moral to little drops rising and falling from the fountain. When man begins to understand life the first thing that he does is to criticize and condemn a person who thinks and acts differently from the standard of moral he is accustomed to know. [10]When he is advanced a little but mislead of condemning others he begins to . . . if it does not . . . with his tender [11] of morals.[10] But when he becomes fully advanced, then he sees the moral of everyone from his point of view, and he understands from that that there are so many grades of human evolution, and every grade of human evolution has its standard, and so, if a thing is not right by one standard it is right by another. Therefore he refrains from condemning anyone in this world. This was seen in the life of Christ, that before the accusation came out of the lips of the accuser, the forgiveness of the Master arose before it. Forgiveness came up first, before justice. From whence it came? [12] Not only from love, because the perfect ones have balance of love and intelligence both.

It is the limitedness of intelligence that is inclined to criticize and condemn. The intelligence which is developed first understands and places all things in their places, but afterwards seeks the reason behind all things. He sees the justification of all things. It is not the one who accuses, who persecutes, who

---

8. (Sz.)Sz.: "right" crossed out
9. In October 1923 the name "Sufi Order" was changed into "Sufi Movement"
10. (Sz.)Sz.: this sentence, which shows two open spaces, was crossed out;
Sk.tp.: this sentence omitted
11. Sz.: the crossed out word appears to be "tender" or "lender", neither of which seems to make sense in the context
12. (Sz.)Sz.: "From whence it came?" changed into "From what came it?";
Sk.tp.: "From what came it?"

is the one who will elevate man. It is the one who understands, who forgives, who will raise man from his standard of evolution. The distinction between good and bad is made by the Sufi by consulting with oneself, for the Sufi realizes that his [13] soul, which is the Divine immanence, is nothing but joy. Joy is its nature. And since it is joy itself, it seeks for it, rightly or wrongly. When it wrongly seeks, it seems to get it, but it does not get it. When it rightly seeks it attains it, for that is the purpose of life.

The Sufi Order does not call renunciation a great virtue, to suffer pain as a great merit. No. It is foreign to the nature of the soul. It cannot be a virtue; it cannot be a merit. Yes, in attaining a certain joy, if it came that one had to go through pain and suffering, that is worthwhile. The strain [14] or [15] suffering or renunciation which leads to that joy to which he wants to attain, then it is no more suffering or pain or renunciation. It is only pain for what one wished to buy. And from this principle the Sufi understands that whatever be the action, if it is productive of joy, if the joy is everlasting, if the joy is dependable, it cannot be anything other than virtue. An action which is pain, which is suffering, however high it may seem, cannot be a virtue, because it is not the seeking of the soul.

In the Vedanta this joy is called . . . [16], a joy which is greater than all the pleasures known to the world, a joy which is independent of all things in this world. And this world, which is called Maya in Vedantic terms, has a tendency to tempt man at every move he makes in life, to make him feel that there is joy, that he goes after it, but finds that the price he has to pay is greater than what he has to purchase. He finds that what seemed for a moment a joy was like the horizon. It seemed it was there, but it was not there. This shows that the life outwards is an assumption of that joy, an illusion which promises that joy, and at every moment breaks its promises [17]. And yet, the soul looking outward cannot find all that serves for its sustenance, since it is joy itself and lives on joy. This is where comes in the whole tragedy of human life. The whole life, it seems, that a person passes in the search for joy and consequently he sees joy hiding behind one thing or another, and every time he tends to discover that illusion, to find it

---

13. (Sz.)Sz.: "his" changed into "the human";
Sk.tp.: "the human" instead of "his"
14. (Sz.)Sz.: "strain" changed into "pain";
Sk.tp.: "pain" instead of "strain"
15. Sk.tp.: "of" instead of "or"
16. Sz.: an open space;
Sk.tp.: "Anand" filled in
17. Sk.tp.: "promise" instead of "promises"

was not the thing he sought after, until he comes to realize that joy within himself, that he finds in himself a spark of that all-sufficient joy where the source of joy is hidden.

No doubt it takes some experience, it takes patience, many sacrifices and disappointments, before one arrives to realize the joy which is within. But at the same time to distinguish what is good and what is bad, that is the best principle to know, that which leads to joy, that is dependable, is virtue, and what leads to trouble and sorrow and suffering, even if it were joy to greet one at the beginning, is a sin. There is no action in this world which can be stamped with sin or virtue. It is its relation with a particular soul which makes it sin or virtue.

Whatever the action, if it is productive of joy, how can it be a sin? If there is a joy which is everlasting, how can it be a sin? Everything in its beginning, in its continuity, and in its result that is joyful, is certain virtue, and that which is the reverse in its beginning and in its continuity, in its result is a sin. In this way a man, by being thoughtful in life, by directing every thought, feeling and action with wisdom, can know for himself the secret of right and wrong, instead of depending upon someone else telling him, and it is this knowledge that will make him know and understand his fellowman better.

Copied from the book The Inner Life, 1st ed.

1

IV

The Realization of the Inner Life

The principle of the one who experiences the inner life, is to become all things to all men throughout his life. In every situation, in every capacity, he answers the demand of the moment. Often people think that the spiritual person must be a man with sad looks, with a long face, with a serious expression and with a melancholy atmosphere. Really speaking, that picture is the exact contrary of the real spiritual person. In all capacities the one who lives the inner life has to act outwardly as he ought in order to fit the occasion; he must act according to the circumstances, and he must speak to everyone in his own language, standing upon the same level, and yet realizing the inner life.

For the knower of truth, the one who has attained spiritual knowledge, and who lives the inner life, there is no occupation in life which is too difficult, as a business man, as a professional man, as a king; a ruler, a poor man, a worldly man, as a priest or monk, in all aspects he is different to what people know and see of him. To the one who lives the inner life the world is a stage, on which he is the actor, who has to act a part, in which he has sometimes to be

---

Documents:

Bk. = the first edition of the book The Inner Life, published by the Sufi Order (Society in England), Southampton, England, in December 1922. It contains ten lectures, given in September 1922 at Katwijk, the Netherlands, during a Summer School, which were taken down by a professional stenographer. No book-preparation of this text or other earlier document has been found to date.

Sk.corr. = some corrections made by Sakina Furnée in a copy of the book The Inner Life, 1st ed.

Notes:

1. From the "Quarterly Magazine for Seekers after Truth": Sufism, edited by Sophia Saintsbury Green, of December 1922, and a hwr. annotation by Sirdar van Tuyll, it is known that this lecture was given at Katwijk, the Netherlands, on Tuesday, 5th September 1922, in the evening (v. Preface).

angry, and sometimes loving, and in which he has to take part both in tragedy and comedy. So also the one who has realized the inner life acts constantly; and like the actor who does not feel the emotions he assumes, the spiritual man has to fill fittingly the place in which life has placed him. There he performs everything thoroughly and rightly, in order to fulfil his outer mission in life. He is a friend to his friend, a relative to his relatives. With all to whom he is outwardly related he keeps the right relationship with thought, with consideration, and yet in his realization he is above all relationships. He is in the crowd and in the solitude at the same time. He may be very much amused and at the same time he is very serious. He may seem very sad, and yet there is joy welling up from his heart.

Therefore the one who has realized the inner life is a mystery to every one; no one can fathom the depth of that person, except that he promises sincerity, he emits love, he commands trust, he spreads goodness, and he gives an impression of God and the truth. For the man who has realized the inner life every act is his meditation; if he is walking in the street it is his meditation; if he is working as a carpenter, as a goldsmith or in any other trade or business, that is his meditation. It does not matter if he is looking at heaven or at the earth, he is looking at the object that he worships. East or west or north or south, upon all sides is his God. In form, in principle, nothing restricts him. He may know things and yet may not speak, for if a man who lives the inner life were to speak of his experiences it would confuse many minds. There are some individuals in the world who from morning until evening have their eyes and their ears focussed on every dark corner, wanting to listen, or to see what they can find out; and they find out nothing. If someone were to tell such people wonders he would have a very good occupation, the whole world would seek him. But such is not the work of the self-realized man. He sees and yet does not look; if he were to look, how much he would see! There is so much to be seen by one whose every glance, wherever it is cast, breaks through every object and discovers its depth and its secret. And if he were to look at things and find out their secrets and depths where would it end, and of what interest is it to him?

The inner life, therefore, is seeing all things and yet not seeing them, feeling all things and not expressing them, for they cannot be fully expressed; understanding all things and not explaining; how far can such a man explain, and how much can another understand? Each according to the capacity he has, no more. The inner life is not lived by closing the eyes; one need not close one's eyes from this world in order to live it, one can just as well open them.

The exact meaning of the inner life is not only to live in the body, but to live in the heart, to live in the soul. Why, then, does not the average man live the inner life when he too has a heart and a soul? It is because he has a heart and yet is not conscious of it; he has a soul and knows not what it is. When he lives in the captivity of the body, limited by that body, he can only feel a thing by touching it, he sees only by looking through his eyes, he hears only by hearing with his ears. How much can the ears hear and the eyes see? All this experience obtained by the outer senses is limited. When man lives in this limitation he does not know[2] another part of his being, which is much higher, more wonderful, more living and more exalted exists. Once he begins to know this, then the body becomes his tool, for he lives in his heart, and then later he passes on and lives in his soul. He experiences life independently of his body, and that is called the inner life. Once man has experienced the inner life, the fear of death has expired, because he knows death comes to the body, not to his inner being. When once he begins to realize life in his heart and in his soul, then he looks upon his body as a coat. If the coat is old he puts it away and takes a new one, for his being does not depend upon his coat. The fear of death lasts only so long as man has not realized that his real being does not depend upon his body.

The joy, therefore, of the one who experiences the inner life is beyond comparison greater than that of the average man living only as a captive in his mortal body. Yet the inner life does not necessitate man's adopting a certain way of living, or living an ascetic, or a religious life. Whatever his outer occupation be, it does not matter; the man who lives the inner life lives through it all. Man always looks for a spiritual person in a religious person, or perhaps in what he calls a good person, or in someone with a philosophical mind, but that is not necessarily the case. A person may be religious, even philosophical, a person may be religious or good, and yet he may not live the inner life.

There is no distinct outward appearance which can prove a person to be living the inner life, except one thing. When a child grows toward youth, you can see in the expression of that child a light beaming out, a certain new consciousness arising, a new knowledge coming which the child has not known before. That is the sign of youth, yet the child does[3] say so; he cannot say it, even if he wanted to, he cannot explain it. And yet you can see it from every movement that the child makes, from his every expression, you can find that he is realizing life now. And so it is with the soul, when the soul begins to realize the life above and beyond this life, it begins to show; and although the man who realizes this may refrain from purposely showing it, yet from his expression, his movement, his glance, his voice, from every action he does, and from every

---

2. Sk.corr.: "that" added
3. Ibid.: "not" added, corr. in the 2nd edition

attitude, the wise can grasp, and the others can feel that he is conscious of some mystery.

The inner life is a birth of the soul; as Christ said that unless the soul is born again it cannot enter the kingdom of heaven. Therefore the realization of the inner life is entering the kingdom of heaven; and this consciousness when it comes to the human being shows itself as a new birth, and with this new birth there comes the assurance of everlasting life.

A typescript made under Sakina Furnée's direction of a question and answer.

Question: *Is it better to give an outlet to one's joy and sorrow or to suppress them?*

Answer: The expression of joy should not be extreme. The wise are never overjoyed, because there is no worldly circumstance that can give them great joy. And also they know that the extreme expression of joy will bring sorrow after it. You can see that in everyday life. If you make a little child laugh very much or enjoy very much for five minutes, in one hour, or in two hours, or before evening, it will feel very unhappy. And if the wise person does not give an outlet to his joy, still less will he give an outlet to his sorrow. Because, not only would that humiliate a person, but to be in extreme sorrow increases the idea of the self. I have seen this with my Murshid. I knew him for years, and often there were circumstances which would have caused great joy, but I never in all those years saw his even cheerfulness altered. The wise person is in the thought of God, and what is there in this world so great that it can move him much? Before that, I had seen the same thing with my father.

Document:

Sk.tp. = a typescript made under Sakina Furnée's direction. In later years Sk. added this question and answer to two answers to questions, given on 22 October 1922 and referring to lectures of 7 and 8 October 1922. It appears, however, that this question and answer refers to the lecture "The Problem of the Day" of 5th September 1922 and probably can be dated 6 September 1922. It is not known from what document Sk. copied it, as no other reporting or copies have as yet been found in the archives.

Wednesday afternoon, September 6th[1]

The Problem of the Day[2]

The Difference between Right and Wrong[2]

All that is directed by love is as a rule right. And all that is directed by hate is most often wrong. In fact at the present time, when the effect of war is prevailing throughout the world, if this principle were thought out and followed, many difficulties might be surmounted. But the hatred that exists today between nations, especially in Europe, in the damaged heart of Europe, and[3] it continued, in a hundred years' time it could[4] enfeeble Europe to an unimaginable condition.

Documents:

Sz. = a reporting by Shabaz Mitchell, mainly in longhand, but with several short passages taken down in shorthand; a transliteration of these passages was made afterwards in the same document.
(Sz.)Sz.: some corr. and add. made by Shabaz Mitchell in his own reporting,
(Sz.)Gr.: one add. to "Sz." by Miss Sophia Green;

O.t. = an old typescript, made from "Sz." by Shabaz Mitchell;
(O.t.)Sz.: one alteration and one add. made in "o.t." by Shabaz Mitchell,
(O.t.)Gr.: one add. to "o.t." by Miss Sophia Green,
(O.t.)Sk.: one corr. made in "o.t." by Sakina Furnée;

Sk.tp. = a typescript made from "o.t." in later years under Sakina Furnée's direction, with corr., add., etc. incorporated
(Sk.tp.)Sk.: two corr. made in "Sk.tp." by Sakina Furnée

Notes:

1. (O.t.)Sz.: "Wednesday 6/9" instead of "Wednesday afternoon", and later "6 Sept." added at the upper right corner of page 1 in hwr.;
   Sk.tp.: "1922" added
2. (O.t.)Gr.: "V" added after the title and after the subtitle, thereby indicating that it was the fifth lecture in this series;
   Sk.tp.: "(5)" added after the subtitle
3. (Sz.)Sz.: "and" changed into "if";
   o.t., Sk.tp.: "if" instead of "and"
4. O.t., Sk.tp.: "would" instead of "could"

And how many people[5] there are today—millions—who will perhaps believe this as a principle but[6] not ready to follow it, ~~nor sure that~~ not willing to follow it.

And what does it show? It shows that hatred has become as the nature of so many souls, as drinking becomes the nature of a drunken man to . . .[7], so that in a few years' time, knowing that it ruins his health, yet he cannot get along without drink. So it is with this feeling of hatred. Directed by this feeling[8] when one does an act of patriotism, can it be worthy? Even an act of worship cannot be worthy if directed by hatred—praying for somebody's destruction. That is the state of today.

The distinction[9] of right and wrong can also be seen by understanding the secret of metaphysics, that every activity has its time and place, which awaits the expression of that activity to give it a place. Therefore all that one does which fits in with the time, the circumstances, the demand of the moment, it is right. And what does not fit in is wrong; and [10] that must be avoided. For instance, at one time laughter fits in with the moment, the moment gives a scope to the smile. There is another time that the same action, laughter or smile, has no place to fit in—it is not the demand of that occasion. Therefore the thing that was right once, does not now fit in with the occasion. It seems ~~that~~ this outward life welcomes a word sometimes, and the same word at another time it does not welcome. The one who keenly watches life, he therefore understands the time and the situation, and accordingly he thinks, speaks and acts. Life is a school for every activity, and when that activity is fitting with the scope, the scope becomes as a world [11] or as a capacity, where every activity is rightly utilised. And every activity done with this understanding is right; if not, it is wrong.

There was a time of war when every activity was directed towards the war. Now the peace is made, and yet there are so many [12], such a large proportion of humanity, in utter misery. Very few in this world know the fact fully, and fewer still work to bring ease to suffering humanity. The only way

---

5. O.t.: "peoples"
6. (Sz.)Sz.: inserted "are" before "not"; o.t., Sk.tp.: "are" added
7. (Sz.)Sz.: "to" and one illegible word crossed out; o.t., Sk.tp.: "to" omitted
8. O.t., Sk.tp.: "of hatred" added
9. Ibid.: "destruction" instead of "distinction", probably a misreading from "Sz."
10. Ibid.: "and" omitted
11. (Sz.)Sz.: "world" changed into "mould"; o.t., Sk.tp.: "mould" instead of "world"
12. (Sz.)Sz.: "nations" added; o.t., Sk.tp.: "nations" added

how the [13] better conditions could be brought about would be to forget that hatred that existed during the war. It must expire with the finishing of the war. A new feeling must now be produced among individuals and in the heart of humanity, without any regard of friend or foe, to sympathise with suffering humanity. That alone can bring about the ideal peace. This can come by the realisation of the moral that the Sufi Message brings, that the whole humanity is as one single body. It is the different sections under the names of races and religions who are its organs; and the pain caused to any [14] organ of the body has its influence, sooner or later, on the whole body. Every individual in this world, every community and nation is united in this universe. Not one single being is pulled alone without [15] every soul there [16] having had a share of that pull. No soul is pressed in this world without some other individual being pressed in some form or other. The whole universe is one, its source is one, its goal is one. This world of variety deludes so as to make [17] our eyes covered from the reality as in a state of dark night. It will not always remain. There will come a moment when every individual will realise it [18], when the multitude, the world will realise it; and the sooner it is realised the better it will be.

It is the spreading of this idea throughout the world which is the main work of the Sufi Order [19], to make man conscious of this oneness of the whole being, of his share with the joy and sorrow of each being [20], [21] is the central theme of the Sufi Message.

The only principle that the Sufi Message gives and asks that one should live, is that each must work and live for all.

---

13. O.t., Sk.tp.: "to" instead of "the"
14. O.t.: "one" instead of "any"
15. O.t.: "with" instead of "without";
    (o.t.)Sk.: "without" written above "with"
16. O.t., Sk.tp.: "there" omitted
17. (Sz.)Sz.: "so as to make" changed into "us so and makes";
    o.t., Sk.tp.: "us so and makes"
18. O.t.: "this" instead of "it";
    (Sk.tp.)Sk.: "this", changed back to "it" in hwr.
19. In October 1923 the official name became "Sufi Movement", and "Sufi Order" became the name for one of its branches: the esoteric school
20. Sk.tp.: "other" instead of "being";
    (Sk.tp.)Sk.: "other" changed back into "being"
21. (Sz.)Sz.: "and this" added;
    o.t., Sk.tp.: "This" added

Copied from the book The Inner Life, 1st ed.

[1]

V

Freedom of Action

As a man grows through the inner life, so he feels a freedom of thought, speech and action which comes as a natural course through his spiritual journey. And the reason why this freedom comes and from whence it comes can be explained by the fact that there is a spirit of freedom hidden within man, covered by outward conventionalities. When man grows out of the outward conventionalities, then the spirit of freedom, which was closed in so far, becomes manifest.

The laws given to humanity are given by those far from such laws,—the Elder Ones. As for children there are certain laws, certain rules necessary, so those who have not yet evolved to look at life from the higher point of view are fixed under certain laws which are taught to them as religion; and they are as necessary for mankind as the rules given to the children in the home. If there were no rules given, the children would become unruly; but when the children become grown up, then they begin to see for themselves the reason why rules were given to them, and the benefit that these rules were to them; then they

Documents:

Bk. = the first edition of the book The Inner Life, published by the Sufi Order (Society in England), Southampton, England, in December 1922. It contains ten lectures, given in September 1922 at Katwijk, the Netherlands, during a Summer School, which were taken down by a professional stenographer. No book-preparation of this text or other earlier document has been found to date.

Sk.corr. = some corrections made by Sakina Furnée in a copy of the book The Inner Life, 1st ed.

Notes:

1. From the "Quarterly Magazine for Seekers after Truth": Sufism, edited by Sophia Saintsbury Green, of December 1922, and a hwr. annotation by Sirdar van Tuyll, it is known that this lecture was given at Katwijk, the Netherlands, on Wednesday, 6th September 1922, in the evening (v. Preface).

can make such rules for themselves as suit them best.

The inner life, therefore, helps a soul to grow up; when the soul evolves from subjection to mastery, then it makes rules for itself. In the East, therefore, no one tries to criticise a spiritual person; no one stands up to judge his action or to accuse him of something which he himself calls wrong. For this reason Jesus Christ has said: "Judge not." But this teaching has been given to point out that "judge not" applies to your equal; for the one who is still more advanced, no one can judge. When man has the tendency to judge one more advanced than himself, the consequence is that spiritual advancement deteriorates, because however advanced he may be, those who have not yet advanced pull him down. Therefore humanity instead of going forward goes backward. What happened in the case of Jesus Christ? He was judged. The liberated soul, the soul which was made free by divine nature, was judged at the court of man. The men less advanced considered themselves sufficiently learned to judge Christ, and not only to judge, but to give sentence.

In whatever period of civilization, therefore, the tendency to judge the one who is advanced has shown itself, there has always come a collapse of the whole civilization. The Sufi Surmad[2], a great Saint, who lived in Gwalia[3], was asked by the Emperor Aurungzeb[4] to attend at the mosque, for it was against the rules of the time that anyone kept away from the regular prayers, which took place in the mosque of the State. Sarmud[5], being a man of ecstasy, living every moment of his day and night in union with God, being God-conscious himself, he perhaps forgot, or refused; a certain time of prayer or a certain place for prayer for him was nothing. Every place for him was a place of prayer; every time was a time of prayer; his every breath was a prayer. When he refused to attend prayers he was beheaded for going against the rules which were made for everyone. The consequence was that the downfall of the whole Mogul[6] Empire can be dated from that time; the entire Mogul civilization, unique in its time, fell to pieces.

The Hindus have always known this philosophy, for the reason that they had a perfect religion, a religion in which one aspect of God was characterized as human, and their various Devas are nothing but various characteristics of human nature, each of them adored and worshipped. In this way not only God, but the whole human nature in all its aspects was adored and worshipped. It is

---

2. Sk.corr.: "Sarmad" instead of "Surmad"
3. Ibid.: "Gwalior" instead of "Gwalia"
4. Ibid.: "Aurangzeb" instead of "Aurungzeb"
5. Ibid.: "Sarmad" instead of "Sarmud"
6. Ibid.: "Moghul" instead of "Mogul"

that which makes the Hindu religion perfect. When people say, "This place is sacred, and the other place is not sacred; that particular thing is holy, and all other things[7] not holy", in this way they divide life into many pieces, the life which is one, the life which cannot be divided.

Therefore those who rise above the ordinary conventionalities of life by their inner development, come to another consciousness. For them worldly laws are the laws for the children. Those who begin to see this difference between the laws they set before themselves and the laws that are observed by mankind, sometimes at first condemn and then disregard the common laws. They criticize them and ask, "What is it all for?" But those who come to the fuller realization of the inner laws, show respect even for the laws of the children; knowing that they are the laws for the children and not for the grown-up, yet they respect them, for they know that it cannot be otherwise. The laws which they know can only manifest to the one whose soul rises to that realization, but before that soul rises it must have some law by which to live in harmony. Therefore advanced souls regard such laws with respect, and observe them when they are in the community. They do not condemn them, they will not criticise them. They realize that harmony is the principal thing in life and that we cannot be happy through life if we cannot harmonize with all those around us. Whatever be our grade of evolution, whatever be our outlook on life, and whatever be our freedom, we must have regard for the laws of the majority.

Now the question is, those who are spiritually advanced, do they have any special conception of morals? Indeed, they have, and their morals are great morals, much greater than the average human being can conceive of. It is not that by becoming free spiritually from the laws of the generality, they become free from their own laws. They have their own laws to bind them, and these are much higher and much greater laws. No doubt, their way of looking at things may be criticised and may not be generally understood. Yet, their law is more akin to nature; their laws are in harmony with the spirit; their laws have their effect as phenomena; and by regarding two morals which are contrary to each other, the morals of the generality and their own morals, they arrive at a plane and a condition where their hands and feet are nailed. That is the symbolical meaning of the nailing of Christ to the Cross.

---

7. Ibid.: "are" added

Shabaz Mitchell's longhand reporting.

Thursday afternoon, September 7th[1]

The Problem of the Day[2]

Distinction between Good and Bad

Man very often overlooks if there were[3] some good hidden under the garb of what he calls bad, or that there may be some evil hidden under what he calls good. Sometimes an action is a cause and sometimes an action is an effect. Often an action which is an effect and which appears bad, may have at the back of it a cause, if that cause[4] were known, one would find it to be good. If one only saw clearly into every action, thought and word, one would see a thousand petals around it and within it, which are perhaps quite different from what it appears outside. Very often the most innocent people in this world are accused of some fault, and often the most wicked by their outward appearance make all they do prove apparently good. Therefore it is not [5]the power of every man to judge another. The ordinary man cannot judge, although he is the man who is ready to judge; and the one who arrives to[6] the state of understanding the[7] life, so that he can judge, or has the right to judge, then he refrains from judging. At this present moment in this world

---

Documents:

Sz. = a reporting by Shabaz Mitchell, mainly in longhand, but with several passages taken down in shorthand; a transliteration of these passages was made afterwards in the same document.
(Sz.)Sz.: corr. and add. made in "Sz." by Shabaz Mitchell;
(Sz.)Gr.: one addition to "Sz." by Miss Sophia Green.

Sk.tp. = a typescript made from "Sz." in later years under Sakina Furnée's direction, with corr., etc. incorporated.
(Sk.tp.)Sk.: one word added to "Sk.tp." by Sakina Furnée.

Notes:

1. Sk.tp.: "1922" added
2. (Sz.)Gr.: "VI" added after the title, thereby indicating that it was the sixth lecture in this series; Sk.tp.: "(6)" added at the end of the line
3. (Sz.)Sz.: "if there were" changed into "that there may be"; Sk.tp.: "that there may be" instead of "if there were"
4. Sk.tp.: "which if it" instead of "if that cause"
5. (Sz.)Sz.: afterwards "in" added; Sk.tp.: "in" added
6. (Sz.)Sz.: "to" changed into "at"; Sk.tp.: "at" instead of "to"
7. (Sz.)Sz.: "the" crossed out; Sk.tp.: "the" omitted

the laws[8] are ever[9] on the increase. The number of lawyers is ever increasing and [10]is never sufficient for the needs of humanity. The light is needed to tell what is in man's heart, how a person is speaking, whereas[11] a lawyer keeps on making right of wrong and wrong of right, and that[12] one who is concerned is speechless because he knows not the man-made law. Man is entirely in the hands of the law, if the law is favourable or unfavourable, if the lawyer has understood the case or has not understood the case. The lawyer is not a psychologist. He does not know the inside of the heart. About the case,[13] what he knows is all[14] the outer signs, which is not all worth anything when a person feels this[15] inner truth of a true case. Mostly in every case the inside is contrary to its outside appearance, and the case is judged in the court from its outside appearance. In that way it has become a profession.

People with wealth are mostly the victims of lawyers. The court is the place where a great deal of their wealth is due. If a little thing is shown to the lawyer he can make [16]it a mountain out of a molehill[16]. If it is a thing which common sense can judge in one moment's time, it must take a year. If it is the case of a rich person it must take much longer. Many witnesses can be hired, and at last he wins[17] very often who has some influence, who has some strength to fight, who has the means; and often the means become his enemy and the case is prolonged because he is rich. The consequence is that there are more and more ~~persons~~ prisons, more people accused of crimes, who have that impression upon their souls, upon their minds.

The interest that the newspapers take in publishing a little fault to the

---

8. (Sz.)Sz.: "laws" changed into "lawyers";
   Sk.tp.: "lawyers" instead of "laws"
9. Sk.tp.: "ever" omitted
10. (Sz.)Sz.) afterwards "there" added
11. (Sz.)Sz.: "whereas" replaced with "while";
    Sk.tp.: "while" instead of "whereas"
12. (Sz.)Sz.: "that" changed into "the";
    Sk.tp.: "the" instead of "that"
13. Ibid.: "About the case" moved to after "what he knows"
14. Sk.tp.: "all" omitted;
    (Sk.tp.)Sk.: "all" reinserted in hwr.
15. Sk.tp.: "the" instead of "this"
16. (Sz.)Sz.: rewritten to read, "a molehill a mountain";
    Sk.tp.: "a molehill a mountain" instead of "it a mountain out of a molehill"
17. Sk.tp.: "comes" instead of "wins", probably a misreading from "Sz."

whole world with every sort of exaggeration and ridicule [18]is most pitiful—to think that at this time of human evolution such a tendency should exist in humankind. At every court the reporter is waiting to get some sensational news, to bring [18] out before humanity the ridicule and laughter, having no regard for the respect due to the individual, and by that proving lack of respect for humanity. And by this strictness of the law and by the ever-increasing judicial activities, do you think the world is any better? It is worse, for that sense of chivalry, that sense of honour which is in man with clearness of conscience which guides man's life, it all becomes ~~blinded~~ blunted, when he finds himself in the crowd where there is no sense of the dignity of the human being.

These people who are sentenced to imprisonment for so many years, what often is got out of it? Have they learned to refrain from doing their wrong-doing again? No. It has only blunted their fineness, their clearness of conscience, their delicate sensibility of looking at an error. Once they have realized themselves degraded before the eyes of humanity, they become more shameless. By a deep study of human nature one will find out that the tendency to make an [19] error is not a crime. It is very often either ignorance or weakness. And this cannot be cured or corrected by sending them to prison or giving them a life sentence. A prison is a home of misery. That will not teach mankind how to live better, how to be better. What is necessary is a school for criminals, not imprisonment. The only sentence which can be given is compulsory attendance at this school, where they are taught by sufficiently advanced people to see for themselves the suitable action and to find out where they have made a mistake, where there was weakness; if there was weakness, then to train them and show them how to develop, and show them how they can get out of it; if it was through ignorance, then sufficient light should be shed [20] upon their minds so that they may realize for themselves that it was their error. When the teacher of the school and those who attend the school both are convinced and satisfied with each other, then he is a free man again. Why all this misery? Who profits by it? Why all this expense that the state has to make without any benefit from it? What a difference if one can only find that there was a time in the ~~past~~ civilization of the past when one wise man, gifted with divine light, who

---

18. (Sz.)Sz.: "it" added;
    Sk.tp.: "it" added
19. (Sz.)Sz.: "an" crossed out
20. (Sz.)Sz.: "should be shed" changed into "to be put";
    Sk.tp.: "to be put" instead of "should be shed"

had keen sight into the matter, judged a case instantly, at first glance. And the case was finished in a moment's time instead of going on for years and years, those in fault having all the time to pay for their faults. And then, [21]for one particular action there are ten people accused, they have the same kind of punishment.

There is a story that four criminals were brought before a wise king, accused of some fault. He look at one and said, "He must be hanged". He look at another and said, "He must be exiled". He looked at the third person and said, "He must be sentenced for the whole life". And he looked at the fourth person and said, "I am sorry to think that you can do such a thing. Go away. Do not show yourself to me any more". All these three went to their punishments, willingly or unwillingly, but this one, the last one, he went home and committed suicide with [22] remorse. Those words of the king were worse than a life sentence; they cut him through. We do not use in everyday life the same whip for [23] the horse as we do on the donkey. This matter is not realized just now—individual temperament, recognition of individual character. The theory of the individual does not seem to exist. It is all a rigid law by which the whole humanity may be governed—whether it is the donkey, or the horse, or the mule. And what it takes away is the progress of humanity towards a higher ideal. It pulls man down to think that he is bound to the rigidity of thoughts and ideas. He cannot feel himself exalted. He feels himself bound to the earth, and there is no way of getting out of it. This is, [24] no doubt, the ways of the periods in the past [25]for this purpose, and the methods of ~~the~~ today are for today, but reform has a scope in every period. It is not necessary that during this period we should follow the methods of the past, but it is most necessary that we should recognize the faults of the age today, so that we can get above them. We must adopt new

---

21. (Sz.)Sz.: "if" added;
Sk.tp.: "if" added
22. (Sz.)Sz.: "with" replaced with "through";
Sk.tp.: "through" instead of "with"
23. (Sz.)Sz.: "for" changed into "on";
Sk.tp.: "on" instead of "for"
24. (Sz.)Sz.: "This is," crossed out;
Sk.tp.: "This is," omitted
25. (Sz.)Sz.: "were" later added;
Sk.tp.: "were" added

methods. One of the best ways of meeting (dealing)[26] with ~~criminals~~ crime is not to take the criminal[27] as a criminal, but to take him as either ignorant or weak. Instead of hating him, instead of insulting him and looking on him with contempt, to feel that feeling of brotherhood, that he is a human being as we ourselves are and that we could have the same fault in us. Only if at this moment he happens to be in fault, it is our duty to lift him up, thinking that some day we are[28] in his place and he may lift us up. It is that feeling of brotherhood which will enlighten the generality, and not the feeling that by the power of a certain office or by[29] a certain law that man can condemn another to imprisonment, and not really having known the cause[30] inside, the cause which was behind his crime.

For a Sufi this is a question of very great importance, for he sees the cause behind the cause, and in this way several causes, one behind the other, until he traces in the particular Cause Whom he calls God, that leading Cause which leads every impulse and every activity, even of the sinners. After rising to the Sufi realization one dare not say one word, whatever he sees. He can only keep his lips closed and do all he can to smooth the condition, to make things better without uttering one word, without arguing, without accusing, without condemning anyone for his fault. Verily, after all, God is working behind every purpose, every impulse.

---

26. Sz.: apparently "meeting" was said, but Shabaz Mitchell suggested to replace "meeting" with "dealing";
    Sk.tp.: "meeting (dealing)"
27. Sk.tp.: "criminals"
28. (Sz.)Sz.: "are" later replaced with "may be";
    Sk.tp.: "may be" instead of "are"
29. Sk.tp.: "only" instead of "or by", probably a misreading from "Sz."
30. (Sz.)Sz.: "cause" crossed out;
    Sk.tp.: "cause" omitted

Copied from the book The Inner Life, 1st ed.

[1]

VI

The Law of the Inner Life

Those who live the inner life begin to see a law which is hidden to the average man. There is the law of nature, which is known as science, and that of life, which is called moral law, but beyond science and morals there is another law. It may be called occult law, or in other words, inner law; a law which can be understood by an open heart and an awakened soul.

[2]This law manifests to the view of the seer in many and varied forms; sometimes it appears in quite a contrary form to the effect that it has later on in its manifestation. The eye of the seer becomes a sword which cuts open, so to speak, all things, including the hearts of men, and sees clearly through all they contain; but it is a cutting open which is at the same time healing.

In the Koran[3] it is said: "He has taught man by the skill of his pen." And what does that mean? It means that to the man who lives the inner life, everything that he sees becomes a written character and this whole visible world

---

Documents:

Bk. = the first edition of the book The Inner Life, published by the Sufi Order (Society in England), Southampton, England, in December 1922. It contains ten lectures, given in September 1922 at Katwijk, the Netherlands, during a Summer School, which were taken down by a professional stenographer. No book-preparation of this text or other earlier document has been found to date.

Sk.corr. = some corrections made by Sakina Furnée in a copy of the book The Inner Life, 1st ed.

Notes:

1. From the "Quarterly Magazine for Seekers after Truth": Sufism, edited by Sophia Saintsbury Green, of December 1922, and a hwr. annotation by Sirdar van Tuyll, it is known that this lecture was given at Katwijk, the Netherlands, on Thursday, 7th September 1922, in the evening (v. Preface).
2. Sk.corr.: Sk. added this paragraph to the first one
3. Ibid.: "Qur'an" instead of "Koran"

a book. He reads it as plainly as a letter written by his friend. And besides this, he hears a voice within which becomes to him a language. It is an inner language; its words are not the same as the words of the external language. It is a divine language. It is a language without words, which can only be called a voice, and yet it serves as a language. It is like music, which is as clear as a language to the musician. Another person enjoys music, but only the musician exactly knows what it says, what every note is, how it is expressed and what it reveals. Every phrase of music to him has a meaning; every piece of music to him is a picture. But this I say only about a real musician.

People profess to have clairvoyance and clairaudience, and very often delude others by giving false prophecies, but the one who lives the inner life does not need to prophesy; he does not need to tell others what he sees and what he hears. It is not only that he is not inclined to do so, but also he sees no necessity for it; besides, he cannot fully express himself. How difficult it is to translate fully the poetry of one language into the poetry of another! Yet it is only interpreting the ideas of one part of the earth to the people of another part of the same earth. How much more difficult then it must be to translate or to interpret the ideas of the divine world to the human world. In what words can they be given, what phrases can be used for them, and after being given even in words and phrases, who would understand them? It is the language of a different world.

Therefore, when the prophets and seers of all ages have given to humanity a certain message and law, it was only the giving of a drop from the ocean which they received into their hearts. And this also is a great difficulty, for even this drop is not intelligible. Does every Christian understand the Bible? Does every Mussulman know Koran[3], or every Hindu Vedanta? No, they may know the words of the verses but not always the real meaning. Among the Mussulmans there are some who know the whole Koran[3] by heart, but that does not suffice for the purpose. The whole nature is a secret book, yet it is an open book to the seer. How can man translate it, how can man interpret it? It is like trying to bring the sea onto the land; one can bring it, but how much?

The understanding of this law gives quite a different outlook on life to the seer, which makes him more inclined to appreciate all that is good and beautiful, to admire all that is worth admiring, to enjoy all that is worth enjoying, to experience all that is worth experiencing. It awakens the sympathy of the seer to love, to tolerate, to forgive, to endure and to sympathize; it gives the inclination to support, to protect, and to serve those in need. But can he say what he really feels, how he really feels? No, he cannot say it even to himself.

Therefore, the one who lives the inner life is all things: he is as a physician who knows things that a physician cannot know; as an astrologer who knows much more than the astrologer; an artist who knows that which an artist could not know; a musician who knows what a musician does not know; a poet who knows what the poet cannot perceive, for he becomes the artist of the entire world, the singer of the divine song. He becomes an astrologer of the entire cosmos, which is hidden to the sight of men. He does not need outer things as the signs of knowing the eternal life. His very life itself is the evidence of the everlasting life. To him death is a shadow, it is a change, it is turning the face from one side to the other. To him all things have their meaning, every movement in this world, the movement of the water, of the air, of the lightning and the thunder and the wind; every movement has a message for him, it brings to him some sign. To another person it is only the thunder, it is only a storm, but to him every movement has its meaning. And when he rises in his development, not only has every movement its meaning, but on every movement there is his command. It is that part of his life which becomes Mastership.

Besides this, in all affairs of this world, of individuals and multitudes, which confuse people, which bring them despair, and cause them depression, which give joy and pleasure, which amuse them, he sees through all. He knows why it comes, from whence it comes, what is behind it, what is the cause of it, and behind the seeming cause what is the hidden cause, and if he wished to trace the cause behind the cause, he could trace back to the primal cause, for the inner life is lived by living with the primal cause, by being in unity with the primal cause. Therefore the one who lives the inner life, in other words, who lives the life of God, God is in him and he is in God.

Shabaz Mitchell's longhand reporting.

Friday, September 8th[1]

[2]Problem of the Day

The Social Problem[3]

Brotherhood has been the central theme of every religious message and social reform, given in every period of the world's history. Although so much is being talked today on the question of brotherhood, yet it appears that the condition today is worse than ever before. Brotherhood is the innate desire of every soul. It is not learned. It is the desire which every soul has been born with, and consciously or unconsciously every soul is striving in its way to realize this desire. It is only the wrong method which is often taken in bringing about the state of brotherhood, which, instead of accomplishing the desire, works against it. Once there existed class difference, which is very much enfeebled now, although the causes of it are yet to be found; but the difficulty which presents itself before humanity today is the activity which is going on in different sections of humanity, which is called brotherhood but is the brotherhood of one section getting ready to work with another section. People of different grades in life develop unions of different professions, uniting together; in this way realizing brotherhood in a limited section and using that unity and strength which is created by it against one another. And the reason is that brotherhood is being formed from outside and not by the help of inner realization. The same thing one finds in the brotherhood of nations. Each nation in itself is realizing the value of patriotism and realizing

---

Documents:

Sz. = a reporting by Shabaz Mitchell, mainly in longhand, but with several passages taken down in shorthand; a transliteration of these passages was made afterwards in the same document;
(Sz.)Sz.: corr. and add. made by Shabaz Mitchell in "Sz.";
(Sz.)Gr.: one addition to "Sz." by Miss Sophia Green.

Sk.tp. = a typescript made from "Sz." in later years under Sakina Furnée's direction, with corr., etc. incorporated;
(Sk.tp.)Sk.: corr. and add. made by Sakina Furnée in "Sk.tp."

Notes:

1. Sk.tp.: "1922" added
2. Ibid.: "The" added
3. (Sz.)Gr.: "VII" added after the subtitle, thereby indicating that it is the seventh lecture in this series;
   Sk.tp.: "Social Development" instead of "The Social Problem"

it as a virtue more and more every day, preparing that strength as a blow against another nation. Also a number of nations joining together form a brotherhood of nations, and in this way increasing power, and[4] each having before their sight their own interest, and in this way dividing the whole humanity, which is one, into parts. It is the spirit of brotherhood which is working behind it all, but at the same time it is working outward; it is not working[5] inward. It may be called a material brotherhood. But material brotherhood will always prove to be a failure in the end. For it is not built on hard rock; it is built on sand. There must be a central ideal in order to form a brotherhood. If it is the nation as the central ideal, then all other nations in the world are foreign. If a profession is a central ideal, then all those who do not belong to that profession are foreign—one is entitled to take the best of others; one is ready to take the side of those belonging to his own profession. If it is a community, then it is only for the interest of the community that every member of the community stands, but at the same time he stands against others. There are commercial unions working in the same manner, the societies of women [6]and[7] pro-suffragette[8] existing, at the same time[6] working against one another; political unions working for their own ideals against one another and calling it at the same time a movement of brotherhood. So that the different religions, churches, societies, have their own interest at heart, at the same time claiming it to be brotherhood. If the ideal of brotherhood works out in its limitations as it is going on just now at times, more and more sections of humanity will be formed, one working against another, and Brotherhood, which is the central theme of the spiritual ideal, will in the end prove to be something undesirable. Even now there are many people who are afraid of the name "brotherhood". They ~~do not~~ cannot bear to listen to it because they have seen so much of it that they feel they should keep away from it. What is lacking in the ideal of brotherhood is the spiritual ideal--in other words, the God-ideal. Whatever be the religion of

---

4. (Sz.)Sz.: "and" crossed out;
   Sk.tp.: "and" omitted
5. (Sz.)Sz.: "is not working" changed into "does not work";
   Sk.tp.: "does not work"
6. Sk.tp.: this part of the sentence omitted: "and pro-suffragette existing, at the same time";
   (Sk.tp.)Sk.: later inserted in hwr.: "and societies of pro-suffragette, existing, and at the same time"
7. (Sz.)Sz.: "societies" added
8. "pro-suffragette": those in favour of women's suffrage (the right to vote for women), a movement which began in the late 19th century

man, as[9] long as he realizes that the source and goal is God, Who is source and goal of the whole humanity, he can easily realize brotherhood, which is not only an intellectual idea for him, but becomes his faith and belief to find [10] himself united, beyond all [11] different boundaries which divide men, in God. And so it is with different nations. When one nation works against another, at that time the interest is all centered in one's own happiness, peace, progress, and benefit. If in the national working also they have [12] realized the spiritual ideal as the centre and, in the spiritual ideal the nation, the community together, it would always work for the betterment of humanity. The theme of the political working would be entirely changed; it would change the outlook of the statesmen today. It does not mean that a particular kind of state must follow, but it only means that the political world of the day should change itself from materiality to spirituality. With the different unions which are formed of those busy with different progress, with different actions, fighting with the world for their own, if there was a God-ideal before their view, a spiritual ideal as the only object in life, the life would be changed. Then each one would be working for another. If the different movements [13] today working for brotherhood would work in the world without thinking that their particular movement must be the only brotherhood in the world, but living [14] behind with [15] that idea or thought [16] that they are the servants of the human brotherhood, that alone being the sacred cause before them, that can be the only right kind of work in bringing about brotherhood.

It must be known that the Sufi movement is not a movement for a Sufi brotherhood; it is a movement for the human brotherhood. It is not our aim in life to bring humanity to belong to our particular society or order. The

9. (Sz.)Sz.: "as" changed into "so";
Sk.tp.: "so" instead of "as"
10. (Sz.)Sz.: "to find" changed into "and he finds";
Sk.tp.: "and he finds" instead of "to find"
11. (Sz.)Sz.: "the" added;
Sk.tp.: "the" added
12. (Sz.)Sz.: "have" crossed out;
Sk.tp.: "have" omitted
13. Sk.tp.: "of" added
14. (Sz.)Sz.: "living" changed into "having", then restored to "living"
15. (Sz.)Sz.: "with" crossed out, then reinserted;
Sk.tp.: "with" omitted;
(Sk.tp.)Sk.: "with" added in hwr.
16. (Sz.)Sz.: "or thought" crossed out;
Sk.tp.: "or thought" omitted

Order[17] we have formed is for convenience, that we may have an opportunity of working in the direction of the human brotherhood, and we are only happy to see other movements working in the same direction and bringing about the results for which we are constantly striving, and devoting our lives to this cause. No doubt, as circumstances are at present, it seems most difficult to alter things immediately, but at the same time the individuals who deeply feel the condition of the world today, and who are willing to give their time and thought to the work and toil in this direction, certainly will make ~~of their lives~~ every moment of their lives valuable.

---

17. "Sufi Order" in 1922 was still the general name for the different Sufi activities

Copied from the book The Inner Life, 1st ed.

[1]

VII

The Object of the Inner Life

Is it power which is the object of the spiritual person, or is it inspiration after which he seeks? It is in fact neither of these things which he pursues, but all such things as power and inspiration follow him as he proceeds on his path toward the spiritual goal. The goal of the spiritual person is self-realization, and his journey is toward the depth of his own being, his God, his Ideal.

Does such a person sacrifice all interests in life, or does he consider the different objects that people have in their lives as something leading astray? Not at all; no doubt his object is the highest that any soul can have, but all other objects which he sees before himself in life do not necessarily hinder him on his path; they become as a staircase on his way, making his path easy to tread. Therefore the person living the inner life never condemns and does not criticize the objects of another, however small or ridiculous they may appear, for he knows that every object in the life of a person is but a stepping-stone which leads him forward if he only wishes to go forward.

There is a time in the life of a soul when it has the desire to play

---

Documents:

Bk. = the first edition of the book The Inner Life, published by the Sufi Order (Society in England), Southampton, England, in December 1922. It contains ten lectures, given in September 1922 at Katwijk, the Netherlands, during a Summer School, which were taken down by a professional stenographer. No book-preparation of this text or other earlier document has been found to date.

Sk.corr. = some corrections made by Sakina Furnée in a copy of the book The Inner Life, 1st ed.

Notes:

1. From the "Quarterly Magazine for Seekers after Truth": Sufism, edited by Sophia Saintsbury Green, of December 1922, and a hwr. annotation by Sirdar van Tuyll, it is known that this lecture was given at Katwijk, the Netherlands, on Friday, 8th September 1922, in the evening (v. Preface).

with dolls; there is a seeking after toys. From the spiritual point of view there is no harm in that, and man sees in time the way that leads to the goal; these are only passing interests leading to others, and in this way man goes forward.

Therefore according to the view of the seer man places before him at different times such objects as riches, pleasure, or a material heaven; the spiritual person starts his journey from the point where these end. The process of evolution is not a straight way,—it is more like a wheel which is ever turning. So the experience of the person who treads the spiritual path begins to show a downward tendency and from that again upwards. For instance, in the spiritual path a person goes backwards, he experiences youth again, for spirituality gives health to the mind and to the body, it being the real life. He experiences vigour, strength, aspiration, enthusiasm, energy, and a living spirit that makes him feel youthful whatever be his age. Then he becomes as a little child, eager to play, ready to laugh, happy among children, he shows in his personality childlike traits, especially that look one sees in children where there is no worry, anxiety, or bitter feeling against anyone; where there is a desire to be friendly with all, where there is no pride or conceit, but readiness to associate with anybody, whatever be the class or caste, nation or race; so the spiritual person becomes like a child; the tendency to tears, the readiness for laughter; all these are found in the spiritual person.

As the spiritual person goes further he shows in his nature infancy. This can be perceived in his innocence; his heart may be lighted with wisdom, yet he is innocent; he is easily deceived, even knowingly, besides being happy under all conditions, like an infant. As the infant has no regard for honour or for insult, neither has the spiritual person. When he arrives at this stage, he answers insult with a smile. Honours given to him are like honours given to a little baby who does not know to whom they are offered. Only the person who has given the honours knows that they have been given to somebody there. The spiritual one is not conscious of it, nor happy with it, nor proud of it. It is nothing to him. The one who has honoured him has honoured himself, since to the baby it is nothing if somebody should speak in favour of him or against him, the baby does not mind, he is ready to smile at both; so is the spiritual soul.

As the spiritual soul proceeds further he begins to show the real traits of humanity; for here humanity really begins, one can see in such a soul the signs which are the pure characteristics of the human being, devoid of the animal traits. For instance, there is a tendency in him to appreciate every little good deed done by anyone; to admire good wherever he sees it in any person, a tendency to sympathize, whatever be the condition of the person, saint or sinner, a tendency to take interest in the affairs of his friends when called upon to do so; a tendency to sacrifice, not considering what he sacrifices, as long as he is moved to do that action. Respect, gratitude, sincerity, faithfulness, patience, endurance, all these qualities begin to show in the character of that man. It is in this stage that truly he can judge, for at this stage the sense of justice awakens.

But as he grows, he still continues to grow backwards. He now shows the signs of the animal kingdom. For instance such a quality as that of the elephant, which with all its strength and power of giant bulk is ready to take the load put upon it; the horse, which is ready to serve the rider; and the cow which lives in the world harmoniously, comes home without being driven, gives milk which is the right of her calf. These qualities come to the spiritual person. The same thing is taught by Christ.[2]

When he goes on further still, there develops in him the quality of the vegetable kingdom, of the plants which bring forth fruit and flowers, patiently waiting for the rain from above. Never asking any return from those who come to gather flowers and fruit, giving and never expecting a return, desiring only to bring forth beauty according to the capability which is hidden in them, and letting it be taken by the worthy or unworthy, whoever it be, without any expectation of appreciation or thanks.

And when the spiritual person advances still further he arrives at the stage of the mineral kingdom. He becomes as a rock, a rock for others to lean on, to depend upon, a rock that stands unmoved amidst the constantly moving waves of the sea of life; a rock to endure all things of this world whose influence has a jarring effect upon sensitive human beings; a rock of constancy in friendship, of steadiness in love, of loyalty to every ideal for which he has taken his stand. One can depend upon him through life and death, here and hereafter. In this world where nothing is dependable, which is full of changes every moment, such a soul has arrived at the stage, where he shows through all these changes that rock-like quality, proving thereby his advancement to the mineral kingdom.[3]

His further advancement is into the "djin"[4] quality, which represents the all-knowing, all-understanding. There is nothing he cannot understand; however difficult the situation, however subtle the problem, whatever be the

---

2. Note in bk.: Gal. vi.2 ["Bear ye one another's burdens, and so fulfil the law of Christ."]
   Sk.corr.: added "New Testament"
3. Note in bk.: Isa. xxxii.2 ["And a man shall be as . . . the shadow of a great rock in a weary land."]
   Sk.corr.: added "Old Testament"
4. See *jinn* in Glossary.

condition of those around him, he understands it all. A person may come to him hardened with faults that he has committed all his life, before this understanding he melts[5] for whether it be a friend or an enemy, he understands both. Not only has he the knowledge of human nature, but of objects as well, of conditions of life in general in all its aspects.

And when he advances still further his nature develops into that of an angel. The nature of the angel is to be worshipful. He therefore worships God in all creatures; he does not feel greater or to be any better or any more spiritual himself than anybody else. In this realization he is the worshipper of all the names and forms there are, for he considers them all the names and forms of God. There is no one, however degenerate or looked-down upon by the world, who is any less in his eyes. In his eyes there is no one but the Divine Being, and in this way every moment of his life is devoted to worship. For him it is no longer necessary that he must worship God at a certain time or in a certain house, or in a certain manner. There is not one moment that he is not in worship, every moment of his life he is in worship, he is before God, and being before God at every moment of his life he becomes so purified that his heart becomes a crystal where everything is clear, everything is reflected there, no one can hide his thoughts from him, nothing is hidden from him, all is known as clearly as it is known to the other person, and more so. For every person knows his own condition and yet not the reason, but the spiritual being at this stage knows the condition of the person and the reason behind it. Therefore he knows more about every person than that person knows himself.

It is this stage in which his progress culminates and comes to its fulness, and concerning this Christ has spoken in the words: "Be ye perfect, as your Father in heaven is perfect." When that stage arrives, it is beyond all expression. It is a sense, it is a realization, it is a feeling, which words can never explain. There is only one thing that can be said, that when a person has touched that stage which is called perfection, his thought, speech, action, his atmosphere, everything becomes productive of God; he spreads God everywhere. Even if he did not speak, still he would spread God; if he did not do anything, still he would bring God. And thus those God-realized ones bring to the world the living God. At present there exists in the world only a belief in God, God exists in imagination, in the ideal. It is such a soul which has touched Divine Perfection that brings to the earth a living God, Who without him would remain only in the Heavens.

---

5. Sk.corr.: a comma added

A copy in the handwriting of Miss Kafia Kerdijk, made from an earlier document, probably her own longhand reporting of the lecture.[1]

[2]

[3]

To the Mureeds

One thing that Mureeds will realise is that[4] Initiation is given, not that they will tell others about it. Keep it in your mind, but do not speak about it. By keeping it secret you show a sacred feeling towards it. My Mureeds will do their exercises without break if they can help, and a few minutes every day they must devote to reading the papers. I wish that my Mureeds will show the character of the Sufi Order by their own example, not speaking with others on any subjects which are uncommon: clairvoyance, spirits, etc. Those who speak

---

Documents:

Kr. = a copy in the handwriting of Miss Kafia Kerdijk, made from an earlier document, probably her own longhand reporting of the lecture
(Kr.)Gd.: indication in the notes for some add. and corr. made in "Kr." by Sherifa Goodenough

Tp. = a typescript made form "Kr.", which shows a few add. and changes, made into a microfiche by Headquarters

Sk.tp. = a typewritten copy made from "Kr." by Sakina Furnée or under her supervision

Notes:

1. (Kr.)Gd.: added, "Reported by Miss ". After comparison of the handwriting in "Kr." with a letter written to Pir-o-Murshid Inayat Khan by Miss Kerdijk on 21 May 1921, which is in the archives, it can be seen that also the document "Kr." shows Miss Kerdijk's handwriting. She was an early Dutch mureed. (See the "Explanation of Abbreviations")
2. (Kr.)Gd.: "1922. Holland" added. Although no complete date is mentioned, this lecture could well have been given at the Summer School, held at Katwijk, the Netherlands, during the first half of September 1922, possibily on Saturday afternoon, 9th September, 1922 when for one day the series of lectures on "The Problem of the Day" was interrupted;
   tp.: "Holland 1922" added
3. (Kr.)Gd.: "Gatheka" later written above; the lecture, however, has not appeared in the series of "Gathekas" or other existing Headquarters' series;
   tp.: "Gatheka. ms. Not published" added
4. Tp.: "the" added

about these things do not realise their real value. Life is sacred, and the idea[5] of life cannot be discussed with everybody. To-day the tendency is to make religion a science, it is our work to make science a religion. People want to drag Heaven to earth, we would[6] to raise earth to Heaven. True religion is an ideal, and the more sacredly we regard the ideal, the more sacred is our religion.

In my absence my Mureeds must assemble and keep[7] exchange of love and harmony; by that they will show their real sympathy and devotion to their Murshid. No doubt my Mureeds will, as they evolve in the spiritual path, understand more and more what the Message is and what responsibility it is. And by realising this, they not only must sympathise, but should show it in a practical realm and see in what way they can share the burden of the responsibility. I do not appeal to my Mureeds, who are busy and have not yet understood the extent[8] of Murshid's responsibility and the importance of his work, but I make appeal to those Mureeds whose hearts are sincerely given to Murshid.

[9]As to myself, I am dedicated to the Cause, and the Mountain I have lifted upon my shoulders I shall carry till my last breath, even if nobody comes to my help.

The mighty [10] Power Whose Message I brought to you and to humanity helps and will continue to help. I wish that Mureeds who have every desire to help may not be deprived of the privilege of helping also to lift this Mountain.

It is not to be explained in one word, in which way help may be given. But where there is a will, there is a way. And as soon as they will realise the greatness of the work, the doors will open before them and then they themselves will understand and see their way. [9]

---

5. (Kr.)Gd.: "idea" changed into "ideal"
6. (Kr.)Gd.: "would" changed into "want"'
   tp., Sk.tp.: "want" instead of "would"
7. Tp.: "help" instead of "keep", which may have been a misreading from "Kr."
8. Ibid.: "nature" instead of "extent"
9. (Kr.)Gd.: the last three paragraphs made into one paragraph with a partly illegible annotation "no[t to be]publish[ed]";
   tp.: one paragraph instead of three paragraphs
10. (Kr.)Gd.: "mighty" changed into "Almighty";
    tp.: "Almighty" instead of "mighty"

A typescript made by Shabaz Mitchell,
probably from his own shorthand
reporting of the questions and answers.

[1]

Questions and Answers

There were two questions asked: What would be the best means of effecting the social and moral progress of the world?

The first thing is to study the question and then set to work. For an instance, when one says social progress,—everybody has perhaps his ideas of social progress, and if each one thinks that what he thinks is the best way of social progress, that will not be the right way, because there would be a conflict between him and others.

Therefore our work in the Sufi Order is to study the question, to see it from all points of view and to find out the best way.

And so it is with the moral question. The standard of morals of every person is different, every person likes to live according to his principles, and if he thought that the whole[2] world should follow his principles, then it would be difficult. Therefore one individual cannot say that that is the right thing, and that the whole world should follow it. But at the same time one must be considerate. That which is called a spiritual message, a divine message, is not only a message for spiritual evolution, but the law that is given from time to time. And the Prophet is to be the reformer, but something more than reformer. Where the

---

Documents:

Sz. = an old typescript, made by Shabaz Mitchell from his shorthand reporting of questions and answers referring to the lectures "Moral Question" of 5th September 1922 and "Social Problem" of 8th September 1922. The few corr. later made by Sz. in "Sz." are incorporated in the basic text here produced, as they are just typing or spelling mistakes.

tp.c. = a typewritten copy made from "Sz." with a few inaccuracies.

Sk.tp. = a later typescript made from "Sz." under Sakina Furnée's supervision.

Notes:

1. Although the above mentioned documents bear no date, it seems most likely that these answers to questions were given on Saturday afternoon, 9th September 1922, at Katwijk in the Netherlands
2. Tp.c.: "whole" omitted

reformer is the child of the civilisation, the prophet is the father of the civilisation, and whenever the prophetic message has put the divine light on the world reform, the world has become much different in all ages, and the ideal conditions in the world[3] have been brought about.

For an instance, there was a time of the Prophet Mohammed, when he came in Arabia, in Persia and in Egypt, there was everything upset; peace was only a word, it was not [4] be traced anywhere. There was vulgarity and perplexity in the intellectual world and superfluousness[5] of life. When the Prophet came it was not an academic, intellectual message he brought, it was a divine message. A person may say, "It was given in Arabia, we do not know anything about it". But, remember, its influence has[6] brought about the Reformation and the Renaissance,—these were the outcome of the Prophet's message. Therefore when the Prophet's message[7] came, it spread throughout the whole world, directly or indirectly.

Then in the time of Jesus, when there was no means of spreading the message, there were a few people around the prophet, very few, and fewer still with education, mostly fishermen without any knowledge. There were not the boats and the railway trains and the conveyances which take books and people from one country to another. But at the same time it was a message that had an influence although it was given to fishermen. The fishermen kept it intact in some form or another, and after many years St. Paul came, whose mind was intuitively capable of conceiving all that came from the fishermen, and at the same time to[8] perceive all that was said at the time by Jesus, and the message reached to the corners of the whole world, and it is the lack of understanding when people discard it.

For an instance, now at present there is a tendency that the opinion of the majority is the opinion worth accepting. One cannot talk about it very much, but the wise man will always find out that the opinion of the minority will supersede the opinion of the majority; he will always find the opinion of the minority having more sense than the opinion of the majority. That shows that there are many children and very few adults in the human family. To depend upon the opinion of the majority, as is the way in the world today, always leads to

---

3. Sz.: the word "world", apparently omitted in typing, added by hand
4. Tp.c.: "to" added by hand;
   Sk.tp.: "to"
5. Sz.: "superficiality" may have been said or meant instead of "superfluousness"
6. Sz.: the type says "was", corr. by hand to "has"
7. Sz.: the word "message", apparently omitted in typing, added by hand
8. Sz.: the word "to", apparently omitted in typing, added by hand

destruction. But what happens is that by the pretence of the opinion of the majority ruling, it is the one person who gets the majority, it is his opinion that the majority accept and think for the moment, "We have our opinion". But the leader among them, he forces his opinion upon the others, and they, being not much advanced themselves, take his opinion, and then they think that it is their own and the opinion of the majority, and therefore it must be carried out. The world-system is wrong in this way. It is not their individual opinion, they are not capable of. . .[9]

---

9. Tp.c.: the last, unfinished sentence was first crossed out, then restored, and completed by Sk. with the words "having an opinion for themselves";
Sk.tp.: the last sentence ("It is not. . .capable of. . .") omitted

Copied from the book The Inner Life, 1st ed.

[1]

VIII

The Attainment of the Inner Life

In the attainment of the inner life there are five things necessary. The first thing that is necessary is the mastery of mind, and this is done by unlearning all that one has learned. The inner knowledge is not gained by adding to the knowledge one has already achieved in life, for it requires a rock foundation. One cannot build a house of rocks on a foundation of sand. Therefore in order to make the foundation of rocks, one has to dig into the sand and build the foundation on the rocks below. Therefore very often it becomes difficult for an intellectual person, who through life has learned things and understood them by the power of intellect, to attain to the inner life. For these two paths are different. The one goes to the north and the other goes to the south. When a person says, "I have now walked so many miles to the south, shall I therefore reach sooner something that exists in the north?" He[2] must know that he will not reach it sooner, but later, because as many hours as he has walked to the south he must walk back in order to reach the north.

Therefore it must be understood that all man learns and experiences in this life in the world, all that he calls learning or knowledge, is only used in the world where he is learning, and bears the same relation to himself as the eggshell does to the chick; but when he takes the path to the inner life that learning and knowledge is of no use to him. The more he is capable of forgetting that

---

Documents:

Bk. = the first edition of the book The Inner Life, published by the Sufi Order (Society in England), Southampton, England, in December 1922. It contains ten lectures, given in September 1922 at Katwijk, the Netherlands, during a Summer School, which were taken down by a professional stenographer. No book-preparation of this text or other earlier document has been found to date.

Sk.corr. = some corrections made by Sakina Furnée in a copy of the book The Inner Life, 1st ed.

Notes:

1. From the "Quarterly Magazine for Seekers after Truth": Sufism, edited by Sophia Saintsbury Green, of December 1922, and a hwr. annotation by Sirdar van Tuyll, it is known that this lecture was given at Katwijk, the Netherlands, on Saturday, 9th September 1922, in the evening (v. Preface).
2. Sk.corr.: Sk. changed "He" to ", he ," continuing the sentence

knowledge, of unlearning it, the more capable is he of attaining the object for which he treads the spiritual path. Therefore it has been a great struggle for those learned and experienced in the outer life, to think that after their great advancement in worldly knowledge they have to go back again. Often they cannot understand; many among them think it is strange and are therefore disappointed. It is like learning the language of a certain country, when wanting to go into another country where that language is not understood, nor[3] the language of the latter country understood by one's self[4]. Just as there is the north pole and the south pole, so there is the outward and the inward life. The difference is still vaster, because the gap between the inner life and the outer life is vaster than the distance between the north pole and south pole. The one who advances to the south is not getting nearer to the north pole, but on the contrary he is going further from it; in order to reach it he must turn right round. However, it is not difficult for the soul that is an earnest traveller on the Path. It is only using the enthusiasm in the opposite direction; to turn the enthusiasm one has for learning something of the world into forgetting and unlearning it, in order to learn something of the inner life.

Now the question is how does one unlearn? Learning is forming a knot in the mind. Whatever one learns from experience or from a person, one makes a knot of it in the mind, and there are as many knots found as there are things one has learned. Unlearning is unravelling the knot, and it is as hard to unlearn as it is to untie a knot. How much effort it requires, how much patience it requires to unravel when one has made a knot and pulled it tight from both sides! So it requires patience and effort to unravel the knots in the mind. And what helps the process? The light of reason working with full power unravels the mental knots. A knot is a limited reason. When one unravels it its limitation is taken away, it is open. And when the mind becomes smooth by unlearning, and by digging out all impressions, of good and bad, of right and wrong, then the ground of the heart becomes as cultivated ground, just as the land does after ploughing. All the old stumps and roots and pebbles and rocks are taken off and it is made into ground which is now ready for the sowing of the seed. And if there are rocks and stones and bricks still scattered there, and still some of the old roots lying there, then it is difficult for the seed to be sown; the ground is not in the condition the farmer wishes it to be.

The next thing in the attainment of the inner life is to seek a spiritual guide,—someone whom a man can absolutely trust and have every confidence in,

---

3. Sk.corr.: "is" added
4. Ibid.: "oneself" instead of "one's self"

someone to whom he can look up, and with whom he is in sympathy, which would culminate in what is called devotion. And if once he has found someone in life whom he considers his Guru, his Murshid, his guide, then to give to him all confidence, so that not a thing is kept back. If there is something kept back then what is given might just as well be taken away, because everything must be done fully, either have confidence or not have confidence, either have trust or no trust. On this path of perfection all things must be done fully.

Now there are the particular ways of the guide, which depend upon his temperament and upon his discrimination in finding for everyone who is being guided a special way. He may lead them to their destination by the royal road, or through the streets and lanes, down to the sea or through the town, by land or by water, the way that to him seems the best under certain circumstances.

The third thing necessary to spiritual attainment is the receiving of knowledge. This being the knowledge of the inner world, it cannot be compared with the knowledge one has learned before. That is why it is necessary to unlearn the former. Man cannot adjust what he receives in this path with the ideas which he has held before; the two things cannot go together. Therefore, there are three stages of receiving knowledge which the one being guided has to go through. The first stage is the receiving the knowledge, when he does nothing but receive. The next stage is the period after this, and that stage is the assimilating of what has been learned. He thinks upon it, he ponders upon it, in order that it may remain in his mind. It is just like eating food and then assimilating it. The third stage is the reasoning it out by oneself. Man does not reason it out as soon as he has received it; if he did, he would lose the whole thing. Because it is like a person who has learned a and b and c at one stage, and then would ask how about words that did not begin with those letters. He would reason it out much sooner than he ought, for he has not yet learned the other letters. There is a time which must necessarily be given to receiving, as one gives the time to eating. While one is eating one does not run about in the street in order to assimilate the food. After he has finished his dinner then he can do everything possible to help digest it. Assimilating is clearly understanding, feeling and memorizing knowledge within one's self. Not only that, but waiting until its benefit and its illumination is coming as a result of achievement.

The third part then to the receiving of knowledge is reasoning; to reason it through, "Why was it like that? what benefit has come to me from that? how can it be made practicable in life? how can it benefit myself and others?" That is the third stage. If these stages are confused then the whole process becomes confused, and one cannot get that benefit for which one treads the spiritual path.

The fourth grade of attainment of the inner life is meditation. If one has unlearned all that he has learned, if one has a teacher, and if one has received the knowledge of the inner life, still meditation is one thing which is most necessary, which in the Sufi word is called "Riazat." In the first place meditation is done mechanically, at an hour which one has fixed upon as the hour for devotion or concentration. The next step is to think of that idea of meditation at other times during the day. And the third stage is continuing meditation throughout day and night. Then one has attained to the right meditation. If a person does meditation only for fifteen minutes in the evening and then forgets altogether about it all day, he does the same thing as going to church on Sunday and the other days of the week forgetting all about it. Intellectual training no doubt has its use in the achievement of the inner life, but the principal thing is meditation. That is the real training. The study of one year and the meditation of one day are equal. By this meditation I mean the right kind of meditation. If a person closes his eyes and sits doing nothing he may just as well go to sleep. Meditation is not only an exercise to be practised. In meditation the soul is charged with new light and life, with inspiration and vigour; in meditation there is every kind of blessing. Some become tired of meditation, but that does not mean that they meditate,—they become tired before having arrived at a stage where they really experience the effect of meditation, like those who become weary of practising the violin,—they are tired because they have not yet played the violin. If once they played they would never be weary. The difficulty is playing the violin and the difficulty is having patience with one's own playing. Patience is required in meditation; why a person gets tired is because he is accustomed to activity throughout the day. His nerves are all inclined to go on and on in that activity, which is not really for his benefit, and yet it is giving him the inclination to go on; and when he sits with his eyes closed he feels uncomfortable, for the mind which has been active all day becomes restive, just like a horse after having had a long run. Then if you want that horse to stand still, it is restive. It cannot stand still, because every nerve has been active, and it becomes almost impossible to keep that horse still. And so it is with man. Once I was with a man who was in the habit of meditating, and while we were sitting near the fire and talking about things he went into the silence, and I had to sit quiet until he opened his eyes. I asked him, "It is beautiful, is it not?" and he said, "It is never enough." Those who experience the joy of meditation, for them there is nothing in this world which is more interesting and enjoyable. They experience the inner peace and the joy that cannot be explained in words, they touch Perfection, or the spirit of Light, of Life and of Love,—all is there.

The fifth necessity in the spiritual path is the living of the everyday life. There are not strict morals which a spiritual guide enforces upon a person, for that work has been given to the outward religions. It is the exoteric side of spiritual work to which the outer morals belong, but the *essence* of morals is practised by those treading the spiritual path. Their first moral is constantly to avoid hurting the feeling of another. The second moral principle is to avoid allowing themselves to be affected by the constantly jarring influences which every soul has to meet in life. The third principle is to keep their balance under all different situations and conditions which upset this tranquil state of mind. The fourth principle is to love unceasingly all those who deserve love, and to give to the undeserving their forgiveness, and this is continually practised by them. The fifth principle is detachment amidst the crowd, but by detachment I do not mean separation. By detachment only is meant rising above those bondages which bind man and keep him back from his journey toward the goal.

A later typescript made under Sakina Furnée's direction, which reproduces the oldest available version.

Katwijk [1], September 10th, 1922

Questions and Answers

Question: *How, without losing intellect, can we bring back the higher state of innocence which existed in the garden of Eden?*

Answer: We do not need to lose intellect, but we need to rise above it. So long as a man is beneath, so to speak, his intellect, he is the slave of his intellect. When he is above [2], he is master. Man is greater than the angels, therefore the world can be a higher place than the garden of Eden if [3] after the achievement of intellect man has [4] power over it. If man [5] were to rise above it instead

---

Documents:

Sk.tp. = a later copy, made under Sakina Furnée's direction, probably from Shabaz Mitchell's copy which he made from his own shorthand reporting; neither the original reporting nor Shabaz Mitchell's copy are currently in the Archives, but this later copy reproduces the oldest version available.

Gr.tp.1 = a typescript by Miss Sophia Green, probably also made from Shabaz Mitchell's typewritten copy (see "Sk.tp." above). On its cover is written in Sirdar van Tuyll's hwr.: "Katwijk 1922". Sophia Green intended to publish these questions and answers in the magazine Sufism, edited by her, and for this purpose "Gr.tp.1" was slightly edited and the order of the questions and answers changed.

Gr.tp.2 = a carbon-copy of "Gr.tp.1" used by Gr. for further editing, putting the q.a.'s in a different order, omitting several q.a.'s, and adding one q.a. which was given after the lecture on Brotherhood on 11th September 1922. On the cover of this document Gr. wrote: "Mag." (= magazine), "Questions and Answers by Inayat Khan".

tp.c. = a typewritten copy made from "Gr.tp.2", with corr., add., etc. incorporated.

Sf. = Sufism, "A Quarterly Magazine for Seekers after Truth," edited by S.E.M. Green, June 1923, page 15 ff.: the q.a.'s here published have been taken from "tp.c.".

Notes:

1. Katwijk, a seaside village in the Netherlands, situated near Leiden.
2. Tp.c., Sf.: "it" added
3. Gr.tp.1: "only" added;
   Gr.tp.2: "only" crossed out
4. Gr.tp.1: "one had" instead of "man has";
   Gr.tp.2: "man has" restored
5. Gr.tp.1: "one" instead of "man";
   Gr.tp.2: "man" restored

of sinking beneath it[6].

Question: *Will you please tell us what is meant by "a soul's stage of evolution"?*

Answer: When the soul is evolved it feels by itself. In other words, it becomes conscious of its purity, of its majesty, of its eternal life, of its bliss, of its inspiration, and of its power.[7]

Question: *Is heaven a place as well as a condition of soul?*

Answer: It is a condition of the soul which can make any place heaven. Not only the earth would be turned into heaven, but even hell could be turned into heaven, if only the soul attained that perfection which is its only goal.

Question: *Is the misunderstanding between Christians and Moslems one of the reasons for bringing Sufism into the Western world?*

Answer: It is not only the misunderstanding between Christians and Moslems, but the misunderstandings among Christians themselves and the misunderstandings between individuals and the misunderstandings[8] between every fighting nation which has brought Sufism into the West. Furthermore, Sufism as a School has come from the East to the West, but Sufism as a Message has not come from the East to the West; it has come from above onto[9] the earth; and in that sense Sufism does not belong to the East or the West. At the same time the word Sufi has its origin in [10] the Persian "Sufa", and the Greek "Sophia"[10], these[11] words representing East and West[12]. Therefore, the Sufi School of

---

6. Gr.tp.1: "standing below" instead of "sinking beneath it";
   Gr.tp.2: "sinking beneath it" restored;
   Sk.tp.: afterwards, without crossing out "sinking beneath it", Sakina Furnée wrote "standing below" underneath
7. Gr.tp.1,2: this q.a. inserted between the second and third one
8. All other documents: "misunderstanding";
   Sk.tp.: afterwards Sk. crossed out the "s"
9. Gr.tp.1,2: "on to" instead of "onto";
   tp.c., Sf.: "on" instead of "onto"
10. Gr.tp.1: reordered to read, "the Greek 'Sophia' and the Persian 'Sufa'";
    Gr.tp.2: restored to "the Persian 'Sufa', and the Greek 'Sophia'"
11. Gr.tp.1: "both" instead of "these";
    Gr.tp.2: "these" restored
12. Gr.tp.1: added, "and the same are in the word 'Sufi';
    Gr.tp.2: the added phrase crossed out

esotericism no doubt has [13] at the back of it the tradition of the ancient Sufi schools which existed in all different periods, but the Sufi Message has its different tradition. It is more than a school; it is life itself: it is the answer to the cry of the whole humanity.

Question: *Why is Confucianism, the Chinese religion, not taken up in the Church of All?*

Answer: In the prayers of the Church of All there come the words "in the names known and unknown to the world", which includes all different Messages that come [14] from time to time; for [15] it has been beyond human power to take note of every one of them. History is limited, traditions are limited, and that unlimited, ever-running stream of the Divine Message which has always come cannot be fully registered in history or in tradition. What the Sufi wants the members of the Church of All to do [16] is not only to recognize the Scriptures which are read during the Service, but the Scriptures which have never been known to the world. [17]Nobody knows about them. Where there is wisdom they respect it and recognize it as the stream coming from above. If it is not mentioned in history, if it is not spoken of in the tradition, it does not matter.[17] [18]You can understand [19] that it would be impossible to include all things known to the world; but at the same time in our heart they are included; nothing is kept out. What is chiefly in the prayers and Service of the Church of All is the Message which is brought by Nabi and fulfilled by Rasoul. The inner meaning of these two words may be understood and can be explained in personal discussion.

---

13. Gr.tp.1: "its tradition" added;
    Gr.tp.2: "its tradition" crossed out
14. Gr.tp.1: "come" afterwards changed into "came"
15. Gr.tp.1: "and" instead of "for";
    Gr.tp.2: "for" restored
16. Gr.tp.1: "know" instead of "do";
    Gr.tp.2: "do" restored;
    Sk.tp.: afterwards Sk. wrote "know" above
17. Gr.tp.2: this passage, "Nobody knows . . . . does not matter." crossed out;
    tp.c., Sf.: this passage omitted
18. Gr.tp.1: "Therefore" added;
    Gr.tp.2: "Therefore" crossed out;
    tp.c., Sf.: "Therefore" omitted
19. Gr.tp.1: "now" added;
    Gr.tp.2: "now" crossed out

[20]*Question:* *Why is there animal worship in the old religion? Old religions say that bad conduct can bring a human being after his death back to the animal kingdom. Was there a point in time when this was true?*

Answer: The reason why animal worship was taught in the religions in the ancient times was to point out to humanity some traits in certain animals which were beneficial for a man to notice. For instance, the Hindus worshipped the cow. The nature of the cow is harmlessness, usefulness; the cowherd [21] takes her into the fields, she lives on the grass and herbs, comes back home, recognizing the places she belongs to. With her two horns yet [22] she is harmless, and harmless to man who takes the greatest share of the milk which is for her calf, without ever thinking about it, without ever appreciating it. He has all delicious dishes made out of the milk but he never thinks of her. Man eats in his delicious [23] food in different forms the essence that she gives of her life without any bitterness, without any enmity, without any selfishness. She returns after the whole day in the forest; in the evening she comes in the same place where the best of her life is taken. [24]

There are morals which one can learn by looking at a tree, by looking at an animal, and by looking at a bird. In the ancient times when there was no printing press, or any other source of giving philosophy or morals in the form of books, the Teachers [25] gave it in this form, and [26]in it one can see God. One does [27] see God in all forms, especially in [28]things which teach [29] lessons,

---

20. Gr.tp.1,2: this q.a. moved to become the tenth q.a.
21. Gr.tp.1: "shepherd" instead of "cowherd";
 Gr.tp.2: "cowherd" restored
22. Gr.tp.1: "yet" omitted;
 Gr.tp.2: "yet" restored
23. Tp.c., Sf.: "delicious" omitted
24. Gr.tp.1: added "And when she is old she is cast out.";
 Gr.tp.2: the added sentence crossed out;
 Sk.tp.: later this sentence was added by Sk.
25. Gr.tp.1: "they" instead of "the Teachers";
 Gr.tp.2: "the Teachers" restored
26. Gr.tp.1: replaced "in it" with "at the same time where it is";
 Gr.tp.2: "in it" restored
27. Tp.c., Sf.: "indeed" added
28. Ibid.: "the" added
29. Gr.tp.1: "can give us some" instead of "teach";
 Gr.tp.2: "teach" restored;
 Sk.tp.: later Sk. added, "can give us some" as a possible replacement of "teach"

which can inspire man and help him [30] in his life, things which are pointed out by Teachers to be looked at and worshipped. So, really speaking they did not say "Worship the cow", they said, "To worship God, look at the cow". Those who see on the surface [31] say: "They are worshipping the [32] cow"; but in reality [33] they are worshipping God.

Then as to this idea that if a person has not lived rightly in life he will go backward to the animal life. Life, really speaking, grows, and a man goes forward. After being wise, man hardly becomes foolish, and if it seem [34] that he become [34] foolish, it is perhaps one step backward, but it does not mean that he goes a hundred steps backward. Man advances; he cannot fall like that. Yes, [35] there are hindrances in the Path which set him back two or three steps; but then again [36] he takes two or three steps forward. But still in those times when the Priesthood or fatherhood [37] spoke, [38] they would speak as to children--"If you are not going to be good you are going to be punished". So this threatening was a very good threatening [39], that they would be turned into a cow, or dog, or cat. At the same time, coming to the real essence of Truth, when one touches the ultimate Truth, then he realizes that there is nothing which is not in him [40]. There is the animal kingdom in him, there is the vegetable kingdom in him, there is the mineral kingdom in him, there is the angelic kingdom in him, and there is the Divine. All that is low, [41]all that is high, all that exists is in man. [41] Every man is a

---

30. Gr.tp.1: "man" instead of "him";
    Gr.tp.2: "him" restored
31. Gr.tp.1: rewritten to read, "have seen from a distance";
    Gr.tp.2: "see on the surface" restored
32. Tp.c.: "the" omitted
33. Gr.tp.1: "in reality" omitted;
    Gr.tp.2: "in reality" restored
34. Sk.tp.: later Sk. changed "seem" and "become" (subjunctive) to "seems" and "becomes" (indicative)
35. Gr.tp.2: "True," instead of "Yes," but later restored to "Yes,";
    tp.c., Sf.: "True," instead of "Yes,"
36. Gr.tp.1: "and then" instead of "but then again";
    Gr.tp.2: "but then again" restored
37. Tp.c., Sf.: "or fatherhood" omitted
38. Gr.tp.1,2: "us" instead of a comma, later crossed out
39. Gr.tp.2: "a very good threatening" crossed out, but later restored;
    tp.c., Sf.: "a very good threatening" omitted
40. Tp.c., Sf.: "man" instead of "him"
41. Gr.tp.2: "all that is high, all that is, exists in man", later changed back to "all that is high, all that exists is in man";
    tp.c.: "all that is that exists in man", later changed by Sk. into "all that is high, all that is, that

miniature of God, and God's constituents are all there, within and without [42], [43]and so in miniature form in man. [43]

[44]*Question:* *Is not the particular view of looking on what we think other people's faults a hindrance?*

Answer: No doubt it is.

[45]*Question:* *Is it the first time that the Sufi Order has been introduced into the West?*

Answer: Yes. But at the same time the Sufi Order as a school has a foundation, but what has followed, which is the Sufi Message, has not only been introduced to the West for the first time, but to the world for the first time.

[46]*Question:* *In the story of Eden are the coats of skins the physical bodies of humanity?*

Answer: Yes.

[47]*Question:* *Is the story of Christ walking on the sea history, or symbolism, or both? Is the Mahabharata history, or symbolism, or both? How can one know which part of the Scriptures is history and which part is symbology?*

Answer: One can distinguish between the two scriptures, the Hinduistic scriptures and the Christian and Jewish scriptures. The scriptures

---

exists in man";
Sf.: "all that is high, all that is that exists in man."

42. Gr.tp.2: "his being" added, but later crossed out;
tp.c., Sf.: "his being" added
43. Gr.tp.2: "and so in miniature form in man" crossed out;
tp.c., Sf.: "and so in miniature form in man" omitted
44. Gr.tp.1,2: this q.a. moved to become the second q.a., but then crossed out in "Gr.tp.2";
tp.c., Sf.: this q.a. omitted
45. Gr.tp.1: this q.a. moved to become the seventh q.a.;
Gr.tp.2: this q.a. removed from the document;
tp.c., Sf.: this q.a. has not been inserted
46. Gr.tp.1: this q.a. moved to become the eighth q.a.;
Gr.tp.2: this q.a. removed from the document;
tp.c., Sf.: this q.a. has not been inserted
47. Gr.tp.1: this q.a. moved to become the ninth q.a.;
Gr.tp.2: this q.a. removed from the document;
tp. and Sf.: this q.a. has not been inserted

of the Hindus have been written, each scripture by one person--for instance the Ramayana[48] and the Mahabharata. They came as scriptures written by different persons and containing the inner wisdom; (predicting the coming of Rama and)[49] giving a picture of the life of Krishna. That being the case they have come from time to time as scriptures given by that particular person. Coming to the question of the stories in the Bible one sees that after hundreds of years certain stories[50] were gathered as they came from time to time by St. Paul, and given in the volume of the New Testament. From having been told from one person to another symbology and history is so mixed up that it is most difficult in a paragraph to define which is symbology and which is history, and especially to define which is the authentic part and which is the part that those who spoke have given. However, the truth is to be found there just the same. But found by whom? By everyone? No. By the sincere seeker after truth who sees that his soul's eyes are open; for him there is truth. But if another person can understand, sometimes it is history; sometimes he makes out of it a miracle; sometimes he calls it symbology and sometimes he calls it the truth. It is not on the truth that people differ in their opinions: it is on the false side of it that people argue and dispute and divide themselves into sections. Why there are so many Christian churches, and so many faiths and beliefs in this world is not because the truth of each is different; it is because the falsehood of each is different. Each has a false conception and he calls it truth. It is not in the truth they differ. In the truth no one differs. For instance, if I were to tell you the symbolical meaning of the walking of Christ on the water, you for yourselves can imagine what makes Christ greater, and by making Christ greater makes humanity greater; and what makes humanity smaller compared with greater. In one case Christ takes humanity upward, in the other case Christ stands aloof and allows humanity to come down. The symbolical picture is that the rise and fall in life, the constant movement, the favours[51] and likes and dislikes, the constant change of mood, the joys and sorrows which go to make up the whole life are a picture of the sea, ever moving, with the wind, with the storm, and then becoming calm. Is it not the condition of life? And

---

48. Gr.tp.1: "Rama Bharata", changed by Sirdar van Tuyll into "Ramayana"
49. Ibid.: parentheses "( )" omitted
50. Ibid.: "stories" omitted
51. Ibid.: "fevers" instead of "favours"

this life sometimes rises and blinds a person; makes a person rather commit suicide than live. These little rises and falls and changes make it difficult for man to go through life--one feels oneself drowned[52] in the sea; one feels oneself sinking in the sea. Sometimes one feels oneself struggling along with great difficulty but being able to swim. Every moment there is danger of sinking to the bottom. In this sea of life that soul which reflects Divine perfection gets that power to walk above these ever-moving waves of life. Rise to him is no rise; fall to him is no fall. The favour of this world does not delight him; its disfavour does not trouble him. Everything comes and goes as rising and falling waves, and he steadily walks through life and that is walking upon the water. This causes man to think that in the soul of the human being there is Divine perfection and when that human soul becomes conscious of that perfection he is blessed with that power by which he can walk over this water. This raises the whole humanity with Christ, whereas when a person says, "Jesus Christ walked on the water", there is a man who says: "It is a sin if I say anything else, because it is written in the Bible". Then comes a materialist and says: "What do you say? I do not believe in religion if religion teaches such a thing". How many have left religion for just such little things. They had no patience to wait and see it symbolically. They said, "If there are these things which cannot appeal to me, there is nothing in religion. I will leave it".

The blessing which they could have gained by the understanding of the traditional teaching which came from ancient times, and which is given period after period in the different Messages, is neglected by the persons who have no patience, but very often it (the blessing) is helped by those who are ready to believe because it is written in the Scripture. Why? Because it is a delicate subject. One can speak yet very little, for there is something which we call regard and respect for all that is sacred, and when one does not observe that law one really offends one's finer nature and many others who have some religious devotional feeling. Therefore, the way of the Sufi is to regard and respect all things, to understand all things for oneself, not to express readily his opinion, for it is not everyone who is ready to understand it. It is good to give in the service of truth, but there is teaching in the Sufi cult to keep one's thoughts secret and sacred, to keep one's realizations secret and sacred. All have not

52. Ibid.: "dragged down by oneself" instead of "drowned"

reached the plane of realization, perhaps one has gone much further and someone is perhaps much behind, and your realization may not suit the one who has gone further or the one who is behind. Every Sufi has a staircase, the different places are as steps and stairs, and the staircase is not made to stand on but to walk upon, to climb upon. From one belief to another belief one climbs and so safely one arrives at one's destiny, and if one wanted to put one leg on the first stair and another leg on the top, one could not do it and one would be disappointed. It is good to strive after truth but we must not think that what we realize is for the whole world. What one individual realizes is for himself. If he finds another person whose thoughts are his own, he can exchange his thoughts with him but not otherwise, because the belief of every person has some good about it and some benefit, and the breaking of that belief is like breaking his God. There cannot be a worse thing than that.

[53]*Question:* *Why are the candles in the Service that are lighted in a ceremonial way, not extinguished in the same ceremonial way?*

Answer: It is in the lighting of the candles that the ceremony consists, not in the extinguishing of the candles. The extinguishing of the candles is a necessity which has no realization [54] to the ceremony at all. [55] Extinguishing of the candles as a ceremony would have a bad influence on the human soul.

---

53. Gr.tp.2: this q.a. has been removed from the document; tp.c., Sf.: this q.a. has not been inserted
54. Gr.tp.1: "relation" instead of "realization"
55. Ibid.: this last sentence is lacking, but was added afterwards by Sirdar van Tuyll

A copy in the handwriting of Shabaz Mitchell, probably made from his own shorthand reporting.

11 September [1]

The Problem of the Day

Brotherhood [2]

The most important part which the ideal of Brotherhood has to fulfil in daily life is not only to bring about a better understanding ~~by forming~~ between different classes, nations and races, but to create a moral ideal in every individual. Man conscious of the principle of Brotherhood can consider the interest of his fellowman. In the schools the most essential teaching of Brotherhood must be that a child should grow to recognize in the other children his brothers and sisters and his obligation to them as ~~he does~~ his obligation[3] to his own brothers and sisters. Children with their development in life grow to recognize in the family their obligation to their brothers and sisters without being especially taught, only the fact that they know they are their brothers and sisters; and therefore naturally that knowledge produces in them a sense of duty to one another and a sense of honour to care for the honour of their brothers and sisters. If the same sense was developed for the youth in children to look upon the child of another also as a brother or sister, to stand by them in their troubles and to guard them in their

---

Documents:

Sz.c. = an edited copy in the handwriting of Shabaz Mitchell, probably made from his own shorthand reporting of the lecture, which is not in the archives.
(Sz.c.)Sz.: a few corr. made by Shabaz Mitchell in "Sz.c."

Sk.tp. = a typescript made from "Sz.c." in later years under Sakina Furnée's direction, with corr., etc. incorporated.

Notes:

1. (Sz.c.)Sz.: later added, "No.10", thereby indicating that this lecture was supposed to be the tenth one in this series;
   Sk.tp.: "1922" added
2. Sk.tp.: at the end of the line, after title and subtitle, added, "(9)", which means that this lecture was supposed to be the ninth in the series "The Problem of the Day". This seems to be right, if the questions and answers given on Sunday 10th September 1922 are considered to be no. 8.
3. (Sz.c.)Sz.: "is" added;
   Sk.tp.: "is" added

difficulties, and to consider their honour one's own honour, the world[4] become much better. When man would grow to manhood, he would have a different outlook on life. He would move about in this world as a human being, as a man. Besides, in business man would realize, not only his material interest, but also his duty to those with whom he has to deal in business. In his profession he would not only think he has to obey the laws of the professional unions or observe their etiquette because he is forced by his profession to do so, but he would feel the interest and honour of the others as his own interest and honour if the feeling of brotherhood were developed in him. Business causes people to have necessary laws, etiquettes, forms of politeness and outward brotherhood, and yet there is always something absent which is most necessary in life. The moral of brotherhood must be realized by understanding the meaning of brotherhood. Brotherhood does not only mean a name. People may call outwardly "brother", and yet behind may talk against each other. The word "brother" has something sacred in it. It is not only a word, but life; there is something living in it. When one calls someone else his brother he stands by him for all his life. A brother is just like one hand to the other hand. When one hand is hurt immediately to its rescue comes the other hand. When one hand is trying to do something the other hand helps it. When one hand is tired the other hand is ready to take up its work; and the rest of both hands is when they are united together. When a person wants to rest, he clasps his hand[5]. That unity is symbolical of brotherhood. If people name the members of a certain institution or society brothers, it means nothing. Instead of members you call them brothers.

Brotherhood is realized by the recognition of three ideas. One idea is that we are brothers because our Source is One—our Father is one. We are brothers because we are working on this earth hand in hand, conditions have brought us together. Our interests are common in their depth when we in this world are so linked together[6] with one another. If we could only see it through the eye then you would find that unhappiness of one individual has its effect in some way or other on all; and the happiness of one individual has its effect on all—more on those who are around him and a little less on those who are distant. Everyone pulled or pushed in life has an effect upon the whole of humanity. The pull is a pull on the whole humanity in proportion. If only humanity were to understand this living doctrine of metaphysics which has always been taught by the prophets.

4. Sk.tp.: "would" added
5. Ibid.: "hands"
6. (Sz.c.)Sz.: "together" crossed out; Sk.tp.: "together" omitted

If only the scientists had been able to tell, the world would have been quite different. And the third idea in which one can realize brotherhood is that the goal is the same. Through whatever way we may reach, through heaven or hell, it is the only goal. It is not a settlement, it is the final goal we have to reach. And therefore we have to meet again. This shows that in the beginning we are brothers because of the source; and we are brothers in the midst of it because we are living on earth, the interest of one depending on others; and in the end the goal of all is the same.

What keeps man ignorant of the ideal of brotherhood is the outward nature of creation, which is of a dual nature. It is the idea of separation--"You are different from me. I am different from you". And that difference and distinction in character, in ways of thinking, in the way of living, in all different forms are dividing men into different classes, different nations, different races, and then the difference which exists between people in their way of looking at things and in their ideas. This impresses man with the thought "I am a separate entity and in no way connected with another". In spirit he is not aware. The only actions he is conscious of are the outward ties such as relationship or some partnership in business, or when they are collaborators in certain work, in learning at school--some occasions like this make them feel they are connected with one another. But these outward actions do not awake the spirit to that inward connection which is stronger and closer[7] and binds one soul to another. All these outer connections make people think there is no inner connection. When an outer tie has been broken a person says, "I have nothing to do with that person". A person thinks it is finished, but it is not finished. You have that person in you and that person has you in him. It is not finished. And if one could see the beginning, where it has begun, then he would never believe that it finishes. It is always there. It is only the outside links which man recognizes as a relation; the inward connection which binds every soul to one another, man does not understand.

What is necessary just now is not only brotherhood to be taught as morals, but brotherhood to be taught as spirit, as a spiritual idea, as the mystery of the whole metaphysics and philosophy[8]. In all ages prophets and sages and seers have realized this law, and yet there is so much in life which works against it, which covers it from the eyes of man. Man's sight is so limited that he see[9]

---

7. Sk.tp.: "and closer" omitted, probably because of the word "closer" not written very clearly in "Sz.c."
8. Ibid.: "philosophies" instead of "philosophy" (a misreading)
9. Ibid.: "sees"

no further than he sees, and he remains in an illusion, in a mist, not knowing with whom he is connected and with whom he is disconnected, only recognizing the outward little connections which seem to bind him here and there, yet not realizing that this whole manifestation is one whole mechanism working, wherein [10] every soul fills in his place, where every soul has its purpose to accomplish and where every soul stands in connection with all souls.

The more you look at the world from the mystical point of view, the more your outlook on life becomes keen, the more one finds that every person one meets [11], every person who goes your way in life, has something to do with you and you have something to do with them. And it is this brotherhood which must be realized, this truth of the whole universe, and by awaking the consciousness of this brotherhood in the world, the ideals of the spirit of brotherhood will come to manifestation.

\- - - - - - -

---

10. Ibid.: "where" instead of "wherein"
11. Ibid.: "you meet" instead of "one meets"

Documents referring to the questions and answers after the lecture:

Gr.tp.1	=	a slightly edited typescript made by Miss Sophia Green, probably from Shabaz Mitchell's transcribed shorthand reporting of the q.a.'s, which is not in the archives.
Gr.tp.2	=	a carbon-copy of "Gr.tp.1", used by Gr. for editing. The q.a.'s given on 10th September 1922 were inserted in "Sf.", to which was added the fifth q.a. from this present lecture.
Sf.	=	Sufism: "A Quarterly Magazine for Seekers after Truth", edited by Sophia Green. In its number of June 1923 the fifth q.a. after the lecture "Brotherhood" of 11 September 1922 has been added on p. 17.
Sk.tp.	=	a later copy, apparently made from "Gr.tp.1" under Sakina Furnée's direction with only two words changed.

A typescript made by Miss Sophia Green.

Monday, September 11th [12]

Question: *What will be the ideal work, the ideal relation, between the work of the different sexes in the future evolution? Is it not wrong that women try to do the work of men?*

Answer: Well, there are two questions in this. I will first answer "Is it not wrong that women should try to do the work of men?" The question is what is the work of man? Very often the work that man is accustomed to do and may be seen doing is considered man's work. The work which woman is not seen doing for a long time, people consider is not woman's work. What woman has been seen for some centuries doing, people think is woman's work. But I should think, that according to the metaphysical point of view, considering woman and her life, the fine work must be for woman, and the rough work must be in the charge of man. But besides this it all depends upon the evolution of man and woman. If woman is evolved enough to do a certain work which wants art and intelligence, why must she not do it? No doubt it is a very great pity to see, especially after the war, women having taken the work of the labouring men which does not in any way suit the life of woman, and which has destroyed many lives from their youth, for their whole life.

Now coming to the next question, what would be the ideal of work for men and women in the future? Just now we are in a period of reaction which is coming from woman's side, and which is caused by man's negligence in the past of the life of woman, and therefore, the conditions today are not normal conditions. Life in the world just now, considering the work of man and woman, is not balanced. Just now it is a revolt or reaction coming from the side of woman in answer to negligence which has passed before, but there will come a time when the

---

12. No year is mentioned, but it was in 1922, as the questions and answers refer to lectures given on 8, 9, 10 (q.a.-class) and 11 September 1922, and Pir-o-Murshid himself in the answer to the seventh question refers to his address of that same day.

conditions of life in the world will adjust themselves, and an ideal time will come when man will realize that as there is co-operation with woman in the home, so there will be in all directions of life, even in the state.

Question: *Has not the promise of Heaven and reward an egoistic purpose?*

Answer: Call it egoistic if you will. Very often a child is induced to work better if he is promised candy. You must remember that man is always a child, if not in one way, in another.

Question: *How many souls that realize the Message are wanted to fulfil the work?*

Answer: As far as I understand this question it means those who have realized the value of the Message--how many of them are needed to fulfil the work of the movement? We shall never have a sufficient number, and therefore, every individual [13] must bear in mind that if life permits him to offer his time, his life, [14] his work, that it will not be too many.

Question: *In what way can we bring this ideal of spiritual brotherhood to mankind?*

Answer: The first way is understanding for yourself, making it clear in your mind. The next process will be to try to explain it to your fellow man and when you find that you have succeeded in making an impression with the ideal in which you sincerely believe, then you must proceed to spread this idea in a wider circle. But note at the same time, that it is the will of God that this be known to the world, and souls who will become channels of this, have this as their life's privilege. Therefore we must consider that there is no doubt that it will spread—only the contribution of our efforts is a life's privilege.

---

13. Gr.tp.1: "individual" changed by Sakina Furnée into "mureed"
14. Sk.tp.: "his life" first omitted, then added in tp. at the end of the line, probably meant to be inserted after "his work"

[15]*Question:* *If the source of all souls is one, do they all proceed from the same source at the same point in time, or are there younger or older souls in humanity?*

Answer: There is such a large variety of younger and older souls and the souls are so numerous that it is most difficult to fix a standard of younger and older souls. Every soul, however young, can find a still younger soul; every soul, however old, can find an older soul. God is unlimited, and so is manifestation.

Question: *What is the reason that enlightened souls must come from the East and why cannot they come from the West if their Message is for the West?*

Answer: One cannot divide the Wisdom of the East and West. In fact, the wisdom does not belong to the East or West. The idea is that among many other reasons there is one reason why the East has remained as a cradle of thought from very ancient times. One can see in all traditions of the Aryan race in ancient times that it went out to spread throughout the world, and especially those who wished to make experiment in the inner life sought for their place of meditation the land of India.

Therefore, for thousands of years the people of that country have devoted their lives to this end. Man must progress in some way. Life cannot exist without progress. And when people think that the Orient has not progressed, that the people of the East have not improved as have the people of the West, it is true. When you compare the present civilization of the West, its order and system, the great progress which the West has made, it is incomparably greater than what one can see in the East. Perhaps just now you can see in the uncivilized parts of the Western countries some forms of Eastern life, and that shows how much the Western world has gone forward in one direction. But at the same time while vast progress in some direction or other—and it is the direction of the multitude that individuals take—when we come to the metaphysical view the whole life is

---

15. Gr.tp.2, Sf.: this fifth q.a. has been added unchanged to "Questions and Answers" of 10 September 1922.

a balance. The sun, moon, the moving of the world itself is all a balance. If there was no balance the world would drop down. If the East had progressed in the same direction as the West, how many more wars would have come in the first place. There would have been guns and cannons all over the world. Just now this is only in this part of the world. God has busied all those in the East and West in a certain work. But no doubt the world will become more balanced if the East will partake of all that is required from the West, and the West will partake of what [16] is required from the East. The more exchange there is of thought and idea, the more balanced the world will be and the greater comfort will come to humanity.

Question: *Does the recognition of brotherhood tend to keep people in contact even on the physical plane?*

Answer: Yes. If the spirit of brotherhood is understood in the way I have explained in my address, it would not only keep people conscious of their contact on the physical plane but people would realize their contact with one another in the spirit.

Question: *What is the meaning of the Virgin Mary standing upon the Crescent Moon? The same symbol is also found in India.*

Answer: The Crescent Moon is the symbol of womanhood as the sun is the symbol of manhood. The crescent moon is the symbol of respondence which is the female attribute of the soul. The crescent moon also is the symbol of the Messenger, for the Message is received by different Prophets in respondence to the voice of God.

---

16. Sk.tp.: "all that" instead of "what"

Copied from the book The Inner Life, 1st ed.

[1]

IX

The Angel-Man

The Hindu word, [2]"*Deva*" denotes an angel-man, and the Sufi term for this is *Faristha-khaslat*[3]. Every soul has as its first expression angelic life, and therefore it is not surprising if man shows angelic traits in his life, for it is in the depth of his soul. The soul coming through different spheres and planes of existence partakes of different attributes, and the attributes of the lower world become so collected and gathered around the soul, that it almost forgets its very first experience of itself, its purest being. The soul that through all the worldly experiences has a tendency to turn towards its origin, its angelic state, shows a different character from the general characteristics of human beings. This soul shows the tendency of the compass that always points in a certain direction, whichever way it is moved

---

Documents:

Bk. = the first edition of the book The Inner Life, published by the Sufi Order (Society in England), Southampton, England, in December 1922. It contains ten lectures, given in September 1922 at Katwijk, the Netherlands, during a Summer School, which were taken down by a professional stenographer. No book-preparation of this text or other earlier document has been found to date.

Fm.corr. = an add. and a corr. in Fazal Mai Egeling's hwr. in a copy of the book The Inner Life, 1st ed., presented to her by Sophia Green on 24th January 1923.

Sk.corr. = some corrections made by Sakina Furnée in a copy of the book The Inner Life, 1st ed.

Notes:

1. From the "Quarterly Magazine for Seekers after Truth": Sufism, edited by Sophia Saintsbury Green, of December 1922, and a hwr. annotation by Sirdar van Tuyll, it is known that this lecture was given at Katwijk, the Netherlands, on Monday, 11th September 1922, in the evening (v. Preface).
2. Fm.corr.: added "Shining-One," before "'Deva'"
3. Sk.corr.: "'farishta-khaslat'". Throughout this chapter, Sk. changed the initial capital letters on "Deva", "Djnayn", "Djin", "Vairâgya" and "Vairâgi" to lower case.

or turned. And it is the same with a soul, whose nature it is to be pointing to the origin and source from which every soul comes.

[4]Now this soul may have the same tendency from childhood, and through youth, and when grown up it may still have the same tendency; it may develop it more and more, but it is a tendency which is born with the soul and its magnetism is great. It attracts every other soul, because it is in contact with its real self, and that real self is the real self of every soul which it contacts, and therefore it acts as a magnet towards these souls. *Deva* is the name of this pure kind of human soul.

The next type of soul to the *Deva* is the *Djnayn*[5], from which comes the word "*djin*"[6]. This is a characteristic of a soul that keeps in contact with the inner region, which is reflected outwardly in all that is beautiful. While the soul of every person is looking for the beauty which is outward, the attention of the *djin*[6] soul is directed not so much to that beauty which is reflected outwardly, as it is to the source of that beauty, which is within.

It is among those who live the inner life that these two characteristic types of the *Deva* or angel and the *Djnayn*[5] or *djin*[6] are mostly to be found, because they are less absorbed in the life of this world, so more attracted to the inner life. It does not mean that they are not occupied with the worldly life; it does not mean that they take no interest in this world; in fact it is the interest in the external life which brings the soul towards it. If the soul were not interested in the world it would not come; it is its interest which brings it. But to such a soul, while the external life is of interest, at the same time it is a disappointment. All that interests a fine soul in this world only interests as long as it does not touch it, once it has touched it this soul loses interest in it, its natural inclination is to withdraw. The things which hold the average soul cannot hold this soul; they can only attract, for this soul is seeking for something, and it sees its reflection outwardly, but when it touches it, it finds it was a shadow, and was not real, and it goes back disappointed, and so the life of the *Deva* or *djin*[6] is spent in this manner.

The characteristic of the hare[7] as described by the poets of India, is

---

4. Sk.corr.: no new paragraph
5. The word *djnayn* is problematical; there is a Sanskrit adjective, *djnyāh*, meaning "wise, knowing, familiar", but this is not related to the Arabic *djin* or *jinn*.
6. See *jinn* in Glossary.
7. Fm.corr.: the word "hare" corr. to "deer" in four different sentences in Fm.'s hwr. It is highly unlikely that Fm. would make such a change on her own initiative, and therefore it may be assumed that Pir-o-Murshid Inayat Khan indicated to her that "hare" was a mistake and "deer" was correct. Sk.'s corr. indicates that she also assumed or knew that the change came from Pir-o-Murshid;
Sk.corr.: "deer" instead of "hare"

that when it is thirsty it runs about in the forests looking for water, and it is greatly delighted on hearing the sounds of thunder, and runs about with a desire to drink; but sometimes it is only thunder and[8] does not rain afterwards, or if it rains it is perhaps only a shower and not enough water to drink and the hare[5] still remains thirsty. And so is the thirst of a fine soul in this world. The soul of the spiritually inclined man is constantly thirsty, looking for something, seeking for something, and when it thinks it has found, the thing turns out to be different and so life becomes a continual struggle and disappointment. And the result is that instead of taking interest in all things, a kind of indifference is produced, and yet in the real character of this soul there is no indifference; there is only love. Although life seems to make this soul indifferent, it cannot really become indifferent, and it is this state working through this life that gives man a certain feeling, for which only a Hindu word is applicable, no other language has a word which can give you this particular meaning so adequately. The Hindus call it "*Vairâgya*" from which the term *Vairâgi* has come. *Vairâgi* means a person who has become indifferent, and yet indifference is not the word for it. It describes a person who has lost the value in his eyes of all that attracts the human being. It is no more attractive to him; it no more enslaves him. He may still be interested in all things of this life, but not bound to them. The first feeling of the *Vairâgi* is to turn away from everything. That person shows the nature of the hare[5], which runs away at the flutter of a leaf, for the person becomes sensitive and convinced of the disappointing results that come from the limitation and changeableness of life in the world. Hurt within, he becomes sensitive, and the first thing that occurs to his mind is to fly, to hide somewhere, to go into a cave in the mountains, or into the forest where he will meet no one. No affair of this world, no relation, no friendship, no wealth, no rank or position or comfort, nothing holds him. And yet that does not mean that he in any way lacks what is called love or kindness, for if ever he lives in this world it is only out of love. When he is not interested in the world it is only love that keeps him here,—the love which does not express itself any more in the way of attachment, but only in the way of kindness, forgiveness, generosity, service, consideration, sympathy, helpfulness, in any way that[9] it can, never expecting a return from the world, but ever doing all that he can, pitying the conditions, knowing the limitedness of life and its continual changeability.

When this *Vairâgi* becomes more developed, then he becomes like a

---

8. Sk.corr.: "it" added
9. Ibid.: "that" crossed out

serpent. He becomes wise like a serpent. He seeks solitude as the serpent seeks solitude. The serpent is never interested in moving among the crowd; it always has its home where it hides itself; it only comes out when it is hungry or thirsty, and once it has taken its food it does not hunger or thirst after more as the dogs and cats do; you can give them food again and again, and they still want more. When the serpent is once fed it goes into its hole and stays there until it wants food again; it has lost all voraciousness. And so has the soul of the *Vairâgi*; he only wants to live in this world for the sake of others, not for himself. His connection with people in the world is to serve them, not asking for their service, to love them, not asking for love; to be friends with them, not asking for friendship. He never allows himself to be deceived a second time, once disappointed is sufficient. Once the *Vairâgi* has come to realize the falsehood of ordinary life he never allows himself to be deceived again. He sees the world with the eye of experience, and he says: "I do not expect anything from you; if I come to you it is to give to you, not to take from you; I do all things for you, but will not be bound to you." That is the watchword of the *Vairâgi*.

When the *Vairâgi* is still more developed in this feeling of *Vairâgya* then he becomes a lion. He is no more the serpent seeking solitude, although he loves it still; he is no more the hare[5], running away from the crowd. He is the lion, who stands and faces all difficulties. No longer sensitive, but with all strength and power, with all balance, with patience he endures, and with a brave spirit he stands in the crowd in the world. For what? To bear all things that come to him; to endure all the jarring influences that the world offers to a sensitive person; to look into the eyes of all, being brave in spirit and strengthened in truth and clear of conscience. It is in this way that the lion-like soul of the *Deva*, the angel-man, comes to the rescue of humanity. What is called the master or the saint, or prophet or sage is this developed *vairagi*[10]. He is like the fruit that has ripened on the tree, helped by the sun. In this way this soul that is ripened by experience in life, and has not allowed itself to become decayed by that experience but has upheld the truth, with balance, with hope and patience, directed by love for humanity and desire to serve God, without any desire for appreciation or return from below or from above, it is that soul of the *Deva* that brings the Divine Message, whenever the Message comes, to a community, a nation, or to the world.

---

10. Bk.: this one time, the word was printed without the initial capital letter or the circumflex over the second "a", presumably the typesetter's error.

An edited, typewritten copy
made by Miss Sophia Green.

Katwijk[1], September 12th, 1922

Questions and Answers

Question: *Does not the present system in schools of working for prizes encourage a spirit of competition which is harmful to children?*

Answer: Yes, it does to some extent, but there are many other sides to the spirit of competition which develops in the world which are still worse. When one rejoices in one's gain which comes to one at the loss of another, and when one pushes one's way through life regardless of pushing another and causing him to fall, all these things close the doors of the heart, the only opening for the soul to breathe, and to look out into the world throwing its light upon life. When the doors of the heart are closed, and when the soul is unable to throw its light and see into the world, then the life, whatever may be man's gain and however much man may be provided with the things of this world, he can never experience happiness, for the true happiness comes from within, for the light and life which is within is the only source of happiness, and even the worldly happiness experienced is increased and added to when the inner life and light have manifested outwardly. And those cannot manifest outwardly so long as the doors of the heart are closed.

Documents:

Gr.tp. = a slightly edited typescript made by Miss Sophia Green, probably from Shabaz Mitchell's transcription of his own shorthand reporting of the three questions and answers, which is not in the archives

Sk.tp. = a later copy, apparently made from "Gr.tp." under Sakina Furnée's direction, with only one word added.

Notes:

1. Katwijk: a seaside village in the Netherlands, situated near Leiden

Question: *Will Brotherhood ever be strong enough to prevent war in the future?*

Answer: Yes. Man will not always remain[2] the same, the child is not always a child, and the youth is not always a youth. As there comes a time in the life of an individual when he thinks better than he thought before, so there comes a moment, a time, in the life of multitudes, of the generality, when they think better than they have thought before. There are many things which the people in the past did, which make us tremble even to hear of, and we experience discomfort at the idea of those happenings in the past; and in the same way when the world has evolved and humanity is different, it will give them a feeling of awe when they hear of what the world has gone through during this period.

Question: *Do you think it possible that some idealists can succeed in awakening the world to the inner reality?*

Answer: One can see the possibility by understanding the nature of every soul which is yearning constantly to awaken to reality. It is not taking before the world something which the world does not want. It is taking something before the world which the world is seeking. Therefore, if this cannot be possible, is there anything else which is possible? This is the first thing which should be possible; only if we realize for ourselves the reality, we shall be taking before the world the water of life, the partaking of which gives life eternal.

---

2. Sk.tp.: "in" added, which would suppose another word following after "same"; or "in" may have been the erroneous repetition of the end of the preceding word, "remain". In both cases it could indicate that Sakina Furnée consulted an earlier ms. (perhaps Shabaz Mitchell's hwr. transcription of his shorthand reporting of the q.a.'s).

Copied from the book The Inner Life, 1st ed.

[1]

X

Five Different Kinds of the Spiritual Souls

Those who live the inner life have to adopt a certain outer form of living in the world amidst people of all kinds. There are five principal ways known which the spiritual souls adopt to meet life in the world, although there are many more ways. Very often they are found in such forms of life that one could never imagine for one moment that they were living the inner life. It is for this reason that the wise of all ages have taught respect for every human being, whatever be the outward character of that person;[2] and have advised man to think who is behind that garb and what it is.

Among the five principal characteristics of the spiritual being, the first is the religious character. This is a person who lives the religious life, the life of an orthodox person, like everybody else, not showing any outward trace of a deeper knowledge or wider view, though he realizes it within himself. Outwardly he goes to his religious temple, or his church, the same as everybody else. He

---

Documents:

Bk. = the first edition of the book The Inner Life, published by the Sufi Order (Society in England), Southampton, England, in December 1922. It contains ten lectures, given in September 1922 at Katwijk, the Netherlands, during a Summer School, which were taken down by a professional stenographer. No book-preparation of this text or other earlier document has been found to date.

Sk.corr. = some corrections made by Sakina Furnée in a copy of the book The Inner Life, 1st ed.

Notes:

1. From the "Quarterly Magazine for Seekers after Truth": Sufism, edited by Sophia Saintsbury Green, of December 1922, and a hwr. annotation by Sirdar van Tuyll, it is known that this lecture was given at Katwijk, the Netherlands, on Tuesday, 12th September 1922, in the evening (v. Preface).
2. Sk.corr.: changed the semicolon to a comma

offers his prayers to[3] Deity in the same form as everybody, reads the Scriptures in the same way that[4] everybody else does, receives the sacraments and asks for the benediction of the church in the same way that[4] everybody does. He shows no difference, no special characteristics outwardly showing him to be spiritually advanced; but at the same time while others are doing all their religious actions outwardly, he realizes them in his life in reality. Every religious action to him is a symbolical revelation; prayer to him is a meditation; the Scripture to him is his reminder, for the holy Book refers him to that which he reads in life, and in nature; and therefore while outwardly he is only a religious man like everybody in the world, inwardly he is a spiritual man.

Another aspect of a spiritual man is to be found in the philosophical mind. He may not at all show any trace of orthodoxy or piety; he may seem to be quite a man of the world in business, or in the affairs of the worldly life. He takes all things smoothly, he tolerates all things, endures all things. He takes life easily with his understanding. He understands all things inwardly; outwardly he acts according to life's demand. No one may ever think that he is living the inner life. He may be settling a business affair, and yet he may have the realization of God and truth at the same time. He may not at all appear meditative or contemplative, and yet every moment of his life may be devoted to contemplation. He may take his occupation in everyday life as a means of spiritual realization. No one outwardly may consider for one moment that he is spiritually so highly evolved, except that those who come in contact with him may in time be convinced that he is an honest person; that he is fair and just in his principles and life; that he is sincere. That is all the religion he needs. In this way his outward life becomes his religion, and his inner realization his spirituality.

The third form of a spiritual being is that of a server, one who does good to others. In this form there may be saints hidden. They never speak about spirituality, nor much about the philosophy of life. Their philosophy and religion are in their action. There is love gushing forth from their heart every moment of their life, and they are occupied in doing good to others. They consider everyone who comes near them as their brother or sister, as their child, and take an interest in their joy and their sorrow, and do all they can to guide them, to instruct them, to advise them through their life. In this form the spiritual person may be a teacher, a preacher or a philanthropist, but whatever form he may appear in, the chief thing in his life is the service of mankind, doing good to another, bringing happiness to someone in some form, and the joy that rises from this is high

3. Sk.corr.: "the" added
4. Ibid.: "that" changed into "as"

spiritual ecstasy, for every act of goodness and kindness has a particular joy which brings the air of heaven. When all the time a person is occupied doing good to others, there is a constant joy arising, and that joy creates a heavenly atmosphere, creating within him that heaven which is his inner life. This world is so full of thorns, so full of troubles, pains and sorrows, and in this same world he lives; but by the very fact of his trying to remove the thorns from the path of another, although they prick his own hands, he rises, giving him that inner joy which is his spiritual realization.

There is the fourth form of a spiritual person, which is the mystic form, and that form is difficult to understand, because the mystic is born. Mysticism is not a thing which is learned, it is a temperament. A mystic may have his face turned toward the north while he is looking toward the south; a mystic may have his head bent low and yet he may be looking up; his eyes may be open outwardly while he may be looking inwardly; his eyes may be closed and yet he may be looking outwardly. The average man cannot understand the mystic, and therefore people are always at a loss when dealing with him. His "yes" is not the same yes that everybody says; his "no" has not the same meaning as that which everybody understands. In almost every phrase he says there is some symbolical meaning. His every outward action has an inner significance. A man who does not understand his symbolical meaning may be bewildered by hearing a phrase which is nothing but confusion to him. A mystic may take one step outwardly, inwardly he has taken a thousand; he may be in one city and may be working in another place at the same time. A mystic is a phenomenon in himself and a confusion to those around him. He himself cannot tell them what he is doing, nor will they understand the real secret of the mystic. For it is someone who is living the inner life and at the same time covering that inner life by outer action; his word or movement is nothing but the cover of some inner action. Therefore those who understand the mystic never dispute with him. When he says "go," they go; when he says "come," they come; when he comes to them they do not say, "do not come," they understand that it is the time when he must come; and when he goes from them they do not ask him to stay for they know it is the time when he must go.

Neither the laughter of a mystic, nor his tears are to be taken as any outward expression which means something. His tears may perhaps be a cover for very great joy, his smile, his laughter, may be a cover for a very deep sentiment. His open eyes, his closed eyes, the turning of his face, his glance, his silence, his conversation, nothing means the same that one is accustomed to understand. Yet it does not mean that the mystic does this purposely, he is so made; no one could purposely do it even if he wished, no one has the power to do it. The truth is that the soul of the mystic is a dancing soul. It has realized that inner law, it has fathomed that mystery for which souls long, and in the joy of that mystery the whole life of the mystic becomes a mystery. You may see the mystic twenty times a day and twenty times he will have a different expression. Every time his mood is different, and yet his outward mood may not at all be his inner mood. The mystic is an example of God's mystery in the form of man.

The fifth form in which a person who lives the inner life appears is a strange form, a form which very few people can understand. He puts on the mask of innocence outwardly to such an extent that those who do not understand may easily consider him unbalanced, peculiar, or strange. He does not mind about it for the reason that it is only his shield. If he were to admit before humanity the power that he has, thousands of people would go after him and he would not have one moment to live his inner life. The enormous power that he possesses governs inwardly lands and countries, controlling them and keeping them safe from disasters, such as floods, and plagues and also wars, keeping harmony in the country or in the place in which he lives, and all this is done by his silence, by his constant realization of the inner life. To a person who lacks deep insight, he will seem a strange being. In the language of the East he is called Madzub. That same idea was known to the ancient Greeks and the traces of it are still in existence in some places, but mostly in the East. There are souls to be found to-day in the East, living in this garb, of a self-realized man who shows no trace outwardly of philosophy or mysticism or religion, or any particular morals, and yet his presence is a battery of power, his glance most inspiring, a commanding expression in his looks, and if he ever speaks his word is the promise of God. What he says is Truth, but he rarely speaks a word, it is difficult to get a word out of him; but once he has spoken, what he says is done.

There is no end to the variety of the outward appearance of spiritual souls in life, but at the same time there is no better way of living in this world, and yet living the inner life, than being *one's self*, outwardly and inwardly. Whatever be one's profession, work, or part in the outer life, to perform it sincerely, and truthfully, to fulfill one's mission in the outer life thoroughly, at the same time keeping the inner realization that the outer life, whatever be one's occupation, should reflect the inner realization of truth.

An edited, typewritten copy made by Miss Sophia Green.

Katwijk[1], September 13th[2], 1922

Questions and Answers

Question: *If a man had not good manners naturally, and tried to adopt good manners as his ideal, would that change his character?*

Answer: No, not at all. On the other hand it would spoil his character. For a good manner is the outcome of a good heart; a graceful manner is produced from beauty of heart; it comes from within. At present there are people who perhaps finish their learning in a way, in what they call a polished manner, and when they go among people they have an outer manner which does not come from their heart, and therefore, has no charm whatever. And with every polished manner something of the rigidity of the heart is expressed in some form or other, and therefore it is never a finished manner. This can be understood better by seeing a dancer who has studied very much outwardly and comparing her dancing with that of another dancer who is inspired from within. It is not an outward study or practice, but it is some beauty inwardly which moves her and inspires her to movement, and every movement is full of charm, beauty, and magic, and so is a beautiful manner.

Question: *You told us that balance was best when one tried to see always the opinion of the other, but is not balance best when one sees both*

Documents:

Gr.tp. = a slightly edited typewritten copy of four questions and answers made by Miss Sophia Green, probably from Shabaz Mitchell's transcription of his own shorthand reporting.

Sk.tp. = a later copy of the four questions and answers in "Gr.tp.", plus a fifth question and answer, the origin of which is not known.

Notes:

1. Katwijk: a seaside village in the Netherlands, situated near Leiden
2. September 13th, 1922 was the last day of the Summer School given at Katwijk

opinions?

Answer: Yes. The psychology is that with two opinions before one, one's own opinion covers, so to speak, one's eyes, hindering one's eyes from seeing properly. Therefore, the just will not let this veil veil his eyes. He will study the opinion of another thoroughly, which is very rarely done. If everyone saw truly the two opinions, a great deal of the conflict of life would be lessened. Those wars and disasters, and the unrest which the world has been going through would certainly cease to a very great extent, and many problems which today such institutions as the League of Nations[3], and other political institutions cannot very well solve, would become easily solved. The difficulty of the present time is not that the problems are different[4]; it is the people who are different. Do you think that the problems were so difficult that they were not solved in Geneva[5], that they had to go to Genoa[6], and then they were not solved, and they had to go to Holland[7], and still they are not solved, and you do not know when they will be solved. Is life's problem so difficult for human intelligence? If man were only simple and just! This world is made for man; he is made master of the creatures. Yet the problem of life is so difficult that he has to go from one land to another land to discuss it and still it is not finished. What does it mean? It means restlessness of conscience, a lack of that just spirit on every side, and that good will to do good to one another. If it were there, if the spirit of humanity were present, the whole difficulty would be solved. People make out of mole-hills mountains, because they want to make mountains of them. When we think where all this trouble comes from, we cannot but see that it comes from a tendency of men only to live the outward life, and not the inner life. It is the awakening of the

---

3. The League of Nations: founded after World War I with its seat at Geneva, Switzerland. See "List of Persons, Places, Works, etc."
4. Gr.tp.: later changed in unidentified hwr. to "difficult";
   Sk.tp.: "difficult"
5. Geneva: in the 1920s was the seat of the League of Nations. See "List of Persons, Places, Works, etc."
6. Genoa: capital of the region of Liguria in Italy, where the "Conference of Genoa" took place in the spring of 1922, in order to discuss the economic reconstruction after World War I of central and eastern Europe, and to improve relations between Soviet Russia and Europe's capitalist regimes.
7. Holland (or The Netherlands) became the seat of the "International Court of Justice", established by the League of Nations after World War I.

spirit that will make men simple and straightforward. And if he were simple and straightforward, all things for him would be simple and straightforward; nothing would be very difficult. It is we who make life difficult. If we did not make difficulties, life would not be difficult. The complexity of life is man's complexity. If he were simple, life would become simple.

Question: Do you think it possible for a small group of persons to form a kind of ideal state?

Answer: Yes, it can be possible, but it will not be stable. As soon as you have an ideal state, many guests will visit you and they will bring their atmosphere there to add to the ideal state of affairs, and the same ideal state will turn into something which will frighten you away from the state and others will occupy it. Therefore, it must not be our idea[8] that a section of humanity may improve and make life good. It will never be possible. What is necessary is a general evolution of humankind and those who really intend to work for a general reform must take before them the whole world as the form at which they have to work.

Question: Will you please tell us what you mean by a soul's purpose in life? Do you mean a certain work to be accomplished in the world, or a certain degree of inner realization to be attained, or both?

Answer: Yes. The purpose is hidden under a purpose: the outer purpose of each soul is peculiar to itself; the inner purpose of all souls is one, and that is spiritual realization.

[9]*Question: Can you explain how sacramental offerings or sacraments can forgive sins?*

Answer: In the first place I am asked a question which the priest should be asked, and to answer this question the priest is responsible, not me. However, I will try to explain for the priest. The idea is that in the

---

8. Sk.tp.: "ideal" instead of "idea"
9. This question and answer occur only in "Sk.tp."; no earlier or original document has been located to date.

ancient times the religions had taken symbolism as its means of expressing their hidden laws. Now what is the flesh of Christ? What is the blood of Christ? Blood represents life; flesh represents light, radiance, and radiance is of the flesh. Therefore, in reality Christ as the symbolical ideal is the Divine Light and Life. And what is sin? Sin is the lack of life, and the lack of light. The thing which is not wise, the thing which is not reasonable is void of light and at the same time void of life. It is life which controls one's actions. It is lack of life when one cannot live up to one's ideal, when one cannot do what one wishes to do. There are only two reasons which lead man to mistake. One reason is that he is perplexed and cannot see what is right. Another reason is that he sees what is right but he is so weak that he cannot *do* what is right. Either is lack of life or lack of light. This symbolism explains the perfection of light and the perfection of life which we have idealized in Christ, the ideal, that by eating it or by partaking of it one may realize it in one's thought. It is only a symbol. It is not in partaking of a symbol, but the mastery is in solving the problem and finding out the inner meaning of the thing. Then one can know that sin can be removed by partaking of light and life which perfects man, which strengthens man, which makes life clear.

Sakina's handwritten copy of which no shorthand or longhand reporting has been found in the archives to date.

1

The Message[2]

Aristocracy and democracy are not two things, but one.

There is but one chief thing, which is hierarchy. When it is right, it is called aristocracy; when it goes wrong, and when there comes a new spirit to rebuild it, this progress[3] is a state of democracy.

It is natural that man is agitated with one thing when he wants to build another thing. He revolts against every thing which[4] was before, and so in rebuilding, this revolting spirit often acts to his disadvantage.

As externally there is a system of government, so inwardly there is a system of government. One can see this government in every family also. There

---

Documents:

Sk.hwr. = a ms. in Sakina Furnée's handwriting, possibly taken down from dictation by Pir-o-Murshid, or copied from a ms. in his handwriting.

tp. = a typewritten copy made from "Sk.hwr." with some editing and a few corr. and add. in Sherifa Goodenough's handwriting.

bk.p. = a preparation by Sherifa Goodenough of the text made from "tp." for publication in The Unity of Religious Ideals (1929), compiled by Sherifa Goodenough.

bk. = 1st ed. of the book The Unity of Religious Ideals, Part III: part of Chapter I: "The Spiritual Hierarchy", p.123 f.f.

Notes:

1. No date is mentioned on the documents, but the subject matter, language and the absence of a reporting point to the Summer School held at Katwijk in the Netherlands during the first half of September 1922, when neither Sakina Furnée nor Sherifa Goodenough was present.
2. Tp.: next to the title, Gd. added in hwr. "Hierarchy", designating its use for a chapter in the book The Unity of Religious Ideals
3. Tp.: "progress" changed by Gd. into "process"; bk.p., bk.: "process"
4. Bk.p., bk.: "that" instead of "which"

is a king in every family; there are ministers, counsels,[5] partakers of his responsibility and servants, who are paid for their work.

Taking the whole universe as one whole, there is also a system of government: as there is a system of government in the sky. There is the sun; then there is the moon which is directly infocussed[6] to the sun, and there are[7] principal planets who[8] surround the moon,[9] and then [10] there are stars.

And on the model of the heaven, the inner and outer governments of the earth are arranged. [11]The same way man's body is arranged: there is one principal factor, then a responsive factor, [12] then there are working factors as servants, then principal ministers, and when one would take [13] the existence of man from his soul to [14] body, it is one complete kingdom, which constitutes all the necessary officials and servants, making one's being as a kingdom. In that way it shows that the king will always exist. No democratic view, however [15] against the aristocratic form, will ever succeed in life without forming the kingdom. The difference is that if he will not call the one his [16] king, he will name him president.

In the spiritual hierarchy there are seven grades of spiritual souls, who form the spiritual standard. And each grade is divided into two classes: Jelal and Jemal; and descending from the combination of these two spirits there comes a third line, as a central line, which is the spirit of prophecy and which is called "the Spirit of Guidance."

---

5. Tp.: "counsels" changed by Gd. into "councils";
   bk.p., bk.: "counsellors"
6. All other documents: "focussed", although "in focus to" may have been said
7. Ibid.: "the" added
8. Ibid.: "which" instead of "who"
9. Bk.: "it" instead of "the moon"
10. All other documents: "then" omitted
11. Tp.: added in Gd.'s hwr.: "In";
    bk.p., bk.: "In"
12. Bk.p., bk.: "then a responsive factor" omitted
13. Ibid.: "takes" instead of "would take"
14. Ibid.: "his" added
15. Ibid.: "much" added
16. Bk.p.: "his" crossed out;
    bk.: "his" omitted

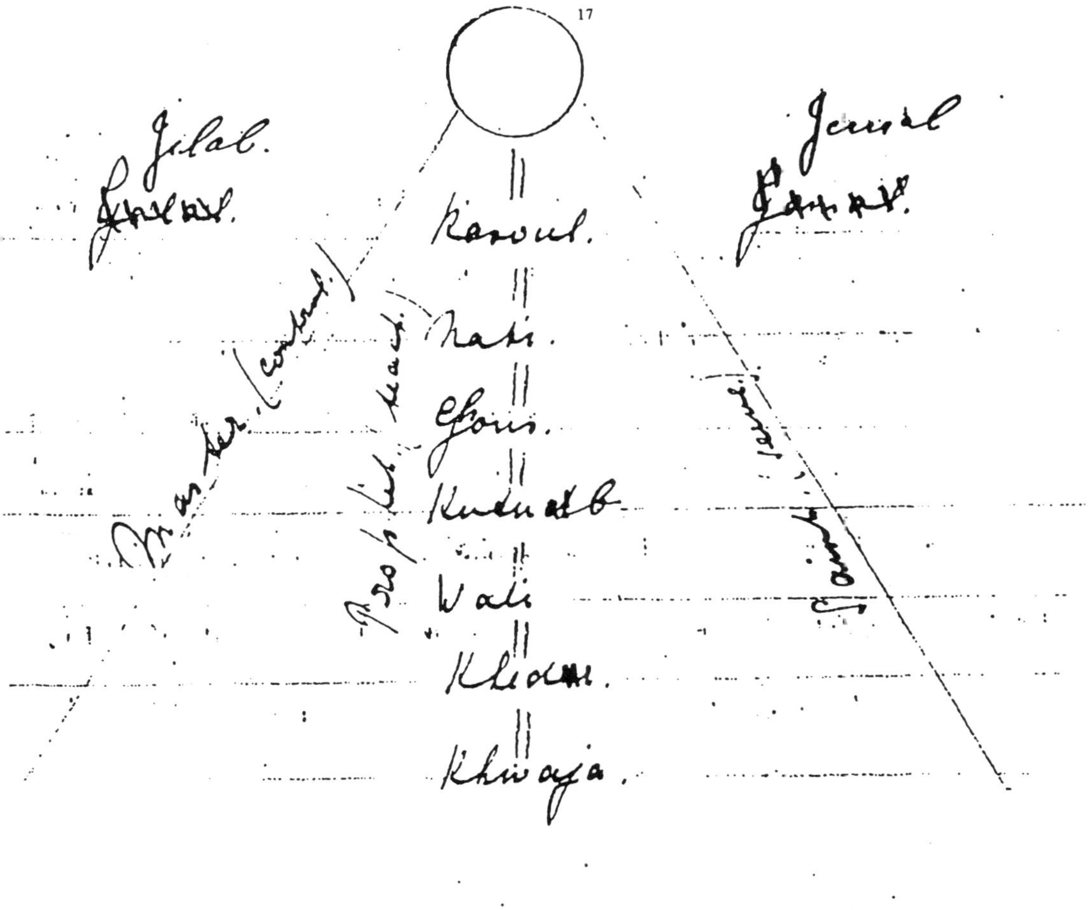

17. The diagram only appears in "Sk.hwr.", although there is a large space for it in the "tp."

It has never been necessary for any of these numbers [18] of the hierarchy to claim [19] themselves, especially for the reason that in this world of falsehood there are false claims, and even the real claims in the worldly life [20] are no more true than [21] false. And also as there has been no reason why the claims should be made, since the holders of these offices can serve the purpose better by being silent than by announcing themselves such and such, [22] and when every office in the world brings ~~about~~ to man a certain amount of vanity, and as the [23] vanity is the greatest enemy of spiritual people, and as there is [24] jealousy of human nature always at work, and as the [23] competition and rivalry is [25] the very source that gives [26] stimulance [27] to the life in the world,—the office has always been concealed by the spiritual office-holders, except by the teachers who had to give the message of God to people and teach them; and how many in the world would not believe unless they knew that [28] he was the office-bearer ~~of~~ from God.

The teachers have [29] their life [30] as the example of their office; except that, they had no other evidence. Miracles are known afterwards, legends are formed afterwards, poems are made afterwards, temples are built afterwards, following has increased afterwards, their words have ben valued afterwards. But during their lifetime they [31]had nothing, but met with oppositions[31] and the constant change of their [32] followers, agreeing one day, running away [33] another day, and all sorts of difficulties they have suffered, even such as the [34] crucifixion.

---

18. Sk.hwr.: by misreading, or by mishearing, "numbers" was written; all other documents: "members" instead of "numbers"
19. Bk.: "acclaim" instead of "claim"
20. Tp.: "life" omitted
21. Bk.p.: "the" added, then crossed out
22. Tp.: In Gd.'s hwr. "such and such" changed into "so and so"; bk.p., bk.: "as so and so"
23. Bk.p., bk.: "the" omitted
24. Ibid.: "the" added
25. Bk.: "are" instead of "is"
26. Ibid.: "give"
27. Tp.: "stimulance" replaced with "stimulus"; bk.p., bk.: "stimulus"
28. All other documents: "that" omitted
29. Bk.p., bk.: "had" instead of "have"
30. Bk.: "lives" instead of "life"
31. All other documents: rewritten to read, "met with nothing but opposition"
32. Bk.p., bk.: "the" instead of "their"
33. Tp.: later Gd. replaced "running away" with "disagreeing"; bk.p., bk.: "disagreeing"
34. All other documents: "the" omitted

The teacher's position is more delicate than [35] of the master [36] or saint, [37] because he must claim and be among people. And being among people is [38] as a bird of a different forest having arrived in a strange land, and all other birds, finding him different from them, wish to fight him, [39] torture him and wish to kill him. That has been the condition of the prophet in all times and the same will always be.

The last one, who [40] left a warning for the coming one, [41] was this: that the prophecy was sealed. He did not mean by this that the work of the Spirit [42] of Guidance was sealed. It was a clue to the successor, and there [43] the claim was sealed, that the work may [44] be done without a claim, and it is the work that is done that should prove its genuineness instead of a claim.

---

35. Ibid.: "that" added
36. Tp.: "martyr", later changed to "Master" in Gd.'s hwr.
37. Bk.p., bk.: "or saint" left out
38. Bk.: "to be" added
39. All other documents: "and" added
40. Bk.p.: "who" crossed out;
    bk.: "who" omitted
41. Bk.p., bk.: "which" added
42. Tp.: "prophet" instead of "Spirit", later replaced with "spirit"
43. Tp.: "and there" changed by Gd. into "now that";
    bk.p.: "that now" instead of "and there" and then changed to "now that";
    bk.: "now that" instead of "and there"
44. Bk.p., bk.: "must" instead of "may"

A text in the handwriting of Kefayat LLoyd, probably copied from her own longhand reporting of the lecture.

Ethical Church[1], 6 October 1922

The Alchemy of Happiness

Beloved ones of God,

My subject this evening is the alchemy of happiness. In Sanscrit terms alchemy is the science of human nature, and the word alchemy[2] comes from [3] originally, from K.[4] [5] alchemy, known in the West as the process by which not only medicine was made, but gold and silver; so this term was used symbolically for that science which was the making of the real silver and gold in the character of man. If one asked, through all the different occupations one sees in this world, making everyone busy, what was the object with which everyone is busy with[6] night and day, what is the incentive that prompts man to action, what is the motive, the object for all this restless activity, the answer is, the object is to attain

---

Documents:

Kf. = a handwritten copy by Kefayat LLoyd, probably copied from her own longhand reporting of the lecture. The English seems to show some editing;
(Kf.)Sd. = some additions by Saida van Tuyll;
(Kf.)Sr. = additions and corrections by Sirdar van Tuyll.

Sk.tp. = a later typescript made from "Kf." by Sakina Furnée or under her direction.

Notes:

1. The Ethical Church was located in the Bayswater section of London
2. v. Glossary
3. Kf.: an open space;
   (Kf.)Sd.: filled in "Arabia";
   Sk.tp.: "Arabia"
4. (Kf.)Sr.: changed "from K." to "Ilm Kimiya";
   Sk.tp.: "Ilm Kimiya"
5. (Kf.)Sr.: filled in "which is changed into";
   Sk.tp.: "which is changed into"
6. (Kf.)Sr.: "with" crossed out;
   Sk.tp.: "with" omitted

happiness. Through every channel, in every walk of life, man is working for happiness; if he is collecting, if he is making money, if he is studying, if he is seeking power, and even the religious spirit working in man, the hidden motive in all this is the attainment of happiness. If one analyzes life one finds that at the bottom of every desire there is only one motive and that is the attainment of happiness. No doubt the word happiness is very often confused with the word pleasure; it is natural that it should be so, for man does not know really what happiness is, he only knows pleasure. The reason why every soul is constantly yearning for happiness, may be answered, because happiness is the real being of man. Happiness is his real nature; so he is uncomfortable in the absence of what is the true nature of his being—he is seeking for something which is natural. He is seeking for something which belongs to him but which in this life he has never experienced, only pleasure. But the soul being itself happiness, happiness is there in the depth. What is called wrongdoing is when the soul seeks to accomplish its object by a method which is mistaken, and so it is disappointed, it does not reach the object for which it is seeking. No action, no thought, nothing has right or wrong stamped upon it by divine decree. Man has made for convenience laws of what he calls right and wrong. In reality if there is wrong, it is that which prompts the soul to [7]action by which it finds something different to what it is really seeking, and so it remains as thirsty as ever.

The difference between happiness and pleasure is called in Sanscrit m [8]. It is like the thirsty hare[9] seeking water in tropical countries, it shows a great joy at hearing the sound of a thunder-storm. And yet very often thunder-storms come and yet it does not rain; so the happiness of the hare is in the expectation, he shows joy in running about and waiting for the coming of the rain. If one studies human nature, one finds that it is like the hare, constantly seeking something; and sometimes at the expectation of some gain, he feels so happy, but he finds no satisfaction, the thirst is still there, it is only the satisfaction of a moment. Man pains[10] riches, honours, rank, all these things he has perhaps worked for and yet he finds no satisfaction, for

---

7. (Kf.)Sr.: "an" added;
Sk.tp.: "an" added
8. Kf.: only the letter "m", followed by a blank;
Sk.tp.: a blank;
perhaps "*maya*", illusion, could have been said
9. Cf. lecture "The Angel-man" of 11th September 1922, note 3
10. (Kf.)Sr.: "for" added;
Sk.tp.: "for" added

satisfaction is somewhere else, and not in this human life.

According to the Yogis and Sufis there are different planes of existence through which the soul experiences life, and the one plane which is the part of man's being which alone he can call his real Self, from there he looks at all the other planes only as instruments through which to experience, and he finds that this true plane is happiness itself. In Vedanta it is called [11], absolute happiness, or real happiness; happiness is therefore buried in one's own heart, and yet man wants to find it outside. Happiness can only be found by digging into the grave where it is buried alive, it is living, and therefore working. The yearning of man for happiness is the yearning for that happiness which is buried; unconsciously often man works for this. There is a cult, a process, a method, by which he can dig and find, and it is this cult which in the terms of the wise of ancient times is called alchemy. Many people thought this meant the scientific process of making gold, and strove all through their lives to discover this secret. And even now there are people seeking to find out the process of turning metals into gold; but even if man made this discovery, he has not found the true alchemy, for he has not turned himself into gold. Wealth is constantly changing from one hand to another. The treasure that man can depend upon is in himself, the gold that can be produced in his own soul is the only real treasure.

There is a story told in the Scriptures that have been held sacred for thousands of years by the Hindus, that a great sage or prophet was[12] through[13] the forest when he met a young robber, whose occupation was to stand in the forest, and attack those travellers who passed by, and take all they had. He came to the prophet N.[14] and said, "Where are you going?" And N. said, "What do you want from me?" And the robber said, "I want all that you have, show me your gold and silver, you have riches." And N. said, "Yes, I have riches, I have plenty of gold and silver." The robber said, "Give them to me, or I will take them." And N. said, "My treasure is that which cannot be seen by you. You must change your eyes and your heart in order to recognize my treasure, you cannot rob me of my treasure, you cannot touch it, it is more precious than gems, or gold and silver." This was the first time the youth had heard such words: words of power, of sincerity. He was

---

11. (Kf.)Sd.: filled in "*ananda*";
Sk.tp.: "*ananda*"
12. Kf.: between the last word at the bottom of one page ("was"), and the first word on the next page, one word has been omitted. Here "roaming" could have been said.
13. Sk.tp.: the omission of a verb was corrected by changing "through" into "in"
14. Kf., Sk.tp.: no name has been filled in here.

always accustomed to hear frightened people speaking, he never before had met a brave soul who stood and said sincerely that he had treasure that never perishes[15], that would always last. The robber was much impressed; he said, "Can you make me understand where I can get this treasure?" And N. said, "Alchemy is the process by which can be made treasure that will last for ever.[16] It is called by different names: mysticism, occultism, morals, religion, but in point of fact all comes from the one source, the one goal, the Wisdom which comes not by study, but by experience: it comes by study, but not by merely book-reading. For the one who becomes the student of life, who studies himself, who studies human nature, for him every moment in life is a revelation; his experience of life, of pain, pleasure, success, happiness, failure or error, all is a valuable study, there is not one wasted moment, he learns through all aspects of life. The only true Teacher of humanity comes in all forms, and is ever present, He is known and unknown, has appeared and disappeared. That Teacher is constantly with man, if he will only be a pupil. The difficulty in the life of the seeker is that he has no patience to be a pupil, he wishes to begin by teaching. If he would know the true life of the Masters, the inspirers of humanity, he will come to understand that God alone is the Teacher. The perfection of pupilship alone constitutes Teachership. It is by being an empty cup, by freeing one's heart from all fixed ideas which keep man back, by making the heart the empty vessel into which the wine of wisdom can be poured. It is only lack of faith which keeps man back from receiving this wine. Life today is so involved in commercialism, in materialism, one sees nothing but competition, prejudice, conflict and disharmony, and the outcome is war, unrest, disaster, there does not seem to be any rest. What does all this show? It shows that in seeking for happiness man has followed the wrong path, the path which can never lead to the joy and peace for which his soul yearns.

Now you will ask me, "What is the way of attainment?" There is a process known in the East, and explained in symbolic words, that out of mercury silver is made. First the ever moving nature of mercury must be stilled, and when it is stilled the same substance turns into silver; next comes the process of turning silver into gold, and for this the essence of a certain herb is poured on to the silver, which has first been melted, and the silver

---

15. Sk.tp.: "perished"
16. Kf.: no quotation mark appears at the end of the quotation;
Sk.tp.: added a quotation mark after "ever", and Sr.(?) indicated that a new paragraph should begin with "It is called. . ."

becomes gold. Many in all ages have sought for this herb, and many have tried to find the way to still mercury, the nature of which is constant movement. The mystical interpretation is, that the nature of mind is like the nature of mercury, constantly moving, it is very difficult to make it still. Those who have practised long concentration know how difficult it is to control the mind. It is very easy to close the eyes and sit still. And often even if the mind is still, when one closes the eyes and tries to concentrate, the mind becomes the more active, because the mind is accustomed to keep still more easily when it is held by external objects. The secret of stilling the mind is to be learnt in the secret or science of Breath. Breath is the essence of life, the centre of life. It is used as the rein is used in controlling a restive horse. The mind, which is more troublesome than a restive horse, is controlled by knowing the proper method of breathing. It is a great pity that since the mystical cult of the East has become known in the West, books have been published, and these methods which have been kept as sacred as religion by the people of the East have been discussed in words which cannot truly explain the mystery of that which is the centre of life. People read and begin to play with Breath, and often they injure health of mind and body, and instead of getting help they get harm. Then there are others who make a business of teaching breathing exercises, and they degrade something which is as sacred as religion. It is the science of life, and it cannot be turned into a business. The science of Breath is the greatest mystery there is. For thousands of years in the schools of the mystics it has been trusted to man as sacred, and that trust has been called initiation.

Once the mind is stilled comes the next process, and that is the turning the silver into gold. If we have only turned the mercury into silver, we have not accomplished all, for the object was to make gold. Often after having gained some power by concentration, man wants to work that power, and not knowing the past and the future, and blinded by the influence of those things which stand nearest to him, he uses that power wrongly to his own disadvantage. The right way of learning the cult of alchemy is[17], after one has acquired nerve control by turning mercury into silver, is to melt the silver, and this melting is done by awakening one's sympathy for humanity by consideration for everyone one meets, by realizing one's responsibility and one's duty towards one's fellow man. It is in this manner that the faculty of feeling is awakened, and love manifests in compassion, forgiveness, sympathy, service, gentleness, meekness and sacrifice. The principles of this

---

17. Sk.tp.: "is" put in parentheses

alchemy were taught by Christ in the Sermon on the Mount—by the practice of these principles the heart is melted, and that which turns it into gold is the Love of God, but one cannot know the love of God, unless love is awakened for one's fellow man. It is when man shows love and sympathy for his fellow man, when he makes sacrifices, when he begins to bear suffering and troubles for those around him, then it is that he becomes capable of loving God. The one who says, I love God, but I do not love mankind, is a liar, for no one can love God except his heart is melted, and the sign of the melted heart is shown every moment in unselfish, loving service. The silver that is not yet melted cannot be turned into gold. When the essence of the herb has been poured on to the melted silver, the herb, the essence of which is the ideal of God, the knowledge of God, when one knows no Friend greater than God, when the One one trusts most in life is God, to Whom all praise is due, when the whole object in life is God, when man has come to this God ideal, the next step is to take the essence from the herb, the knowledge of God, and the knowledge of God is the realization of God as the perfection of all beauty in every form, of all power, strength and might, of wisdom in all its forms, literature, art, science, poetry. In God is the perfection of all that is. The more one lives in this knowledge, the more one is in Paradise. Sorrows, distresses of life are forgotten, one is no longer lonely, for the Friend is always there, in the crowd or in the solitude, He never leaves, the Friend Who is more beautiful than anything in the world, more precious, more wise, for all beauty, treasure, wisdom, are His, and He Himself is the perfection of all. Constantly contemplating makes one grow into God and one comes closer and closer to God, Who is the goal and the aim of life.

A typescript, probably by Nargis Dowland.

---

7 October 1922

Man, the Master of his Life

There are numberless complaints that the souls living on earth have to make of all kinds—lack of health, of wealth, or[1] power, or[1] position. Every soul has some complaint, and if one were to find the solution for every complaint many centuries would be necessary; perhaps as many centuries as there are souls in this world would be necessary to find the solution for the complaint of each person. But when one sees the underlying mystery that is hidden beneath all these complaints, one finds there is one tragedy of life which manifests in various forms. Therefore, when the complaint is explained the complaint of every man is different, but when the complaint is seen through, analysed, the bottom of every complaint is one and the same thing. Outwardly one sees there are many reasons; in the depth there is only one reason, and that reason of the tragedy of life is limitation. All the pain, sorrow, disappointment, discouragement—all this comes from one thing, limitation in its various forms.

And there arises the question—if it is the nature of man to be limited, why then must this nature become a tragedy in his life? But in reality it is not his original nature. Limitation is man's acquired nature. No doubt if this question was[2] to be more explained and analysed one would have to explain

---

Documents:

Ng. = a typescript probably by Nargis Dowland, perhaps made from her own longhand reporting of the lecture, with some editing. The original reporting is not in the archives;
(Ng.)Gr.: corr. made in "Ng." by Miss Sophia Green.

Sk.tp. = a later typescript, copied from "Ng." by Sakina Furnée or under her direction with the corr. incorporated.

Notes:

1. (Ng.)Gr.: "or" changed into "of";
Sk.tp.: "of" instead of "or"
2. (Ng.)Gr.: "was" changed into "were";
Sk.tp.: "were" instead of "was"

what personality is. But every [3] personality is not man's original self; it is an acquired self. It is, therefore, that man finds himself in a position in which he finds his life placed in a situation which is not his own. He finds that he is not himself, but he does not realise. When a person says: "I am not well", or "Some part of my body is in pain", or perhaps he cannot move or use that part of his body—what does it suggest to him? It suggests "I am not myself". If one inquired what he would have if he were himself, he would have mastery over that particular part of his body. When he can move his body properly he is master of his body. This shows that what is natural is mastery; what is unnatural is limitation. Everything which causes discomfort, therefore, is limitation. Now the question is: Where does this limitation come from? This limitation comes from the process through which the soul involves itself into physical manifestation. The soul comes forward in a limited form and finds itself limited. Therefore in the sacred tradition of the ancient Sufis of Persia one reads of the grief of the soul. In the poetry of Rumi one reads of the soul lamenting for its captivity on Earth. If the nature of the soul was limitation or inability it would not have grieved. By coming on Earth it is grieved. It seems as if someone who was happy and free and master of himself and perfect in himself had come into a form and finds himself in a position where he finds himself limited in every direction. In experiencing happiness, in accomplishing certain things, in experiencing life as the soul wishes to experience it, the soul feels limited. But the greatest grief of the soul is not only the limitation, the forgetting of that perfection which only remains, so to speak, in its sub-conscious [4]. There is that yearning, that desire which is the only proof to the soul that "once I was happy, that once I was perfect, that once I was master of myself, that once I was pure from all sorrow and sadness and jealousy". The very reason that the soul yearns for these things shows that the soul is acquainted with perfection and knows the perfection it had; only as soon as the soul is born on Earth, it sees nothing but limitation, and therefore the soul cannot dare say "I ever was a perfect being"; he [5] cannot dare believe it will be happy. It thinks it is always limited, that "I am nothing but a limited being. See, I am only a bubble. I have never been the sea", although the bubble has sprung from the sea. This causes it to realise itself as a bubble. It only

---

3. (Ng.)Gr.: "every" crossed out;
   Sk.tp.: "every" omitted
4. (Ng.)Gr.: "sub-conscious" changed into "sub-consciousness";
   Sk.tp.: "sub-consciousness"
5. (Ng.)Gr.: "he" changed into "it";
   Sk.tp.: "it"

knows itself to be a bubble. Compared with itself, when it looks at the sea it is so vast that it forgets it has sprung from the sea. It is not only a part of the sea, but it has the being of the sea. It constitutes the sea. And this realisation is worse than limitation. The actual limitation which the nature of life presents is not alone the cause of the tragedy of life. For instance, when a person is ill he sees that no medicine, no treatment, nothing "does any good because the illness has taken a hold on me and perhaps nothing will cure me". There are many who after a long illness are impressed with the idea that no doctor, no healer, no one can help. Not only have the conditions made limitation, but besides the limitation which the condition of life has brought, the person is holding the limitation in his consciousness, making still more limitation to his own disadvantage. There are many others who say: "Yes, I get angry, I cannot help it. I become impatient, but I cannot help it. It is my habit". Or "I get out of control, I cannot help it. It is in me. It is my nature". What does this in me[6] show? That it is not only the condition but that it is also the belief that makes a man more limited than he is. How many people in this world come through miseries all through life, find lack of enthusiasm, lack of spirit, lack of vigour, which is always caused by that which they have got in their mind—"I am good for nothing. I am not capable of accomplishing anything in life". So one leads a life of depression, conscious of one's defect, conscious of one's weakness; causing that weakness to become greater and greater. It deepens one's weakness to say "I cannot help it". It is wrong because it is against the nature of the soul. The soul has the desire to progress. The soul has the desire to overcome all difficulties. The soul has the desire to prosper through life and to achieve things in life. The soul has the desire to gain knowledge. The soul has the desire to be good and show goodness. It is the love of beauty.

Man forgets that it is his divine heritage, it is his birthright to attain, to gain what his soul is yearning for; for the soul itself in its essence is pure. It is seeking after love, harmony, and beauty, of[7] good qualities. The soul is robbed of all goodness and all beauty, and it constantly yearns for them, and when it is deprived of what it constantly yearns for then it becomes disappointed and experiences tragedy in life. Very often people make of their troubles and sorrows and destructions[8] of different forms, as[9] some

---

6. Sk.tp.: "in me" put in quotation marks
7. (Ng.)Gr.: "of" first changed in to "all", then changed into "and" instead; Sk.tp.: "and" instead of "of"
8. (Ng.)Gr.: first "destructions" changed into "depression", then "destruction" restored; Sk.tp.: "destruction"

virtue, religious or mystical. If a person is going through some suffering or pain he thinks it is something religious. But this is a wrong conception that pulls down religion and philosophy and mysticism to the ground. Life is not sent for unhappiness, life is not sent for weakness; life is not sent for lack of enthusiasm. The problem of life is to attain, to accomplish what the soul has come for in accomplishing; to realise what it has lost; to realise what is really beautiful; to realise what is truly dependable. To be sad, to live with a long face is not religion. And to think "I cannot do this", or perhaps "I cannot accomplish that; it is my habit; I cannot help it"--all these are limitations which should not be, are a habit that should not be, are a nature which you do not like, which you do not love, which you do not admire. Your nature must be what you like, what you admire, what you wish it to be. Christ has said, "If you ask for bread the Father will not give you a stone". If a person has a certain ideal of life, he wants to make his life according to that certain ideal, why should he not strive and experience that ideal. There are people who grieve over others not listening to them—"my friend does not listen to me", or "my mother is cross with me", or "my daughter does not pay attention to what I say", or "my friend", or "my beloved does not listen to me". If we ask "Do you listen to yourself?" the whole question would be solved. If our own soul does not listen to us then who else will listen to us? When we do not ourselves believe in ourselves, in our ideal, in our thought, how can other persons believe? Therefore in order to gain mastery the first thing is that man must become sincere and must live a true life. What he believes thoroughly he must do; what he does not believe he must not do. What he knows he must say; what he does not know he must not say. Often you find people arguing and discussing things they do not know. For the very reason they do not know they argue on the subject. They do not wish to agree; they wish to argue. If they knew the subject they would not wish to. There would be no reason. Very often people with great strength dispute and argue; but at the same time the tendency to argue proves that he does not believe it—he believes it half: perhaps it is, perhaps it is not. If he knows he does not want to argue. There are many in this world who know what is wrong and what is right; what they must do and what they must not do; and very often they do against their wish, against what they believe, against their ideal. What is it? It is lack of mastery. A man, suppose, who is addicted to drink, after experiencing that it has a bad influence on his life, has a bad effect on his

9. (Ng.)Gr.: "as" crossed out;
Sk.tp.: "as" omitted

body, his health, after realising that, sees it and wishes for drink, longs for it. This man, knowing this way is not right, that it is not good for him and not for his benefit, and yet he still goes and does it. He ruins himself. All the follies and mistakes and all the errors through which humanity is going are not always caused by ignorance—they are caused by lack of mastery. The soul who has attained mastery, he reaches to that state where he is commander of himself. He is commander of his mind and body, and one who is commander of the mind and body of man is the commander of his life.

According to the mysticism of the East, there are moments when the influence of man, when the influence of soul has a bad effect upon one's affairs, and there are moments when it has a good effect on one's affairs. I have been very interested in that question. The whole mysticism of the East is based upon that principle. Every soul has a planet and that planet has an influence, and that[10] not only an influence on oneself but on one's affairs, on one's surroundings and one's environment. As large the planet, so large is its influence; as large his soul, so large is its influence. All the horizon of his influence is affected at every moment according to the change of the condition of the soul. Think then that every failure is caused by a certain condition of the soul at a certain time; and so on the surface. Now by reasoning and by study and by analysing one finds the cause which is most logical. And the cause is that the physical body is only an instrument. It is the soul which has[11] a planet, or as the being of a person, is taking this instrument and experiencing life; and all that belongs to the soul, the house, farm or palace or factory or business or profession—all these belongings are in some form or other attached to it; and it is the change of its condition from moment to moment which has its influence on the whole environment which is under the influence of that soul. Therefore, the ordinary person, not knowing this, says "What does it matter if I do not control myself; if I do not have mastery of life? I have so much in the bank. Is it not enough? What does it matter if I do not control my life? If I am not master of myself? I occupy a high position; I am a big person". But he does not know that if he is a big person he has still greater difficulties. If he has much money in the bank there are others looking at it at the same time. He thinks others do not know it is in the bank, but many others know it and are

---

10. (Ng.)Gr.:"that" crossed out;
Sk.tp.: "that" omitted
11. (Ng.)Gr.: the "h" of "has" crossed out, making "as";
Sk.tp.: "has", but the "h" later crossed out

looking for the moment to come. Power, position, wealth or health are all[12] dependable, all these conditions will change in one moment. One storm can sweep them away. Are these things to be depended upon? And yet many in this world from morning to night are delighted and absorbed in the things of this world, in the pursuit of all the things of the world, forgetting the real mastery, the kingdom of God, which is in the heart of man. Spirituality apart, even for worldly benefit, for worldly affairs mastery is the most important thing. No doubt in the practice of mastery there seem a great many restrictions, a great many principles to be observed, but if there is any freedom, the freedom is in mastery. In these modern times when there is so much talk about freedom, if man only knew that the real freedom can be found within oneself. It is the freedom of soul, the liberation of soul, captive on Earth, which really gives freedom. In order to attain this freedom one has to realise first mastery of self, to realize whether I am captive or whether I am king; and once he has worked it out to live in this realization and make the whole life this realization. There is a story, a fable, which explains this idea better:

Among many sheep there was a little young one, a lion, playing together. And a lion happened to pass that way and saw this young lion playing as though he were a little sheep. The sheep did not understand and began to run; and this young lion also ran with the sheep. But this big lion pursued them and stopped this little lion and asked him: "What are you? Will you tell me?" The little lion answered, "I am a sheep. I am trembling. I am afraid of you". He said, "You are afraid of me? You are a lion: why are you afraid of me"? He said: "I am not a lion; I am a sheep. I am trembling". The lion said, "You need not tremble; all the sheep have run away and you are a lion". The lion said: "I will show you and prove to you that you are a lion, so come with me". The little lion was afraid of the big lion, but they came to a pool of water, and there the lion said to the young lion, "Look at your reflection in the water. Are you a sheep or are you a lion"? And he looked and he said, "I think I am a lion". And the lion said, "It is not enough that you only think you are a lion. You know you are a lion; you must realise you are a lion". Just now with a little book knowledge people begin to read and say a great many things. Even they do not hesitate to claim "I am God". They do not know that this is not a thing to be said. Those who have arrived at some knowledge have not got it by claims. They have arrived at their knowledge by meditation, by

---

12. (Ng.)Gr.: "all" changed into "not";
Sk.tp.: "not" instead of "all"

contemplation, by realizing. To read in a book that "I am God", or to claim that all is God, is nothing but impertinence. Man with his limitation, standing in the place of slave of the Divine Being, for him to claim what he doesn't deserve, is nothing but imprudence[13]. At these times when religion seems to fade away and materialism to abound, many who do not believe in God, many who are in doubt if there is any such thing as God, and many who are in the pursuit of the Divine Knowledge, they begin to make claims which should not be made, and waste their time in analyzing and studying something which cannot be acquited[14] by study alone, but by love, by devotion, by one's service to one's fellow man, by humility and modesty shown in one's character, by awakening sympathy for those around us, by having consideration in every word, every deed, by showing meekness and showing tenderness, by sharing the pain and suffering of another. It is by this that the Spirit of Divine Fire in the heart is awakened into a blaze, and then by contemplation of that blaze and that light, it is that which brings man to a realization of God, perhaps to such a degree that man's limited self remains no more, no longer before his view—then he attains to mastery which is the only object of the yearning of every soul.

---

13. (Ng.)Gr.: the "r" crossed out to make "impudence";
    Sk.tp.: "impudence"
14. (Ng.)Gr.: the "t" crossed out and replaced by "r", making "acquired";
    Sk.tp.: "acquired"

Kefayat LLoyd's longhand reporting.

London, 8 October 1922

[1]

Beloved ones of God, [2]

I wish to speak this morning on the subject of life being a constant struggle. For the foolish person that struggle is with others, but for the wise person it is with himself. The wise all through his life struggles with himself; he is constantly tuning himself to that note, which is his ideal, and for which his soul is always yearning: he tries to raise himself to the ideal which he holds in his mind. The one who lacks wisdom is discontented with everyone and everything, with the wise, with the foolish, with friend, or foe, with good and bad, everything has a jarring effect upon him, all is wrong, and always he struggles with the life outside, wastes his time and energy and wears himself out and he becomes a burden to himself. By a deep study of life, of human nature, we shall find that those who make the greatest appeal to our hearts are those in whom the self is not intensely assertive—where the self is gentle, mild[3], or as it is called in the Bible, poor in spirit, the self that is not like a rock but like water, fluid, pliable, ever running. There are times when one finds the self within like a rock, and times when it is a stream of running water, and if one studied one would find that the moments when the self is like running water are the moments when one is satisfied with life, and with all around one, while when we are like a rock, a stone, we are neither happy nor do we make those around us happy. This shows that man is a

---

Documents:

Kf. = a longhand reporting by Kefayat LLoyd of a sermon given in the Church of All.

Bk.p. = a book-preparation of the second part of this lecture, to which Gd. gave the title "Jacob Wrestling with the Angel."

Bk. = The book The Unity of Religious Ideals, Part V, chapter XIII (1st ed. 1929). The book was compiled and prepared for publication by Sherifa Goodenough.

Notes:

1. Kf.: added by Kf. "Church of All"
2. Ibid.: later added by Kf. "Symbolic interpretation of Jacob, struggling (wrestling) with the angel."
3. Ibid.: later "mild" put in parentheses by Kf.

mystery, that which in man claims to be I, the ego, is the greatest of all mysteries, and if this mystery is solved, then all the mystery of life is understood. The mystery of the ego is the mystery of the universe. In the beginning this ego comes out of darkness, as it is said in the Koran, "We have created the world from darkness". Ignorant of the knowledge of life and of human nature, the soul comes on earth, and acquires a knowledge which makes it more ignorant, learned in one direction, but ignorant of the very truth of life. This ignorance feeds and helps the ego to grow, and when it is grown, the man calls himself "I": I am a separate individual, separate from my fellow man, I am <u>an</u> individual, I am separate from God. My inheritance, my rank, my position, my wealth, my separate self stands apart from all I love or hate, from those I know, and those I do not know, those who belong to Heaven, and those who belong to earth. In terms of the Sufis this development of the ego is called *nufs*, which means that man with all his learning, experience, strength, power, is yet limited, ignorant, blind. The Scriptures have said that Satan is always with man, that he is never away, but I should say that it is not that Satan is <u>with</u> man, but that he is <u>in</u> man. The ignorant ego claiming the separated I, blind to the mystery of life, is the cause of all the tragedy of life, the blind activity of the ego, *nufs*. But through all this the Father in Heaven is constantly guiding man, and especially those who seek His guidance. The man who is called from within, to understand life and to make others understand, is the prophet. We read in the Scriptures of Jacob fighting with a man, all night long he wrestled. This story is a symbolical representation of the idea I want to explain. The awakening soul looks about, and asks, who is my enemy? And while the ignorant soul thinks it is my neighbour, my relative[4] who is my enemy, the awakened soul says "it is myself, my ignorant ego is my enemy" and it is the struggle with this enemy that will bring me light, and raise me from the denseness of the earth. [5]The wrestling of Jacob was the wrestling of the soul with the ego.[5] Night is symbolically the time when the darkness of ignorance causes confusion, one feels sorrow, loneliness, depression, one sees no way out, one is burdened on all sides, chained, there seems no freedom for the soul, for this is the time of night. But when the soul can fight the ego, then it rises above the chains and attachments of this world; as was[6] said in the Bible first Jacob left all his belongings, he came away from them. This means that he was indifferent to

4. Bk.p., bk.: "relation" instead of "relative"
5. Ibid.: this sentence was moved back to before "The awakened soul. . ."
6. Ibid.: "it is" instead of "was"

all to which he once felt attached. The Sufi looks at this from another point of view—he thinks that to leave all he possesses and to go to the forests or mountains is not true detachment. The true detachment is in the heart of man. One can be surrounded by beauty, comfort, wealth, position, love, all these things, and yet be detached from them, be no slave to them, rise above them. [7] So there is a little difference in the methods which the Sufis and the Yogis practise. The Yogi says "all is false, all things of the earth make the burden of life greater", and these form[8] his detachment and indifference to life is shown by dwelling in the solitudes, away from all these things. The struggle of the Sufi is greater, he stands in the midst of all these attachments and yet rises above them, nothing can hold him, he is detached and yet in the midst of the crowd.[7] Jacob left all, and came to the solitudes[9], into the silence, and there he wished to fight the deluded self, the ego which blinds man to the truth. And what was the result? The daybreak came, and that man or angel who had fought with Jacob wished to leave him[10], depart; this means that the ego wanted to leave, there was no more ego, no more I, but with the daybreak a new light, a new inspiration, a new revelation came. The very ego which Jacob saw as his greatest enemy in the daylight he recognised as God Himself. The One with Whom all night he had fought; he bowed before Him, he asked His blessing; he asked His Name, for he saw then no longer I, but Thou. And the name could not be told, for that was the unveiling of the Unity of God and man; and in this realization names and forms are lost.

---

7. Ibid.: this passage omitted
8. Kf.: afterwards Kf. replaced "these form" with "therefore", "these form" probably because she thought what she wrote was misheard
9. Bk.p., bk.: "solitude"
10. Ibid.: later "leave him" crossed out by Kf.

Miss Salima Wiseman's longhand reporting.

Brighton, 10 October 1922

1

I wish to bring to the notice of my mureeds two great duties which every one of them must consider it most important to perform. The first duty is towards himself, the second is towards God and humanity. The first and most important is towards himself. It must be known and understood that the Sufi Order does not give particular principles, tenets, or doctrines[2]; nor does it impose any particular belief. He keeps[3] you free to make your lives really happy, that others may share your happiness. This happiness[4] can be attained by thoroughly studying the nature of happiness, finding out what it is that gives true happiness, for so often in seeking happiness[5] the soul is deceived and deluded and so remains without happiness[6]. The mureeds must take care that their bodies are strong, healthy, vigorous, and ready to work[7], that their minds are balanced, sound and clear, then they can have happiness and give

Documents:

S.W. = a longhand reporting by Miss Salima Wiseman, a mureed from Southampton, England;
(S.W.)Gr.: some corr. made in "S.W." by Miss Sophia Green

Kf. = another longhand reporting made by Kefayat LLoyd, nearly identical in wording to "S.W."

Sk.tp. = a later typescript made from "Kf." by Sakina Furnée or under her direction.

Notes:

1. S.W.: "Members' Meeting" written above by Miss Wiseman;
   Kf.: "Members Meeting" written above by Kefayat LLoyd;
   Sk.tp.: "Mureeds' Class" instead of "Members' Meeting"
2. Sk.tp.: "dogmas" instead of "doctrines", but later Sk. added "doctrines" before "or dogmas"
3. (S.W.)Gr.: "He keeps" changed into "It leaves";
   Kf.: "He keeps" changed into "It keeps";
   Sk.tp.: changed "It keeps" into "It leaves"
4. (S.W.)Gr.: "happiness" crossed out;
   Sk.tp.: "happiness" later put in parentheses
5. (S.W.)Gr.: "happiness" replaced with "it"
6. Ibid.: "without happiness" changed into "unhappy"
7. Kf.: "and ready to work" first omitted, but then reinserted

it to those around them. If in this time of great distress, every mureed would realize that[8] he is a volunteer in an army, working for the peace of souls, a great work would be done.

The second duty, towards God and humanity is to show their devotion to the cause, to Murshid, and to God, by some service. You ask, what service can you do for the cause? You can create an interest in the Message in those around you, in your friends, you may for instance bring your friends to this centre, where[9] sometimes there are readings, and so you will help the movement, and by so doing, you may help humanity and the cause of God.

A person may attend the classes for years, and yet not be useful, but the one who is desirous to serve can do much; for a cause like this needs all kinds of help; do not think that in order to create interest, you must have a certain authority in the Order; no, if the heart is blessed with the ideal of the Sufi Order; if the message is deep in your heart, you are certainly authorized by God, and you can do great service. One can spare half an hour to give to one's[10] friends in one's house, to call them together and to[11] read to them from "The Persian Rose Garden"[12] or some other book, to tell them what you can, and so enlarge the interest in the cause.

And, remember, that the more there are who will unite in this service, the more force there is for the furtherance of the cause, and remember also, that there is no separation from Murshid, if he is miles away, once you are initiated, you are in the spirit always with your Murshid, no distance can separate, the blessing of Murshid is always with you; the more you are conscious of this, the more it will benefit your life, and the influence you receive, you can spread around you.

Remember, it is not only a work done in this Order, it is a world movement, the responsibility of which is too great for words to express, and if anything can give you an idea of its greatness, you will show it by sympathy for Murshid and appreciation for the teachings which[13] are given to you. Words say little, and the service must not be done in order to oblige Murshid, it must be done for God and for humanity. You must consider it as your most sacred task, given by God, therefore most important to fulfil, and the main purpose of your life.

---

8. Sk.tp.: "that" omitted, but later added
9. Kf., Sk.tp.: "when" instead of "where"
10. Ibid.: "one's" omitted
11. Ibid.: "to" omitted
12. The correct title is *In an Eastern Rose Garden*, published in 1921.
13. Ibid.: "that" instead of "which"

A report of a lecture in the
magazine *Sufism* of December 1922.

1

The Alchemy of Happiness
2

Beloved ones of God,

My subject to-night is the Alchemy of Happiness. The soul in the Sanskrit language and in the terms of Vedanta is called *Atman*, which means happiness or bliss itself—not that happiness belongs to the soul, but that the soul itself is happiness. To-day we often confuse happiness with pleasure. Pleasure is only an illusion of happiness, a shadow of happiness, and in this delusion man perhaps passes his whole life, seeking after pleasure, and never

---

Documents :

Sf. = Magazine *Sufism*, December 1922, in which the lecture appears on pp. 2-6. No original document has been found in the archives.

Bk. = an exact, typewritten copy of the lecture, made from "Sf." and published as a separate booklet by Sufi Book Depot, Southampton, England.

Sk.tp. = an exact, typewritten copy, made from "bk." under the direction of Sakina Furnée, probably with the purpose of storing the lecture in a file in the archives.

Tp. = a later typescript made from "Bk.", not known by whom, and nearly identical to "Bk.".

A translation of the lecture into French appeared in the monthly magazine *Soufisme*, nr. 1 of January 1926, published by Le Mouvement Soufi in Paris.

Notes:

1. Although the lecture bears no date, in the same December 1922 issue of the magazine *Sufism* (see "Sf." under Documents), it is mentioned that Pir-o-Murshid had been lecturing in London, Brighton, Southampton and other places from 5 to 16 October 1922. On 6th October a lecture on "The Alchemy of Happiness" was given in London, and the present lecture--on the same subject matter--could well have been given at Southampton on 16th October 1922, the day before Pir-o-Murshid's return from there to the Continent (by ship), on 17th October.
2. Bk., Sk.tp.: added under the title: "A Verbatim Report of a Lecture given by Inayat Khan." In "Sk.tp." this same addition is put in parentheses;
   tp.: on top of page 1 added in tp.: "A verbatim report of a lecture, printed as a booklet by Sufi Book Depot, Southampton. + 1921." This date, however, appears to be incorrect.

finding satisfaction. There is a Hindu saying that man looks for pleasure and gets pain. Every pleasure which is seeming happiness in outward appearance promises happiness, for it is the shadow of happiness, but just as the shadow of a person is not the person and yet represents the form of the person, so pleasure represents happiness but is not so in reality. According to this idea one finds that there are rarely souls in this world who know what happiness is; they are constantly disappointed in one thing after another, but the nature of life in the world is such—it is so deluding that if man were disappointed a thousand times, he would still take the same path, for he knows no other. The more we study life, the more we realize how rarely there is a soul who can honestly say, "I am happy." Every soul almost, whatever his life's position, will say that he is unhappy in some way or another, and if you ask for a reason he will say perhaps, "I cannot attain to the position, power, property, possessions or rank for which I have worked for years." He is craving for money perhaps, and does not realize that possessions give no satisfaction; or perhaps he says he has enemies, or those whom he loves do not love him; there are a thousand excuses for unhappiness that the reasoning mind will make. But is even one of these excuses ever[3] entirely correct? Do you think even if they gained their desires they would be happy? If they possessed all, would these things suffice? No; for still they would find some excuse for unhappiness, and all these excuses are as coverings before man's eyes, for deep within is the yearning for the true happiness which none of these things can give. The one who is really happy is happy everywhere: in a palace or a cottage, in riches or poverty, for he has discovered the fountain of happiness which is situated in his own heart; so long as a person has not found that fountain, nothing will give him real happiness. The man who does not know the secret of happiness often develops avarice. He wants thousands; and when he gets them they do not satisfy, and he wants millions; and still he is not satisfied—he wants more and more. If you give him your sympathy and service he is still unhappy; all you possess is not enough—even your love does not help him, for he is seeking in a wrong direction, and life itself becomes a tragedy.

Happiness cannot be bought or sold, nor can you give it to a person who has not got it. Happiness is in your own being, your own self, that self that is the most precious thing in life. All religions, all philosophical systems, have taught man in different forms how to find it by the religious path, or the mystical way, and all the wise ones have in some form or another given a

---

3. tp.: "ever" omitted, but later reinserted by Sk.

method by which the individual can find that happiness for which the soul is seeking. Sages, and mystics, have called this process Alchemy. The stories of the Arabian Nights which symbolize these mystical ideas are full of the belief that there is a philosopher's stone that will turn metals into gold by a chemical process. No doubt this symbolic idea has deluded men both in the East and West; many have thought that a process exists by which gold can be produced. But this is not the idea of the wise; the pursuit after gold is for those who are as yet children. For those who have the consciousness of reality gold stands for Light or Spiritual inspiration. Gold represents the colour of Light, and therefore an unconscious pursuit after Light has made man seek for gold. But there is a great difference between real gold and false. It is the longing for true gold that makes man collect the imitation gold, ignorant that the real gold is within. He satisfies the craving of his soul in this way, as a child satisfies itself by playing with dolls. But a man does not depend upon age for this realization. A person may have reached an advanced age and be still playing with dolls: his soul may be involved in the search for this imitation gold, while another in youth may begin to see life in its real aspect. If one studied the transitory nature of life in the world, how changeable it is, and the constant craving of everyone for happiness, one would certainly endeavour, whatever happened, to find something one could depend upon. Man placed in the midst of this ever-changing world yet appreciates and seeks for constancy somewhere—he does not know that he must develop in himself the nature of constancy; the nature of the soul is to value that which is dependable. But think: Is there anything in the world on which one can depend, which is above change and destruction; all that is born, all that is made, must one day face destruction; all that has a beginning has also an end; and if there is anything one can depend upon it is hidden in the heart of man, it is the Divine spark, the true philosopher's stone, the real gold, which is the innermost being of man. A person who follows a religion, and has not come to the realization of truth, of what use is his religion to him if he is not happy? Religion does not mean depression and sadness. The spirit of religion must give happiness. God is happy. He is the perfection of Love, Harmony and Beauty. A religious person must be happier than the one who is not religious. If a person who professes religion is always melancholy, in this way religion is disgraced, the form has been kept, but the spirit is lost; if the study of religion and mysticism does not lead to real joy and happiness, it may just as well not exist, for it does not help to fulfil the purpose of life. The world to-day is sad and suffering as the result of the terrible war; the religion which answers the demand of life to-day is that method of morals which invigorates and gives life to souls, which illuminates the heart of man with the Divine Light which is already there, not by the outer form necessarily, although for some a form is helpful, but the first necessity is the showing forth of that happiness which is the desire of every soul.

Now as to the question of how this method of Alchemy is practised, the whole process was explained by the alchemists in a symbolical way. They say gold is made out of mercury; the nature of mercury is to be ever moving, but by a certain process the mercury is first stilled, and once stilled it becomes silver; the silver then has to be melted, and on to the melted silver the juice of a herb is poured, and then the melted silver turns into gold. Of course this method is given in outline, but there is a detailed explanation of the whole process. Many child-souls have tried to make gold by stilling mercury and melting silver; they have tried to find the herb, but they were deluded, they had better have worked and earned money. The real interpretation of this process is that mercury represents the nature of the ever-restless mind, realized especially when a person tries to concentrate; the mind is like a restive horse, when it is ridden it is more restive, when in the stable less restive. Such is the nature of mind, it becomes more restless when you desire to control it, it is like mercury, constantly moving. When by a method of concentration one has mastered the mind, one has taken the first step in the accomplishment of a sacred task. Prayer is concentration, reading is concentration, sitting and relaxing and thinking on one subject are all concentration. All artists, thinkers, and inventors have practised concentration in some form; they have given their minds to one thing, and by focussing on one object have developed the faculty of concentration; but for stilling the mind a special method is necessary, and is taught by the mystics, just as singing is taught by the teacher of voice production; the secret is to be learnt in the science of breath.

Breath is the essence of life—the centre of life—and mind, which is more difficult to control than a restive horse, may be controlled by a knowledge of the proper method of breathing. For this, instruction from a teacher is a necessity, for since the mystical cult of the East has become known in the West, books have been published, and teaching, which had been kept as sacred as religion, has been discussed in words which cannot truly explain the mystery of that which is the centre of man's very being; people read the books and begin to play with breath, and often instead of receiving benefit they injure both mind and body; there are also those who make a business of teaching breathing exercises for money, and so degrading a sacred thing. The science of breath is the greatest mystery there is, and for thousands of years in the schools of the mystics has been kept as a sacred trust.

When the mind is under complete control, and no longer restless, one can hold a thought at will as long as one wishes. This is the beginning of phenomena; some abuse these privileges, and by dissipating the power, before turning the silver into gold they destroy the silver. The silver must be heated before it can melt, and with what?—with that warmth which is the Divine essence in the heart of man, which comes forth as love, tolerance, sympathy, service, humility, unselfishness, in a stream which rises and falls in a thousand drops, each drop of which could be called a virtue, all coming from that one stream hidden in the heart of man—the love element—which when it glows in the heart, the actions, the movements, the tones of the voice, the expression, all show that the heart is warm. The moment this happens the man really lives; he has unsealed the spring of happiness which overcomes all that is jarring and inharmonious. The spring has established itself as a Divine stream.

After the heart is warmed by the Divine element, which is love, the next stage is the herb, which is the Love of God; but the love of God alone is not sufficient, knowledge of God is also necessary. It is the absence of the knowledge of God which makes man leave his religion, because there is a limit to man's patience. Knowledge of God strengthens man's belief in God, throws light on the individual and on life. Things become clear; every leaf on a tree becomes as a page of a holy book to one whose eyes are open to the knowledge of God. When the juice of the herb of Divine love is poured on to the heart, warmed by the love of his fellow man, then that heart becomes the heart of gold, the heart that expresses what God would express. Man has not seen God, but man has then seen God[4] in man, and when this is so, then verily everything that comes from such a man comes from God Himself.

---

4. Ibid.: "Gold" instead of "God", later changed back by Sk. into "God"

In Miss Sophia Green's handwriting,
from her notebook of October, 1922.

London[1]

The nature of a vampire is another form of greediness or voraciousness. The vampire is never satisfied for[2] all he receives. The magnetism of the presence of atmosphere of mind or of [3]body[4] the lower kind of vampire absorbs the vitality of the body, the second[5] who is somewhat higher absorbs the vitality of mind and the third kind absorbs the vitality of the emotional nature—[6] of heart. A vampire may extract all vitality by holding a hand[7], by the meeting of the glance, by merely sitting in the presence of a person he can breathe in all the vitality of another person[8]. In kissing or embracing a vampire can take the whole life out of a person; a vampire lives on the vitality of those who come[9] in contact with him, making it as [10] his desired food. No doubt so [11] depending upon the vitality of others often he gets a magnetism which he cannot digest and in which

---

Documents:

Gr. = a copybook of Miss Sophia Green, in which she took down in longhand or sometimes copied what seem to be answers given to questions referring to the lectures given on 7th and 8th October, 1922. On the first page of this notebook Gr. wrote: "London, October 1922."

Ng. = a copy in the handwriting of Miss Nargis Dowland, made either from her own hastily written down longhand reporting or from somebody else's.

Sk.tp. = a typescript copied from "Ng." under Sakina Furnée's direction.

Notes:

1. Ng.: added "Dictated by Murshid on October 22nd, 1922, at Inverness Court Hotel, London."; Sk.tp.: copied the heading as in "Ng."
2. Ng., Sk.tp.: "with" instead of "for"
3. Sk.tp.: "the" added, but later crossed out by Sk.
4. Ng., Sk.tp.: added a semi colon after "body"
5. Ibid.: "kind" added
6. Sk.tp.: "dash" omitted
7. Gr.: "a hand" changed by Gr. into "hands"; Ng., Sk.tp.: "hands"
8. Ng., Sk.tp.: "person" omitted
9. Ibid.: "are" instead of "come"
10. Ibid.: "as" omitted
11. Ibid.: "No doubt so" replaced with "So,"

lies his [12] destruction.

----

[13] There is always one spirit working against [14] and not allowing man [15] to get the mastery over his own kingdom. He makes [16] first his appearance through one's own mind and if one [17] did not recognize him one would think it is [18] himself [19]; but it is not one's true self, [20] if it were to be called a self [20] it is the false self; the shadow is not the body although it has the exact appearance of the body. When once [21] man recognizes this spirit in himself and fights with him and wishes to drive him out knowing that his continual striving is to bring man [22] down from his throne and deprive him of his right and command over his domain, then he works through the mind of another and comes before man under a thousand guises, as a friend, as a lover, as a beloved, as a support, and a defence trying to make man weak in some way or the [23] other; ~~enfeeble~~ rob him ~~in some dire~~ of his power and enfeeble him. He comes with money when man is in poverty; he comes as a sympathizer when man is troubled and confused, he often comes to lull man to sleep; comes to caress him when he is in tears, he [24] is the Satan. When one detests him within and without then he is fought and conquered.

---

12. Ibid.: "own" added
13. Ng.: added by Ng.' "Dictated by Murshid on October 22nd, 1922, at Inverness Court Hotel, London.";
    Sk.tp.: copied Ng.'s heading as in "Ng.";
    Gr.: at a later date Gr. added above the answer to a second question: "Sangatha I. Suluk."
14. Ng., Sk.tp.: "man" added
15. Ibid.: "him" instead of "man"
16. Ibid.: "makes" moved to after "first"
17. Gr.: "one" afterwards changed into "we"
18. Ng., Sk.tp.: "was" instead of "is"
19. Ibid.: "oneself" instead of "himself"
20. Ibid.: "if it were to be called...self" omitted
21. Ng., Sk.tp.: "once" omitted
22. Gr.: afterwards Gr. changed "man" into "him"
23. Ng., Sk.tp.: "the" omitted
24. Ibid.: ". He" instead of ", he"

Lakmé van Hogendorp's handwritten copy
of a dictation by Pir-o-Murshid Inayat Khan.

[1]November 1922

[2] The most ancient conception of *shruti*[3] that existed in India was a mystical one. The musicians of the ancient times had twenty-two *shruti*s in the octave. Between *sa* and *re* four; from *re* to *ga* three; between *ga* and *ma* two; between *ma* and *pa* four; between *pa* and *dha* four; between *dha* and *ni* three, and between *ni* and *sa* two, which made twenty-two.

This seems to be the most natural scale; it was derived by the anatomical study of the natural voice production from the different centres of the body.

The power of *raga*s had its mystery in the production of these natural notes. The influence of foreign music on the original music of India has worked to a great disadvantage in this particular direction, and it has changed the value of [4]notes which they originally had in their music.

Compared to this arrangement, the octave recognized in European music seems to be too mechanical, with the intervals of a tone and half a tone. When sound is so evenly divided, it becomes cut into even pieces; it is more natural when it is wavelike, ~~that~~ when it has positive and negative shades. The intervals of four, three and two *shruti*s make a great variety. There is not too much variety, ~~and~~ yet it makes music more pliable.

Documents:

Lm. = a handwritten copy made by Lakmé van Hogendorp from her own longhand reporting of a dictation given by Pir-o-Murshid Inayat Khan.

O.t. = an old typewritten copy made from "Lm."

Sk.tp. = a typescript made from "o.t." by Sakina Furnée or under her supervision.

Notes:

1. In Lakmé's copybook, before this series of lessons on music, appears in her hwr.: "Dictations given in Geneva, November 1922." This must have been during the <u>first half of November</u>, as Pir-o-Murshid Inayat Khan is known to have been on a lecture tour during the second half of November 1922.
2. O.t., Sk.tp.: added "Music" and joined this lesson and the three following into one.
3. See *sruti* in Glossary.
4. Lm.: later "the" was added by Lm.;
   o.t., Sk.tp.: "the"

Lakmé van Hogendorp's handwritten copy
of a dictation by Pir-o-Murshid Inayat Khan.

---

[1]November 1922

Every *raga* is like a dominion where each note has a certain role to perform. Each note has a position which gives it a particular distinction among the other notes. There is one note in the *raga* which is called *mukhya* or keynote.

Then there is *vadi*, which is a prominent note and considered as a king.

There is *samavadi*[2], the note which responds in harmony to the *vadi* ~~note~~; this note is considered to be a minister.

There is *tri vadi*[3], which acts as an opponent to *vadi*, and has a distinct position in the *raga*. It is considered to be an enemy.

There is another note, which is silent; it does not strike, but blends with the other notes. It is called *anuvadi*, which is a picture of the servant.

For a musician this analogy is not merely imagination, but[4] something living. He sees the notes act as individuals in *raga*, just as individuals in a certain dominion. It is far-reaching imagination to picture a note as a human being, but there is nothing more living than a sound. Audibility is the sign of life. Besides, all human beings are as[5] notes in the symphony of life in the world, and to see life in the realm of music is the most advanced thought.

Documents:

Lm. = a handwritten copy made by Lakmé van Hogendorp from her own longhand reporting of a dictation given by Pir-o-Murshid Inayat Khan.

O.t. = an old typewritten copy made from "Lm."

Sk.tp. = a typescript made from "o.t." by Sakina Furnée or under her supervision.

Notes:

1. In Lakmé's copybook, before this series of lessons on music, appears in her hwr.: "Dictations given in Geneva, November 1922." This must have been during the first half of November, as Pir-o-Murshid Inayat Khan is known to have been on a lecture tour during the second half of November 1922.
2. See *samvadi* in Glossary.
3. *Tri vadi* is not a known musical term; see *vivadi* in Glossary.
4. O.t., Sk.tp.: "it is" added
5. Lm.: "like" written by Lm. above "as"; o.t., Sk.tp.: "like"

Lakmé van Hogendorp's handwritten copy
of a dictation by Pir-o-Murshid Inayat Khan.

[1]November 1922

In Indian music all *raga*s have their position. Some *raga*s are used in higher music, and other *raga*s are popular, [2]found in every music, and[3] known to every person.

Therefore at[4] the courts and in the high society some special *raga*s are appreciated, such as *Kanera*, *Malkaus*, *Malahari*,[5] etc. and a *raga*[6] such as *Kalangra*[7], *Pilu*, *Bhairavi* are sung everywhere.

Even in the high society these other *raga*s are liked for conventionality's sake, but whenever there is a moment that they can get away from conventionality, they take a great delight in the popular *raga*s.

The student of Indian *raga*s can distinguish the reason why certain *raga*s are held as superior to the popular ones. They are different by reason of their weight. The popular ones are selected for light music.

The ancient music of India was of two kinds, the temple music and

---

Documents:

Lm.	=	a handwritten copy made by Lakmé van Hogendorp from her own longhand reporting of a dictation given by Pir-o-Murshid Inayat Khan.
O.t.	=	an old typewritten copy made from "Lm."
Sk.tp.	=	a typescript made from "o.t." by Sakina Furnée or under her supervision.

Notes:

1. In Lakmé's copybook, before this series of lessons on music, appears in her hwr.: "Dictations given in Geneva, November 1922." This must have been during the first half of November, as Pir-o-Murshid Inayat Khan is known to have been on a lecture tour during the second half of November 1922.
2. O.t., Sk.tp.: ". These are" instead of ","
3. Ibid.: "are" added
4. O.t.: "in" instead of "at";
   Sk.tp.: first "in", then changed back to "at"
5. See *kanhada*, *malkos*, abd *malhara* in Glossary.
6. Lm.: "a raga" changed into "ragas" by Lm.;
   o.t., Sk.tp.: "ragas"
7. See *kalangada* in Glossary.

the court music. In a later period a third kind was added to these, it[8] *marhal*[9] music. At the religious ceremonies at the court songs were sung, called *Chanda*[10], *Prabandha*, *Gita* and *Kavitta*.

In the temple *Kirtanas* and *Kritas*[11] were sung.

The *marhal*[9] music was partly instrumental and partly vocal. The *marhal*[9] songs are named *Dharu*, *Dhurpad*[12], *Dhuwa*[13] and *Matha*.

---

8. O.t., Sk.tp.: "the" instead of "it"
9. Ibid.: "martial" written by mistake instead of "*marhal*"; see *marga* in Glossary (the English letters "g" and "h" are easily confused by speakers of Dutch)
10. See page 144 for further discussion of *chanda*.
11. See *kriti* in Glossary.
12. A variant spelling of *dhrupada*, q.v. in Glossary.
13. See *dhova* in Glossary.

Lakmé van Hogendorp's handwritten copy
of a dictation by Pir-o-Murshid Inayat Khan.

---

[1]November 1922

During the Mogul period the ancient songs of the court began to disappear, owing to the want of appreciation, and[2] a new kind of music appeared[3]: an Indian music with Persian colour.

Hindi *raga*s with Mogul technique, that music was named *khayal*[4], meaning imagination. The[5] Mahomet Shah[6], Emperor of India, who himself was a musician, called his compositions *khayal*. In the words of his songs his pen-name is included, which is Sadarang[7].

After the form of *khayal* a still lighter form was introduced in Indian music, which was called *asthar*[8]. The whole construction of *asthar* was consistent of no more than two phrases of music and words, upon which a

---

Documents:

Lm. = a handwritten copy made by Lakmé van Hogendorp from her own longhand reporting of a dictation given by Pir-o-Murshid Inayat Khan.

O.t. = an old typewritten copy made from "Lm."

Sk.tp. = a typescript made from "o.t." by Sakina Furnée or under her supervision.

Notes:

For the rendering of the Indian musical terms, see Preface.

1. In Lakmé's copybook, before this series of lessons on music, appears in her hwr.: "Dictations given in Geneva, November 1922." This must have been during the first half of November, as Pir-o-Murshid Inayat Khan is known to have been on a lecture tour during the second half of November 1922.
2. Lm.: later added "we find" in Lm.'s hwr.;
   o.t., Sk.tp.: "we find"
3. Lm.: later changed "appeared" into "appearing";
   o.t., Sk.tp.: "appearing"
4. Lakmé wrote "*geal*" in her hwr., attempting (in Dutch orthography) to approximate the sound; see *khyala* in Glossary
5. O.t., Sk.tp.: "The" omitted
6. Now generally known as Muhammad Shah
7. "Sadarang" is known as a singer in the court of Muhammad Shah, rather than as a pen-name of the Emperor
8. Perhaps "*asthai*" was said, q.v. in Glossary

building of extemporizations was built. This gave a great facility to Indian voice culture, for it gave every singer full liberty to[9] express his skill in improvisation. Unfortunately, in many cases, singers took more liberty than was necessary, thereby confusing the standard of Indian vocal culture.

This epoch gave rise on one side to Indian vocal culture, but on the other side [10] it [11] made it almost too individualistic, and so rooted out the uniformity which is the strength of every cult. It was Shori who introduced a new form of *khayal* in Indian music.

In Panjabi an improvement [12] upon *khayal* was made[12], a song strongly coloured with Persian music, yet produced in Indian ~~music~~ *raga*s, [13]called *tappa*. This had a captivating influence upon the hearers.

Later, still another branch of Indian music sprang forth. It was a kind of renewal of the folklore. It was taken up by the king Wajid Ali Shah of Luknow, who was [14]a gifted musician himself, and poet; he called his songs *thumari*. These songs were sung with movements [15], gestures, and they became part of [16]dancing music.

After the Mogul [17]~~period~~ Empire an improvement was made in the temple music of India. A song with modifications was used not only in religious services, but also in meditative gatherings, and this was called *bhajan* [18].

There was a great Mogul poet, Khusrau, who introduced Sufi music in India. ~~He made . . . popular in meditative circles. Songs which are called~~ He made the different forms of songs, which represented Persian music in India, [19]popular in meditative circles, songs [20] called *kalbana narsheguli* [21],

---

9. O.t., Sk.tp.: added "extemporize and"
10. Ibid.: "hand" instead of "side"
11. Ibid.: "this" instead of "it"
12. Ibid.: changed the sequence into "was made upon *khayal*"
13. Ibid.: "it was" added
14. Ibid.: "himself" added before "a gifted musician" and omitted after it.
15. O.t.: "These songs were sung with movements" omitted;
    Sk.tp.: first this part of the sentence was omitted, then reinserted in Sk.'s hwr.
16. O.t., Sk.tp.: "the" added
17. Ibid.: "Empire" omitted and "period" restored
18. See *bhajana* in Glossary.
19. O.t.: "songs" added;
    Sk.tp.: first "songs" added, then crossed out by Sk.
20. O.t.: "songs" replaced with "these were";
    Sk.tp.: "these songs were" instead of "songs"
21. See *qalbana naqsh-i kul* in Glossary.

tarana, etc. Some ~~among~~ of these songs were in Persian and others [22]in special symbolical words of the Sufis, which the initiate alone could understand.

Besides this, Amir Khusrau invented an instrument which was practically a modification of the *vina*, but could be played with more facility, and called it *sitar*, meaning three strings.

Of course in time many other strings were added to this instrument and it became popular all over ~~the world~~ India, and was greatly appreciated. Amir Khusrau also made a language of this instrument, which gave a great facility to those who composed music for the *sitar* and for those who played it.

He also improved upon the words which already existed in India as a language of *mridanga*[23], the ancient drum of Hindus, which was mostly played in temples and with which [24]god Ganesha is pictured.

Amir Khusrau divided the ancient *mridanga* into two parts, calling it [25] *tabla* and *bahya*, and thus [26] gave a great facility to the drum-players. By making a language of it, he made *tabla* playing a most interesting and advanced art.

---

22. O.t., Sk.tp.: "were" added
23. See *mrdanga* in Glossary
24. Ibid.: "the" added
25. Ibid.: "it" changed into "them"
26. Lm.: later added "by his invention" in Lm.'s hwr.; o.t., Sk.tp.: "by his invention"

Lakmé van Hogendorp's handwritten copy
of a dictation by Pir-o-Murshid Inayat Khan.

[1]November 1922

[2]. . . the development of Indian music has been chiefly along the vocal lines, not necessarily instrumental.

The ancient songs which were sung in the Sanskrit age were named *Chanda*, *Prabandha*, *Gita*, *Kavitta*.

CHANDA means a metre. There are different metres which make in themselves various rhythms; these metres put to[3] song are called *Chanda*s[4]. Every such metre has a particular name, and in this way there are numberless metres.

Note. (among modern composers it is Mula Bux[5] who rendered the various metres to music, in his work called *Chando manjari*.)

PRABANDHA means any[6] metre which. . .[7]

[continued]

Documents:

Lm. = a handwritten copy made by Lakmé van Hogendorp from her own longhand reporting of a dictation given by Pir-o-Murshid Inayat Khan.

O.t. = an old typewritten copy made from "Lm."

Sk.tp. = a typescript made from "o.t." by Sakina Furnée or under her supervision.

Notes:

For the rendering of the Indian musical terms, see Preface.

1. In Lakmé's copybook, before this series of lessons on music, appears in her hwr.: "Dictations given in Geneva, November 1922." This must have been during the first half of November, as Pir-o-Murshid Inayat Khan is known to have been on a lecture tour during the second half of November 1922.
2. Lm.: the beginning of this page appears to be the continuation of something earlier in the notebook, no longer available, as the first sentence does not begin with a capital letter.
3. O.t., Sk.t.: "into" instead of "to"
4. O.t., Sk.tp.: "Chanda"
5. Properly Maula Bakhsh, Pir-o-Murshid Inayat Khan's grandfather and a renowned musician
6. O.t., Sk.t.: "a" instead of "any"
7. Here the transcription of the dictation ends abruptly; later it was crossed out

An old typewritten copy (o.t.) from an unknown source.

---

[8]. . . must not necessarily be particular metre recognized by a certain name; such a metre rendered to music is called *Prabandha*.

GITA need not be a set rhythm; words which are rendered to music make *Gita*. The music is made first and the words are then added.

KAVITTA is a poetry rendered to music.

From the above-said songs, one will notice the close relationship which the people of India recognized between music and poetry, which they named *Sahitya Sangita*.

In the age of the Prakrit language, 4000 years from now, another phase of music came into manifestation: four different songs became known in the country. *Dharu*, *Dhurpad*[9], *Dhuwa*[10] and *Matha*.

DHARU was a song that was used as martial music by the warriors. They sang it as they marched on the battle-field. The words of this song were written by skillful poets, and encouraged the warriors through the battle. The music of this song was also appropriate for the occasion.

DHUWA[10] was a song which was sung in the praise of the King, and spoke of the kingly grandeur.

DHURPAD[9] was a song which is now considered classical, and which really showed the technicality of music. *Dhurpad* constitutes four parts: the first part as an introduction to the raga; the second part an explanation of the raga; the third part further explains the raga, and in the fourth part the rage is finished. There is a drum called *Mhurdanga*[11], which accompanies *Dhurpad*[9], showing its emphatic rhythm. The words of *Dhurpad* are philosophical, or some other subject pertaining to beauty and nature. They may also be of a mythological character. The ancient technicality of voice culture had a great scope in *Dhurpad*. There are several rhythms in which *Dhurpad*s are composed, such as [12]*Sulfa*, *Djaptala*, *Djimra*, *Teevra*, *Teala* and

---

8. Here begins the part of which no original document is available in the archives. Perhaps owing to the difficulty of spelling of the many foreign words, Lakmé van Hogendorp abruptly stopped copying the dictated text. For the rest, we have only the typed text, probably made by Mahtab van Hogendorp, Lakmé's mother.
9. A variant spelling for *dhrupada*, q.v. in Glossary.
10. See *dhova* in Glossary.
11. See *mrdanga* in Glossary.
12. According to Dr. Mehta, these terms should read: "*sulapha* (properly *sulaphakhta*), *jhapatala*, *dhamar*, *tevra*, *titala* and *ata chautala* ", q.v. in Glossary.

Ara Chautala[12], but *Dhurpad*s are mostly found to be composed in *Chautala.*

MATHA was the folk song which the men in the street sang and enjoyed.

An old typewritten copy
from an unknown source.[1]

---

[2]November 1922

ASTHAI[3] was a new way of singing the *khayal*[4], more popular, and which showed a great voice culture. In the *Asthai* there is facility of improvisation, and of showing the flexibility of the voice. *Asthai* may be called the female aspect of *khayal*; it was very much like the Oratorio in the West. The inventor of the above-mentioned song was presented before the Emperor of India[5], and he sang at the court to the Emperor's great satisfaction. But when the Emperor asked the great Master Nayak Gopal what he thought about it, he said: "Yes, your Majesty, it is beautiful, undoubtedly, yet this marks the decline of Indian solemn music". His prophecy came true, for the people have since that time revelled continually in lighter music till the music of India fell beneath its best-time glory.

Documents:

O.t. = an old typewritten copy which may have been made from a document dictated by Pir-o-Murshid Inayat Khan.

Sk.tp. = a typescript made from "o.t." by Sakina Furnée or under her supervision, identical to "o.t."

Notes:

1. This is the second section of a series (known as "Indian Music") on Indian vocal music; the first section is the preceding entry.
2. This must have been during the first half of November 1922, as Pir-o-Murshid Inayat Khan then was in Geneva, where he dictated lessons on music to Lakmé van Hogendorp. In the second half of November 1922 Pir-o-Murshid is known to have been on a lecture tour in Switzerland.
3. See *astai* in Glossary.
4. In this document, *khayal* is rendered as "gheal"; see *khyal* in Glossary.
5. This must have been the Emperor Akbar.

An old typewritten copy
from an unknown source.[1]

---

[2]November 1922.

3

TAPPA. In the new way of singing which came during the Mogul period, came also a new significance of India's music. *Tappa* showed Persian vocal culture wedded to Indian raga. This brought out the best from both countries, yet in a light form, light but not easy, and full of art. *Tappa* was invented by Shori, one of India's greatest composers, and this form of music took a distinct place. In Delibes' "Lakmé" there is a duet which is exactly the imitation of *Tappa* (a duet on the subject of *amour*).

THUMRI[4]. A further step was taken along the line of *Asthai*[5]. The *Asthai* was modified, and brought to the folklore, and this was called *Thumri*. The dancers interpreted the words of *Asthai* in gestures, so making the dance of India rich; Wajid Ali Shah, the king of Lucknow, was one of the great propounders of *Thumri*. He was so absorbed in enjoying music, that after some time, he did not give the needed attention to his kingdom, and in the end he lost his country; but even in prison he continued to compose and his

---

Documents:

O.t. = an old typewritten copy which may have been made from a dictation by Pir-o-Murshid Inayat Khan

Sk.tp. = a typescript made from "o.t." by Sakina Furnée or under her supervision

Notes:

For the rendering of the Indian musical terms, see Preface.

1. This is the third in the series on Indian vocal music beginning on p. 144.
2. This must have been during the first half of November 1922, as Pir-o-Murshid Inayat Khan then was in Geneva, where he dictated lessons on music to Lakmé van Hogendorp. In the second half of November 1922 Pir-o-Murshid is known to have been on a lecture tour in Switzerland.
3. Sk.tp.: typed above the lecture: "Indian Music", and at a later date added "(and Composers of India)".
4. *Thumri* is also written *thumari*, q.v. in Glossary.
5. See *astai* in Glossary.

compositions became popular in the whole country. *Thumri* is mostly made of four phrases; it is a love-song, love between Krishna and the girls of Radha.

DADRA[6] is another form of *Thumri*. It is composed in 6/8 time, and a peculiar character is produced by its rhythm.

KAHERVA[7] is a *Thumri* which is used by the dancers who sing while dancing. Its rhythm is of 2/4, but this rhythm is so emphasised by the *Tabla*, a special drum of India, that it has a tickling effect on human nerves.

LAVANI is a folksong composed by amateur poets. It is sung, and yet it is not the music which is important, but the poetry. Often there is a competition among bards who compose and sing *Lavani*.

CHAKRA is another form of *Lavani*, the rhythm of which is more pronounced; there is a play of sarcasm in its poetry.

---

6. See *dadara* in Glossary.
7. See *kaharva* in Glossary.

An old typewritten copy
from an unknown source.[1]

---

[2]November 1922

There are four schools of vocal culture in India, which are called *Bhainis*[3]: *Gandharva*[4], *Deva*, *Dadha* and *Miras*.

GANDHARVA BHAINI is called the language of Paradise. It is a style which has ancient technique of voice-culture, simple but definite. It is like a decorative art of singing, and wants a great pliability of the voice to produce it perfectly.

DEVA BHAINI is a style which is more ancient still. The technique of this style depends upon breath-control. In this style, *Gayatri Mantras*, the sacred chants, were sung, the effect of which is said to be a miracle.

DADHA[5] *BHAINI* is a style of folklore among the uncultured people, the poetry of which lacks the rhythm, or rather, the rhythm and form are most odd. This *Bhaini* is most successfully pictured by the composer Leoncavallo in his Opera *Pagliacci*.

MIRAS[6] *BHAINI* is the artist's popular interpretation of the folklore, but it is a folklore coloured by the artist's personality, and so it becomes a finished popular music.

Documents:

O.t. = an old typewritten copy which may have been made from a document dictated by Pir-o-Murshid Inayat Khan

Sk.tp. = a typescript made from "o.t." by Sakina Furnée or under her supervision

Notes:

1. This is the fourth in a series on Indian vocal music beginning on page 144.
2. This must have been during the first half of November 1922, as Pir-o-Murshid Inayat Khan then was in Geneva, where he dictated lessons on music to Lakmé van Hogendorp. In the second half of November 1922 Pir-o-Murshid is known to have been on a lecture tour in Switzerland.
3. See *bani* in Glossary.
4. The typescripts have "*Ghandara*".
5. The word *dadha*, according to Prof. Mehta, is not known in the context of music; in Hindi the word *dadha* exists, dialectical for "fire"; see *dadara* in Glossary.
6. See *mirasi* in Glossary.

An old typewritten copy from an unknown source.[1]
[2]

Composers of India

The most ancient composers of India were Narada and Thumbara[3], who were considered as prophets, spiritual messengers. Narada inspired Valmiki, who wrote *purana*s, the *Ramayana* and *Mahabharata*, the most sacred legends, which the Hindus consider as the Holy Scriptures. These Scriptures were not only poetical, but musical, for *purana*s are sung. Although in the course of time the compositions of Narada and Thumbara were lost, their names are celebrated. In India composers have always been artists at the same time, for the Hindus have always believed that it is the artist alone who can be a truly great composer; for how can a person compose music who cannot perform it fully. For instance, how one can compose for the voice without knowing all the intricacies of vocal culture, and one cannot really know vocal culture by merely studying its technique. It is practice which makes perfect.

Among the musicians of Karnatic there have been two most well-known composers who lived in the . . . [4] century: Tyagarajah and Dikshitar. Their compositions are called *Kirtana*s. Modification and shortening of these *Kirtana*s produce one more melody which is called *Kriti*. The development of Karnatic music brought out another kind of melody called *Pallavi*; it is one theme upon which the whole construction is made by improvisation. This gives great scope for the artists of Karnatic to show their skill in rhythm and *svara*s, which is the special talent of the Karnatic musician.

Documents:

O.t. = an old typewritten copy of unknown origin, handed down by Mahtab van Hogendorp to the Biographical Department. She may have copied the text from a dictation given to her daughter Lakmé by Pir-o-Murshid Inayat Khan.

Sk.tp. = a typescript made from "o.t." by Sakina Furnée or under her supervision.

Notes:

1. As can be seen from the contents of this lecture, it apparently belongs to the series on Indian Music dictated by Pir-o-Murshid Inayat Khan in Geneva in November 1922.
2. This must have been during the first half of November 1922. In the second half of November 1922 Pir-o-Murshid is known to have been on a lecture tour in Switzerland.
3. See Tumbara in List of Persons, etc.
4. The composers Tyagarajah and Dikshitar lived in the 18th/19th century.

The[5] Hindustani composers of the . . . century[6] were: Nayak Bhaiji Bhawer[7] and Nayak Gopal[8], who composed *Dharu*, *Dhurpad*[9], *Dhuva*[10] and *Matha*; but very few of their compositions are now to be found. Then followed Nayak Madhal[11], who followed along the lines of the ancient composers.

Tansen[12], the great singer of Akbar's Court, was at the same time a composer, and some of his compositions are still to be found. After that, Mahomet Shah[13], the Emperor of India whose name was known in the musical world as Sadarang[14], composed *khayal*s[15] which created a revolution in Indian music. His compositions are majestic, there is something noble in them, and they require a highly cultured voice to sing them correctly. These *khayal*s made all the ancient art of India appear colourless, for there was something so striking in the colour they gave to Indian music.

Then there was Amir Khusrau, a great poet and a gifted musician, being a Sufi, his inspiration brought a great revival in the music of India. He invented the *sitar* on the model of the *vina*, and made a system of practising the instrument, by making special alphabets to make the system easy. This helped the students of music very much, especially in the absence of a proper notation. He made also alphabets for *vina*, and for *mhurdanga*[16], *phakavaj*[17] and *tabla*, the Indian drums. This method opened a wide scope for the development of this art, and from this time the artistic side of Indian music has developed immensely. He also made words as a special musical language of the Sufis, and composed songs in that language, which was interesting for the non-initiated to hear, and comprehensible to those who were initiated in the Sufi art.[18]

---

5. O.t.: added "greatest" in hwr., probably by Mahtab van Hogendorp; Sk.tp.: "greatest"
6. Sk.tp.: "of the ... century" omitted. It should be "13th, 14th century" as the two composers first mentioned, Nayaka Baiju Bavara and Nayaka Gopala, were from that time
7. See Baiju Bavara, Nayaka in List of Persons, etc.
8. See Gopala, Nayaka in List of Persons, etc.
9. A variant spelling for *dhrupada*, q.v. in Glossary.
10. See *dhova* in Glossary.
11. No reference to this musician has been found to date.
12. See Tan Sen in List of Persons, etc.
13. See Muhammad Shah in List of Persons, etc.
14. The name by which the Emperor Muhammad Shah was known was *Rangila*, meaning "bright, merry, colourful"; Sadarang was a singer in the Emperor's court.
15. See *khyala* in Glossary.
16. See *mrdanga* in Glossary.
17. See *pakhawaj* in Glossary.
18. O.t.: at the end, in parentheses, the word "Note:" appears; however, the note itself is missing.

A simultaneous translation into German by Sherifa Goodenough
of a lecture which may not have been reported in English.

Basel, 16 November 1922
Great Hall of the museum, afternoon

Die Botschaft des Sufiordens[1]

2

Die Botschaft, die der Sufiorden den Westländern sandte, sollte nicht einer besonderen Gemeinschaft, ja nicht einem bestimmten Volk, einer Rasse gelten, sondern der ganzen Menschheit. Die Menschen müssen von innen heraus zur Einheit kommen; der Vollkommenheit, die jeder Religion zugrunde liegt der einen Weisheit der einen Wahrheit, sollen sie sich nicht verschließen, indem sie aus menschlicher Unvollkommenheit die Grenzen der Religion enge machen. Im Menschen liegt ein Göttlicher Funke; den durch Gebet, Meditation, Streben nach der Weisheit und Wahrheit, Glauben anfachen, das ist Religion. Solchermaßen aufgefasst, wird die Religion nicht eine Trennung bewirken, sondern durch gegenseitige Duldung und gegenseitiges Verständnis

---

Documents:

Gd. = a typewritten copy of a simultaneous translation into German, sentence by sentence, by Sherifa Goodenough. Probably no one reported this lecture as it was spoken in English, and therefore this German translation is the oldest available text.

tp. = a translation back into English, signed "P.", made from "Gd." or a newspaper article in the "Basler Nachrichten", Basel, Switzerland, of 17th November 1922 (the full text of this document is printed following the German text).

Notes:

1. Here the word "Order" indicates the different Sufi activities, not just the esoteric school. In October 1923, the official name became "Sufi Movement."

2. Gd.: It is not known who added the following introduction to the lecture: "Inayat Khan was received in perfect silence, following his wish. Then, after a few moments of concentration, he performed before the large gathering a song in Arabic, the text of which was not communicated, but its warm simplicity captivated the audience.";
tp.: these words do not appear in the newspaper article.

werden die Menschen zur Einheit kommen; die Grundlage des gegenseitigen Verständnisses ist aber eines jeden Erkenntnis seiner Selbst, wie es von Philosophen und Religionen gefordert wird. Daß wir einen göttlichen Funken in uns tragen, geht aus dem Worten Christi hervor: "Seid vollkommen, wie euer Vater im Himmel auch vollkommen ist."

Wichtig ist die Erkenntnis, daß die Menschen von einander abhängig sind; daß alle nicht glücklich sein können, so lange ein Teil leidet. Der Mangel an Einmütigkeit ist es, aus dem heraus die Unruhen und die Not unserer Zeit entstanden sind. Nicht kommerzielle, politische, soziale Einheit kann uns helfen, sondern gegenseitiges Verständnis. Wir aber sollten, anstatt dem Feuer neue Nahrung zuzuführen, es löschen. Und das können wir, indem wir die Weisheitslehren unserer Religion, die einfachen, ewigen Worte Christi in die Tat umsetzen.

Der Ruf der Sufibotschaft ergeht an alle: in ihrer eigenen Religion nach der innersten Wahrheit zu streben; mit den Mitteln der eigenen Religion die Mißbräuche abzuschaffen, die in Haß und Verachtung und Unduldsamkeit gegenüber Andersgläubigen bestehen. Die meisten Kriege der Vergangenheit waren Religionskriege, und auch heute ist noch ein Schatten von Religion hinter Krieg und Revolution; nicht der Zusammenschluß aller Menschen zu einer Sekte ist zu verlangen; sondern die Anhänger aller Religionen und Glaubens-bekenntnisse sollen zum Erkennen und Befolgen der Wahrheit erweckt werden. Der Sufismus will nicht für sich Vorteile erwerben, sondern allen denen wie ein Freund zur Seite stehen, die nach der tiefsten Wahrheit suchen. Die Welt soll erkennen, daß <u>ein</u> Gott ist und die Menschen alle Brüder sind; aller Wohlsein besteht im Glück der Gesamtheit, und das Leben und Arbeiten für einander ist der größte Dienst.[3]

---

3. Gd.: It is not known who added this passage at the end: "Inayat Khan's dignified simplicity contained the mark of what his conviction expresses. And this can even be said of the excellent translator of the English lecture. The public, which followed the words of the speaker with great attention, is grateful to the students for the opportunity to hear this lecture. In conclusion, the chairman of the board of the Faculty of Philosophy I, who had introduced the guest, indicated that Inayat Khan would give a lecture that same evening, Friday, at 8:15, in the Great Hall of the School of Science on the subject, 'The Desire of the World.'"

   tp.: "The gentle simplicity of Inayat Khan's presence evoked most vividly the spirit hidden behind his words."

A typed translation of a German newspaper article.

TRANSLATION.

"Basler Nachrichten." Basel, Switzerland.
November 17th. 1922.[1]

The Message of the Sufi Movement.

A lecture given by Inayat Khan
in the Aula of the Museum.

The Message brought to the West by the Sufi Movement is not destined to any one special community, race, or country. It is meant for the benefit of the whole world. It is through this Message that mankind will learn the realisation of Unity. The perfection that lies at the base of every religion—the one wisdom, and the one Truth,—cannot be found while human imperfection continues to build up barriers round all religions. There is a divine spark hidden in man. Religion is in reality a striving after wisdom and truth, the continued fanning of the flame of faith, through prayer and meditation. If understood in this sense, religion ought not to bring about separation, but rather, mutual comprehension and tolerance. And the basis of such an understanding is for man to learn first of all to know himself, as is taught in all philosophy and religion. The words of Christ, "Be ye perfect as your Father in Heaven is perfect"[2], are a further proof that the Divine Spark is hidden in the heart of man. And no less important is the fact, that the whole of mankind is bound by a complete mutual interdependence. Humanity as a whole cannot be happy while any one part of it suffers. It is lack of common agreement that has brought about the present state of unrest and distress. The cure lies not so much in political and social unity, than in a mutual understanding. Therefore, instead of feeding the flames, we should first of all,

---

Document:

Tr. = a translation back into English, signed "P." (it is not known who this might be), of a newspaper article, apparently based on "Tp." (see previous entry), but with the introduction omitted and the conclusion shortened.

Note:

1. This is the date of the newspaper article; the lecture was given on the previous day.
2. Matt. v.48

endeavor to quench them. And this may be accomplished by putting into practice the teaching of our own religion: the words of Christ.

All spiritual life holds alike moments of illumination, coming sooner or later, and such moments change a person's whole outlook on life. They are therefore responsible also for the corresponding change brought about in that person's life and actions. The Sufi Message is the same for all people; it urges them to seek the innermost truth of their own religion, and abandon such abuse of the principles of religion as lead only to hate, contempt, and intolerance of the followers of other faiths and creeds. Most of the wars of olden times were caused by religion, and even nowadays, there still remains a shadow of religion behind every war or revolution. The union of all peoples in one sect or faith is not desirable. But the followers of all sects and creeds must awake to the whole-hearted recognition and practice of Truth. Sufism does not seek to gain any advantage for itself; it merely wishes to prove a friend in need to all earnest seekers after Truth. The world must come to the realisation that there is but one God, and that all men are brothers. The well-being of the whole humanity depends upon the happiness of the totality of its members. The greatest service lies in living and working for each other.

The gentle simplicity of Inayat Khan's presence evoked most vividly the spirit hidden behind his words.

(signed)
P.

A typescript of a German translation of a lecture
(no original reporting has been found in the archives to date).

Zürich, 21 November 1922

Die gegenseitige Abhängigkeit des inneren und des äußeren Lebens

Die Menschen im allgemeinen haben sich gewöhnt, das Leben ausschließlich vom äußeren Standpunkt aus zu betrachten, der Mystiker aber betrachtet es vom inneren Standpunkt aus. Es gibt eine Welt, die der Mensch erlebt und eine andere Welt gibt es, die der Mensch innerhalb seiner selbst erstehen läßt. Diese Welt ist es, die von den Mystikern Herz genannt wird. In der Sprache der Mystiker bedeutet "Herz" nicht jener Klumpen Fleisch, der sich in der Mitte des Körpers befindet, sondern die Welt, die der Mensch innerhalb seiner selbst erstehen läßt. Diese Welt bildet er und stellt er zusammen aus den Eindrücken, die er von aussen erhält, aus Eindrücken, die er ohne es zu wollen empfängt, und auch aus solchen, die er mit Absicht in sich aufnimmt.

Es kommt oft vor, daß einem äusserst intelligenten, hochbegabten Menschen ein Misserfolg nach dem anderen zu Teil wird und andererseits geschieht es manchmal, daß ein sehr einfacher Mensch mit weniger Erfahrung im Gebiet der Industrie und des Handels einen größeren Erfolg erreicht, als einer, der sehr bewandert und sehrt begabt ist. Der Erfolg hängt nicht immer[1] von den Fähigkeiten des Menschen, von seinen Geistesfähigkeiten, seinen intellektuellen Errungenschaften, ab[1] ; es gibt etwas, das hinter dem Erfolg versteckt ist. Wäre das nicht der Fall, so würden die sehr vernünftigen[2], sehr gescheiten Leute immer einen Erfolg erlangen, die einfachen aber würden zu[3]

Document:

Tp. = a typescript on foolscap. Most probably this typewritten copy has been made from a simultaneous translation of the lecture into German by Sherifa Goodenough. No original reporting in English seems to exist, which is understandable, as Gd. was occupied with translating;
(Tp.)Gd.: corrections and improvements made by Sherifa Goodenough on "Tp."

Notes:

1. (Tp.)Gd.: "ab" inserted after "immer" and "ab" at the end of the sentence crossed out
2. (Tp.)Gd.: "die" inserted
3. (Tp.)Gd.: "zu" crossed out

keinen Erfolg gelangen[4] können. Es gibt etwas, was darauf hindeutet, was hinter Erfolg und Mißerfolg versteckt ist: die Tatsache nämlich, daß manchmal ein Erfolg nach dem andern eintrifft und man auch sehr häufig von einem Mißerfolg zum andern schreitet.

Zu dieser Zeit, wo die Vernunft, der Verstand des Menschen sich so sehr entwickelt hat, scheint es, als sei allgemein ein großer Wunsch vorhanden, etwas über das Leben zu wissen und zu verstehen. Leider aber sucht man nicht immer auf dem richtigen Wege nach der Wahrheit. Heutzutage lesen die intellektuellen Leute und solche, die studieren, in Büchern nach und suchen dort nach etwas Tiefem, etwas merkwürdigem, das ihnen einen Einblick ins Leben verschaffen könnte. Und andere, die vielleicht[5] einen einfachen Glauben, eine einfache Auffassung besitzen, bemühen sich mittels solcher Experimente, die jetzt so häufig gemacht werden, den tiefen Grund des Lebens zu erforschen. Ein großer Teil der Menschheit gibt sich heute mit solchen Experimenten ab und sucht auf diese Weise nach Wundern und wunderbaren Erscheinungen. Keine aber von diesen Lehren kann den Menschen zum richtigen Ziele führen. In Büchern kann man Dinge dieser Welt studieren.

Wer Wunder sehen will, braucht nicht die Geister der Toten heraufzubeschwören, er soll nur einen tiefen, richtigen Blick in das Leben tun. Je tiefer sein Einblick, desto größere Wunder werden sich ihm offenbaren. Warum soll man nach Wundern suchen bei denen, die vorgeben, das innere Gesicht zu besitzen, oder die Geister der Toten heraufbeschwören zu können? Wer Wunder sehen wollte, der konnte solche während der vergangenen Jahre des Krieges und der Leiden beobachten. Es ist in diesen[6] Jahren des öfteren vorgekommen, daß Mütter, deren Söhne im Krieg standen, ohne daß sie Nachricht erhalten hätten, wußten, wann den Sohn die größten Gefahren umgaben, wann er qualvolle Leiden ausstehen mußte. So wurden oft solche, die eine aufrichtige und innige Freundschaft miteinander verband, der gegenseitigen Verhältnisse oder des Schicksals gewahr. Wer in der Freundschaft aufrichtig ist, wessen Gewissen rein, wessen Liebe tief ist, der braucht die Wunder nicht zu suchen, er erlebt sie im Zusammenhang mit jedem Einzelnen den er begegnet. Was beweist uns dieses? Es beweist, daß der Mensch an sich selbst ein Wunder ist und dennoch sucht der Mensch die Wunder ausserhalb seiner selbst!

---

4. (Tp.)Gd.: "gelangen" replaced by "erreichen"
5. (Tp.)Gd.: "die vielleicht" replaced by "solche etwa die"
6. (Tp.)Gd.: "diesen" replaced with "jenen"

In der Sprache der Sufi wird das Herz der göttliche Spiegel genannt, in dem sich alles was auf Erden und[7] Himmel ist, widerspiegelt. Dieses Herz, welches einem Spiegel gleicht, wird der Außenwelt ausgestellt und alles, was es in der Außenwelt gibt, spiegelt sich im Herzen wieder. Doch, nachdem dieser Spiegel ein lebendiger Spiegel ist, ist seine Natur eine etwas andere, als die eines leblosen Gegenstandes. Dieser Spiegel sammelt, sammelt alles was vor ihm erscheint, alles, was er an sich heranzieht. Der Mensch, der immer die Fehler anderer sieht, zieht alle Fehler anderer an sich heran und sammelt diese und mit der Zeit merkt er, daß er alles was er verachtete, alles, was ihm zuwider war, in sich aufgenommen hat. Sehr oft wird man wahrnehmen können, daß jemand, der an seinem Freunde einen Fehler beobachtet hat, selber den nämlichen Fehler besitzt, und nicht nur daß er ihn besitzt, sondern daß der Fehler bei ihm sogar in verstärktem Maße auftritt. Dieses bedeutet, daß die Außenwelt vom Menschen selber erschaffen wird und er sammelt aus dieser alles, was er zusammenraffen kann und schafft sich daraus seine Innenwelt. Wenn jemand die Beobachtung macht: jener ist häßlich, der andere grob, ein Dritter ungeschickt, so hat er dieses nur beobachtet, sein Herz aber hat die Photographie alles dieses aufgenommen und er besitzt von nun an selber alle die Fehler, die er nur an anderen beobachtet zu haben glaubt. Man merkt sehr oft, daß wenn man gedacht hat: mein Bruder, meine Schwester, mein Mann, meine Frau, waren unfreundlich, kalt zu mir, man diesen Eindruck in sein Herz aufgenommen und dann auf andere übertragen hat. Im Herzen des einen Menschen Spiegelt sich alles, was das Herz eines andern enthält, wieder. Wenn einer dem andern mißtraut, erweckt er auch im Herzen des andern das Mißtrauen. Wenn jemand an seine Arbeit geht, sei es im Handel, im Beruf oder in der Industrie, und den Gedanken in sich trägt: "Werde ich Erfolg haben oder nicht? Werden die, die mir helfen sollen ehrlich oder unehrlich sein?" so wirft er durch sein Mißtrauen, seine Zweifel, einen Schatten auf die Herzen der andern. Es gibt viele Menschen, die, bevor sie irgendein Werk beginnen, an ihrem Erfolg zweifeln; ja, es hat Leute gegeben die, bevor sie in den Krieg zogen, sich sagten, "Vielleicht werde ich nicht zurückkehren, vielleicht ist mir das nicht beschieden." Und sehr oft glaubt man, ein Unglück habe geschehen müssen, denn man habe es ja im voraus wahrgenommen. Ein solcher Standpunkt ist jedoch ein der mystischen Auffassung ganz entgegengesetzter. Der Mystiker wird sagen: "Dadurch, daß er glaubte, er werde aus dem kriege nicht zurückkehren, bewirkte jener, daß er nicht zurückkehrte". Der Mystiker wird

7. (Tp.)Gd.: "im" inserted

sagen: "Die Tatsache, daß dieser[8] bevor er das Unternehmen begonnen hat gesagt hat, ich werde keinen Erfolg haben, hat bewirkt daß er auch keinen gehabt hat." Diese zwei Teile des Lebens, das Innenleben und das Aussenleben, werfen gegenseitig Schatten aufeinander. Ein Künstler, ein Maler, der großen Erfolg hat in seiner Kunst, verdankt ihn dem Umstande, daß er die Schönheit beobachtet und in sich aufgenommen hat; wenn er ans Werk des Malens geht, gibt er diese Schönheit wieder von sich in einem schönen Gemälde. Bei einem Musiker, einem Komponisten, ist es ebenso. Wenn ein Kind so erzogen würde, daß es nie einen musikalischen Laut zu hören bekäme, so wäre es selbst bei einer auch noch so großen angeborenen musikalischen Begabung, unfähig, seinem Talent Ausdruck zu verleihen. Dieses beweist, daß die Gabe, die ein Mensch in sich birgt, in den[9] Werke des Menschen [10] seinen klarsten Ausdruck gewinnt. Die Seele des Künstlers kann man in seiner Kunst schauen, wie man die Seele des Musikers in seiner Musik hören kann; die Seele eines jeden Menschen kann man aber in dem was er tut wahrnehmen. Als ich einmal die Witwe eines großen Künstlers besuchte und diese mir die Gemälde ihres verstorbenen Mannes zeigte, die schönsten, die sie von ihm besaß, kam mir beim ersten Anblick dieser Bilder sofort der Gedanke: "Das war ein Herz, das zerrissen worden war, das im Leben schwere und traurige Erfahrungen gemacht hatte". Ich sagte zu dieser Dame, "die Bilder interessieren mich so sehr, daß ich gerne einiges über das Leben Ihres Mannes erfahren möchte". Sie antwortete mir: "Die Qualen die mein Mann im Leben durchzumachen hatte, waren so entsetzliche, daß ich nie davon erzählen kann, ohne daß ich selber wieder sehr leiden muss". Wenn man mit klarem Blick und tiefer Einsicht die Werke aller großen Dichter, Musiker und Künstler betrachten und studieren würde, so könnte man in ihnen das Leben des Künstlers erkennen. In einem Gedicht des großen Persischen Dichters Omar Khayyam, heißt es, "der Himmel sei der Anblick der erfüllten Wünsche und die Hölle der Schatten einer brennenden Seele"; das bedeutet, der Mensch erschaffe in sich selber den Himmel und die Hölle, in denen er dann lebt. Der Mensch braucht gar nicht abzuwarten, um den Himmel und die Hölle im Jenseits zu erleben, er braucht nur die Augen zu schließen, um gewahr zu werden dessen, was in seinem Herzen vor sich geht; dann wird er wissen, ob er im Himmel oder in der Hölle ist. Daher darf man auch wohl den großen Richter weder tadeln noch loben, denn der Mensch hat sich selber seinen Himmel und seine Hölle erschaffen. Es gibt Seelen, die

8. (Tp.)Gd.: "Mensch" added
9. (Tp.)Gd.: "den" replaced with "seinem"
10. (Tp.)Gd.: "des Menschen" crossed out

immer leiden, die sich beständig in Qualen befinden. Es kann ihnen ein Palast zum bewohnen gegeben, eine paradiesische Umgebung geschenkt werden, trotzdem werden sie immer leiden, denn ihr Innenleben entspricht dem äußeren nicht. Für die aber, welche ihr Innenleben aus Liebe, aus Schönheit zusammengestellt haben, für [11] wird es immer ~~noch so~~, und wenn sie auch in einer noch so elenden Umgebung sich befinden mögen, etwas geben, auf das sie bauen können, das ihnen Trost und Freude gewährt.

Die Macht des Herzens ist eine solche, daß ein jeder, der mit einem Menschen zusammenkommt [12]die Tore dessen Herzens offen stehen, erleben wird, daß die Tore seines Herzens sich öffnen werden. Wer aber einem begegnet, dessen Herz verschlossen ist, wird erleben, daß die Tore des eigenen Herzens sich schließen werden. Dieses ist der Grund warum man manchmal, wenn jemand ins Haus eintritt, das Gefühl bekommt, man möchte davon laufen und wiederum, wenn man andern Menschen begegnet, die Empfindung hat, als sei man mit ihnen seit zwanzig Jahren befreundet. Der Mensch, der diese Tatsache nicht erkennt hat, verschließt eigensüchtig die Tore seines Herzens und klagt dann über andere und sagt: "Der andere hat sich gegen mich verschlossen", und weiß dabei nicht, daß sein eigenes Herz verschlossen ist.

Und vom religiösen Standpunkt sind die Herzen derer, die gegen ihre Mitmenschen verschlossen sind, auch gegen Gott verschlossen. In der Bibel wird ein Schlüssel zu diesem Gedanken gegeben, im Gebet, wo gesagt wird, "Vergib uns unsere Schulden, wie auch wir vergeben unseren Schuldnern." Was heißt dieses? Es heißt daß das Vergeben, Vergeben anzieht, und Rache, Rache. Wenn ein Mensch die Handlungen anderer ihm gegenüber wie eine Rechnung aufschreibt, so werden auch seine Handlungen aufgeschrieben werden. Hinter diesem Leben, das voller Falschheit und Ungerechtigkeit ist, ist vollkommene Gerechtigkeit und vollkommene Wahrheit verborgen. Und hätten die Augen des Herzens nur die Macht, dieses Leben zu durchblicken [13], so würden sie jene vollkommene Wahrheit und vollkommene Gerechtigkeit gewahren. Der Einfluß des selbstsüchtigen Menschen läßt einen jeden, dem er begegnet selbstsüchtig werden und der Selbstlose kann alle andern zu selbstlosen Wesen machen. Einer der zweifelt, bewirkt, daß alle andern an ihm zu zweifeln beginnen und einer der Vertrauen hat, daß alle andern Vertrauen haben in ihn. Derjenige der Voreingenommen ist gegen andere, erzeugt in den Herzen anderer Voreingenommenheit und einer der andern mit

11. (Tp.)Gd.: ""die" added
12. Perhaps "dem" should be added here
13. (Tp.)Gd.: "blicken" at the end of "durchblicken" replaced by "schauen"

Liebe begegnet, erweckt in den herzen der andern Liebe.

Im Leben ist eine so große Gerechtigkeit und ein so großes Gleichgewicht, die man erkennen würde, wenn man einen ganz tiefen Blick hinein tun könnte! Wenn man aber nicht tief genug blicken kann, werden einem diese Gerechtigkeit und dieses Gleichgewicht nie klar werden. Wie wenig Menschen gibt es unter den vielen die tagsüber ihren Beschäftigungen nachgehen und [14] die ganze Nacht von ihrer Arbeit träumen, welche das Ziel ihrer Arbeit kennen und wissen zu welchem Zweck sie auf Erden gekommen sind! Wie viele gibt es auf dieser Erde, die wie Maschinen von früh bis spät arbeiten und immer nur arbeiten. Und wenn man sie fragen würde "Was haben Sie erreicht?" so wüßten sie auf diese Frage keine Antwort zu geben, sie wissen ja selber nicht, was sie mit dem allen bezwecken! Was bedeutet das Bibelwort: "Dein Wille geschehe auf Erden, wie im Himmel?" Es bedeutet, daß jener Vollkommene seinen Traum, sein Traumgesicht, zur Vollendung führen will, seinem Ideal gemäß, und was ihn daran hindert, ist die Unwissenheit des Menschen, seine Unkenntnis des Zieles seines eigenen Lebens. Darum besteht die wahre Philosophie, die wahre Weisheit darin, daß man ausfindig macht, was das wahre Ziel des Lebens ist, durch daß das Verlangen des Menschen erfüllt wird. Und wenn [15] jener Augenblick gekommen sein wird [16], in dem der Mensch von hier scheiden muß, [17]werden es nicht der Ruhm, nicht der Reichtum sein, nicht die Annehmlichkeiten, der Rang, die Stellung die er erworben hat, die ihm Trost werden [18] spenden können, sondern nur allein das Bewußtsein, den Zweck, zu dessen Erfüllung er auf Erden gekommen war, erreicht zu haben. Der Mensch der ein wahrhaftes Leben führt, dessen Mitgefühl erwacht ist, der bereit [19] seinen Mitmenschen zu dienen, ihnen zu helfen, ist sicher auf dem rechten Wege und es wird gewiß ein Augenblick kommen, wo er erwachen wird. Das Werk des Sufi-Ordens besteht nicht darin Aberglauben zu lehren oder neue Theorien zu bringen, denn Salomo hat ja gesagt, es gebe nichts Neues unter der Sonne. Der demütige Dienst, den er leisten kann, ist dieser, den Menschen an diese kleinen, einfachen Sachen zu erinnern, die ihn im Taumel des Lebens nüchtern erhalten können. Indem er dieses tut, erfüllt der Sufi-Orden seine Aufgabe.

---

14. (Tp.)Gd.: "dann" added
15. (Tp.)Gd.: "wenn" replaced with "ist einmal"
16. (Tp.)Gd.: "sein wird" crossed out
17. (Tp.)Gd.: "so" inserted
18. (Tp.)Gd.: "werden" cossed out
19. (Tp.)Gd.: "ist" inserted

A typewritten copy made
by a professional reporter.

Lausanne, Salle Jean Muret, 22 November 1922,
from 8.40 to 9.45 p.m.

The Alchemy of Happiness

In the reverence of God, [1] my subject of this evening is the Alchemy of Happiness.

Happiness is the seeking of every soul, whether saint or sinner, whether he goes in the right path or in the wrong path, he seeks after happiness; the only difference is that one knows what is real happiness and one is still in illusion.

Very often these two things, happiness and pleasure, are confused by people, and it is not only in the language that one speaks every day that they are confused, but in the thought. If it was made clear to us all what happiness is, what pleasure is, then one has already advanced through life.

In the East, especially in India and in other parts of tropical countries, there exists an idea which they call . . . [2] It is an illusion, and like the thirsty hare [3] in the forest, looking for water. There are heavy clouds and thunder;

Documents:

Tp.r. = a typewritten copy presented by the professional reporter who took down this lecture. It shows several inaccuracies and omissions. In Sherifa Goodenough's handwriting is written above: "Very incomplete". She wrote this same annotation above all four lectures given on 22, 23 afternoon and evening, and 24 November 1922, and taken down by the same professional reporter, although only the present lecture should perhaps be called "very incomplete".

Sk.tp. = a later typescript made by Sakina Furnée from "tp.r." and nearly identical to it

Sr.Sk. = an extensive errata list on which in later years Sakina Furnée and Sirdar van Tuyll exchanged comments on revisions made in the texts.

Notes:

1. Tp.r.: "In the reverence of God," mistaken by the reporter for "Beloved ones of God," Pir-o-Murshid Inayat Khan's regular mode of address
2. Ibid.: Perhaps "maya" could have been said. See note 8 on page 97.
3. Cf. note 5 on page 80.

the hare is thirsty in the heat of the sun, and when it hears the thunder, awaits the rain that will come, and is delighted, and rejoices, running about. But there is only a little thunder, that is gone, and there is no rain, no water, only thunder. And that is the condition of man through life. From childhood he is attracted to all that seems to him beautiful, in colour and form; he is after it and yet never satisfied. This childish condition remains with many, even when he is grown-up. He does not play with the toys of his childhood, but has other things which he thinks will give him happiness, but they never give it.

If one stops and thinks, and sees into life, how every soul is doing, from morning to evening, some good or bad action, and that his motive in that action is only to seek some happiness. But it is always like that. The cup of wine is at our lips, but we never have a moment to drink it. A still deeper study of life will show that the more one seeks after happiness, the more one finds that instead of happiness he has attracted a still greater trouble to himself. If we find seekers after happiness in the world, and study their life, we see how in this life they find responsibilities, anxieties and cares. At each step a person seeking happiness feels disappointed, and does not find the reason why happiness does not come to him, but if he will only go forward he will find it. It is an intoxication of life, so that if man is disappointed every day, he will still go on and think that he will suddenly find it, because he is intoxicated and does not know what he is doing. Man does not think today that it is worth while to give some thought to the deeper study of life. He gives great importance to material efforts, to business, and has no moment to spare to think about the deep subject of life. In order to think deeply in the matters of life, it is not necessary that man should become unselfish to begin with; in order to think deeply on life it does not mean that man should look on it . . . even from a selfish point of view, even from a business point of view.

What is pleasure, what is pain, what is happiness? Man will always find that what he calls happiness costs more and gives less. Yes, at certain moments it costs the full price, man receives what he seeks, but in many other cases he has to pay . . .

Besides, when man is seeking after happiness, and when he has got it, he is never satisfied, he thinks that now there is something else. The object he was seeking is not ample enough, he wants more of it, such as money, power, or something else.

What has upset the whole world today is this cupidity . . . developed in human nature, seeking after happiness which does not belong to it. Think how nations today are against nations, races against races, and the bitterness of one for another, the individual against the community. It is beyond explanation; the struggle between capital and labour; the . . . of governments in different countries just now. It shows man that it is not only the fault of the collectivity, but it is the fault . . . It shows that the whole education of the world has become different. It seems that the whole of progress seems to be superfluous, and that side, which is the only side that must be developed, seems to be neglected, and therefore, any benefit derived is worthless; it may seem for a moment of some use, but in the end it is of no use. As it says in the Bible: "Where your treasure is, there will your heart be also". [4]

When man has taken this illusive happiness, a happiness which is not real, as his motive, he will only find disappointment and change: he can't get happiness out of it, nor bring happiness to his fellow-men. But all people's best intentions, working for material gains for themselves or for others, do not come any way near that object for which their soul constantly longs. [5] In the first place, what is called sin and what is called virtue may be reckoned according to the natural point of view at understanding the nature of happiness.[5]

What takes one to real happiness is virtue, and whatever creates an illusion of happiness is sin. It is not a certain action which can be stamped as virtue or sin, as every preacher of different religions has to show. In reality, every action, every thought, whatever it is and whatever its appearance, can be both sin and virtue. What brings real happiness is virtue; what takes men away from happiness is sin, and therefore there is no better (?) way of understanding real sin or virtue, only man must know and find out by himself what gives real happiness.

Now there is a question we may ask. What is happiness? Where does it come from? And the answer will be: happiness is man's innermost being, man's real self; the soul of man is happiness. As the soul of man is happiness itself, it seeks for happiness; as the body is made of matter, its joy and pleasure is in matter, its sustenance is matter. As matter is sustained by matter, so the spirit, which is happiness, is maintained by happiness.

Why has the world today gone from bad to worse? Because the soul seems to have been buried in matter. Man today is not conscious of himself as a soul, he thinks of himself as body, just that. If it was not so, would there be all these great restaurants and cafés, and hotels, where every day

---

4. Matt. vi.21
5. Even though this sentence does not make sense as written, it is so in the original.

feasting is going on? During the war, and after the war, during the[6] peace, it is always the same. Man seeks joy in life. Some religious buildings I have seen many during my travels are now being used to greater profit as cinemas. There cannot be greater profit. Man is becoming more and more material. Among those who seem to be seeking after something spiritual are two kinds. No doubt there is a great deal going on about a new awakening in the world, but when you inquire what the awakening is, and what direction it takes, you will find two distinctive directions: 1. There is a tendency to study in a book about spiritual things; the want to study a spiritual idea which a word can never explain; a book is a dead thing and has no power to explain fully; words are the names of things we can touch, see, hear and comprehend. What can be felt and made comprehensible cannot be explained by words. Of course there are many people today who are bolder to discuss and argue about things that people in ancient times felt were too sacred to talk about.

2. People are drawn to a spiritualistic idea; good people are trying mystically to raise the dead, in fact they are making experiments and wonder-working phenomena with the dead.

Friends, when we are living on this earth, there is so much for us to study in life. Study the living beings, there is so much to study, but instead of that, people want to study the dead! Think, every person we meet from morning to evening, every person with whom we come into contact, in the affairs of business, or otherwise, is a book to study. Human physiology and expression form a great study. To feel the influence of a person in life, whether straight or crooked, is such an interesting study and stimulates the intelligence so much that there is no need to make experiments with the dead. It is coming to such an extremity that people have now another invention, and that is to photograph spiritually[7] those who are dead. There is so much to photograph among the living! Those in the West can communicate with friends in the East, but it is not enough for us to communicate with one another[8] here, we want to communicate with the stars, the planets. It is not only the simple people, but those who are intellectual who try to raise the dead. They want to make spirit a substance. If that is called an awakening, a spiritual awakening in the world, I don't[9] know where this spiritual awakening will lead humanity. Do we want a new religion today? No, not

---

6. Sr.Sk.: "the" crossed out
7. Marking on the text indicates reversal of the order of "photograph spiritually"
8. Tp.r.: "brother" typed over "another" by the reporter;
   Sk.tp.: "brother"
9. Sk.tp.: "do not" instead of "don't"

at all. Solomon has said: "There is nothing new".[10] What we want today is to study the simple things, such as you find in the Bible (Matt. vi). There is all wisdom, the wisdom that is found in simplicity and not in complexity. He who will search will find it; the condition is to search for it. But today man thinks of, and becomes much attracted by, and interested in something that he cannot understand. He says: "It is something worth thinking about, because I cannot understand it." It gives an opportunity to those who walk in the path of falsehood and to those who attract others in their path. One has to find truth within one's self.

In ancient times the people in the East were seeking after truth . . . or what they call in the Eastern language . . . Of course those seeking after material gold have for many years, even in the East, taken this symbol to mean searching and making gold . . . but in reality the symbolical meaning of gold is "light", or that which is more precious than mere metal. They say that mercury is made still by putting the juice of some herbs on it, and when it has become still then it is burnt and turned into ashes. When the ashes are again put together with another juice that holds them, they become a metal which is gold. Now, the mystical interpretation of this is that the mind has the quality of mercury which is never still but is always moving, always active; it can only be made still by one thing, and that is concentration. Prayer is concentration, silence is concentration; there are many different concentrations which are learnt and understood in the school of mystics. It is no material concentration that can make the mercury still, it is the mind, the sacredness of concentration that gives the mercury stillness; it is the Divine herb which stills the mercury. I have very often the experience of some coming to me and saying: "We don't believe in any God or any Divinity, but we believe there is some power in concentration, and if you can tell us some way we shall be very glad". I have always told them: "Your doctor is somewhere else. All things change, all things will be destroyed some day, how can they give you stillness? The whole secret is in the Divine ideal. A concentration on the Divine ideal produces that Divine power".

There are jarring influences that come from round us in life. A sensitive person feels the jarring effects and throws it upon somebody else, and that person does the same, so in that way one match struck can burn the whole city. It will not be very difficult to see the explanation of this idea in studying the beginning of the recent war, how from a little match-striking the whole world was burnt. Therefore the mind, the spirit, which is turning into

---

10. Ecclesiastes i.9 (no longer believed by scholars to be by Solomon).

gold, takes all the flame to itself and turns . . . into ashes. This process is taught by Christ, Who told men not to resist evil.[11] What gain is there? Do not throw this flame upon another person. Stand it and endure it patiently. The effect of which is that it turns one to ashes. In the Bible we read: "Blessed are the poor in spirit".[12] That spirit which is turned into ashes, but the ashes must not remain in atoms, these must be joined together and become one. These atoms are united again by another juice, and what is that juice? That juice is the knowledge of God, in the language of Sufi . . . and in Hindu . . . . The truth is one, whatever name you give it; it is the knowledge of God which is realized in the union of all life; it is this which makes the false true.

Thank you all for your sympathetic response. God bless you.

---

11. Matt. v.39
12. Matt. v.3

A typewritten copy made
by a professional reporter.

Clarens, Villa Vincent, 23 November 1922,
from 4.05 to 4.40

Dreams

In the reverence of God, [1] my subject this afternoon is Dreams. A dream is an inspiration, according to the point of view of the Sufi. There are four kinds of dreams.

1. [2] The soul dream. That dream is the actual vision of something that has passed, or that is going to happen, or that will happen.

2. The heart dream. In this dream there is a feeling more dominant than when one sees. The feeling itself is expressive of what has happened or will happen.

3. The symbolical dream, the mind dream. This dream comes to a man of artistic mind or mystical spirit, when in the language of dreams, so to speak, he knows the past, present and future.

Documents:

Tp.r. = a typewritten copy presented by the professional reporter who took down this lecture. It may have undergone some editing, but on the whole it seems to be near to the words as spoken. In Sherifa Goodenough's handwriting is written above: "Very incomplete". She wrote this same annotation above all four lectures given on 22, 23 afternoon and evening, and 24 November 1922, and taken down by the same professional reporter, although only the lecture of 22 November 1922 could perhaps be called "very incomplete".

Sk.tp. = a later typescript made by Sakina Furnée from "tp.r.", on which Sk. copied Sherifa Goodenough's note: "Very incomplete".

Notes:

1. Tp.r.: "In the reverence of God" substituted by the reporter for "Beloved ones of God", Pir-o-Murshid Inayat Khan's regular mode of address;
   Sk.tp.: "Beloved ones of God,"
2. Sk.tp.: the numbers omitted

4. The dream of the mind. Whatever the mind is impressed with during the day, the mind goes on repeating it, and the dream is the same . . . [3] impression. Every person has that kind of dream, either clear or confused, but the mystical artist dreams the dream which is symbolical, the dream of a person who is tender, kind and sympathetic.

The soul dream comes to a spiritual person. [4]At the same time to some persons some of these four dreams happen, or each of these dreams may be manifested to him. If I were to define the cause of dreams, it would take perhaps a long time, but what I mean to say just now is that according to the stage of man's spiritual development he receives the knowledge of the unseen world. [4]Now, coming to the idea of inspiration. It is a general word and is known to many, but they don't [5] know that the inspiration of each person has a certain source. The inspiration of the artist, painter, is not the same as that of the poet, and the inspiration of the poet is different from that of the musician. The inspiration of the philosopher is different from that of the mystic. The inspiration of the adventurer is different from that of the prophet, and the reason is that they touch different planes and their inspirations have different lines in different directions, though the spirit and soul of all inspirations is one. It depends how far the soul approaches nearer to that source, and according to that state is the inspiration of form. Behind all religions in this world there is one spirit and there is one inspiration, and men, not having known this, have fought and quarrelled and disagreed on the points of religion. If they only knew the meaning of the words Christ spoke: "I am Alpha and Omega, the first and the last", [6] they would never have reason to dispute and to despise one another.

Very often those who think that they are the greatest friends or followers of Christ in this world go further astray than the simple (?) [7] ones because, out of love for Christ they close the door to Christ Himself. If they knew, there is no form through which Christ does not manifest Himself; in the gentleness of a loving mother, in the kind feelings of a loving father, and in the smiles of a little infant the true lover of Christ sees Him and recognizes Him. In the sincere friendship of a friend and in the true teaching of a teacher one sees Christ, but the one who hesitates, the one who revolts and will not see the hand of Christ so manifested, does not realize Him.

---

3. Ibid.: Sk. filled in "(kind of)" in ink
4. Ibid.: Here Sk. indicated the beginning of a new paragraph
5. Ibid.: "do not"
6. Revelation xxii.13
7. Ibid.: The "(?)" inserted by the reporter crossed out by Sk.

The Scriptures of the past (The Old Testament) combine all the visions and inspirations which came to the different prophets. In the whole Bible there are different legends, explanatory of the dreams and visions which came from time to time. But those who make it limited, do they mean to say that after this Book was finished the visions, the Light of Christ was finished? Or do they mean to say that before the time that these Scriptures were compiled there was no inspiration or vision, or light, that the world was without it? And if they think that before this, and after the Book was finished, the world was without the Light, how can they support the very words of Christ: "I am Alpha and Omega . . . the first and the last"? [6] The message of Christ has come to a certain community, and they are receiving it everywhere, so to speak, and are charged with new life, new intelligence, new inspiration and new blessing.

What happens when it is refused and not recognized? They keep their original beliefs and religions, and refuse what comes fresh and is necessary, and in that way they have lost the new life which comes to refresh them.

Jesus Christ said of the Pharisees that they were hardened in their own religious feelings and refused His message. It is just like people saying: "The rain which came last year was the sacred rain, we shall not receive this year's rain but stop it". Friends, so to speak, the message of God which comes from above is the rain of Divine mercy; rain comes every autumn and so the message comes at the time necessary, then the cycle is changed. But people think little of messages, they think of personalities; they give importance to the personality.

In all ages what has been the conflict between men? Only this: "I am the follower of Moses, Abraham, Christ, Mahomet, Buddha; you are different. I am different". Can they not honestly say: "We are followers of God's Divine Light, His message, whether it comes from one name or another name"? Who knows in which name a person adores someone? For instance, what a confusion there would be if a man from the East were to come here and say: "I am . . . Will you tell me what is your religion"? And a man were to answer: "But here we are not followers of . . . [8] we are followers of Jesus Christ"; and they fought and quarrelled together and killed each other, and in the end it would be found out that . . . [8] is the name of Jesus Christ in the East. Human beings are like children; they fight about names and forms, and from childhood they fight for the historical facts, the history which every community has put in different words.

The true Christian is he who realizes Christ in his soul, and hears the word of Christ rise in his heart. This hearer will see Christ in all forms, in all His messages; in whatever period they come, he will respond to them.

---

8. Perhaps "`Isa", the name for Jesus in Arabic, known throughout the Islamic world

The Sufi movement in the world is an answer to the cry of humanity at the present time, and the more the souls will respond to it, the more they will be convinced that it is not a human enterprise, it is the promise of Christ and of God. Those whose heart is clear and open, those whose soul is awake, for them in this message is the voice of Christ. The message is to heal the wounds of the world at the present moment caused by war and destruction, by human materialism and selfishness at the present epoch. And those who will answer the call in this message will answer the call of God. For the moment has come when those who feel and teach should unite and spread the knowledge of truth against the superstition and ignorance which has spread far and wide. The time has come that the spirit of Divine heritage in man must be awakened in this world, and it is this aim for which the whole activity of the Sufi movement is working.

Thank you for your sympathetic response. May God bless you.

A typewritten copy made
by a professional reporter

Montreux, Hotel Splendide, 23 November 1922
from 8.40 to 9.30.

[1] In the reverence of God, my subject of this evening is

The Inner Voice

In this age the signs [2] of instinct is an admitted fact. Material man today admits that the animals choose their food, and what they must ~~leave~~ not eat, they leave. Also he admits the fact that the birds without being taught, fly, the fish without being taught, swim, and the sparrows without being taught, make their nests. But in spite of admitting this he is ready to deny the source from which this instinct comes. It is the same source from which intuition comes, inspiration and the revelation of other kinds of things; the same source from which instinct

Documents:

Tp.r. = a typewritten copy presented by the professional reporter who took down this lecture. It may have undergone some editing but on the whole it seems to be near to the words as spoken.
In Sherifa Goodenough's handwriting is written above: "Very incomplete". She wrote this same annotation above all four lectures given on 22, 23 afternoon and evening, and 24 November 1922, and taken down by the same professional reporter; this lecture, however, although a few words may have been missed, seems to be substantially complete.

Sk.tp. = a later typescript made by Sakina Furnée from "tp.r.", on which Sk. copied Sherifa Goodenough's note "Very incomplete report".

Sr.Sk. = a list with some corr. in Sk.'s handwriting, probably suggested by Sirdar van Tuyll and accepted by Sk.

Notes:

1. Tp.r.: "In the reverence of God," substituted for "Beloved ones of God," Pir-o-Murshid Inayat Khan's regular mode of address;
   Sk.tp.: "Beloved ones of God,"
2. All documents: "signs", but "science" must have been said

has come. This shows[3] a mystic that God is the teacher of the whole creation, even of the lower creation; but to a man God teaches more, man being the finest of all creation. Besides, man is more capable to learn and therefore he is taught more. In the East religion says that God has made man as His representative in the whole creation. What does it mean? It does not[4] mean that man represents heaven or something Divine, but it means that man is the miniature of God. That man is capable of showing the perfection of His wisdom can be seen in the example of Christ. If that perfection were not possible for man it would not have been written in the Bible: "By ye perfect even as your Father in heaven is perfect".[5]

Someone may ask: "What is the reason that the warning of certain happenings is given by horses, by dogs, and cats in the house, and man remains ignorant?" Many who have some experience with animals, who understand the signs of the animals, they will without difficulty admit the fact that especially such happenings as a great illness or death are known by the animals in the house, they give man warning. Besides there are several birds that give warning of great happenings. No doubt the experience of these things has become more material[6] because man is living crowded in a city; he is in less contact with the Divine and his life is artificial, he does not know, does not notice these things. The reason why man does not know is not that he is incapable of knowing, it is only that he has so many things on his mind. He has lost his real power of concentration, his power of stilling the mind, and in that respect he becomes worse than the horses, dogs and cats. No doubt as human nature, he is the most active among all the creatures, and this activity is the right thing for him if he could keep it under control. Instead of that, life is made artificial, and every day it becomes increasingly artificial; a man has not remained a man, he has become a machine; his thought, his mind, is constantly working, and for what? For nothing. Think of the feeling that one gets in the large cities today. The trams running and the buses, the motor-cars running over one another. Under the ground there are vibrations going on, and on the earth there are automobiles running, and now, since the war has taken place, now even the sky is not free for us to breathe the pure air; there also aeroplanes you see every day. If you go near the water there are steaming ships making noise, if you go into the country you have the noise of the factory from morning till evening, and in the town there

3. Sk.tp.: added by Sk. in hwr.: "to"
4. Perhaps "only" was missed by the reporter
5. Matt. v.48
6. Sr.Sk.: "rare" instead of "material"

are machines. Impressed by all these things, if you ask a man, talk to him something about the inner voice, about spiritual ideas, he will answer: "What is it? I don't understand". It is only necessary to hear the voice which is within, it is not necessary to study something; what is necessary is to become like nature, but man has become artificial and he must become natural in order to hear the voice within. But the unfortunate thing is that this artificial life has become necessary to man and when they tell him about natural life, spiritual life, God ideal, natural thought, he thinks it is something against his nature: [7] "I can't bear it".

When an illness becomes spread all over, it becomes common, it becomes the standard of health; therefore, today's illness of humanity is materialism, and that materialism has become natural. In order to find an example in support of this argument you need not look for a saint or saints. You can see this in a fairly good person, a righteous person of tranquil mind and good intentions, sympathetic. You can see this in his life. The first thing that a sympathetic heart with a clear conscience perceives is an impression; every person he meets during the day, he feels not only what that person says but what is behind it. This can increase. When a person comes into a certain room he feels a kind of atmosphere. He goes to visit someone, he feels the atmosphere in the house, of the people, of the family. He feels in his heart whether his friend's enterprise will be a success or a failure, distinctly or indistinctly. He feels what is happening. That person feels the pleasure, the displeasure of his fellowmen without having spoken; that person can understand if there is a smile outwardly and a cry inside, he hears it; and that person understands if there are tears outside and inside there is nothing. You may ask: "Is that faculty to be cultivated, and if it is to be cultivated, in what manner"? I will answer, "Yes". A sympathetic person who has taken a spiritual path will naturally progress and that faculty will develop. But what is most necessary before wanting to develop that faculty is that one's life has become true. It is sincerity, trueness, good living, a quieter thought, which prepare man for the voice which is within. But with all this goodness every person is not spiritually inclined, every person does not concentrate his mind towards that ideal which is necessary; he will be still, so to speak, blocked, not open to receive and hear the voice.

The next step of inspiration after impression is intuition. Intuition is a distinct feeling; it is not only a convinced feeling that perhaps it will happen so, but a distinct feeling that it must happen so. An intuitive person feels if somebody is writing him a letter from a distance. The intuitive person thinks

---

7. Ibid.: "; he says:" instead of a colon only

about somebody and meets him in the street; he had thought about him. The intuitive person [8]feels that perhaps when he goes to table the fish will be brought him, because intuition was going on[8] in the mind of the cook, and he has foreseen this. An intuitive person becomes a kind of thought-reader, what they call clairvoyant. Although today there seems to be such a lot of that clairvoyance, it has become a business, there are so many clairvoyants! The most amusing thing is this, that it has become such an ordinary thing to have clairvoyance that very often friends ask if you have some clairvoyance[9] power, if you are psychic. It is just like asking a person: "Have you a pen or paper?" Neither the one who asks nor the one who answers realizes how sacred the subject is, and how that subject may be treated. It is amusing to see how many people in these days talk so freely about having that power; if they only knew, that when there is such a power one has to be modest about it, close one's lips and look down. When, therefore, a man develops, he experiences what is called inspiration. It may come as an inspiration to paint, of music,[10] poetry, and the[11] difference between inspiration and the work of a lifetime is, that the one has done his work with much thought, and in the case of inspiration it comes easily, one has only to write it down, and it is there. What comes by inspiration cannot be corrected. Only[12] wanting to help it or correct it you spoil it instead of making it better, because it is not the person who has made it, it has been given him, although a person with materialistic ideas will not be ready to admit the fact. But ask any musician of some depth, or a poet who has really written something, and he will tell you that when he has the intention to write, he cannot, but the moment comes when it is all like rain coming from above.

When still further[13] a soul develops it does not only receive inspiration but it has what is called visions. All that he has to create, all that he produces in form of music or poetry, it is distinctly given to him. There are visions one sees while asleep; one gets into a condition of being in a kind of half sleep; and there are visions which one gets even when wide awake. When this intuitive faculty fully develops it becomes like a searchlight, and this searchlight is thrown upon a body and not only shows it clearly to man but he has the power to open

---

8. Ibid.: rewritten to read: "may feel when going to table that fish will be served him, because he felt by intuition what was going on"
9. Sk.tp.: "clairvoyance" changed by Sk. to "clairvoyant"
10. Sr.Sk.: "or" instead of a comma
11. Ibid.: ". The" instead of ", and the"
12. Sk.tp.: added in ink by Sk.: ", by";
    Sr.Sk.: added "By" and "only" moved to before "spoil"
13. Sr.Sk.: "still further" moved to after "a soul develops"

that body so that man sees the secret of that body, and it is this which is called revelation. Inspiration, intuition, or revelation are grades of the development of this entire (?)[14] power. You may ask me where does this power come from? In[15] answer: the Divine spirit is hidden in the heart of man, and the more the heart is disclosed, the more the Divine spirit finds the chance of rising to its fulness. The great prophets, saints, and sages who have given wisdom to the world, have not got this wisdom from intellectual resources but from the inner voice.

The whole tragedy of humanity today is that lack of the inner voice, and the cause of this is that the soul seems to be buried under matter. A person with a living heart goes with a torchlight to find somewhere someone who can understand what he says. What the condition of the world is, it is hard to find. When one person among thousands comes to some understanding, more realization of life, the first thing he feels is like running away from the whole crowd and never coming back to it again. For the ignorant, perhaps, life here is a joy, but for a person of understanding, a person of wisdom, it is the greatest tragedy to live. [16]At this state of worse condition the Sufi message[17] comes to humanity as an answer to humanity's cry. Its main theme is to waken in humanity the idea of the divine[18], of the human soul. The religions[19] that this message brings is to tolerate the beliefs of one another, and the moral, or rule, or doctrine, that the Sufi order[20] has brought to the world is to consider that the whole inner voice is one. As the happiness of the body depends on the health of the organs, so the happiness of the whole world depends on the . . .[21] of all nations. The Sufi order[20] welcomes such souls who have now arrived to a realization of the truth, the truth which will solve all questions of life, and that truth which alone can be called the ultimate truth.

Thank you for your sympathetic response. God bless you.

---

14. Ibid.: "entire (?)" omitted
15. Sk.tp.: corr. by Sk. into "I would"
16. Sr.Sk.: rewritten to read, "In this bad condition"
17. Sk.tp.: "message" capitalized by Sk.
18. Ibid.: "divine" capitalized by Sk.
19. Ibid.: "religion" instead of "religions"
20. Ibid.: "order" capitalized by Sk., which in 1922 still was the name for all Sufi activities, later (October 1923) re-named "Sufi Movement"
21. Ibid.: Sk. filled in "(well-being)" in ink

A typewritten copy made
by a professional reporter.

Vevey, Hotel d'Angleterre, 24 November 1922,
from 3.00 to 4.05

The Power of Silence

[1] In the reverence of God,[2] my subject of this afternoon is the power of Silence.[1]

The present condition of the world and of humanity has reached a state where there seems to be no limit to activity. Machinery is used in life every day for man's convenience and comfort, so the life of man has become more mechanical. It seems that at the present time very few in the world realize that man needs besides food and water something else of which his soul is the receptacle, and that which is indeed for his life more than material food and drink, the Divine substance, that substance which is all over, in space and

---

Documents:

Tp.r. = a typewritten copy presented by the professional reporter who took down this lecture at Vevey, Switzerland. It may have undergone some editing, but on the whole it seems to be near to the words as spoken.
In Sherifa Goodenough's handwriting is written above: "Very incomplete". She wrote this same annotation above all four lectures given on 22, 23 afternoon and evening and 24 November 1922 in Switzerland and taken down by the same professional reporter, although only the lecture of 22 November 1922 might be called "very incomplete";
(tp.r.)Gd. = editing by Sherifa Goodenough, for which she used the "tp.r."

Sk.tp. = a later typescript made by Sakina Furnée from "tp.r." with most of the editing by Sherifa Goodenough--"(tp.r.)Gd."--incorporated, also copying her note "Very incomplete"

Sr.Sk. = an extensive errata list on which in later years Sakina Furnée and Sirdar van Tuyll exchanged comments on revisions made in the texts.

Notes:

1. (Tp.r.)Gd.: the first sentence crossed out
2. Tp.r.: "In the reverence of God" substituted by the reporter for "Beloved ones of God", Pir-o-Murshid Inayat Khan's regular mode of address;
   Sk.tp.: "Beloved ones of God,"

everywhere, all prevailing[3]. But human nature is such that it gives a[4] greater importance to things which man needs in life, which are man-made, to jewels and gems, than to pure water and the air[5] needed for life; these cost nothing. The Divine spirit, which is the very essence of the whole of[6] creation, and which is mostly[7] needed to nourish the soul, is found everywhere. The nature of living[8] allows man to receive, so to speak, in his soul, in his spirit, that Divine spirit unconsciously, but the life we see today is far from nature. People[9] living in large houses[10] are just like pigeons in pigeon-holes, instead of living in large spaces. Besides this the restlessness of life has increased so much that there are many who have to work from morning till evening, and others, who have not got to work, also get into the habit of working all the time; without working they cannot feel rested. Besides man gets into the habit of talking; he is never tired, morning till evening; if he cannot talk it is monotonous. In time it becomes a kind of passion and the only relief he finds is in talking. He finds a subject to talk upon, and if there is no subject, then gossip. Sometimes one meets very amusing examples of this. I have very often amused myself by stimulating the conversation of one[11] very fond of talking, just by one word, and then being quiet. Besides this I have often amused myself by taking the same point of view as a person and not giving him the trouble to dispute[12] the question. But that person is never pleased; on the other hand he is sorry, because he has expected a contrary point of view which would have stimulated the argument, and[13] so[14] he could have argued for the sake of arguing. Such people will always take the

---

3. (Tp.r.)Gd.: "prevailing" changed to "pervading";
   Sk.tp.: "pervading"
4. (Tp.r.)Gd. "a" crossed out;
   Sk.tp.: "a" omitted
5. (Tp.r.)Gd., Sk.tp.: "that is" added
6. (tp.r.)Gd.: "of" crossed out;
   Sk.tp.: "of" omitted
7. (Tp.r.)Gd.: "mostly" changed into "most";
   Sk.tp.: "most"
8. (Tp.r.)Gd.: "The nature of living" changed into "The natural life";
   Sk.tp.: "The natural life"
9. (Tp.r.)Gd., Sk.tp.: "are" added after "people" and omitted after "houses"
10. (Tp.r.)Gd.: "houses" changed into "towns";
    Sk.tp.: "towns" instead of "houses"
11. (Tp.r.)Gd., Sk.tp.: "someone" instead of "one"
12. (Tp.r.)Gd.: "to dispute" changed into "of disputing";
    Sk.tp.: "of disputing"
13. (Tp.r.)Gd.: "and" crossed out;
    Sk.tp.: "and" omitted
14. (Tp.r.)Gd., Sk.tp.: "that" added

contrary point of view, whether they believe in it or not. Very often a person gets into the habit that he wants to talk, whether you say something in which he agrees or not; he always wants to say something in order to talk a little more.

In the Bible one reads the words of Christ against vain repetitions[15], and if one understood [16]it rightly one would be sparing of words[16]. How very[17] often two friends who really love each other cannot continue their friendship because of argument and misunderstanding. And how often a tendency to talk gives a kind of superficiality to the character, as when people meet at an evening party[18] and talk on subjects which are of no importance, [19]no use to anyone. Another thing is this, that[20] those ~~are~~ we meet in life, those we know and those who are strangers to us, we don't[21] always know how far they are developed, what we can say and what we must not say.

Besides, the [22]world is intoxicated[23], and people in the course of conversation get enthusiastic and say things that afterwards they feel they should not have said. A talkative person can tell another his secrets without knowing it, and then he repents. Self-discipline is the main lesson that one has to learn,[24] to attain mastery, [25]one must practise silence.

There are so few in the world who really understand and know the value of the breath one breathes. One does not only breathe air but the fine properties of the air, which are the radiance, or the Divine essence, which[26] one breathes in[27] every breath one takes. When a person speaks he speaks at the expense of

---

15. Matt. vi.8
16. (Tp.r.)Gd.: rewritten to read, "the meaning rightly it is sparing of words";
    Sk.tp.: "it rightly, it is: sparing of words";
    Sr.Sk.: to be left unchanged: "it rightly one would be sparing of words."
17. (Tp.r.)Gd.: "How very" crossed out, making the sentence begin with "Often";
    Sk.tp.: "How very" omitted
18. (Tp.r.)Gd.: "an evening party" changed into "a party";
    Sk.tp.: "a party"
19. (Tp.r.)Gd., Sk.tp.: "of" added
20. Ibid.: "with" added
21. Ibid.: "do not" instead of "don't"
22. Ibid.: "life in the" added
23. (Tp.r.)Gd.: "intoxicated" changed into "intoxicating";
    Sk.tp.: "intoxicating"
24. (Tp.r.)Gd.: the comma crossed out, changing the meaning;
    Sk.tp.: the comma omitted
25. (Tp.r.)Gd., Sk.tp.: "and for this" added
26. (Tp.r.)Gd.: "which" changed into "that";
    Sk.tp.: "that" instead of "which"
27. (Tp.r.)Gd.: "in" changed into "with";
    Sk.tp.: "with" instead of "in"

that light which he collects through the breath. You will always find a talkative person is[28] weak of nerves, irritable. He makes others irritable and restless. Often a person entering a room[29] upsets everyone sitting there. What is the reason of this? The person does not hold himself in his[30] hand. When he does not control his nerves, he is upset inwardly, and the influence of the vibrations spreads round[31], making the whole atmosphere nervous. It is strange, but at the same time true, that there is a greater progress in the medical world and a greater increase in diseases. Looked[32] at[33] from a psychical point of view one sees that nervousness is a common disease and therefore nobody observes it, notices it, as a disease, but all other diseases coming from it are recognized as diseases. I must say that[34] there are many diseases in the world which come from nervousness.

In ancient times it was the work of religion to teach concentration, prayer, meditation, and in that way silence was taught. Now things are different. The habit of taking a retreat seems to have gone. Man works all day, and when he goes home in the evening he rests in his armchair, thinks of his work and is never really quiet. No doubt activity is a sign of life, but silence is life itself.

In the East perhaps you have heard about the Yogis who lived very long. They lived apart and their soul became nourished, they retained their youth longer than others. The Arabs too, whatever they may be doing, in their profession, in their everyday life, pray five times a day and all the energy spent in working is given back to them. In the language of the Hindus breath is called . . .[35] the very life, and every word one speaks robs man of that very life which is the most important part in man's being. The wise of all ages have considered sparing of the[36] words the [37]most wise thing. In the ancient religion of the Christians, the

---

28. (Tp.r.)Gd.: "is" crossed out;
    Sk.tp.: "is" omitted
29. (Tp.r.)Gd., Sk.tp.: added, "without saying one word"
30. (Tp.r.)Gd.: "his" crossed out;
    Sk.tp.: "his" omitted
31. Sk.tp.: "around" instead of "round"
32. (Tp.r.)Gd.: "Looked" changed into "Looking";
    Sk.tp.: "Looking"
33. Sk.tp.: "it" added
34. (Tp.r.)Gd.: "I must say that" crossed out;
    Sk.tp.: "I must say that" first omitted, then reinserted by Sk.: "I must say";
    Sk.Sk.: "I must say that" to be left in
35. (Tp.r.)Gd., Sk.tp.: "Prana" filled in
36. (Tp.r.)Gd.: "the" crossed out;
    Sk.tp.: "the" omitted

monks used to have their retreat, their silence, and in the silence they heard the voice of God.

Now, coming to the spiritual point of view. [38]The nature of man, the receptacle.[38] Man is expressive, [39] also receptive; he can't [40] express if he has not received. Before man stand two worlds to receive from: one which is before him, and one of which he does not know. For the ordinary man that other world does not exist. The believer has read in the Scriptures and heard that there are two worlds, and he believes that it is so, [41] but in order to know the other world one need not wait till the coming of death. It is manifest when the eyes and the heart are closed to this world, but not when the eyes and heart are still open to the world outside. This can be accomplished by silence, but if the nerves are restless, if [42] always active and there is no stillness in the heart, how can the peace of the inner world become manifest to humanity? The difficulty today is that everybody is interested in learning spiritual things from books, and [43] it would be better to learn from one's self. Silence is natural to man, but as he has been accustomed to activity it has become different to [44] his nature, and therefore the manner of silence is learnt [45]; the process of obtaining that peace which is the peace of the inner world is called concentration, meditation, or any other name like [46] Yogas [47]. The more one realizes the value of that peace, it [48] is life itself and all happiness, the more one sees how less important [49] all other things are compared to that ideal

---

37. (Tp.r.)Gd.: "most wise" changed into "wisest";
    Sk.tp.: "wisest"
38. (Tp.r.)Gd.: this phrase was crossed out;
    Sk.tp.: this phrase omitted
39. (Tp.r.)Gd., Sk.tp.: "and" instead of a comma
40. (Tp.r.)Gd.: "cannot" instead of "can't";
    Sk.tp.: "can not"
41. (Tp.r.)Gd., Sk.tp.: added, "and that one day he will experience the other world"
42. Ibid.: "one is" added
43. (Tp.r.)Gd.: "and" changed into "while";
    Sk.tp.: "while" instead of "and"
44. (Tp.r.)Gd.: "to" changed into "from";
    Sk.tp.: "from" instead of "to"
45. (Tp.r.)Gd., Sk.tp.: "by mystics" added
46. (Tp.r.)Gd.: "like" replaced with "such as";
    Sk.tp.: "such as" instead of "like"
47. (Tp.r.)Gd.: "Yogas" changed into "Yoga";
    Sk.tp.: "Yoga"
48. (Tp.r.)Gd.: "it" changed into "which";
    Sk.tp.: "which" instead of "it"
49. (Tp.r.)Gd.: "how less important" changed into "how much less important", then Gd. added "of" before "how", omitting to change "important" into "importance";
    Sk.tp.: "of how much less importance"

of man [50]. The difficulty today is this: it is [51] not that man cannot [52] attain to a certain [53] peace, or to [54] develop a certain [55] faculty of intuition, but that he cannot keep silence. If there was an advertisement that an eternal peace could be easily given, there [56] would come many people [57]. But you will say, has man lost his power of persevering? No, that is not so. He works for his daily bread because he is sure of his wages. But when he embarks for an unknown destiny he doubts, and after taking a few steps he doubts again and says: "Shall I go back"? What is lacking is faith. Without faith, whatever be his object, whatever enterprise, material or spiritual, he cannot accomplish it. Spiritual attainment is much less difficult than material attainment because it is within man himself; he has not to pursue it, it is not far from his reach. If there is any difficulty it is only lack of faith. The main activity of the Sufi movement in the world [58] is to extend a helping hand to those seekers after truth who wish to know more about the manner of silence and the achievement that one desires [59] by silence. Although the general object of the Sufi movement is to work [60] in humanity the tolerance for [61]religions and beliefs and thus bring about a better understanding, the Sufi Order [62] is composed of the followers of different faiths who are one people in God [63]. Those who find [64] silence have [65] that peace of which no man is deprived,

---

50. (Tp.r.)Gd.: "of man" replaced with "state";
Sk.tp.: "state" instead of "man"
51. (Tp.r.)Gd.: "this, it is" crossed out;
Sk.tp.: "this, it is" omitted
52. (Tp.r.)Gd.: "cannot" replaced with "does not wish";
Sk.tp.: "does not wish to"
53. (Tp.r.)Gd.: "a certain" crossed out;
Sk.tp.: "a certain" omitted
54. (Tp.r.)Gd.: "to" crossed out;
Sk.tp.: "to" omitted
55. (Tp.r.)Gd.: "certain" crossed out;
Sk.tp.: "certain" omitted
56. (Tp.r.)Gd.: "there" crossed out;
Sk.tp.: "there" omitted
57. (Tp.r.)Gd.: reordered to read, "many people would come";
Sk.tp.: "many people would come"
58. (Tp.r.)Gd.: "in the world" crossed out;
Sk.tp.: "in the world" omitted
59. (Tp.r.)Gd., Sk.tp.: added "to attain"
60. Ibid.: added, "to bring about"
61. Ibid.: "all" added
62. "Sufi Order" was the name for all different Sufi activities, officially changed into "Sufi Movement" in October 1923
63. (Tp.r.)Gd.: "are one people in God" replaced with "unite in this common aim";
Sk.tp.: "unite in this common aim"

for that peace comes from God, Who is the God of all men and not of any particular sect of humanity.

[66]Thank you all for your sympathetic response. God bless you.[66]

---

64. (Tp.r.)Gd.: "find" first replaced with "keep", then "keep" was crossed out and "attain to" written instead;
    Sk.tp.: "attain to" instead of "find"
65. (Tp.r.)Gd.: "have" replaced with "attain";
    Sk.tp.: "attain" instead of "have"
66. (Tp.r.)Gd.: this last sentence was crossed out

Sakina Furnée's shorthand reporting.

Morges[1], [2]November 1922

[3]

Beloved ones of God,[4]

[5]My subject of this evening is the Sufi's aim in life.[5]

The aim of[6] every individual in the end is the same. In the beginning

---

Documents:

Sk.sh. = Sakina Furnée's shorthand reporting, with several blanks where she missed one or more words. No later transcription by Sakina has been found,and the lecture has, like all the lectures taken down in shorthand, been retranscribed by Munira van Voorst van Beest.

E.t. = a typescript, not known by whom, based on "Sk.sh.", but made in later years and substantially edited;
(e.t.)Gd.e.: further editing by Sherifa Goodenough on "e.t." to prepare the lecture to be inserted in the series of Social Gathekas, in which it has become nr. 28.

Hq.st. = a stencilled copy made from "(e.t.)Gd.e." at International Headquarters, Geneva.

Hq.t. = a typescript made at International Headquarters, Geneva, nearly identical to "Hq.st."

S.Q. = The Sufi Quarterly of December 1928, Vol IV, nr. 3, taken from "Hq.st."

The lecture has also been published in The Sufi, "a quarterly journal of Mysticism", of January 1936, Vol. II, nr. 1, but this version shows many omissions and inaccuracies, and is not cited in the notes.

Notes:

1. Morges is situated near Lausanne in Switzerland
2. The complete date: 25 November 1922, appears on the "e.t." and was crossed out by Gd. when she prepared the lecture to become a "Social Gatheka"
3. (E.t.)Gd.e.: added in hwr., "(Rep. by: S.Furnée)", later crossed out by Gd. when preparing the lecture for the Social Gatheka series
4. All other documents: "Beloved ones of God," omitted
5. (E.t.)Gd.e.: the first sentence replaced with "The Sufi's Aim in Life" as a title, and later added above: "Social Gatheka";
   Hq.st., Hq.t., S.Q.: "The Sufi's Aim in Life" as a title instead of the first sentence
6. E.t.: "in" instead of "of";
   (e.t.)Gd.e.: "of" restored

the aim of every individual is different. In the end man comes to a stage when his object becomes the object of his soul. And, as long as he has not arrived at this object, he has several objects before him. But the accomplishment of any motive is not satisfactory for long.

According to the philosophy of the[7] Hindus there are four motives in life. One motive is what they call *dharma*, which means duty. There are some who consider[8] virtue[9] in performing their duty, and when [10]that particular duty that [11] is before them they perform,[10] they feel that that [12] is the [13] accomplishment of their life. But [14] after another is—[14] if one duty is accomplished, another is waiting. Life is full of duties. [15]When one accomplished one duty, there is another waiting. [15] When the [16] girl is young . . . [17] she says: my mother, [18] father is my duty. Then a time comes that [19] the pleasure of her husband is her duty. And as time goes on, there is a [20] duty of the mother towards the children. But even there it does not end; there comes the duty of the grandmother. There is no phase of life that the [21] duty

---

7. E.t.: "the" omitted;
   (e.t.)Gd.e.: "the" restored
8. (E.t.)Gd.e.: "that" added;
   Hq.st., Hq.t., S.Q.: "that"
9. (E.t.)Gd.e.: "lies" added;
   Hq.st., Hq.t., S.Q.: "lies"
10. (E.t.)Gd.e.: reordered to read, "they perform that particular duty which is before them";
    Hq.st., Hq.t., S.Q.: as in "(e.t.)Gd.e."
11. All other documents: "which" instead of "that"
12. E.t.: "this";
    (e.t.)Gd.e.: "this" changed back into "that"
13. (E.t.)Gd.e.: "due" added;
    Hq.st., Hq.t., S.Q.: "due"
14. All other documents: "after another is--" omitted
15. E.t.: "When one accomplishes one duty, there is another waiting.";
    (e.t.)Gd.e.: this whole sentence crossed out;
    Hq.st., Hq.t., S.Q.: this sentence omitted
16. (E.t.)Gd.e.: "the" changed into "a";
    Hq.st., Hq.t., S.Q.: "a" instead of "the"
17. Sk.sh.: one word illegible;
    all other documents: a comma
18. (E.t.)Gd.e.: "my" added;
    Hq.st., Hq.t., S.Q.: "my"
19. (E.t.)Gd.e.: "that" changed into "when";
    Hq.st., Hq.t., S.Q.: "when"
20. (E.t.)Gd.e.: "a" changed into "the";
    Hq.st., Hq.t., S.Q.: "the"
21. All other documents: "in life in which" instead of "of life that the"

expires. It begins in form one[22] and it[23] goes on in another. [24]The one who considers duty a pleasure, for him duty is his[25] pleasure. [26]Who considers it a virtue, it is a virtue, but for the one who considers duty as[27] a captivity or a pain, for him it is a pain. For one person it becomes a virtue, [28]for another it becomes an ache. For one it is[28] a privilege, for another a crime.

In the Hindu language . . .[29]: *arth*[30], which means the acquirement[31] or collecting of wealth; it begins with the need of daily bread, and it culminates in millions, and is never.finished. The more one has, the less he[32] feels he[32] has. [33]The more he . . . that it could be placed for . . . .[33] The attainment of wealth is never fully satisfactory. There is always a lack.

And then[34] there comes a third motive, which is pleasure. For this ~~a sacrifice~~ one neglects, one sacrifices which[35] is the main object in life, but at[36] the same time pleasure is such a thing that that[37] desire is never satisfied.[38] The more one experiences the pleasures of this earth, the more there comes a[20] desire to experience[39]. [40]Pleasure is not lasting and costs

---

22. Ibid.: "one form" instead of "form one"
23. Ibid.: "it" omitted
24. Ibid.: "For" added
25. Ibid.: "a" instead of "his"
26. Ibid.: "For him" added
27. (E.t.)Gd.e.: "as" crossed out;
    Hq.st., Hq.t., S.Q.: "as" omitted
28. All other documents: "for another . . . it is" omitted
29. Sk.sh.: an open space;
    all other documents: "there exists the word" filled in
30. Sk.sh.: written in lh. by Sk.: "arth";
    all other documents: erroneously copied as "ardh"
31. E.t.: "acquisition" instead of "acquirement";
    Hq.st., Hq.t., S.Q.: "acquisition"
32. All other documents: "one" instead of "he"
33. E.t.: the incomplete sentence was left out;
    Hq.st., Hq.t., S.Q.: without the incomplete sentence
34. All other documents: "then" omitted
35. Sk.sh.: especially in the early years of lecturing Pir-o-Murshid used "which" instead of "that which";
    e.t.: "; it" instead of "which";
    Hq.st., Hq.t., S.Q.: "; it"
36. E.t.: "in" instead of "at";
    (e.t.)Gd.e.: "in" restored to "at"
37. All other documents: "this" instead of "that"
38. E.t.: the full stop replaced with "and";
    Hq.st., Hq.t., S.Q.: "and"
39. All other documents: "them" added

more[41] than it is worth.

And there is the fourth desire, which is of a different character, and that is in[42] a kind of reward in the hereafter. It is[43] for the attainment of a paradise or reaching some bliss which one does not know. It is a desire for some kind of gain or happiness, bliss or exaltation, which one does not know, but one hopes to experience some day. But even that, if it were vouchsafed, it[23] would not be fully satisfactory, [44]~~for it would not~~ for man would. . . .[44]

And from that[37] the Sufi derives[45] that from[46] all these four different things that humanity is pursuing[47], that[48] there is no stage where he can say, it is finished; it has no end. Therefore his effort is to arrive[49] above these four different desires that humanity has, and the moment he rises above these four desires, there comes only one desire, and that desire is the search for Truth. Not only Sufis, but every person disappointed in this world [50]has this only desire. . . .[50]

A[51] seeker after Truth goes out in[52] the world, and he finds so many sects,[53] so many different religions, he does not know where to go. Then the

---

40. Ibid.: "This" added
41. Ibid.: ", usually," added
42. Ibid.: "for" instead of "in"
43. Ibid.: a comma in place of ". It is"
44. E.t.: the incomplete phrase omitted and the comma after "satisfactory" changed into a full stop;
    Hq.st., Hq.t., S.Q.: the phrase omitted
45. (E.t.)Gd.e.: "derives" changed into "deduces";
    Hq.st., Hq.t., S.Q.: "deduces"
46. (E.t.)Gd.e.: "from" changed into "in";
    Hq.st., Hq.t., S.Q.: "in"
47. All other documents: "after" added
48. Ibid.: "that" omitted
49. E.t.: "to arrive" changed into "to rise";
    Hq.st., Hq.t., S.Q.: "to rise" instead of "to arrive"
50. Sk.sh.: a blank after "desire";
    e.t.: "who has been through a disillusionment, a suffering, or a torture" added after "in this world", although it may have been said after "desire";
    (e.t.)Gd.e.: "every person" first added before "who has been", then crossed out;
    Hq.st., Hq.t., S..Q.: as in "e.t."
51. All other documents: "The" instead of "A"
52. (E.t.)Gd.e.: "in" changed into "into";
    Hq.st., Hq.t., S.Q.: "into"
53. (E.t.)Gd.e.: the comma replaced with "and";
    Hq.st., Hq.t., S.Q.: "and"

desire is to find out which is beyond [54], hidden under which are [55] these sects, these different religions. And therefore [56]he finds that object which he wishes to gain in time, to find from wisdom.[56] Wisdom is a veil over [57] Truth, but wisdom even cannot be called the Truth. God alone is Truth, and it is Truth Who [58] is God. And Truth neither can be [59] studied nor taught nor learnt. It is to be touched, it is to be realised, and that [60] can be realised by the unfoldment of the heart.

For a Sufi belief in God is not sufficient. A belief which has no foundation underneath is just like a scrap of paper [61]. When there is no air [62], it will fall on [63] the ground. How many in this world with all their belief give in [64] when there is a strong influence in their surroundings [65] who does not believe. If belief is such a thing which [66] can be erased, then what use can that belief be for [67]? Really speaking, it [68] is not only belief; the next step one takes after belief is the love [69] of God. [70]The one who only believes in God,

---

54. E.t.: "which is beyond," replaced with "what is" (for "which" see note 35);
    Hq.st., Hq.t., S.Q.: "what is"
55. All other documents: "which are" omitted
56. E.t.: rewritten to read, "he begins to seek that object which he wishes to gain through wisdom";
    Hq.st., Hq.t., S.Q.: as in "e.t."
57. E.t.: "of" instead of "over";
    (e.t.)Gd.e.: "of" changed back to "over"
58. All other documents: "that" instead of "Who"
59. E.t.: reordered to read, "can be neither";
    Hq.st., Hq.t., S.Q.: "can be neither"
60. E.t.: "that" replaced with "this";
    (e.t.)Gd.e.: "this" replaced with "it";
    Hq.st., Hq.t., S.Q.: "it" instead of "that"
61. (E.t.)Gd.e.: "floating" added;
    Hq.st., Hq.t., S.Q.: "floating in the air" added
62. (E.t.)Gd.e.: "air" replaced with "breeze";
    Hq.st., Hq.t., S.Q.: "breeze" instead of "air"
63. (E.t.)Gd.e.: "on" changed into "to";
    Hq.st., Hq.t., S.Q.: "to" instead of "on"
64. E.t.: "it up" instead of "in";
    Hq.st., Hq.t., S.Q.: "it up" instead of "in"
65. E.t.: "of one" added;
    Hq.st., Hq.t., S.Q.: "of one"
66. S.Q.: "that it" instead of "which"
67. All other documents: "for" omitted
68. S.Q.: "there" instead of "it"
69. E.t.: "loving" instead of "love";
    (e.t.)Gd.e.: changed back to "love"
70. (E.t.)Gd.e.: "In" added;
    Hq.st., Hq.t., S.Q.: "In" added

in him God is not living. [71]Who loves God, in him [72] God is living.

But even that is not sufficient. For what is human love? He [73] is limited, his love is limited. The more one has seen the world, the more one knows human nature, the more one knows the falsehood of human love. Even one being [74] who cannot be constant to a human being who is around [75] him, how can he be true in his love for the Beloved [76]Who is never . . . ? [76] Therefore even what man calls the love of God, that [77] is not sufficient. What is necessary is the knowledge of God, for it is the knowledge of God which gives the love for God. And it is the knowledge and love of God which give a perfect belief of [78] God. No one can have the knowledge of God and have no love of [79] God. But one can have a love for God and no knowledge of God. No one can have the knowledge of God, [80] love in [81] God, and no belief in God. But there can be someone who has a belief in God, but no love in [81] God ~~nor~~ .

Therefore for a Sufi these three stages are necessary for the attainment of his aim in life. In the first place he accomplishes with [82] his belief a [83] respect for the beliefs [84] of others. A complete believer is he who does not [85] himself believe, [86] but he [87] respects the belief of others. For a Sufi

---

71. S.Q.: "In the one" added
72. Hq.st., Hq.t., S.Q.: "in him" omitted
73. E.t.: "The human being" instead of "He";
    Hq.st., Hq.t., S.Q.: "The human being"
74. E.t.: "Even one being" replaced with "The one";
    Hq.st., Hq.t., S.Q.: "The one"
75. E.t.: "near" instead of "around";
    Hq.st., Hq.t., S.Q.: "near"
76. Sk.sh.: a blank after "Who is never";
    e.t.: "Whom he has never seen?" instead of "Who is never. . .?";
    Hq.st., Hq.t., S.Q.: "Whom he has never seen?"
77. (E.t.)Gd.e.: "that" crossed out;
    Hq.st., Hq.t., S.Q.: "that" omitted
78. All other documents: "in" instead of "of"
79. Ibid.: "for" instead of "of"
80. Hq.t.: "and" added
81. All other documents: "for" instead of "in"
82. (E.t.)Gd.e.: "accomplishes with" changed into "attains by";
    Hq.st., Hq.t., S.Q.: "attains by"
83. (E.t.)Gd.e.: "a" crossed out;
    Hq.st., Hq.t., S.Q.: "a" omitted
84. All other documents: "belief"
85. Sk.sh.: afterwards Sk. added "only" in sh.;
    all other documents: "only" added
86. All other documents: "believe himself"

in this world there is no one, heathen or[88] pagan, who is to be despised. For he believes in that God Who is not the God of one, a[89] chosen sect. He is[90] the God of all the[91] world. He does not believe in the[16] God of one nation[92], of all nations. [93]For to him different houses where people worship, to him, if he stands in the street, it makes no difference.[93] It[94] is the holy place where he worships[95] . . . he[96] leaves sectarianism to the sect[97]. He has respect for all . . .[98, 99] He is not prejudiced against any, not despising[100], [101]feels sympathy for all.

[102]Now about the love of God.[102] The idea of the Sufi is that the one who does not love his fellow man, he[103] cannot love God. He thinks, as

---

87. E.t.: "who" instead of "he";
    (e.t.)Gd.e.: "who" crossed out;
    Hq.st., Hq.t., S.Q.: "he" omitted
88. (E.t.)Gd.e.: "neither heathen nor" instead of "heathen or";
    Hq.st., Hq.t., S.Q.: "neither heathen nor"
89. All other documents: ", a" omitted
90. (E.t.)Gd.e.: ". He is" changed into ", but";
    Hq.st., Hq.t., S.Q.: ", but"
91. Sk.sh.: "all the" later changed by Sk. into "the whole" in sh.;
    all other documents: "the whole"
92. E.t.: "but" instead of a comma;
    Hq.st, Hq.t., S.Q.: "but"
93. E.t.: rewritten to read, "To him God is in all the different houses where people worship Him; if they stand in the street and pray, it makes no difference to Him.";
    (e.t.)Gd.e.: "Even" added before "if they stand";
    Hq.st., Hq.t., S.Q.: "To him God is in all the different houses where people worship Him. Even if they stand in the street and pray, it makes no difference to Him."
94. All other documents: "that" instead of "It"
95. E.t.: "He is worshipped" instead of "he worships . . .";
    Hq.st., Hq.t., S.Q.: "He is worshipped"
96. E.t.: "The Sufi" instead of "he";
    Hq.st., Hq.t., S.Q.: "The Sufi"
97. (E.t.)Gd.e.: "sects" instead of "sect";
    Hq.st., Hq.t., S.Q.: "sects"
98. Sk.sh.: in her notebook, at the bottom of the page, Sk. wrote in lh.: "forms or ceremonies", perhaps meant to be included after "all" (see note 99)
99. Sk.sh.: a blank after "all";
    all other documents: a full stop after "all"
100. E.t.: "not despising any";
    (e.t.)Gd.e.: "does not despise any";
    Hq.st., Hq.t., S.Q.: "does not despise any"
101. All other documents: "he" added
102. (E.t.)Gd.e.: this sentence crossed out;
    Hq.st., Hq.t., S.Q.: this sentence omitted
103. (E.t.)Gd.e.: "he" crossed out;
    Hq.st., Hq.t., S.Q.: "he" omitted

Christ has said, "Love your neighbour, love your enemy" [104]; and what does it mean? It means not, "Love him because you consider him [105]enemy", but "Love him because in God you are relative [106] to [107] him", . . . [108] human bond. If humanity had belief [109] in this simple and worthy, [110] most valuable teaching, these wars would not have taken place. Do they [111] think that all ~~that~~ this hatred that exists, one nation against the other, one party against the other, there seems to be a conflict . . . [112], do they think . . . [113]? If the world [114]had believed, it[114] would not have taken place. Is it the work of the [115] political people [116] or of business? [117] No, it is the work of the Church, of the [118] religion. But when [119] [120]religious authorities will make for [121]

---

104. See Matt. v.43-44
105. All other documents: "as your" added
106. E.t.: "related" instead of "relative";
    Hq.st., Hq.t., S.Q.: "related"
107. (E.t.)Gd.e.: "to" changed into "with";
    Hq.st., Hq.t., S.Q.: "with" instead of "to"
108. Sk.sh.: a blank, completed by Sk. with "there is a";
    all other documents: this part of the sentence left out
109. E.t.: "believed" instead of "belief";
    Hq.st., Hq.t., S.Q.: "believed"
110. E.t.: "worthy" omitted;
    Hq.st., Hq.t, S.Q.: "worthy," omitted
111. E.t.: "you" in place of "they";
    Hq.st., Hq.t., S.Q.: "you"
112. Sk.sh.: a blank;
    e.t.: filled in: "everywhere";
    Hq.st., Hq.t., S.Q.: "everywhere"
113. Sk.sh.: an open space;
    e.t.: filled in "this would have been if this teaching had been followed?";
    Hq.st., Hq.t., S.Q.: as in "e.t."
114. E.t.: "would have believed it, it";
    (e.t.)Gd.e.: "had believed this teaching, all this" instead of "had believed, it";
    Hq.st., Hq.t., S.Q.: "had believed this teaching, all this"
115. All other documents: "the" omitted
116. (E.t.)Gd.e.: added, "to bring this ~~teaching~~ home to men?";
    Hq.st., Hq.t., S.Q.: "to bring this home to men?"
117. E.t.: "of business?" changed into "the work of commerce?";
    Hq.st., Hq.t., S.Q.: "the work of commerce?"
118. (E.t.)Gd.e.: "the" crossed out;
    all other documents: "the" omitted
119. E.t.: "when" changed into "as long as";
    all other documents: "as long as"
120. (E.t.)Gd.e.: "the" added;
    Hq.st., Hq.t., S.Q.: "the" added
121. All other documents: "for" changed into "of"

themselves a sect, and divide it [122], and looking upon each other . . . [123], then the [124] Truth, brought by Christ, is not practised.

You [125] must know that every change that takes place in the multitude, in times [126] comes among the[115] individuals. For an [127] instance, if two nations are against one another, opposed to one another, working to hurt one another, what will be the consequence? The result will be that in those nations there will be parties that will oppose each other. [128]And when they will come, the same opposition will come in the families [128], and you will find [129] that in time that [130] spirit will be found in a family of two people. Two people living in a [131] house, and both in conflict . . . [132] each other. And where will it culminate? It will culminate in the [133] individual [134] in conflict with himself.

Where does [135] Sufi learn this? He learns it in the wisdom of God. The man who does not recognise God in His creation, never will recognise Him [136] in . . . . [137] [138] Man who . . . divine . . . where this whole creation

---

122. E.t.: "it" changed into "religion";
Hq.st., Hq.t., S.Q.: "religion" instead of "it"
123. Sk.sh.: a blank;
e.t.: "with prejudice" filled in;
Hq.st., Hq.t., S.Q.: "with prejudice"
124. E.t.: "this" in place of "then the";
Hq.st., Hq.t., S.Q.: "this"
125. (E.t.)Gd.e.: "You" changed into "We";
Hq.st., Hq.t., S.Q.: "We" instead of "you"
126. All other documents: "time"
127. (E.t.)Gd.e.: "an" crossed out;
Hq.st., Hq.t., S.Q.: "an" omitted
128. E.t.: rewritten to read, "and then there will come the same opposition in the family";
(e.t.)Gd.e.: "and then there will come the same opposition in families";
Hq.st., Hq.t., S.Q.: as in "(e.t.)Gd.e."
129. (E.t.)Gd.e.: "find" changed into "see";
Hq.st., Hq.t., S.Q.: "see"
130. All other documents: "this"
131. Ibid.: "one" instead of "a"
132. Sk.sh.: a blank;
e.t.: "with" filled in;
Hq.st., Hq.t., S.Q.: "with"
133. E.t.: "the" changed into "every";
Hq.st., Hq.t., S.Q.: "every"
134. All other documents: "being" added
135. Ibid.: "the" (or "The") added
136. E.t.: "the God" instead of "Him";
Hq.st., Hq.t., S.Q.: "the God"
137. Sk.sh.: a blank;
all other documents: filled in, "Heaven"

stands before him and . . . .[138] It is[139] all right for those simple believers in God and ~~guidance~~ religion, who quietly . . .[140] and did not meddle with the world. But now the conditions have changed. Now there is a great battle between Truth and . . .[141] Illusion of matter is in the fulness of the rôle[142] that it is performing in life. Therefore there is a greater battle that the[115] life is fighting with the Truth, than religion has . . . .[143] On one side science cries: matter, matter, matter! On the other side the[115] politicians[144] are crying: self- self- self-interest! The religions are crying: sect, sect, sect! And where must[145] man stop thinking about[146] the ultimate Truth that is the only thing that[147] the soul seeks?

[135]Sufi Message, therefore, has its mission, not for a particular race, nor for a particular nation, nor for a particular Church. It is a call to unite in wisdom, which is *Sophia* in Greek words[148], and which we call Sufi. [149]The Order of the Sufis, the movement of the Sufis,[149] is a group of people, belonging in different religions, who have not left their religion[150], but have

---

138. Sk.sh. an incomplete sentence;
 all other documents: this fragmentary sentence omitted
139. (E.t.)Gd.e.: "is" changed into "was";
 Hq.st., Hq.t., S.Q.: "was"
140. Sk.sh.: an open space;
 e.t.: filled in, "went to church and said their prayers, and came back with a feeling of exaltation,";
 Hq.st., Hq.t., S.Q.: as in "e.t."
141. Sk.sh.: an open space;
 e.t.: "life" filled in;
 Hq.st., Hq.t., S.Q.: "life"
142. (E.t.)Gd.e.: "rôle" changed into "part";
 Hq.st., Hq.t., S.Q.: "part"
143. Sk.sh.: an open space;
 e.t.: filled in "ever had to fight";
 Hq.st., Hq.t., S.Q.: "ever had to fight"
144. E.t.: "politics" instead of "politicians";
 Hq.st., Hq.t., S.Q.: "politicians"
145. (E.t.)Gd.e.: "must" changed into "could";
 Hq.st, Hq.t., S.Q.: "could"
146. All other documents: "to think of" instead of "thinking about"
147. Ibid.: All other documents: "which" instead of "that"
148. (E.t.)Gd.e.: "the Greek word";
 Hq.st., Hq.t., S.Q.: "the Greek words"
149. All other documents: "The Sufi Movement" instead of "The Order of the Sufis, the movement of the Sufis"
150. (E.t.)Gd.e.: "religions";
 Hq.st., Hq.t, S.Q.: "religions"

learned to . . . [151] their religion. And their service [152, 153] in life is [154] the service [152] for God and humanity instead of [155] a particular section. The principal work that the Sufi Order [156] has to accomplish is to bring about a better understanding between East and West, and between the nations [157] of this world. And the note that the Sufi m . . . [158] is striking at the present [159] is the note which sounds [160] the divinity of [135] human soul, [161] to wake humanity to re . . . .[161] If there is any . . . [162] principle that the Sufi movement . . . [163] it is that the whole humanity is as one body. And any organ of that body, hurt or troubled, can cause trouble to the whole body indirectly. And as the health of the [164] body depends upon the health of the whole body, so the health of the whole world depends upon the co . . . [164] of every nation. Besides that [130], [165] to the souls who are being awakened [165], and who [166] feel now there [167] is a [168] moment that [169] they feel like knowing [170] the

---

151. Sk.sh.: a blank, but Sk. added in the margin in sh.: "better understanding";
all other documents: "understand them better" filled in and "their religion" omitted
152. E.t.: "love" instead of "service", as clearly written in Sk.sh.;
Hq.st., Hq.t., S.Q.: "love" instead of "service"
153. (E.t.)Gd.e.: "is" added;
Hq.st., Hq.t., S.Q.: "is"
154. (E.t.)Gd.e.: "is" changed into "as";
Hq.st., Hq.t., S.Q.: "as"
155. All other documents: "for" added
156. (E.t.)Gd.e.: "Order" changed into "Movement";
Hq.st., Hq.t., S.Q.: "Movement"
157. Sk.sh.: added in the margin in sh.: "and races";
(E.t.)Gd.e.: "and races" added
158. Sk.sh.: just an "m", which may stand for "movement";
all other documents: "Message"
159. (E.t.)Gd.e.: "time" added;
Hq.st., Hq.t., S.Q.: "time" added
160. (E.t.)Gd.e.: "which sounds" crossed out with a question mark, and "of" written above;
Hq.st.: "which of sounds"
161. All other documents: "to make human beings recognise the divinity in the human soul" instead of the incomplete sentence, "to wake humanity to re . . ."
162. Sk.sh.: one word illegible, which is not "moral";
all other documents: "moral"
163. Sk.sh.: a blank;
all other documents: "brings"
164. All other documents: rewritten to read, "whole body depends upon the health of each part, so the health of the whole humanity depends upon the health"; the "co . . ." cound represent "condition" or "cooperation"
165. E.t.: "those who are awakened" instead of "to the souls who are being awakened";
(e.t.)Gd.e.: "to those who are wakening,";
Hq.st., Hq.t., S.Q.: "to those who are wakening"
166. All other documents: "who" omitted

deeper side of life, of truth, to them the Order extends [171]its help . . . ,[171] without asking them[172] [173]what religion, sect,[174] dogma they belong. The knowledge of the Sufi is helpful to every person, [175]not only in living his life aright, but in his own religion.[175] The Sufi Order[176] does not call man away from his belief,[177] Church[178], he[179] calls man to live it. In short, it is a movement intended by God to unite humanity in brotherhood, in wisdom.

[180]Thank you all for your sympathetic response. May God bless you.[180]

---

167. Ibid.: "that now" instead of "now there"
168. Ibid.: "a" changed into "the"
169. Ibid.: "when" in place of "that"
170. E.t.: "inclined to know" instead of "like knowing";
Hq.st., Hq.t., S.Q.: "inclined to know"
171. E.t.: "a helping hand" instead of "its help . . . ";
Hq.st., Hq.t., S.Q.: "a helping hand"
172. All other documents: "them" omitted
173. Ibid.: "to" added
174. S.Q.: "or" added instead of the comma
175. Hq.t.: reordered to read, "not only in his own religion, but in living his life aright"
176. (E.t.)Gd.e.: "Order" changed into "Movement";
Hq.st., Hq.t., S.Q.: "Movement" instead of "Order"
177. All other documents: "or" added instead of the comma
178. S.Q.: "religion" instead of "Church"
179. (E.t.)Gd.e.: "he" changed into "it";
Hq.st., Hq.t., S.Q.: "it"
180. All other documents: closing words omitted

A text in the handwriting of Sherifa Goodenough.

1

Indian Music

In Indian music, when several instruments are played together, the effect is not produced by the chord[2], by harmony, but by melody. Each instrument has the melody.

[3]When music is played before a thousand or ten thousand people, then, of course, many instruments are needed.[3]

In the West brilliant[4], impressive, lively, by the chords. We make it so by the melody alone.

Documents:

Gd.h. = a handwritten copy of an earlier ms. (her own or someone else's), made by Sherifa Goodenough for the purpose of editing, showing corr., changes and add. In a few places she wrote the numbers 1 and 2 on the ms., the significance of which is not apparent.

Ng.t.1 = a typewritten copy made by Nargis Dowland of "Gd.h.", incorporating the editorial and other changes in "Gd.h." made by Sherifa Goodenough;
(Ng.t.1)Gd.e.: further editing and corr. by Gd. hand-written on this typescript.

Ng.t.2 = another typewritten copy made by Nargis Dowland, made from "Ng.t.1" and incorporating Gd.'s further editing--"(Ng.t.1)Gd.e.";
(Ng.t.2)Sr.c.: further handwritten corr. by Sirdar van Tuyll, to whom Miss Dowland handed on her typescripts.

Sk.t. = a typewritten copy of "Ng.t.2", made by Sakina Furnée or under her supervision, including Sirdar's corr.--"(Ng.t.2)Sr.c."

Notes:

1. Although undated, this lecture is quite similar in subject matter to the lectures on music given in Geneva, Switzerland, in the first half of November 1922. As Paderewski is mentioned in the lecture, and Pir-o-Murshid probably met him for the first time during his lecture tour in Switzerland in the second half of November 1922, it could well have been given when Pir-o-Murshid returned to Geneva after the tour, at the end of the month. (In the Biography or Pir-o-Murshid Inayat Khan, East-West Publ., London/The Hague, 1979, the meeting with Paderewski and several of the lectures given in the autumn of 1922, appear erroneously under 1923.)
2. Ng.t.1: "chords";
(Ng.t.2)Sr.c.: "chords" changed back to "chord"
3. (Ng.t.1)Gd.e.: this sentence moved to the end of the following paragraph;
Ng.t.2, Sk.t.: put at the end of the following paragraph
4. Gd.h.: "brilliant" changed into "the music is made brilliant";
all other documents: "the music is made brilliant"

When music is played before a few hearers[5] only, then three or four instruments[6] are needed, or only one.

When it is used for concentration, then one instrument, one[7] voice is quite enough. If ten[8] instruments each play a note, then there can be no concentration, the mind is drawn to the ten notes.

[9]The mystics, especially the Sufis, have used music in their prayers, in their meditations. It was a part of their devotions. Khwaja Moinuddin Chishti, [10]Banda Nawaz, [11] and [12] made great use of music. I have practised and experienced myself the use of music in meditation, and I have understood that it is the best means of meditation, the quickest means of freeing the consciousness.

Sound has been called God, Nada Brahm [13], ~~by~~ in the Vedanta. In the Gospel of St. John it is called the Word, from which all things have come. ~~First there~~

[14]When the poet imagines a lake and a mountain, he has the forms, the lake and [15] the mountain, before the eyes of his mind. When the ~~poet~~ musician thinks of ~~the~~ a melody, he has no form, no name before him. He is a plane higher than the poet.

First there was the sound, God was sound. And from the sound, by the

---

5. Gd.h.: "hearers" changed into "listeners";
   All other documents: "listeners"
6. Gd.h.: "only" added;
   All other documents: "only"
7. Ng.t.1: "or" instead of "one";
   (Ng.t.1)Gd.e.: corr. to "one";
   Ng.t.2, Sk.t.: "one"
8. (Ng.t.1)Gd.e.: "two" instead of "ten", changed back into "ten";
   Ng.t.2, Sk.t.: "ten"
9. (Ng.t.1)Gd.e.: a mark in the margin to indicate a new paragraph;
   Ng.t.2, Sk.t.: a new paragraph
10. Gd.h.: added "Haji";
    (Ng.t.1)Gd.e.: "Haji" changed into "Khwaja";
    Ng.t.2, Sk.t.: "Khwaja"
11. Gd.h.: a small open space;
    All other documents: no space left open
12. Gd.h.: a space left open, in which one or two illegible words were written in later;
    (Ng.t.1)Gd.e.: "and" crossed out, no space left;
    Ng.t.2, Sk.t.: "made great use of music" right after "Banda Nawaz", with no space
13. (Ng.t.1)Gd.e.: "Brahma";
    All other documents: "Brahma"
14. (Ng.t.1)Gd.e.: this paragraph, three sentences, moved to the beginning of the previous paragraph;
    Ng.t.2, Sk.t.: put at the beginning of the previous paragraph
15. Ng.t.1: "and" crossed out

sound all this world was manifested.

The story [16] tells that when man was created, first the soul was unwilling to enter the body, saying, "This is a prison, it is dark, and I have always been free." Then God commanded the angels to sing. When they sang, the soul was in such an ecstasy that it entered the body, not knowing where it was going. By music, also, it can be freed from the physical consciousness.

The mother's voice, when she says, "Sleep, sleep", puts the child to sleep, and her voice awakens it again.

In ~~old~~ ancient times music was the sacred art. The great musicians were great mystics. Such were Tansen, ~~of~~ whose miracles are known all over India, Tumbara and Narada [17].

[18, 19]Music produces so great an ecstasy.[19] Even among those musicians who were not mystics, such as Beethoven and [20] Paderewski, you may see that their ecstasy is so great that they have not [21] attention left even to arrange their hair. To brush their coat becomes a very difficult matter for them. In the West and in the East also it is so. In the East you may see a musician going out to play and leaving his sitar at home. His abstraction is so great that even the instrument is forgotten. [18]

By music the highest state, the state of [22] *samadhi* [23], can be produced much more quickly than by any other means.

[24]There are many different practices, but music is the best mystical practice. [24]

---

16. (Ng.t.1)Gd.e.: "story" changed into "Scripture";
    (Ng.t.2)Sr.c.: "Scripture" changed back into "story"
17. Gd.h.: indicated a change in the sequence of "Tumbara and Narada";
    (Ng.t.1)Gd.e.: changed into "Narada and Tumbara";
    Ng.t.2, Sk.t.: "Nerada and Tumbara"
18. (Ng.t.1)Gd.e.: this paragraph, six sentences, moved to the beginning of the previous paragraph;
    Ng.t.2, Sk.t.: put at the beginning of the previous paragraph
19. (Ng.t.2)Sr.c.: this sentence first omitted, then restored
20. Gd.h.: "and" replaced with "or";
    All other documents: "or"
21. Gd.h.: "not" changed into "no";
    all other documents: "no"
22. Gd.h.: "of" changed into "called";
    all other documents: "called"
23. Gd.h.: "by the Yogis" added;
    all other documents: "by the Yogis"
24. (Ng.t.1)Gd.e.: this sentence moved to the beginning of the previous paragraph;
    Ng.t.2, Sk.t.; put at the beginning of the previous paragraph

[25]At the present time, in the East, music has sunk very low. It has been regarded as an amusement, as a diversion. It was regarded as a national possession, as a source of pride [26]to the ego, to the *nafs* [26]. That [27] ~~inheritance of~~ heritage of their fathers, that which had been built up with so great an effort, with so much care, is now being lost, by carelessness, by negligence. In the West, also, music is being brought down. The musician who advertises himself very much, is a great artist. The one who [28]does not advertise [28] is nothing. All [29] is done for money. It is [30] commercialized and degraded. That which should be valued highest is brought down to the lowest circles.

[31]Our work is not only to speak before you, to lecture before you, to bring you the Sufi message in the books and lectures, but to bring it to you also in music, to play before you, to sing before you, ~~to explain before you its~~ , [32]to bring the truth before you [32] in [33] music. In ancient times it was very difficult to speak openly of the truth. The governments [34] were so strict, the religions were so narrow in their interpretation, in their understanding. Especially it was difficult for the Sufis. Many of them have been beheaded for speaking the truth.

The mystics therefore invented a way of speaking the truth in music, in

---

25. (Ng.t.1)Gd.e.: a mark in the margin to indicate a new paragraph;
Ng.t.2, Sk.t.: a new paragraph
26. Gd.h.: first "ego" replaced with "nation", then "ego" restored before "nation", to which was added in Sakina's hwr. "of the" between "ego" and "nation" (to th"e ego of the nation");
Ng.t.1: "to the nation, to the nufs";
(Ng.t.1)Gd.e.: "nufs" changed into "race";
Ng.t.2: "to the nation, to the race";
(Ng.t.2)Sr.c.: "to the ego of the nation, to the *nufs*";
Sk.t.: "to the ego of the nation, to the *nufs*"
27. Gd.h.: "That" changed into "The";
all other documents: "The"
28. Gd.h.: changed into "cannot afford to advertise enough";
all other documents: "cannot afford to advertise enough"
29. Gd.h.: "All" changed into "So much";
all other documents: "So much"
30. Gd.h.: "It is" crossed out, but again restored;
Ng.t.1: "It is" omitted;
Ng.t.2: "It is" omitted;
(Ng.t.2)Sr.c.: "It is" again written in
31. (Ng.t.1)Gd.e.: a mark in the margin to indicate a new paragraph;
Ng.t.2, Sk.t.: a new paragraph
32. Gd.h.: this part of the sentence has been re-ordered to read: "to bring you the truth";
all other documents: "to bring you the truth"
33. Gd.h.: "the realm of" added;
all other documents: "the realm of"
34. Gd.h.: "governments" changed into "governing authorities";
all other documents: "governing authorities"

words [35] that had apparently no meaning [35], such as *tum*, *dim*, *tarana*, *la*, [36], so as to be understood by the initiates, while to the uninitiated it seemed [37] merely a meaningless song. At the present time, even in the East, there are many who do not know that such words have any meaning. They know that the song is called *tarana*; they do not know what it means.

---

35. Gd.h., (Ng.t.1)Gd.e.: indicated that this part of the sentence should be moved after "la"; all other documents: put after "la"
36. Gd.h.: one or two illegible words
37. (Ng.t.1)Gd.e.: "sounded", changed back to "seemed"

Sakina Furnée's shorthand reporting.

Paris [1], [2] December 1922

[3]

[4] Beloved ones of God,

My subject of this evening is "The Word That Was Lost". [4]

This is a symbolical phrase, a paradox [5] of the mystics, which has existed in the East and . . . [6] the wise for ages. Many schools of [7] spiritual cult, of mystical cult, have been formed to understand this particular problem. But the condition is this, that whoever wishes to solve the problem, after he has solved [8]

Documents:

Sk.sh. = Sakina Furnée's shorthand reporting.

E.t. = a copy made from an early typescript of Sk.'s transcription of her shorthand reporting ("Sk.sh.") with some alterations, and in later years preserved by Headquarters, Geneva, on a microfiche.

Sf. = Magazine *Sufism* of September 1923, p. 8-12, an edited version made from "e.t."

Sk.l.tp. = a later typescript made by Sk. from her shorthand reporting, a new transcription made in the 1950's.

Gru.1 = a typescript by Dr. O. C. Gruner of Leeds, England, probably made form "Sf.", with his revisions.

Gru.2 = a second typescript by Dr. Gruner with the corr. and add. incorporated.

As the documents "Gru.1" and "Gru.2" were meant as a preparation of a series of lectures to be published on Pir-o-Murshid's request as a book, *In an Eastern Rosegarden II*, which was never realized, they have not been mentioned in the notes.

Notes:

1. E.t.: "Paris" omitted
2. Sk.sh.: above this lecture in Sk.'s shorthand copybook appears a general date for the lectures which follow, later added by Sk.: "December 1922". After this lecture Sk. took down a lecture dated "3 December 1922, (afternoon)", and therefore it can be assumed that "The Word that was Lost" has been given on 1 or 2 December 1922.
3. Sf.: "THE WORD THAT WAS LOST" as a title;
   Sk.l.tp.: "THE WORD THAT WAS LOST", and added under the title, "(published in Magazine *Sufism* of September 1923)"
4. Sf.: the introductory words ("Beloved . . . that Was Lost'.") omitted
5. Ibid.: ", a paradox" omitted
6. Sk.sh.: first a space, later filled in "on" in sh.;
   e.t., Sf., Sk.l.tp.: "among"
7. Sf.: "the" added
8. All other documents: "it" added

can say[9] very little about it.

There is an ancient story told in the East, [10] that there was a wall of mystery, an ancient wall. And the tradition was that whenever anyone tried to climb upon the wall and looked at[11] the other side of the wall[12], he, instead of coming back, smiled and jumped to[13] the other side, and never came again. But . . .[14] in[15] that country began to become very curious to know what mystery was behind that wall. They thought they must make some arrangement to pull the person back, to tie his feet with chains when he looks at[16] the other side of the wall, [17] when he wishes to go there, to pull him back.[17] There was someone trying to climb on the wall, curious to see what was[18] the other side of the wall[19]. When[7] people saw him climb, they put him seven[20] chains at[21] his feet and held him, [22] that he may[23] not go to[13] the other side of the wall. When he looked at[24] the other side and[25] was delighted with[26] what he saw, and smiled, and those standing [27] at this side, curious what he had to say, the others at this side of the wall[27] pulled him back. But to their great disappointment, when he came back, he lost[28] speech.

The mystery of the whole life has a great charm ~~and~~. Every soul is curious about it, but when one wants to explain the mystery of life, words are [29] not adequate enough to explain[29]. There are many reasons for this

---

9. E.t., Sk.l.tp.: "says" instead of "can say"
10. Sf.: "which tells" added
11. E.t., Sk.l.tp.: "look at";
Sf.: "look on"
12. Sf.: "of the wall" omitted
13. Ibid.: "on" instead of "to"
14. Sk.sh.: an indecipherable word;
e.t., Sk.l.tp.: "people" filled in;
Sf.: "the inhabitants" filled in
15. Sf.: "of" instead of "in"
16. Ibid.: "looked on" instead of "looks at"
17. Ibid.: rewritten to read, "so as to pull him back when he wished to go there"
18. Sk.l.tp.: "on" added
19. Sf.: "of the wall" omitted
20. Ibid.: "him seven" omitted
21. Sk.l.tp., Sf.: "on" instead of "at"
22. Sf.: "so" added
23. Ibid.: "might" instead of "may"
24. Ibid.: "on" instead of "at"
25. Ibid.: "he" instead of "and"
26. Ibid.: "at" instead of "with"
27. Ibid.: rewritten to read, "on the hither side, curious to know what he would have to say"
28. Ibid.: "had lost his" instead of "lost"
29. Ibid.: rewritten to read, "inadequate to explain it"

speechlessness, for this silence. The first thing is that the man who has seen the other side of the wall, finds himself among children. [30] The one who has seen the other side of the wall, [31] to him all things that the[31] people attach great importance and value [32], seem nothing. For that person Truth and fact are two things. For everybody [33] Truth and fact are the same. The followers of different faiths and religions and different opinions and of [34] different ideas, dispute and argue and differ from another [35]. Do they dispute and differ in the realization of Truth? No. All the differences and disputes are caused by the knowledge of [36] various facts, different from one another [37]. There are many facts and one Truth. There are many stars and one sun. When the sun has risen, the stars become pale. [38] The one before whom the sun has risen, the Truth has manifested, for him fact makes little difference. The Light of the Truth falling upon the facts, makes them disappear [39]. It is very interesting to notice that there are many who are deaf and dumb at the same time, and this shows that deafness and dumbness has connection [40]. And according to a certain point of view it is the same thing to be deaf and [41] dumb. It is just like two ends of one line. When you look at the ends, you may say: deaf and dumb. When you look at the line, it is one. Another thing [42] in the same way: [43] perception and expression are the two ends of one line. In other words the faculty of speaking and the sense of hearing is [44] the same. If one is lost, the other is lost. The difference between science and mysticism is very little [45]. Only [46] the difference is that one goes so far and the

---

30. Ibid.: "To" added
31. Ibid.: "all the things to which" instead of "to him all things that the"
32. E.t., Sk.l.tp.: "to" added
33. Sf.: "else" added
34. Sk.l.tp.: "of" omitted
35. Sf.: "each from the other";
    Sk.l.tp.: "from one another"
36. Sf.: "knowledge of" omitted
37. Ibid.: "one from the other" instead of "from one another"
38. Ibid.: "For" added
39. Sk.sh., e.t., Sk.l.tp.: a small blank;
    Sf.: a full stop after "disappear"
40. Sf.: "are connected" instead of "has connection"
41. Ibid.: "to be" added
42. Ibid.: "Another thing" omitted
43. E.t.: "a" added in tp., afterwards replaced with "that" in Sk.'s hwr.;
    Sf.: the colon omitted;
    Sk.l.tp.: "that "added
44. Sf.: "are" instead of "is"
45. Ibid.: "slight" instead of "little"
46. Ibid.: "Only" moved to after "is"

other goes further still. Considering the idea of creation from a material point of view, a scientist goes as far as realizing that there are certain elements that cause the creation and form it into various ~~forms~~ objects. And when he goes further still, he says [47] he goes as far as atoms [48], ~~radiance~~ molecules, electrons, and then he comes to vibrations, and at this end he stands still. He says [49] the basis of the whole creation must be movement, and the finest aspect of movement is called vibrations [50].

When you could [51] come to the mystics, the Vedanta [52] which has existed thousands of years before [52], has said [53], "Nada Brahma", [54] the Word or the Sound or the Vibration was[54] the creative aspect of God. He is not much different [55] from the scientist who says that movement is at [56] the basis of the whole creation. When we read [57] in the Bible, it is said, "First was the Word [57] and the Word was God". When we read in [58] the [59] Qur'an, it is said [60], "*Kul fa kun*" [61], that when [62] the Word manifested, creation followed. [63] Then we find that in reality . . . of [63] the scientist of the day [64] and the conception of the mystics, Teachers of the ancient times [65], one begins to agree with Solomon, that there is nothing new under the sun. [66] Only [67] the difference is that those of

---

47. Ibid.: "he says" omitted
48. Ibid.: "atoms" moved to after "molecules"
49. Ibid.: "that" added
50. Ibid.: "vibration"
51. Ibid.: "could" omitted
52. Ibid.: rewritten to read, "the mystic science of thousands of years ago"
53. Ibid.: "says" instead of "has said"
54. Ibid.: rewritten to read, "Sound-God, or the vibrations are"
55. Ibid.: "He does not differ much" instead of "He is not much different"
56. Ibid.: "at" omitted
57. Ibid.: rewritten to read, "the Bible, we find, 'In the beginning was the Word,' " [John i.1]
58. Ibid.: "in" omitted
59. Sk.l.tp.: "the" omitted
60. Sf.: "we find it says" instead of "it is said"
61. E.t.: "*kulfa kun*";
    Sf.: "*kaunfa u kum*";
    Sk.l.tp.: "*kul fa kum*", then replaced with the correct quotation: "*kun fa yakun*" (Qur'an ii.117 and other Suras)
62. Sf.: "When" instead of "that when"
63. E.t.: later added in Sk.'s hwr. in the open space: "this similarity between";
    Sk.l.tp.: "Then we find in reality . . . of" changed in Sk.'s hwr. into, "When we find this similarity between"
64. Sf.: "today" instead of "the day";
    Sk.l.tp.: "the day" changed by Sk. into "today"
65. Sf.: "the Teachers of ancient times";
    Sk.l.tp.: "the" added before "Teachers"
66. See Old Testament, Ecclesiastes i. 9

the[68] ancient times did not make a limit at this end, which is called movement or vibration, but they have[69] traced its source in the divine Spirit. Now according to the point of view of a mystic, what existed before creation was the Perfect Being. Perfect, not in the sense of the word, but in the sense of the spirit of the word. Because in our everyday conversation "perfect" in[70] many things which are limited. And the spirit of the meaning[71] "perfection" is beyond words. [72] Divine perfection by a mystic is meant by the perfect[73] of [74] wisdom, power, p.[75] of love, p.[75] of peace.[72] But at the same time, when there are eyes, there must be an object to look at, to admire. That is where the purpose of the eyes is fulfilled. When[76] there are ears, there must be a sound to hear and to enjoy[77] its beauty. There is the fulfilment of its[78] existence. Therefore it was necessary for the Perfect Being[79] to realise His Own Perfection, to create a limited perfection to[80] His Own Being. And this is accomplished by One Being[81] divided into three aspects, which is really the secret behind the idea of Trinity: the seer, the seen and the sight. No doubt[82] it is the work of the biologist to explain in detail[83] the gradual development of the creation. But the outline that the mystics[84] of all ages made, was that first[85] was the creation of the mineral

---

67. Sf.: "Only" omitted
68. Ibid.: "the" omitted
69. Ibid.: "have" omitted
70. Sf.: "we use the word perfect of" instead of "'perfect' in";
    Sk.l.tp.: "the word 'perfect' is used in"
71. Sf., Sk.l.tp.: "of" added
72. Sf.: rewritten to read, "By 'Divine Perfection' a mystic means the perfection of beauty, of wisdom, of power, the perfection of love, the perfection of peace.";
    Sk.l.tp.: "Divine perfection by a mystic is meant by the perfection of beauty, wisdom, power, perfection of love, perfection of peace."
73. E.t.: Sk. added "ion" to "perfect" to make "perfection"
74. Sk.sh.: "beauty" inserted by Sk. in lh.;
    e.t., Sk.l.tp.: "beauty," added before "wisdom"
75. "p." filled in by Sk. to read: "perfection"
76. Sf.: "Where" instead of "When"
77. Ibid.: "to be heard and to be enjoyed in"
78. Ibid.: "their" instead of "its"
79. Ibid.: "in order" added
80. Ibid.: "of" instead of "to"
81. "Being" (or "being": there is no capitalization in sh.) could be either a noun or a verbal form
82. Sf.: "No doubt" omitted
83. Ibid.: "the details," instead of "in detail"
84. Sk.l.tp.: "mystic"
85. Sf.: "there" added

kingdom, then[49] of the vegetable, then[49] of animal[86], then[87] of man. But that through all this process of development there has been[88] certain purpose that has led the creation on to the fulfilment of a certain[89] object. But when one[90] studies the whole process, the mineral kingdom, the vegetable[91], the animal[91] and the[92] man, he[93] finds something which was missing and then appearing as the development goes on further. And what is it what[94] was missing? It is the expression and perception, and it is this which the mystics have pointed out in their[95] symbolical expression that[96] "the Word was lost". And what makes[97] them say that the word was lost,[98] was that the Word was[99] in the beginning, there was movement[100], there was the consciousness of the Perfect Being. The rocks are[101] not made, even from a scientific point of view[102], before vibration manifests[103]. It was vibration first and the rocks following[104] after. Only the difference between the mystical and scientifical[105] point of view is this: that the scientist said[106] that from the rock . . . [107] the mystic will say, "No, the rock was

---

86. E.t., Sk.l.tp.: "the animal";
Sf.: "the animal kingdom"
87. Sf.: "and then that" instead of "then"
88. All other documents: "a" added
89. Sf.: "definite" instead of "certain"
90. Ibid.: "he" instead of "one"
91. Ibid.: "kingdom" added
92. E.t., Sk.l.tp.: "then" instead of "the";
Sf.: "the" omitted
93. Sk.sh.: "he" replaced by Sk. with "the seer";
E.t., Sk.l.tp.: "the seer" instead of "he";
Sf.: "then the seer"
94. Sf.: "that" instead of "what"
95. Ibid.: "the" instead of "their"
96. Ibid.: "that" moved to after "Word"
97. Ibid.: "made"
98. Ibid.: a question mark instead of a comma and "It" added
99. E.t.: "the Word was" omitted, then Sk. added "there was" in hwr.;
Sk.l.tp.: "the Word was" omitted, later added by Sk. in ink
100. Sk.sh.: afterwards Sk. added "vibration" in sh.;
e.t.: "vibration," after "movement", then Sk. added "there was" in hwr. before "vibration";
Sf.: ", vibration," added
101. Sf.: "were" instead of "are"
102. Ibid.: "even from a scientific point of view" put in parentheses
103. Ibid.: "manifested"
104. Ibid.: "following" omitted
105. Ibid.: "the scientific" instead of "scientifical"
106. Ibid.: "says" instead of "said"
107. Sk.sh.: a space of half a line;
e.t., Sk.l.tp.: later filled in by Sk. in hwr.: "by a gradual process intelligence developed,";
Sf.: "by a gradual process intelligence developed"

only a grave [108] of intelligence. Intelligence was first and the rock came afterwards."

The whole process of the[68] manifestation suggests that it is working towards some object and that object is [109] one and the same. Yes, there are two points of view to look at [110]. One will say, a mountain will some day . . . [111] into [112] volcano, or, a tree will bear some day fruits [113], and there the object of its being is fulfilled. But again there is another point of view, which is perhaps more perfect [114]: that the stone [115] and trees and animal [116] and man, all are working towards one object and the whole process of the[68] creation is working towards it. And what is that purpose towards which every aspect of this [117] creation is working? What is it that the silent mountains are waiting [118] [119] in the wilderness? What is it that the woods, the trees, are silently [120] waiting[119], what moment, what object? And what is it that all [121] the animals are seeking and searching after besides their [122] food? And what is it that is giving [123] importance to man's every activity, and after the fulfillment of his activity [124] and after every activity[124] draws him to another? It is one object, but covered under many forms. It is the search after that Word, the Word that was lost. The further the creation develops, the greater [125] it longs to . . . [126] this word.

But as there is a gradual process from [7] mineral to [7] human kingdom, so

---

108. Sf.: "grade" instead of "grave";
    Sk.l.tp.: "grave" changed into "grade" by Sk. in ink
109. Sf.: "is" was skipped by mistake in the typesetting
110. Ibid.: "from whence to look at it" instead of "to look at"
111. All other documents: "turn" added
112. Ibid.: "a" added
113. Sf.: reordered to read, "fruits some day"
114. Ibid.: "which is perhaps more perfect" omitted
115. Ibid.: "stones"
116. Ibid.: "animals"
117. Ibid.: "the" instead of "this"
118. Sk.l.tp.: "awaiting" instead of "waiting";
    Sf.: "waiting for"
119. Sf.: "for" added after "waiting";
    Sk.l.tp.: this part of the sentence ("in the wilderness? . . . silently waiting") omitted by mistake in copying the text, and "or" added before "what moment, what object"
120. Sf.: "silently" omitted
121. Ibid.: "all" omitted
122. Ibid.: "their" omitted
123. Ibid.: "gives" instead of "is giving"
124. Ibid.: this phrase omitted
125. Ibid.: "more greatly" instead of "greater"
126. Sk.sh.: a little blank, then filled in "hear" by Sk. in sh.;
    all other documents: "hear" filled in

there also [127] is a gradual process from a certain state of human evolution to a perfect [128] state of human [129] perfection. What is it that gives man [7] inclination to hear a word of admiration, a word of praise which satisfies him? What is[8] that pleases him in hearing the voice, the word of his friend? What is it which [130] charms him in music, in poetry, that gives him a [131] joy? It is the same Word that was lost, appearing in different forms. It seems that creation in its beginning is deaf and dumb--I mean, in the beginning of the material creation. And who feels that [132] pain of realizing to be [133] deaf and dumb? It is that spirit of perfection who [134] has been perfect in perception and ~~inclination~~ expression. The explanation of the soul which Jelal-ud-din Rumi, the great poet, gives in [135] Masnavi, explains [136] this idea in a [137] poetic [138] form. He says, "The soul is as [139] a bird in a cage, deprived of that freedom and that joy which it was accustomed to experience". This also explains the main tragedy of life. Although every man, every soul, has a [140] pain to a certain degree, and the cause of that pain every soul will describe differently, [141] but behind the different causes[141] is one cause, and that cause is this [142] captivity of the soul, in other words, that the Word was lost.

While [143] souls of different stages of evolution wish to search after that [144] Word that was lost in the form in which they are accustomed to search, ... [145] and [146] the ways which are made to search for that[144] Word have become the right

---

127. Sf.: "also" moved to after "is"
128. Ibid.: "perfect" omitted
129. Ibid.: "human" omitted
130. Ibid.: "that" instead of "which"
131. Ibid.: "a" omitted
132. Ibid.: "this" instead of "that"
133. Ibid.: "being" instead of "to be"
134. Ibid.: "which" instead of "who"
135. Ibid.: "his" added
136. Ibid.: "expresses" instead of "explains"
137. Sk.l.tp.: "a" omitted
138. Sf.: "poetical"
139. Ibid.: "like" instead of "as"
140. Ibid.: "suffers" instead of "has a"
141. Ibid.: rewritten to read, "Yet beneath the different causes there"
142. All other documents: "that" instead of "this"
143. Sf.: "While" omitted;
    Sk.l.tp.: "While the", later crossed out by Sk.
144. E.t., Sk.l.tp.: "this" instead of "that"
145. Sk.sh.: a space of half a line;
    e.t., Sf.: a comma instead of an open space;
    Sk.l.tp.: the open space replaced by Sk. with a comma
146. Sf.: rewritten to read, "ways have been made for searching, and these ways have become right ways and wrong ways, sins and virtues"

ways and the wrong ways, and sins and virtues[146]. It is therefore that the wise are[147] tolerant to all, for he sees that every soul has his own way to ~~look~~ follow, his own purpose to accomplish. But in the accomplishment of each[148] purposes is the same[149], and that[132] is the Word which[150] was lost. But no soul will [151]come to get satisfaction unless he will touch that perfection which is ~~meant~~ named[151] in the Bible, "Be you[152] perfect as your Father Who is in Heaven"[153]. Plainly speaking it means that the spirit of God itself has gone through different phases[79] to realize that perfection which, though[154] is[155] limited[156] the perfection of God's own Being, but is[157] intelligible and the satisfaction is there[158].

Now you may ask[159] what explanation you[160] will give to[80] this[161] perfection, what is it, what experience is it? This perfection is which[162] words can never explain, except[163] that the eyes of the soul become open and that from all sides that Word which[162] was lost comes to the ears of his[164] soul. The poets of the East have pictured it in a[131] beautiful imagery in the[68] stories like the[165] Rama and Sita. The joy of this perfection they have explained as a lover who has[166] lost his beloved, who has found[167] her again. But I should say that no imagery can better explain this idea than this picture, that a man who had lost his

---

147. Ibid.: "is" instead of "are"
148. Sk.sh.: "each" cancelled by Sk. and "all these" written by Sk. in sh. instead; all other documents: "all these"
149. Sk.sh.: "same" replaced by Sk. with "one purpose" in sh.; all other documents: "one purpose"
150. Sf., Sk.l.tp.: "that" instead of "which"
151. Ibid.: rewritten to read, "obtain satisfaction unless he touches that perfection which is spoken of"
152. E.t.: "you" crossed out; Sf.: "ye" instead of "you"
153. Sf.: "in Heaven is perfect" instead of "Who is in Heaven" (Matthew v.48)
154. Sk.l.tp.: "though" omitted, later "though it" written in ink by Sk.
155. E.t.: "has" instead of "is"; Sf.: "it" added before "is"; Sk.l.tp.: "has" instead of "is"
156. Sf.: added, "in comparison with"
157. Ibid.: "is yet" instead of "but is"
158. Ibid.: "of the soul is in that" instead of "is there"
159. Sk.l.tp.: "will say that:" instead of "may ask"
160. Sf.: "you" moved to after "will"
161. Ibid.: "that" instead of "this"
162. Ibid.: "what" instead of "which"
163. Ibid.: added, "in saying"
164. Ibid.: "the" instead of "his"
165. Sf.: "that of" instead of "the"; Sk.l.tp.: "the" omitted
166. Sf.: "had" instead of "has"
167. Ibid.: "finding" instead of "who has found"

soul has found it again. Wisdom cannot be called truth. Wisdom is a form in which the souls[49] have realized, have tried to perceive or [168] interpret the world [169] in [170] life to themselves. It is this [171] wisdom which is called in the Greek language *Sophia*, [172] in Persian [173] *Sufi*. Wisdom is the interpretation of life made by someone whose point of view has become different by looking at life in the sunlight.

By the Sufi Message it [174] is meant the Message of Wisdom. It is more a point of view than any teaching or dogmas [175] or ceremonies [176]. Of course [177] one arrives at this point of view, not only by study, but by association of those of [178] that particular point of view. Besides, by diving deep into life, that [179] one comes to the realization of Truth. And for diving deep into life there is a way or [180] process. It is possible that with some difficulty or ease one might [181] find out a place one is looking for in a town, [182] but by asking one who knows, one can find it sooner. [183]Sufi movement therefore gives [184] the[68] facility of studying, of [185] coming into [186] contact with those of the same point of view, and of knowing [187] ways [188], by [189] which one comes to realization [190], which are [191]

---

168. Ibid.: "and to" instead of "or"
169. E.t.: Sk. wrote "Word" instead of "world";
Sk.l.tp.: "Word" instead of "world"
170. Sf.: "and" instead of "in"
171. Ibid.: "this" omitted
172. Ibid.: "and" added
173. Sk.sh.: it is not clear if "Persia" or "Persian" was written in lh.;
Sk.l.tp.: "Persia", later changed by Sk. into "Persian"
174. Sf.: "it" omitted
175. Ibid.: "dogma"
176. Ibid.: "theory" instead of "ceremonies"
177. Ibid.: "Of course" omitted
178. Ibid.: "with those who have" instead of "of those of"
179. Sf., Sk.l.tp.: "that" omitted
180. Sf.: "or a" instead of "or";
Sk.l.tp.: "of" instead of "or"
181. Sf.: "may" instead of "might"
182. Ibid.: added, "one may look for it in different directions and at last find it."
183. All other documents: "The" added
184. Sf.: "to each" added
185. Sk.l.tp.: "or"; later changed by Sk. into "of"
186. Sf.: "in" instead of "into"
187. Sk.l.tp.: "of knowing" changed by Sk. in ink into "it knows"
188. Sf.: "the process" instead of "ways"
189. Ibid.: "through" instead of "by"
190. Sf.: "that realisation" instead of "realization";
Sk.l.tp.: "realizations"
191. Sf.: "is" instead of "are"

necessary in the Path.

[192] Thank you all for [193] sympathetic response.

May God bless you. [192]

---

192. Ibid.: the closing words omitted
193. E.t.: "your" added by Sk. in hwr.; Sk.l.tp.: "your" added

Sakina Furnée's shorthand reporting.

Paris[1], December 3rd, 1922

2

Beloved ones of God,[3]

My subject of this afternoon is "The Alchemy of Happiness".

This phrase, alchemy of happiness, is not an unusual phrase to the East. For as[4] everything in the outer world is made and can be made by a chemical process, so[5] there is a chemical process also by which the things of the inner life can be made. If one looks at life from this point of view, one will find that the whole world is working according to some chemical process. But in the oriental language chemistry is specially[6] understood as a process of making gold, gold which is the most valuable of all metals. And making of the[7] gold of life is like making the[8] life most valuable. Besides, gold is [9]a symbolical expression of[9] light. And what does it suggest? It suggests that even a material person, who

---

Documents:

Sk.sh. = a transcription of Sakina Furnée's shorthand reporting.

E.t. = a copy made from an early typescript of Sk.'s shorthand reporting (Sk.sh.) with some alterations, and in later years preserved by Hq., Geneva, on a microfiche.

Sk.h. = a hwr. copy made by Sk. either by again transcribing her shorthand reporting, or by copying her first transcription (e.t.), with a few light corr.;
(Sk.h.)Sk.: Sk.'s later editing, for which she used the "Sk.h."

Sk.l.tp. = a later typescript made by Sk. or under her direction from "e.t." Only a part of the later corr. and add. in "(Sk.h.)Sk." has been incorporated in this typescript; mostly it goes back to "Sk.sh." and e.t."

Notes:

1. Sk.h.: "Paris" replaced with "*Au Musée Guimet*"
2. Sk.h.: title added, "The Alchemy of Happiness";
   (Sk.h.)Sk.: added above the lecture by Sk., at different times: "In handwriting Sakina", "reported by Sakina", "typed and sent to Hq."
3. (Sk.h.)Sk.: "Beloved ones of God" crossed out
4. Sk.h.: "as" omitted
5. (Sk.h.)Sk.: ", so" changed into ". So"
6. Ibid.: "especially"
7. Ibid.: "of the" crossed out
8. Ibid.: "the" crossed out
9. Ibid.: reordered to read, "an expression symbolical of"

is after [10] the pursuit of gold, is really after[10] the[8] pursuit of light. In short, all those material [11] or spiritual [12], directly or indirectly are searching for light.

Now the question is, what is happiness, what can be the definition of the word? There cannot be [13] better definition of happiness than the feeling of one's natural self. As the body is made of matter, its sustenance is matter, so the soul of man is happiness itself and it is happiness which sustains it. In the Vedanta of the Hindus, the soul's existence is called *ananda*, which means happiness. But in our everyday life we confuse these words, such as happiness, pleasure and joy. We do not always use them in their [14] place. And owing to that [15] confusion in the [16] language man, so to speak, gets out of touch with that happiness which is the seeking [17] of his soul. The greatest tragedy of [18] life is man's search for happiness in the domains where his happiness does not exist. The life outside responds to his inner yearning of [19] happiness, but responds for how long? For a moment. But the intoxication that the life outside produces in man is so great that if all through life man had failure after failure, he would still remain in this [20] intoxication, ~~he would not see~~ The nature of the life of illusion which is before man is such as if there is [21] a cover under a cover of illusion, and when one cover is removed, there is another cover to . . . [22] man. To [23] a person who would stand outside of life and look at the life as a spectator [24], and not [25] one in the world, will find that man is continually seeking after what he does not know. For [26] instance: [27] take a continually grudging life[27] and give him what he wants.

---

10. Ibid.: "after" changed into "in"
11. E.t.: "materially" instead of "material" (referring to "searching" and not to "those"); Sk.l.tp.: "materially"
12. E.t.: "spiritually" instead of "spiritual" (referring to "searching" and not to "those"; Sk.l.tp.: "spiritually"
13. Sk.h.: "a" added
14. Sk. added "proper" in sh.; all other documents: "proper" added
15. E.t., Sk.l.tp.: "this" instead of "that"
16. (Sk.h.)Sk.: "the" crossed out
17. Sk.h.: "language" instead of "seeking" (misreading the sh.?)
18. Ibid.: "in" instead of "of"
19. Ibid.: "of" replaced with "for"
20. All other documents: "that" instead of "this"
21. (Sk.h.)Sk.: "is" changed into "were"
22. Sk.sh.: an open space; all other documents: "delude" filled in
23. Sk.l.tp.: "To" crossed out
24. Sk.h.: "picture" instead of "spectator"
25. Sk.sh.: a small blank between "not" and "one"; Sk.l.tp.: Sk. added "as" in the margin
26. E.t., Sk.h., Sk.l.tp.: "an" added; (Sk.h.)Sk.: "an" crossed out

Next day you will see him pursuing after something else, unhappy just the same. Give him . . .[28], next day he will again be unhappy. What does it mean? It means that man in this life is like a drunken man. Give him one glass, he wants another; give him another and he wants another. He is never satisfied. He is not to be blamed for it, because man in this world is limited and his soul belongs to [29]unlimited. And that spark of that perfect being, which man represents in his soul, can never be satisfied in this life. But not only that reason, but there is a reason besides; and that is the key to[30] which his soul constantly yearns as[31] a secret, and everyone does not find[32] it. And it is that key which is called "alchemy of happiness" in the words of [33]mystics. Those who have understood its real meaning, they have tried their best to get that key. Those who have not ~~found~~ understood its meaning have tried to find the real[34] gold. And both have attained to it, for even [35]making the[8] gold, it is necessary for making it[36] to know the key. The process of making gold as explained in the symbolical language of the Hindus, is as follows: the first thing that the alchemist does, is that he tries to make the m. mutery stan[37], and he does it by putting into it the juice of a certain herb. When once the mercury becomes still, then he puts it into the fire, until it turns into ashes. He takes those[38] ashes again and puts into it a certain juice of herbs, and the grains of the ashes become[39] together, and turn into gold. Now this is the explanation of all the alchemists, those striving[40]

---

27. (Sk.h.)Sk.: rewritten to read, "take one who is continually grudging in life, grumbling, complaining and dissatisfied", but later "complaining" crossed out;
Sk.l.tp.: as in "(Sk.h.)Sk." without "complaining"
28. E.t.: "again" filled in;
Sk.h.: "again what he asks for, and" added;
Sk.l.tp.: "again next day what he asks for, and" added
29. (Sk.h.)Sk.: "the" added;
Sk.l.tp.: "the"
30. (Sk.h.)Sk.: "to" changed into "for";
Sk.l.tp.: "for"
31. E.t., Sk.l.tp.: "is" instead of "as"
32. Sk.sh.: Sk. wrote "possess" above "find" in sh.;
all other documents: "possess"
33. Sk.h., Sk.l.tp.: "the" added
34. All other documents: "material" instead of "real"
35. (Sk.h.)Sk.: "for" added
36. Ibid.: "for making it" crossed out
37. Sk.h.: "mercury . . . " instead of "m. mutery stan";
(Sk.h.)Sk.: "mercury steady";
Sk.l.tp.: "mercury still"
38. All other documents: "these" instead of "those"
39. (Sk.h.)Sk.: "become" changed into "come"
40. E.t.: "after" added;
Sk.h.: a blank, (Sk.h.)Sk.: filled in "after";
Sk.l.tp.: "after"

their[41] ideal spiritual[42] or material[43]. And the mystical interpretation of this[44] theory is that mind is like mercury. The mind feels itself alive when it is active in thinking, in imagining, and therefore [45]mind has never rest during day or night. In the day man works, at night he dreams; both times the mind is at work. Now if this m.[46] is made still, then the first process is that it turns into silver, which means, when[47] the mind becomes still, ~~is the moment~~ man's life becomes valuable. He need not be [48]a spiritual man or a . . .[48]; [49]be he a businessman, . . . whatever be his occupation in life[49], [50]he will be more valuable in life[50]. And if[51] man is pious, religious, spiritual, whose mind is not still, he is not really spiritual, he does not know the secret of . . .[52]. What is the reason? The reason is that every soul has its own domain, and that[45] soul is supposed to be the king of that domain. And it is[53] the extent of the power that man has to make his mind still, according to that he can control and rule his domain in life. And when man [54]lacks to control and rule[54] his domain, whatever be his external position in life, he cannot experience happiness in life. According to the idea of the mystic, wrong is that ~~what~~ which is not in its time and not in its proper place. When man cannot control and rule his domain, then, whatever he does with good intention or evil intention, is wrong. Nothing he will do which is right, nothing he will do which is good. Even if he had an intention to do good, he cannot do good, for he is not the king of his kingdom. If [55]individual ~~se~~

---

41. E.t.: "the" instead of "their";
    Sk.h., Sk.l.tp.: "the"
42. E.t., Sk.l.tp.: "spiritually"
43. Ibid.: "materially"
44. Sk.h.: "that" instead of "this"
45. Ibid.: "the" added
46. All other documents: "mercury"
47. Ibid.: "the moment" instead of "when"
48. Sk.sh.: in the small blank after "a spiritual man or a" appears the first letter of a word in sh., which may well be a "p", so "pious man" may have been said;
    e.t.: "a spiritual man or a pious man";
    (Sk.h.)Sk.: "~~as~~ a religious man or a spiritual man";
    Sk.l.tp.: "a spiritual man or a pious (religious) man"
49. (Sk.h.)Sk.: "if he be a businessman, or in whatever walk in life"
50. Sk.sh.: "become" written above "be";
    e.t., Sk.h., Sk.l.tp.: "he will become more valuable in life";
    (Sk.h.)Sk.: "his life becomes more valuable"
51. (Sk.h.)Sk., Sk.l.tp.: "a" added
52. Ibid.: "happiness" filled in
53. (Sk.h.)Sk.: "to" added;
    Sk.l.tp.: "to"
54. (Sk.h.)Sk.: rewritten to read, "is lacking in controlling and ruling"
55. E.t., Sk.l.tp.: "individuals realise";
    Sk.h.: "an individual realises", (Sk.h.)Sk.: "individuals realise"

realizes[55] that great lack in themselves [56], what do you think that the condition of this world today will be [57]? What has caused this [58] present upheaval of nations and of races and of the world in general? What is it that has caused such an upset in the business world? It seems that nowhere there seems to be a satisfactory . . . [59] It all shows that man has lost the key to his [60] domain. And as he cannot get it himself, he wants to snatch the key out of the hands of others, and there is a conflict in life. A man who would look at life from a different point of view, whose sight is deep, [61] will see the picture as I explained [62] the picture before you [63]: [64] as the drunken man[64] pushing up against each other, snatching out of each other's hand [65], not knowing what they are doing, what they are, what they will [66].

Life has various interests, and numerous [67] occupations, and life has one theme, and if that theme is not right, the whole life becomes spoiled. It seems that man today has lost touch with his own soul. He is seeking for something which he does not know, and in that [68] way he is out of sorts [69]. And the lack of this all [70] which results into [71] a loss to the world in general in one way or another; it is [72] all caused by that wrong theme.

But now we have come in explaining [73] the process as far as[73] stilling [74]

---

56. Sk.h.: "himself";
    (Sk.h.)Sk.: "themselves"
57. (Sk.h.)Sk.: "be" changed into "become"
58. Sk.h.: "the" instead of "this"
59. Sk.h.: a blank;
    (Sk.h.)Sk.: first filled in "answer", then "answer" replaced with "state of things";
    Sk.l.tp.: ". . . of things(?) . . .", then in hwr. filled in the word "state" before "of things(?)"
60. E.t.: "this" instead of "his"
61. Sk.h.: "whose sight is deep," omitted
62. E.t., Sk.l.tp.: "explain"
63. Sk.h.: "it before to you" instead of "the picture before you"
64. E.t.: "as the drunken men";
    Sk.h.: "as that of the drunken man", (Sk.h.)Sk.: "man" changed into "men";
    Sk.l.tp.: "as that of the drunken men", with "the" later put in parentheses by Sk.
65. All other documents: "hands"
66. (Sk.h.)Sk.: "will" changed into "want"
67. E.t.: "amusements" instead of "numerous", probably a misreading of the shorthand
68. Sk.h.: "this" instead of "that"
69. Sk.sh.: "source" was taken down, but Sk.'s later corrections show that she must have been unfamiliar with this English idiom;
    Sk.h.: an open space;
    (Sk.h.)Sk.: "control" filled in;
    Sk.l.tp.: "source", with "tune?" written by Sk. in the margin
70. Sk.h.: "is" instead of "all"
71. (Sk.h.)Sk.: "into" changed into "in"
72. All other documents: "is" moved to after "all"
73. (Sk.h.)Sk.: reordered to read "as far as the process"

the mind. But [75]once the mind is stilled[75], man has got power over his domain to make his life more valuable, more is needed. He may benefit by it and he may lose it, because after all it is power; power which is not balanced with wisdom [76]can no longer exist[76]. The man who possesses power [77]is 2 more drunk[77]; in the first place power makes him drunk [78] and ~~the~~ next the life in exterior . . . [79] There are many people who make success in business, success after success. And [80] there comes a moment [81] when [82]it drops down[82] in a [83] moment. Very often one sees a person go [84] higher and higher in his position [85], and [86] reach [87] a place from where he drops down again. It is like a child, give [88]in his hand as[88] a toy, a sword, he will go in the garden, cutting each tree [89], till [90] the sword is broken in his hand.

The idea of every soul in this soul [91] is to attain to that perfection, [92] as

---

74. Ibid.: "of" added
75. Sk.sh.: in sh. the sign for "still" is also used for "stilled";
    Sk.h.: "but" followed by a short illegible word, "the mind is still";
    (Sk.h.)Sk.: "But when the mind is stilled"
76. (Sk.h.)Sk.: "can not exist long";
    Sk.l.tp.: "cannot exist long"
77. E.t., Sk.l.tp.: "is twice more drunken";
    Sk.h.: "is got more drunk; (the number "2", written in "Sk.sh." may have been read for a sh. "g", hence "got");
    (Sk.h.)Sk.: "is the more drunken"
78. E.t., Sk.l.tp.: "drunken"
79. (Sk.h.)Sk.: "exterior" omitted and filled in "the world is in itself intoxicating";
    Sk.l.tp.: "the world is in itself intoxicating", but Sk. added "exterior" in the margin, before "world"
80. Sk.h.: "And" replaced with "then"
81. Ibid.: "moment" replaced with "time"
82. E.t.: "down" first omitted, then inserted in hwr.;
    Sk.h., Sk.l.tp.: "they drop down" instead of "it drops down"
83. Sk.h., Sk.l.tp.: "one" instead of "a"
84. Sk.h.: "goes";
    (Sk.h.)Sk.: the "s" on "goes" crossed out, probably intending "go";
    Sk.l.tp.: "goes"
85. (Sk.h.)Sk.: "and rank" added;
    Sk.l.tp.: "and rank"
86. (Sk.h.)Sk.: "then" added;
    Sk.l.tp.: "then"
87. E.t., Sk.l.tp.: "reaches";
    Sk.h.: "reaches";
    (Sk.h.)Sk.: "reach"
88. Sk.h.: "him in his hand as";
    (Sk.h.)Sk.: "put in his hand"
89. (Sk.h.)Sk.: "and slashing at the trees" instead of "each tree"
90. Ibid.: "until" instead of "till"
91. Sk.h.: "in this soul" omitted;
    e.t., Sk.l.tp.: "in this world"
92. Sk.h.: "as is spoken of";
    (Sk.h.)Sk.: "which is spoken of"

is spoken[92] in the Bible: "Be you [93] perfect as is your Father in Heaven". [94] It does not matter what be his occupation in life, in what way he is going, only [95] the idea is to reach [96] perfection upon all that perfection which [97] is the *but* [98] of the [99] soul born on earth. When going to explain [100] the process . . . [101] after it is made into silver, it goes [102] into the fire. That [103] fire is a natural fire, which is in the heart of man, and that is love. Its first aspect is warm, its next aspect is hot, its third aspect is flame or light. In the first aspect, when this fire is beginning to burn, a person feels sympathetic towards those around him, with those with whom he comes into [104] contact. He appreciates music, he enjoys poetry, he feels living [105] all things around him. But when it turns hot, it is not only that he is enjoying, but he is suffering [106] with those who are suffering [107]pain, with those who have pain [107], [108]he feels with all those, the suffering of the whole universe [108]. When this[44] fire becomes more [109], it rises as a flame and that flame becomes as a torch in the path of man. And when mind which is stilled is put in this fire, then its true nature which is love, which is God, comes

---

93. All other documents: "ye" instead of "you"
94. Matt. v.48
95. (Sk.h.)Sk.: "only" moved to after "the idea is"
96. Ibid.: "that" added
97. E.t.: "and that perfection" instead of "upon all that perfection which";
    Sk.h.: "upon all that perfection" omitted;
    Sk.l.tp.: "and in that perfection" instead of "upon all that perfection which"
98. Sk.sh.: the French word "but" ("end, purpose") was written;
    e.t., Sk.l.tp.: "purpose";
    Sk.h.: "goal"
99. (Sk.h.)Sk.: "the" changed into "every"
100. Ibid.: "coming to the explanation of" instead of "going to explain"
101. E.t.: filled in "of the alchemist";
    Sk.h., Sk.l.tp.: "of the alchemist"
102. (Sk.h.)Sk.: "goes" changed into "is put"
103. All other documents: "This" instead of "That"
104. E.t.: "into", changed in hwr. to "in";
    (Sk.h.)Sk.: "in" instead of "into"
105. (Sk.h.)Sk.: "to" added;
    Sk.l.tp.: "to"
106. (Sk.h.)Sk.: "is suffering" changed into "suffers"
107. E.t.: ", has pain with those who have pain";
    Sk.h.: "he feels pain with those that have pain";
    (Sk.h.)Sk.: "He feels pain with those who are in pain";
    Sk.l.tp.: "He feels pain with those who have pain"
108. Sk.h.: "He feels the suffering of the whole humanity (universe)";
    (Sk.h.)Sk.: "He feels the sufferings of the whole humanity of the universe";
    Sk.l.tp.: "he feels the suffering of the whole humanity of the universe"
109. (Sk.h.)Sk.: "more" replaced with "increased"

out. After having gone through this process, after the heart has . . .[110] into the grains of ashes, [111]when the divine knowledge of unity which unites all nations, all races, the grains join together and turn into gold.[111]

What [112]this whole process suggests?[112] It suggests that it is wisdom, not only an intellectuality, but wisdom in its pure essence, which is the key to true happiness. Wisdom which is called in the Eastern or Western part of the world [113]*Sophia* or *Sufia*[113], it [114] is the means by which the nations, the races and the people of different parts of the world may come together to [115] a [116] better understanding. Therefore the work of the Sufi movement in this world is only devoted to bring about that understanding by the means of spreading ~~that~~ wisdom. [117]While working to bring about [118] better understanding[117] [119]those who wish [120] perhaps a deeper knowledge, a greater explanation of . . . [121], [122]they are given a helping hand [122].

[123]Thank you all for your sympathetic response.

May God bless you.[123]

---

110. (Sk.h.)Sk.: "turned" filled in;
Sk.l.tp.: "turned"
111. (Sk.h.)Sk.: rewritten to read, "then the realization of the divine knowledge of the unity of all nations, races of the whole universe unites the grains and turns them into gold";
Sk.l.tp.: "then the divine knowledge of unity which unite all nations, all races, of the whole universe, the grains join together, and turn into gold."
112. (Sk.h.)Sk.: "does this whole process suggest?"
113. All other documents: "Sufi or Sophia"
114. E.t., Sk.l.tp.: "it" omitted
115. (Sk.h.)Sk.: "to" changed into "in"
116. E.t.: "a" first omitted, then inserted in hwr.
117. (Sk.h.)Sk.: this phrase was crossed out
118. Sk.h., Sk.l.tp.: "a" added
119. Sk.h.: "And" added
120. Sk.h.: "for" added;
(Sk.h.)Sk.: "for" crossed out
121. E.t.: "this world" added;
Sk.h.: "this work" filled in;
Sk.l.tp.: "this work (world)?"
122. All other documents: "to them a helping hand is given"
123. Sk.h.: the closing sentences omitted

Sakina's Furnée's shorthand reporting.

6[1] December 1922. Dinsdag. Rue St. Séverin[2]

3 [4]This evening I would like to speak on music.

Documents:

Sk.sh. = Sakina Furnée's shorthand reporting of the beginning of a lecture, taken down on 5th December 1922 on page 17 of one of Sk.'s shorthand copybooks of 1922/1923. Later Sk. added in the margin: "Beginning of 'Music' " In the same copybook, on page 20, appears a lecture on music, given on 18th or 19th December 1922. In the margin is written in Dutch: "begin 2 blz. eerder", meaning "beginning 2 pages back"

Lf. = a later hwr. copy made by M.lle Lefèbvre from her reporting of the lecture "Music" of 5th December 1922, in a simultaneous French translation, sentence by sentence, combined with the simultaneous French translation of the lecture on music of 18/19 December 1922. She put the combined texts under the date of 19 December 1922. Differences between this translated reporting and Sakina's shorthand reporting are not mentioned in the notes.

Hq.st.1 = a stencilled copy made from "Sk.sh." at headquarters, Geneva, in the form of a Social Gatheka, of the combined texts of the lectures on music of 5th and 19th December. It became nr. 23 in the series "Social Gathekas"

Gd.t. = a later copy of the by Sherifa Goodenough edited text of "Sk.sh." of 5th and 19th December 1922, made after 1927 on Gd.'s typewriter with large letters into one lecture

Hq.t. = a later typescript copied from an earlier "Hq.t.", with some editing, made at Headquarters, Geneva, in the form of a Social Gatheka from "Hq.st.1" and "Gd.t.", in which the lectures of 5th and 19th December 1922 appear as one lecture.

Hq.st.2 = a second stencilled copy, made from "Gd.t." at Headquarters, Geneva, in the form of a Social Gatheka. It became nr. 37, probably erroneously added to this series a second time. Also this document shows the texts of 5th and 19th December 1922 on music as one lecture.

Notes:

1. Sk.sh.: later Sk. corrected "6 Dec." to "5 Dec.", which was a Tuesday ("Dinsdag", the Dutch word for "Tuesday") written above by Sk.
   Gd.t.: the date of 19th December was given to the combined texts of 5th and 19th December 1922.
2. An annotation in Sk.'s hwr. in one of her copybooks from 1922 reads: "Saturday, Monday, Tuesday: lectures Rue St. Séverin 16."
   Gd.t.: "Paris" added
3. Gd.t.: "PUBLIC LECTURE" added above;
   Hq.st. 1, Hq.t.: "SOCIAL GATHEKA Number 23" followed by the Invocation;
   Hq.st. 2: "SOCIAL GATHEKA. Number 37" followed by the Invocation.
4. All other documents: this first sentence omitted and added "Music" as a title

Many in the world take music as a source of amusement or[5] pastime, and to many music is an art, and a musician an entertainer. Yet no one has lived in this world who had[6] thought and felt, and had[7] not considered music as the most sacred of all arts[8], for the fact that what the art of painting cannot clearly suggest, poetry explains it[9] in words, but that which even a poet finds difficult to express in poetry, is expressed in music. But by this I do not only say that music is superior to art[10] and poetry, but[11] in the point of fact music excels religion, for music rises[12] the soul of man even higher than[13] so called external form of religion. But by this it must not be understood that music can take[14] place of religion. For every soul is not necessarily tuned to that pitch that[15] can really benefit by music. Nor[16] every music is[16] necessarily so high that it will exalt a person who will hear[17] it more than the effect that religion will make[18] upon him. However, those who follow the path of the inner cult, for them music is most essential for their spiritual development. The reason is that the soul who is seeking for truth[19], is in search of the formless God. Art no doubt is most elevating, but at the same time[20] contains form. Poetry has words, names suggestive of forms[21]. [22]

---

5. Gd.t.; Hq.st.2: "or" replaced with a comma
6. All other documents: "has" instead of "had"
7. Hq.st.1, Hq.t.: "has" instead of "had"
8. Ibid.: ". For the fact is" instead of ", for the fact"
9. All other documents: "it" omitted
10. Hq.st.1, Hq.t.: "art" changed into "painting"
11. Hq.st.1, Hq.t.: "in fact" instead of "in the point of fact"; Gd.t.: "in point of fact"
12. All other documents: "raises"
13. Ibid.: "the" added
14. Hq.st.1, Gd.t., Hq.st.2: "the" added
15. All other documents: "it" added
16. Ibid.: "is" moved to after "Nor"
17. Hq.st.1., Hq.t.: "will hear" changed into "hears"
18. Ibid.: "make" changed into "have"
19. Gd.t., Hq.st.2: "that" instead of "truth"
20. Ibid.: "it" added
21. Ibid.: "form" instead of "forms"
22. All other documents: here begins the text of the lecture on "Music" given on 19th December 1922, q.v.

Sakina Furnée's shorthand reporting.

1 2

Sadhana, or the Attainment.[3]

The secret of the working of the whole universe is in [4]duality of

---

Documents:

Sk.sh.	=	Sakina Furnée's shorthand reporting, taken down in a small green copybook containing reportings of lectures given in November and December 1922 in Paris.
Hl.	=	a reporting by Mademoiselle C. Hulot of a simultaneous translation into French of the lecture given in English, sentence by sentence. This document is not mentioned in the notes.
Hl.t.	=	a typewritten and edited copy of "Hl.", not mentioned in the notes.
Sk.t.	=	a typescript made from "Sk.sh.", in which the corr. made by Sk. in her shorthand reporting have been incorporated.
Sk.l.tr.	=	Sakina Furnée's later transcription in handwriting of her shorthand reporting, with several inaccuracies; (Sk.l.tr.) Gd.e.: corr. and alterations in light blue ink made by Sherifa Goodenough.
tp.c.	=	a typescript made from "Sk.l.tr." with "(Sk.l.tr.) Gd.e." incorporated.
Hq.st.	=	a stencilled copy issued by International Headquarters, Geneva, made from "tp.c."
Sk.c.tp.	=	a neat, typewritten copy made by Sk. in later years from "Sk.t."

Notes:

1. Sk.sh.: afterwards Sk. added above the lecture an indication that it had been included in the "Gita" series as "Series II,4";
   (Sk.l.tr.) Gd.e.: later added, "Series II. Number 1." Afterwards Sk. changed "1" into "4" with the annotation in pencil, "In stencilled copy issued from I.Hq. this has become "Series II no. 4.";
   tp.c.: added "Series II, Number 4.";
   Hq.st.: added "Series II. GITHA. Number 4.", followed by the Invocation
2. Sk.t.: "December 1922, Paris", and later added a "6" by Sk. in hwr. before "December";
   tp.c.: later added by Sk. in ink: "Paris, December 1922";
   Sk.c.tp.: "December 1922, Paris"
3. Sk.sh.: "I" added before the title; later Sk. added in lh. after the title the first part of the first sentence: "The secret of the working of the whole universe...";
   Sk.t.: later written in ink after the title, "(has become Gita II,4).";
   Sk.l.tr.: "Sadhana I or the Attainment."

nature[5]. In all aspects of nature these two forces are working, and it is the working of these two forces which balances life. Therefore in the [6] attainment not only power, which manifests as enthusiasm [7] or action, is sufficient, but besides power (enthusiasm), knowledge and the capability of working is necessary.

Very often a person fails to attain success, with all his enthusiasm and power of [8] will, and the reason is [9] either by the power he has he pushes along his object, like a ball, or with his strength he hammers the rock, which he really needs as a whole, and not into [10] pieces. Power is, no doubt, most necessary in the[6] attainment, but in absence of knowledge the power may become [11] helpless and . . . . [12] By power I mean power in all aspects: the power that one possesses in the outward life, and the power of mind and body. It is the power of mind which is called will power. No doubt, many with knowledge, but lacking [13] power, also ~~come to~~ meet with failure. If an object is pulled [14]both sides, by power and [15]knowledge, then also there will

---

(Sk.l.tr.) Gd.e.: "I or" crossed out and changed the title into, "Sadhana. The Path of Attainment.";
tp.c.: the title omitted;
Hq.st.: "SADHANA. THE PATH OF ATTAINMENT.";
Sk.c.tp.: "SADHANA, the ATTAINMENT."

4. (Sk.l.tr.) Gd.e.: "the" added;
tp.c., Hq.st.: "the"
5. Sk.l.tr.: "matter" instead of "nature", later restored by Sk. to "nature"
6. (Sk.l.tr.) Gd.e.: "the" crossed out;
tp.c., Hq.st.: "the" omitted
7. Sk.l.tr.: "attainment", afterwards changed back by Sk. to "enthusiasm"
8. Sk.l.tr.: "and" instead of "of";
tp.c.: "and", changed back to "of" in ink by Sk.;
Hq.st.: "and"
9. Sk.sh.: afterwards Sk. added "that" in sh.;
all other documents: "that" added
10. (Sk.l.tr.) Gd.e.: "into" changed to "in";
tp.c., Hq.st.: "in" instead of "into"
11. Sk.sh.: afterwards Sk. replaced "become" in sh. with "prove";
all other documents: "prove" in place of "become"
12. Sk.sh.: the end of the sentence was missed;
Sk.t., Sk.l.tr., Sk.c.tp.: "and" omitted and a space left open;
(Sk.l.tr.) Gd.e., tp.c., Hq.st.: "and" omitted and no space left open
13. Sk.l.tr.: first written "will-power", then Sk. crossed out "will"
14. (Sk.l.tr.) Gd.e.: "from" added;

not be a success. It is the cooperation of these two powers which is the secret of all success. Success, be it of the[6] material character or of some other nature, it[16] is always a success. Success, however small, is a step forward to something great, and failure, however small, it[16] is a failure; it leads to something still worse. Success must not be valued from its outer value, it must be valued from what it prepares in oneself[17]. And failure, however small, has[18] an undesirable impression in oneself. That[19] shows how very necessary it is to keep the balance between power and knowledge.

It is of a very great value to try and develop in life power and knowledge in attaining one's object. Therefore[20] are two[21] people who become tired of the life in the world: [22]one who has risen above the world, and the one who has fallen beneath the world.[22] The former has attained his object, but the latter, even if he left the world, any other life would not satisfy him. His renunciation of worldly things means nothing. It only means incapability[23]. It is the conqueror of the[24] life of the world who has the right to give up the struggle of the world if he wishes to. But [25]from whose hands the life of the world is snatched away from[26] his fellow-man[27], and who is

---

tp.c., Hq.st.: "from"
15. (Sk.l.tr.) Gd.e.: "by" added;
tp.c., Hq.st.: "by"
16. (Sk.l.tr.) Gd.e.: "it" crossed out;
tp.c., Hq.st.: "it" omitted
17. Sk.l.tr.: "one's life self", then changed back to "oneself"
18. (Sk.l.tr.) Gd.e.: "has" changed into "makes";
tp.c., Hq.st.: "makes", but written by Sk. in the margin of tp.c.: "(has)", as was said, but indicating that "makes" would be better
19. All other documents: "This" instead of "That"
20. Sk.sh.: although "Therefore" seems to be written in the sh.r., all other documents have "There"
21. Sk.l.tr.: "kinds of" added in parentheses; (Sk.l.tr.)Gd.e.: the parentheses omitted;
tp.c., Hq.st.: "kinds of" added
22. Sk.l.tr.: this phrase, "one who has risen . . . beneath the world." was skipped when the lecture was again transcribed, but later added by Sk. at the bottom of the page
23. (Sk.l.tr.) Gd.e.: "incapability" changed into "incapacity";
tp.c.: "incapacity", but Sk. added "(incapability)" in the margin, as was said, indicating, however, that "incapacity" might be the right word to be used here;
Hq.st.: "incapacity"
24. Sk.l.tr.: "the" omitted, but later added by Sk.
25. (Sk.l.tr.) Gd.e.: "he" added;
tp.c., Hq.st.: "he"
26. (Sk.l.tr.) Gd.e.: "from" changed into "by";
tp.c., Hq.st.: "by" instead of "from"
27. Sk.t., Sk.c.tp.: "fellow-men", although in Sk.sh. "fellow-man" is clearly taken down

incapable of holding it, who cannot progress, who cannot attain in life what he wishes to attain, if he left the world, it is not renunciation, it is simply poverty. It is not by any means selfishness or avaraciousness [28] to want to succeed in life. For by success man is climbing [29] upward. Only, when intoxicated by his worldly success, he closes his eyes to the further path, [30]he stands still, and that standing still is like death.

The many successful people, whom we see in this world, who [31] do not spiritually [32] progress, it [33] means that ~~they do not continually progress~~ they did not ~~travel~~ continue in the path of success. In reality all roads lead to the same goal: business, profession, science [34], art, religion or philosophy. When people do not seem to have arrived at the [35] proper destination, it is not because they have preferred one path to another path. It is that they have not continued [36] the path. Very often people lacking knowledge, and with strength more than necessary, destroy their own purpose. While wanting to construct, they cause destruction. The greatest fault of human nature is that every man thinks that he knows the[6] best, and when he speaks to another person, he thinks that he [37] knows half, and when he is speaking about a third person, he thinks that he [38] knows only [39] a quarter. And some few who do

---

28. (Sk.l.tr.) Gd.e.: first "avaraciousness" changed into "avarice", then crossed out and "covetousness" written above;
tp.c.: "covetousness", but Sk. wrote "avaraciousness" in the margin, as was said;
Hq.t.: "covetousness"
29. Sk.l.tr.: "inclined", although in "Sk.sh." "climbing" is clearly taken down;
tp.c.: "inclined", replaced by Sk. in ink with "climbing";
Hq.st.: "inclined"
30. Sk.l.tr.: "and" added, later crossed out by Sk.
31. (Sk.l.tr.) Gd.e.: "who" crossed out, but restored by Sk.;
tp.c.: "who" omitted, but added by Sk. in the margin in ink;
Hq.st.: "who" omitted
32. (Sk.l.tr.) Gd.e.: "spiritually" moved to after "progress";
tp.c., Hq.st.: "progress spiritually"
33. (Sk.l.tr.) Gd.e.: "it" crossed out, but restored by Sk.
34. Sk.l.tr.: "or" added, crossed out by Sk.; (Sk.l.tr.) Gd.e.: "or" added;
tp.c.: "or" added, but crossed out by Sk.;
Hq.st.: "or" added
35. Sk.l.tr., tp.c., Hq.st.: "their" instead of "the"
36. (Sk.l.tr.) Gd.e.: "on" added;
tp.c., Hq.st.: "on", but crossed out in "tp.c." by Sk.
37. (Sk.l.tr.) Gd.e.: "he" changed into "the other";
tp.c., Hq.st.: "the other" instead of "he"
38. (Sk.l.tr.) Gd.e.: "he" changed into "that third person";
tp.c., Hq.st.: "that third person" instead of "he"
39. Sk.t., Sk.c.tp.: "only" omitted

not rely upon their knowledge, they are then dependent upon the advice[40] of others. Therefore their success or . . . [41], or thinking[42], depends upon the advice of others.

It is most difficult in life to have power, to possess knowledge, and together with it to have clear vision. And if there is any possibility to keep[43] the vision clear, it is of[44] keeping[45] balance between power and knowledge.[46]

---

40. Sk.l.tr.: "advices"; (Sk.l.tr.)Gd.e.: plural 's' of "advices" crossed out
41. Sk.sh.: one word missed, and later filled in by Sk. "faillite" (the French word for "failure"); Sk.t., Sk.c.tp.: "success or failure"; Sk.l.tr.: "failure or success"; tp.c., Hq.st.: "failure or success"
42. Tp.c., Hq.st.: "thinking" in Sk.l.tr., which had been crossed out in ink and then restored, erroneously read as "their being"
43. (Sk.l.tr.) Gd.e.: "to keep" changed into "of keeping; tp.c., Hq.st.: "of keeping"
44. (Sk.l.tr.) Gd.e.: "of" first changed into 'in", then "in" changed into "by the"; tp.c., Hq.st.: "by the" instead of "of"
45. Tp.c., Hq.st.: "of" added
46. Three questions and answers referring to this lecture, but given at a later time on the same day, can be found beginning on page 206

Sakina Furnée's shorthand reporting.

1 2

In the prayer of the Christian Church, there is a phrase[3]: "Thy Will

---

Documents:

Sk.sh. = Sakina Furnée's shorthand reporting, taken down in a small green copybook containing the reportings of lectures given in November and December 1922 in Paris.

Hq.st.1 = an early stencilled copy issued by Headquarters, Geneva, but without the number of the Religious Gatheka typed in, and without the Invocation.

Hq.t. = a typescript issued by Headquarters, Geneva, restricted in number, but without the number of the Religious Gatheka typed in (later added in hwr.) and the first three words of the Invocation written above by Sk. As the wording of this document is identical to the one of 'Hq.st.1", it has not been mentioned in the notes, except in notes 1 and 20.

Hq.st.2 = a later stencilled copy issued by Headquarters, Geneva, with the number of the Religious Gatheka and the Invocation incorporated. Its wording being identical to Hq.st.1, it has not been mentioned in the notes, except in note 1.

Bk.p.1 = an old typescript made form "Hq.st.1" and used by Sherifa Goodenough as a first preparation for a chapter in the book *The Unity of Religious Ideals*.

Bk.p.2 = a second book-preparation on Gd.'s typewriter with large letters, made from "bk.p.1" with a few slight alterations.

Bk. = the book *The Unity of Religious Ideals*, compiled and prepared by Sherifa Goodenough (1929), in which the lecture appears under Part V, chapter VIII, last section.

Notes:

1. Sk.sh.: later added "Religious Gatheka 6. (486)" in Sk.'s hwr. "(486)" refers to Sk.'s file-numbering;
   Hq.st.1: "RELIGIOUS GATHEKA" added above, and as a subtitle: "Thy Will be done, on earth as it is in Heaven." Later "No. 6" was written in the upper right corner;
   Hq.t.: "RELIGIOUS GATHEKA. Number " (later filled in "6") and added as a subtitle "Thy Will be done, on earth as it is in Heaven.";
   Hq.st.2: "RELIGIOUS GATHEKA. Number 6.", and as a subtitle: "Thy Will be done, on earth as it is in Heaven.";
   bk.p.1: "RELIGIOUS GATHEKA" crossed out and the subtitle used as a title: "Thy Will be done on earth as it is in Heaven.";
   bk.p.2: added as a title: "THY WILL BE DONE, ON EARTH AS IT IS IN HEAVEN.";
   bk.: "Thy Will be Done, in Earth as it is in Heaven," added as a title
2. Although no exact date was added by Sk. above this lecture, nor on the other documents, it follows in her sh. notebook after the lecture "Sadhana or the Attainment", of which

be done on earth as[4] in Heaven."[5] That[6] gives a great key to metaphysics; it gives a hint to the seer that His will, which is easily done in Heaven, has a[7] difficulty to be[8] done on earth. And who stands against His will? Man. And where lays[9] the will of God? In the innermost being of man. And what stands as an obstacle? The surface of the heart of man. And this means struggle in man himself. In him there is the will of God, [10]and in him there is the obstacle. The sphere within him, in which there is the will of God,[10] is the [11] Heaven, and where there is [12]obstacle to it, there is the earth.

By this prayer man is prepared to remove the obstacle which stands before the will of God. Now [13], how to [14] distinguish between these two aspects of will, the will of God, and the obstacle, which is the will of man? It is easy for a person of [15] [16]clear mind and open heart to distinguish it [17], if he only knew [18] the secret of it. For [19] that which is the will of God, to it [20] his whole being responds [21], and in doing His will, his whole being becomes satisfied. When it is his will, then [22] only one side of his being is perhaps satisfied for a certain time, and there comes a conflict in himself. He himself

---

"Sk.t." bears the date "6 December 1922, Paris". Some answers to questions were taken down by Sk. in the same notebook, clearly and directly referring to the lecture "Sadhana or the Attainment", and which would seem to have been given on the same day. Consequently the lecture "In the prayer of the Christian Church...", appearing in Sk.'s notebook between the lecture "Sadhana or the Attainment" and questions and answers referring to it, must also have been given on that same day: 6 December 1922

3. All other documents: "sentence" instead of "phrase"
4. Ibid.: "it is" added
5. Matt. vi.10, Luke xi.2
6. All other documents: "This" instead of "That"
7. Ibid.: "a" omitted
8. Ibid.: "in being" instead of "to be"
9. Ibid.: corr. to "lies"
10. Bk.p.1,2, bk.: this passage omitted ("and in him . . . the will of God,")
11. Ibid.: "is the" replaced with "as in"
12. All other documents: "the" added
13. Bk.p.2, bk.: "Now," omitted
14. All other documents: "can we" in place of "to"
15. Ibid.: "with" instead of "of"
16. Bk.p.1,2, bk.: "a" added
17. All other documents: "it" omitted
18. Bk.: "knows" instead of "knew"
19. All other documents: "to" added
20. Ibid.: "to it" omitted
21. Hq.st.1, Hq.t.: "respond", changed by Sk. in "Hq.t." into "responds"
22. Hq.st.1: "the" instead of "then";
    bk.p.1,2, bk.: "then" omitted

criticises[23] his idea or action. He himself feels dissatisfied with his own being. The wider[24] he sees his idea or his action, the more dissatisfied he will become. [25]In this manner by the x-ray of intelligence, when[25] one sees life, one begins to distinguish between his will and the will of God. The Kingdom of God which is in Heaven, then comes on earth. It does not mean that it disappears from Heaven, but it only means that not only Heaven remains as a Kingdom of Heaven, but even earth becomes a Kingdom of Heaven.

The purpose behind all this creation is that Heaven [26]may be realised on the[27] earth. And if one did not realise it on earth, he cannot realise it in Heaven. One may ask, what do I mean by Heaven? Heaven is that place where all is the choice of man, and everything moves at his command. Heaven is the natural condition of life. When on earth life becomes so entangled that it loses its original harmony, Heaven ceases to exist, and the motive of the soul is that[28] the Kingdom of Heaven which the soul[29] has lost, to gain in life[28]. Nothing one attains[30] in life which will give that satisfaction, which can only be attained by bringing Heaven on earth.

---

23. All other documents: "finds fault with" instead of "criticises"
24. Ibid.: added: "the scope in which"
25. Ibid.: rewritten to read, "When in this manner, by the ray of intelligence"
26. Bk.p.1: "be made" instead of "may be"
27. Bk.p.1,2, bk.: "the" omitted
28. All other documents: "that" omitted and "to gain in life" moved to before "the Kingdom of Heaven"
29. Bk.: "it" in place of "the soul"
30. All other documents: "does one attain" instead of "one attains"

[2]

Question: Knowledge: knowledge gained by the life in the world, or knowledge by intuition?

Answer: No, in this I have only said, knowledge gained in the world. Knowledge [3]not complete, unless it is kindled with the light of intuition.

Question: That[4] balance of power and knowledge, what is the best way of attaining to that[4] balance?

Answer: Man generally gets unbalanced: if there is a power, one wants to exert power, one is always involved in the reasoning; in that way one loses a sort of balance.

[5]*Question: Then ~~comes~~ . . . to judge whether one gives too much importance to*

Documents:

Sk.sh. = Sakina Furnée's shorthand reporting of three questions and answers above which Sk. later wrote the annotation: "questions and answers belonging to Sadhana II, 4, page before" (referring to Sk.'s copybook).

Sk.l.tp. = a later typescript made by Sk. from "Sk.sh." in which the second and third question and answer have been made into one.

Sk.c.tp. = a neat, typewritten copy, made by Sakina in later years from "Sk.l.tp.", in which the second and third question and answer have been made into one.

Notes:

1. Although undated on the documents, these three questions and answers refer clearly to the lecture "Sadhana or the Attainment" of 6 December 1922, and seem to have been given sometime on that same day. (See also note 2 after the lecture "In the prayer of the Christian Church . . ." of 6 December 1922, page 203f.)
2. Sk.l.tp.: added above: "after GITHA SADHANA II, 4.";
   Sk.c.tp.: added on the same document after the lecture which bears the title "SADHANA, the ATTAINMENT"
3. Sk.l.tp, Sk.c.tp.: "is" added
4. Ibid.: "That" changed into "This"
5. Ibid.: "Question" and the question mark omitted, and the incomplete sentence added to the previous answer

power, not cultivating enough knowledge?

[6]Answer: Yes.[6] For an instance, there is a man who is perhaps very much enthusiastic in a certain business, and he ~~is~~, just with his will power, he wants to get as much money as he can, without any thought of how it will be used. He has only the strength of the purpose: "I must succeed". And he gives all his energy in it without thinking about it. And in that way he may come[7] to a success, but still there is always a danger. And then there is another man, who is thinking out a thousand things before taking a step in an affair, and contradicting all things with his own knowledge. What one must do is this, that if one takes one step in power, another step in knowledge, another step in power, another step in knowledge. And so there is balance. Then it becomes rhythmic. Just like in the two-four time in accent, there is an accent, then a weak accent; then there is power, then there is thinking.

---

6. Ibid.: "Answer: Yes." omitted, and the following passage added to the answer to the second question
7. Ibid.: "might go" instead of "may come"

A longhand, edited version by Sherifa Goodenough, possibly from her own longhand reporting of the lecture.

[1]

Man, the Master of his Destiny [2]

When one understands--one studies, the question of the source and the goal of man one finds that man starts his life from perfection and finds himself in limitation. The whole tragedy of life is caused by man's limitation. All that gives pain or trouble to man is that which he cannot understand, which he cannot accomplish, which he cannot attain; and the reason why it should give him trouble or pain is not only that he cannot accomplish, attain, understand, the reason is that there is the desire to accomplish, to understand, to attain; and the very fact that man desires to understand, to accomplish and to attain shows that he has in him the latent power. In plain words, no one in this world desires something which he is not capable of attaining, nor does he desire something that he has not in himself the perception to understand. This shows that all that man desires that is his capability [3], that is within his

Documents:

Lf. = a reporting by Mademoiselle Lefèbvre of a simultaneous translation into French of the lecture, sentence by sentence, but with several blank spaces. As this document seems to be less complete than "Gd.h." (even though it is not always possible to know which words and parts of sentences were actually said by Pir-o-Murshid and what has been added later by Gd.), "Lf." has only been mentioned in notes 1 and 2, and in those cases where Lf.'s text seems to be closer to Pir-o-Murshid's actual words.

Gd.h. = a copied and edited text in Sherifa Goodenough's handwriting, possibly made from her own longhand reporting of the lecture, or possibly translated from the French reporting above, with editorial changes;
(Gd.h.)Gd.e.: further editing by Gd. on the same document.

Tp.c. = a typescript made by Sakina Furnée or under her direction of "Gd.h.", with "(Gd.h.)Gd.e." mostly incorporated.

Notes:

1. Lf.: "Musée Guimet, 10 Décembre 1922", which shows that the lecture was given in Paris
2. Lf.: the lecture began with "Bien aimés de Dieu, mon sujet aujourd'hui sera l'homme, maître de sa destinée";
   Gd.h., tp.c.: "Man, the Master of his Destiny"
3. (Gd.h.)Gd.e.: "is his capability" changed into "he is capable of";
   tp.c.: "he is capable of"

reach; and if he does not attain to it that is a different question. For a mystic the word "impossible" has no meaning. He says, "Yes, I see the impossibility which stands before me as a wall, but it has no reality before[4] me." And what makes the mystic think in this way? It is that the mystic traces in himself the spark of the Divine Being, the[5]: [6]Before Him there was nothing, and all became possible. According to the idea of a mystic all that is done by consequences and all that is done by man is all toward[7] the accomplishment of one single destiny.[6] What human beings accomplish as individuals and what human beings accomplish as a multitude and what takes place by consequences, all this [8]sums up in one object[8]. Only the difference is that two souls travel the same way--one knows toward[7] what he is going, the other does not know; for instance, the horse and the rider: the rider knows where he is going and what he wants to accomplish, the horse does not know. Plainly speaking, the soul who is the master of his kingdom, is born on earth as a slave, but to rise again to attain to that destiny. And this we can study by studying the life of an ~~individual~~ infant. On one side, how helpless the infant is! For its food and for all its needs it depends upon others. But[9] at the same time the infant feels it to be its right to ask for all that seems beautiful and good. Whether the thing belongs to its parents or whether it does not, the infant's idea is to demand it and get it. And what does this show? It shows to the mystic the picture of a king in the captivity of the physical body. The Sufis of Persia, who were the greatest of the poets of the time, have explained in their poetry this idea, that all the sorrow and pain that man has in his life is of the captivity that he feels. Although every man does not look all around, every man looks at one part, and that part is what he himself needs. It shows that if he happens to look at the moment at his hands, which seem to be tied, he thinks, "If only my hands were freed!" But

---

4. (Gd.h.)Gd.e.: "before" changed into "for";
   tp.: "for" instead of "before"
5. Gd.h.: something more must have been said, but only "the" is written;
   (Gd.h.)Gd.e.: "the" crossed out
6. Lf.: referring to the Divine spark, the following words were taken down: "par laquelle tout est possible, sans laquelle tout est impossible. Les mystiques croient à la loi de causalité, que tout vient d'une chose déjà faite, et prépare une autre, non faite." (tr.: with which all is possible, without which all is impossible. The mystics believe in the law of causality, that all derives from something already done, and prepares something else, not yet done.)
7. Tp.: "towards"
8. Lf.: "est résultat de cause antérieure" (tr.: is the result of a previous cause)
9. (Gd.h.)Gd.e.: "But" replaced with "And";
   tp.c.: "And" instead of "But"

if his hands were made free, if he looked at his feet he would find that on his feet also there are chains. It is from the lack of clear vision that man does not see the whole life; and therefore he looks at one part and sees that one part and does not see the chains all around. The very greatest poet of Persia has said, "Man himself has entered this captivity, and he himself has the power to rise above it." The more one sees the picture of life the more one feels oneself in a kind of puzzle, and if on one side he gets out of it, he finds he is in another part of the puzzle. And if man does not give proper attention, and does not study the psychology of life, he may go from one part of this puzzle to another part, with a view to becoming free, but this cannot give him freedom. ~~In the ordinary sense of the words,~~ Those who have reached their majority are distinguished from minors (in the sense in which these words are ordinarily used), by their having reached a certain liberty; and you will find the same difference among individuals. Some individuals, you will find, whatever be their age, are minors and others have reached their majority. And whatever be the age of a person yet a minor, instead of a person he is a kind of machine. And there is another person—he may be quite young, but there is initiative, enthusiasm, optimism, hope; he has reached majority. There is so little known about diseases of the mind. What physicians know is mostly about the diseases of the body. There are many in this world, besides those who have not yet reached a mature state of mind, who suffer from a disease which may be called a kind of paralysis of the mind. And this begins with a kind of hopelessness, of pessimism about life. If you tell them about progress, they will say, "Where is progress under such conditions? What progress? How can we hope for it?" If you tell them about success, they will say, "Success? Far away! [10]How can we hope for[10] a success?" If you tell them about their cure from their illness, they will say, "Impossible! Illness is my nature. It is . . . ." [11] And to cure them is much more difficult than to cure the bodies, that are ill, by medicine. The person whose mind becomes paralysed does not go forward, does not show enthusiasm, does not show hope, because it is paralysed, it is dying. And sometimes, of course, such a disease goes on in families for generations. But at the same time we must know that our longing for happiness, our yearning for peace, shows that our being is happiness, our being is peace. And we can

---

10. (Gd.h.)Gd.e.: rewritten to read, "There is no hope of making"; tp.c.: "There is no hope of making"
11. (Gd.h.)Gd.e.: "It is . . . ." crossed out; tp.c.: "It is . . . ." omitted

only attain that which our soul constantly seeks by attaining that mastery for which our soul was born.

And now the question is how to attain that mastery, or the dominion which man has lost? It is never too late, if ever a person made up his mind to attain, whatever be his condition in life. Yes, first an [12] understanding of life is necessary. One must first know what are the obstacles that stand before man when he wishes to attain mastery. There are two obstacles, very great obstacles. The first obstacle is the selfish nature in oneself, the second is the selfish nature of those around one. And what man ordinarily does is that he forgets the selfish nature in himself, but he observes the selfish nature of his fellow men and then he wants to fight with it. And this fight brings about the most undesirable result, because the selfish nature is such that the more you fight with it, the stronger it becomes. It is just like fighting with the devil and with every fight giving the devil more and more strength. But there is not only one loss by this fight, there is another loss also. This fight feeds one's selfish nature also. If we think about the whole world's condition just now, what is it? It is a fight against selfishness, the very thing against which all the great preachers of humanity have preached and have taught at all times. For instance, the words of Christ are, "Resist not evil". [13] The selfishness of another one calls evil; one's own selfishness one does not call evil. If anyone knows it, he does not wish to call it selfishness, he calls it cleverness, practicality. When another person wants to take advantage of him he says that is evil; when he wants to get the better of another person he thinks that is cleverness. If man only knew the secret of the psychology of human nature he could manage the affairs of life much better. The secret is that the heart of man is made of wax, and unselfishness is like fire; selfishness is just like snow, or ice. Therefore, when a person is selfish and he comes in contact with the [14] selfish people, he makes their heart still harder; therefore, his battle becomes still more difficult, although he thinks, "By my selfishness I am ready for fighting", and he pities the unselfish. The influence of the unselfish person upon the selfish person is just like the influence of fire upon the heart that is made of wax. Unselfishness never fails to make an effect upon the selfish heart, it is only a matter of time. It is only man's lack of knowledge of the psychology of human nature that makes him fail. An unselfish person, not knowing this secret, when he sees

---

12. (Gd.h.)Gd.e.: "an" crossed out;
tp.c.: "an" omitted
13. Matt. v.39
14. (Gd.h.)Gd.e.: "the" crossed out;
tp.c.: "the" omitted

a selfish person, becomes selfish too. Friends, hidden [15] under all this falsehood and hidden under all the thorns that pierce from the surface of life, there is something most wonderful and marvelous hidden under life. And now the question is when does man arrive; what makes man arrive at the state where he can touch [16] the surface and reach the inner side of life. There are two powers which should be cultivated, self-denial and consideration for others. There are very few to be found in this world who are having [17] self-denying, and fewer still who are considerate. There is a talk in this world about saints and sages and supermen and masters of life. If one becomes self-denying and considerate, he does not need to seek for any others, he will find all these in his own soul. Even if one met in one's life a saint, a sage, a prophet, an angel, that does not suffice the purpose; if one has not made of oneself that which was necessary to be made, that will not suffice his purpose. I do not mean by this that association has not an influence. Association can help a great deal in life. But it is not only association, one must try oneself to practise in one's life. Man gives all importance in life to his everyday needs, and to his work, his business, his profession; very little he has left to think of his soul's development. And therefore, with all the success he may make in the world, he remains still deprived of that happiness for which his soul constantly yearns [18].

And now you might ask me how to set to work . . . . [19] Is there anything one should study or is there anything one should do in order to attain to this mastery? No doubt the association of a person . . . [20] also meditation, and study, all these things help. But that which helps more is one's own effort in that direction. For instance, if one [21] in his everyday life,

---

15. (Gd.h.)Gd.e.: "hidden" crossed out;
tp.c.: "hidden" omitted
16. (Gd.h.)Gd.e.: "touch" changed into "break through";
tp.c.: "break through" instead of "touch"
17. (Gd.h.)Gd.e.: "who are having" crossed out, afterwards "who are" restored;
tp.c.: "who are" instead of "who are having"
18. (Gd.h.)Gd.e.: "yearns" replaced with "longs";
tp.c.: "longs" instead of "yearns"
19. Lf.: "pour attaindre cet ideal?";
(Gd.h.)Gd.e.: filled in "for the attainment of this";
tp.c.: "for the attainment of this"
20. (Gd.h.)Gd.e.: afterwards filled in: "experienced in these things";
tp.c.: "experienced in these things" added
21. (Gd.h.)Gd.e.: "one" crossed out;
tp.c.: "one" omitted

[22]all that he does from morning till evening, if he[23] thought after every day whether he . . . [24] in doing all that he does[25], he no doubt can improve. He need not be disappointed at continually increasing errors, for the finer his perception will become, [26]so he will find himself in more errors[26]. Error belongs to Adam, and therefore error is something that one must not think a soul can be free from. Only, what one can do is to try to make an effort in that direction. And besides that self-discipline[27], to think, "My body and my mind are as my instruments, and if these instruments are not in order, in tune, then I am not master of these instruments"; to look at one's life as one would look at another person's, to watch it carefully from morning to evening and to see where one has failed and where one has gained [28]and where one has . . . .[28]

The difference between an ordinary person and an adept is this, that an ordinary person blames another for having done something wrong; an ordinary person blames, and follows something[29], because he says, "Because you have done so, I do so also". But[30] the adept, his mind[31] is full of his own errors; he has no time to think of the errors of another person; he is judging all the time himself, his own actions.

And do not think that it is selfish to make the personality an ideal personality. It is the purpose of life, it is this that was meant by the Creator. And those who think, "But . . .[32] and for one to progress[33], . . .[34] will it not

---

22. (Gd.h.)Gd.e.: "in" added;
    tp.c.: "in" added
23. (Gd.h.)Gd.e.: "if he" replaced with "a person";
    tp.c.: "a person"
24. (Gd.h.)Gd.e.: later filled in: "was considerate";
    tp.c.: "was considerate"
25. (Gd.h.)Gd.e.: "does" replaced with "did";
    tp.c.: "did"
26. (Gd.h.)Gd.e.: rewritten to read, "the more errors he will find in himself";
    tp.c.: "the more errors he will find in himself"
27. (Gd.h.)Gd.e.: "is needed" added;
    tp.c.: "is needed" added
28. (Gd.h.)Gd.e.: "and where one has . . . ." crossed out;
    tp.c.: "and where one has . . . ." omitted
29. (Gd.h.)Gd.e.: "something" replaced with "that thing himself";
    tp.c.: "that thing himself"
30. (Gd.h.)Gd.e.: "mind of" added;
    tp.c.: "the mind of" added
31. (Gd.h.)Gd.e.: "his mind" crossed out;
    tp.c.: "his mind" omitted
32. (Gd.h.)Gd.e.: later filled in, "there are others who are not progressing";
    tp.c.: "there are others who are not progressing" added

be a kind of fault, a kind of sin, for one to progress beyond the others?" This is no doubt a wrong attitude. By this attitude one keeps not only one's own self, but also others, from progress; from the other attitude one goes forward and drags [35]friends and surroundings [35] with one.

Friends, it is this progress which is necessary at this time of the world's greatest misery that has ever been seen. Amidst all the activities that are working towards the reconstruction of the world, the Sufi Message is working towards the progress of human beings to becoming [36] human. The central theme of the Sufi Message is to awaken in the consciousness of humanity the divinity which is the [37] of man. And this can be realised by a [38] progress, a progress . . .[39], to [40] attainment of that perfection which is spoken of by Christ.[41]

---

33. (Gd.h.)Gd.e.: "and for one to progress" crossed out;
tp.c.: "and for one to progress" omitted
34. (Gd.h.)Gd.e.: later "then" added;
tp.c.: "then" added
35. Lf.: "toute la race, et l'aide à progresser" (tr.: the whole race, and helps it to progress.);
Gd.h., tp.c.: "friends and surroundings"
36. Tp.c.: "become" instead of "becoming"
37. (Gd.h.)Gd.e.: later added, "heritage";
Lf.: "dans le coeur";
tp.c.: "heritage" added
38. (Gd.h.)Gd.e.: "general" added;
tp.c.: "general"
39. (Gd.h.)Gd.e.: later filled in, "for every soul, whatever be his evolution";
tp.c.: "for every soul, whatever be his evolution" added
40. (Gd.h.)Gd.e.: "toward the" instead of "to";
tp.c.: "towards the"
41. Lf.: "Soyez parfaits comme votre Père céleste est parfait." (tr.: Be perfect as your Father in Heaven is perfect.) Matt. v.48

Sakina Furnée's shorthand reporting.

1

Towards the One, the Perfection . . .[2]

Sadhana, the Attainment [3]

Documents:

Sk.sh. = Sakina Furnée's shorthand reporting, taken down in a small green copybook containing reportings of lectures given in November and December 1922 in Paris.

Hl. = a reporting by Mademoiselle C. Hulot of a simultaneous translation into French, sentence by sentence, of the first part of the lecture, given in English. This incomplete document has only been mentioned in note 26.

Hl.t. = a typescript made from "Hl.", not mentioned in the notes.

Sk.t. = a typescript made from Sakina's transcription of her shorthand reporting at Headquarters, Geneva.

Sk.l.tr. = Sakina Furnée's later transcription in handwriting of her shorthand reporting, with some inaccuracies;
(Sk.l.tr.)Gd.e.: Sherifa Goodenough's later corrections and editing, in light blue ink, partly taken from "Gd.hwr."

Gd.hwr. = a copy in Gd.'s handwriting, made from "Sk.l.tr." with extensive editing.

Hq.p. = a second copy in Gd.'s handwriting, made as a preparation for the "Hq.st."

Hq.t. = a typescript made at Headquarters, Geneva, made from "Gd.hwr.", but on which Sk. later restored most of the changes made by Gd., back to "Sk.t."

Hq.st. = a stencilled copy issues by Headquarters, Geneva, made from "Hq.p."

Sk.c.tp. = a neat, typewritten copy made by Sk. in later years from "Sk.t."

Notes:

1. Sk.sh.: later Sk. added "Dec. '22" above;
   Sk.t., Hq.t., Sk.c.tp.: "December 1922" added;
   Gd.hwr.: "Dec. 11th 1923", instead of "Dec. 11th, 1922"
2. Sk.sh.: Sk. took down the first words of the Invocation in sh.;
   all other documents except the "Hq.st.": the Invocation omitted
3. Sk.sh.: later Sk. wrote in lh. above the lecture: "Sadhana. For worldly attainment or spiritual attainment . . ."; some years later Sk. added "I", indicating the series of the Gitas where it was included;
   Sk.t.: "SADHANA, THE PATH OF ATTAINMENT". Some years later Sk. added in hwr.: "(has become Githa II,5.)";
   Sk.l.tr.: "Sadhana II or the Attainment". Later Sk. added "nr.5" in pencil; (Sk.l.tr.)Gd.e.: "Sadhana II or The Path of Attainment.";
   Gd.hwr.: "Sadhana" as a title. Added later: "Series II. Number ~~5~~ 6"; afterward "5" was restored;

For[4] worldly[5] attainment, or spiritual attainment, the first thing is to attain[6] self discipline. Many experience and few know that things go wrong when one's self is not disciplined[7]. Those who give way to anger, passion, to emotions easily[8], they may[9] seem for a moment successful, but they cannot continually succeed in life. Very often misfortunes follow an illness or a failure, and the reason is that one[10] weakness gives a[11] way to another, and so the[12] person who goes down, goes down and down and down. It is natural that a step one may take downward[13], for the path of life is not even. But the wise thing is that [14]if one step is gone down, the next step is[15] taken upward. It is, no doubt, a[16] resisting against the force that pulls one downward. But [17]that

---

Hq.p.: "Sadhana. The Path of Attainment. Series II. Number ~~7~~ 5";
Hq.t.: "Sadhana. Series II. Number 5.";
Hq.st.: "Series II. GITHA Number 5." "SADHANA. THE PATH OF ATTAINMENT.";
Sk.c.tp.: "SADHANA, THE PATH OF ATTAINMENT."

4. Gd.hwr.: "In" instead of "For";
Hq.t.: "In", changed back by Sk. to "For";
Hq.p., Hq.st.: "In"
5. Sk.sh.: the sh.-sign for "world" may mean "worldly" as well;
Sk.l.tr.: "world"; (Sk.l.tr.)Gd.e.: "worldly"
6. Sk.sh.: apparently Sk. read "gain" for "attain", although "attain" was taken down;
Sk.t., Sk.c.tp.: "gain";
Hq.t.: "attain" changed by Sk. into "gain"
7. (Sk.l.tr.)Gd.e.: "disciplined" changed to "in discipline";
Gd.hwr., Hq.p., Hq.t., Hq.st.: "in discipline", but in Hq.t. changed back by Sk. into "disciplined"
8. (Sk.l.tr.)Gd.e.: "easily" moved to after "Those who"
9. Sk.t.: "may" omitted;
Hq.t.: "may" crossed out
10. Sk.l.tr.: "a", changed back to "one" by Sk.;
Hq.p., Hq.t., Hq.st.: "a", but changed back by Sk. in "Hq.t." into "one"
11. Hq.p., Hq.t., Hq.st.: "a" omitted
12. Sk.l.tr.: "a"; (Sk.l.tr.)Gd.e.: "the";
Hq.p., Hq.t., Hq.st.: "a", but changed back to "the" by Sk. in "Hq.st."
13. Gd.hwr., Hq.p., Hq.t., Hq.st.: "downwards"
14. (Sk.l.tr.)Gd.e.: "if one has gone down" instead of "if one step is gone down";
Gd.hwr.: "if one has gone down", then added "step" after "one" and again crossed out;
Hq.t.: "one step one has gone down", to which Sk. later added "if" before the first "one";
Hq.p., Hq.st.: "if one step one has gone down"
15. (Sk.l.tr.)Gd.e.: "is" changed into "may be";
Gd.hwr., Hq.p., Hq.t., Hq.st.: "may be", but in "Hq.t." changed back by Sk. to "is"
16. (Sk.l.tr.)Gd.e.: "a" crossed out;
Gd.hwr., Hq.p., Hq.t., Hq.st.: "a" omitted, but reinserted by Sk. in "Hq.t."
17. Sk.l.tr.: "this" instead of "that"; (Sk.l.tr.)Gd.e.: rewritten to read, "only that resistance secures the path of man's life";
Gd.hwr.: "that resistance only secures the path of man's life";
Hq.p., Hq.t., Hq.st.: "that resistance only secures the path of one's life", but in "Hq.t." Sk. changed back "the path of one's life" to "the safety of man's life"

resistance only secures the safety of man's life[17].

What generally happens is that man does not mind a little mistake, he does not take notice of a small weakness. He underestimates a little failure, and [18] this [19] way in the long run he meets with a great failure. The wise thing, therefore, is [20]—to whatever depth one has fallen—to fix one's eyes upward [21]; [22]try to rise instead of falling. It is very interesting to observe that God or Heaven is always pointed upward [23], although in reality God is everywhere, and so is Heaven. And what makes one think that God is upward [24] or Heaven is upward [25], is that natural impulse which is a divine impulse in man, [26]which gives an inclination . . . [26]

And this shows that success, its attainment [27], is [28] divine pleasure. Failure and its experience is displeasure of God [29]. . . [30] people who blame destiny for their failure, take the path of least resistance. [31]But there are more

---

18. Sk.l.tr., Gd.hwr., Hq.p., Hq.t., Hq.st.: "in" added
19. Sk.l.tr.: "that"; (Sk.l.tr.)Gd.e.: "that" restored to "this"; Hq.p., Hq.t., Hq.st.: "that"
20. Gd.hwr., Hq.p., Hq.t., Hq.st.: "is" moved to before "therefore", but in "Hq.t." Sk. restored "is" to after "therefore"
21. (Sk.l.tr.)Gd.e.: "upwards"
22. Gd.hwr., Hq.p., Hq.t., Hq.st.: "to" added, but "to" crossed out by Sk. in "Hq.t."
23. Sk.t., (Sk.l.tr.)Gd.e., Gd.hwr.: "upwards"; Hq.p., Hq.t., Hq.st.: "to upward", but changed by Sk. in "Hq.t." to "upwards"
24. Gd.hwr.: "upwards"
25. (Sk.l.tr.)Gd.e., Gd.hwr.: "upwards"
26. Sk.sh.: a blank, afterwards filled in by Sk. with "to rise above" in sh.;
    Hl.: "d'aspirer aux choses d'en haut" (tr.: to aspire to things from above) in place of the open space;
    Sk.t., Sk.l.tr.: "to rise above" after "inclination";
    Gd.hwr.: "which gives an inclination" omitted, "to rise above" added;
    Hq.p., Hq.t., Hq.st.: "to rise above" added, but in "Hq.t." with a question mark by Sk.;
    Sk.c.tp.: "to rise above" added, but indicated by Sk. that it is uncertain if these words were said by Pir-o-Murshid.
27. (Sk.l.tr.)Gd.e.: "its attainment" changed into "the attainment of success"
28. Ibid.: "the" added
29. (Sk.l.tr.)Gd.e.: "displeasure of God" changed into "the divine disappointment";
    Gd.hwr., Hq.p., Hq.t., Hq.st.: "the divine disappointment" instead of "displeasure of God", but on a copy of "Hq.t.", Sk. replaced "the divine disappointment" with "displeasure of God"
30. Sk.sh.: a space left open before "people";
    all other documents: instead of the open space: ". People"
31. Sk.sh.: some parts of this sentence were missed by Sk.;
    Sk.t., Sk.c.tp.: "But there are no difficulties that appear to be...", although in "Sk.sh." "more" was taken down, which in sh. is nearly identical to "no". "Appears" was taken down in "Sk.sh.", which would indicate that something else has been said after "difficulties" ("in the path", as in "Gd.hwr."?);
    Sk.l.tr.: this incomplete sentence omitted; (Sk.l.tr.)Gd.e.: added the sentence as in "Gd.hwr.";

difficulties that appears to be . . .[31], for [32]man who struggles with life [33]lessens his difficulty[33] as he goes forward. [34]The one who takes easy his path, for him the difficulties grow more as he goes on[34]. By this . . .[35] it[36] is nct meant that one should choose in life a path of more[37] difficulties[38]. By this it is only meant that in the path of attainment difficulties must not be counted. Difficulties rise over his head[39], who looks at them with awe, and the same difficulties fall beneath[40] his feet[41] who does not take notice of them. Man[42] who fails in the world, fails to attain the[43] spiritual bliss also[44]. Man is the king of his domain[45];

Gd.hwr.: "but there are more difficulties in the path that appears to be of least resistance";
Sk.t.: later changed and completed by Sk. in ink to the sentence as it appears in "Gd.hwr.";
Hq.p., Hq.t., Hq.st.: as in "Gd.hwr."

32. Hq.p., Hq.t., Hq.st.: "the" added
33. Sk.t., Sk.c.tp.: "the less his difficulty", later changed by Sk. in "Sk.t." into "lessens his difficulties"; Sk.l.tr.: "his difficulties lessen"; (Sk.l.tr.)Gd.e.: "lessens his difficulties"; Gd.hwr.: "lessens his difficulties"; Hq.p., Hq.t., Hq.st.: "his difficulties lessen"
34. Sk.sh., Sk.c.tp.: Sk. wrote "are added" in sh. above "grow more"; Sk.t.: "are added" in parentheses in tp. after "grow more"; Sk.l.tr.: "easily" instead of "easy"; (Sk.l.tr.)Gd.e.: rewritten to read, "The one who takes the easiest path increases his difficulties"; Gd.hwr.: the same sentence as under (Sk.l.tr.)Gd.e., but preceded by a comma and a small 't'; Hq.p., Hq.t., Hq.st.: "the one who takes the easy path, for him the difficulties grow more as he grows on", but in "Hq.t." changed back by Sk. into: "the one who takes easy his path, for him the difficulties grow more as he goes on"
35. Sk.sh.: a small gap; all other documents: no space left open
36. (Sk.l.tr.)Gd.e.: "it" crossed out
37. Sk.t.: "no", although "more" was taken down in "Sk.sh." (see note 31). Afterwards Sk. corr. "no" to "more"; Sk.c.tp.: "no" instead of "more"
38. (Sk.l.tr.)Gd.e., Hq.p.: "difficulties" changed into "difficulty"; Gd.hwr.: "difficulty"
39. (Sk.l.tr.)Gd.e.: "his head" changed into "the head of him"
40. Sk.t., Sk.c.tp.: "down", although "beneath" was taken down in "Sk.sh." (The sh. signs for "down" and "beneath" are very similar; all other documents: "beneath"
41. (Sk.l.tr.)Gd.e.: "his feet" changed into "the feet of him"
42. (Sk.l.tr.)Gd.e.: "Man" changed into "The one"; Hq.p., Hq.t., Hq.st.: "The man"
43. (Sk.l.tr.)Gd.e.: "to" added, "the" omitted; Gd.hwr., Hq.p., Hq.t., Hq.st.: "to" added, "the" omitted
44. (Sk.l.tr.)Gd.e.: "also" moved to before "fails"
45. Sk.l.tr.: "kingdom", later changed back by Sk. into "domain"

his coming on earth takes away . . .[46] his kingdom. During that[47] trial he is tested if he uses that human virtue which helps him to attain the mastery over[48] his kingdom. Whatever be man's[49] life, he will not be satisfied, for his soul's satisfaction is in fulfilling his purpose[50]. The day when he arrives to[51] that mastery, the day when he has gained the kingdom he had[52] lost, he can say that[53] "Thy will is[54] done on earth as[55] in Heaven". And in this is[56] the fulfillment of man's being born . . . .[57]

The question[58], what is it to be self-disciplined[59]? It is to be able to say "I can" and not that[60] "I can not[61]". Of course, very often the words "I can

---

46. Sk.sh.: a few words missed by Sk.;
    (Sk.l.tr.)Gd.e.: filled in ", bit by bit";
    Gd.hwr., Hq.p., Hq.t., Hq.st.: ", bit by bit," but crossed out by Sk. in "Hq.t."
47. (Sk.l.tr.)Gd.e.: "that" changed to "this";
    Gd.hwr., Hq.p., Hq.t., Hq.st.: "this" instead of "that"
48. (Sk.l.tr.)Gd.e.: "over" changed into "of";
    Gd.hwr.: "of" instead of "over"
49. Sk.l.tr.: "man be in" instead of "be man's"; (Sk.l.tr.)Gd.e.: "man be in", changed back to "be man's"
50. Sk.sh.: "(fulfilling his purpose) . . .";
    Sk.l.tr.: "the fulfillment of his purpose"; (Sk.l.tr.)Gd.e.: "his" changed into "this";
    Gd.hwr., Hq.p., Hq.t., Hq.st.: "the fulfillment of this purpose", changed back by Sk. in "Hq.t." into "fulfilling his purpose"
51. (Sk.l.tr.)Gd.e.: "to" changed into "at";
    Gd.hwr., Hq.p., Hq.t., Hq.st.: "at" instead of "to"
52. Sk.l.tr., Gd.hwr., Hq.p., Hq.t., Hq.st.: "has" instead of "had", but in "Hq.t." changed back by Sk. to "had"
53. Gd.hwr., Hq.p., Hq.t., Hq.st.: "that" replaced with a comma
54. Ibid.: "be" instead of "is", but changed back by Sk. in "Hq.t." into "is"
55. Sk.l.tr., Gd.hwr., Hq.t., Hq.st.: "it is" added;
    Hq.p.: "it is" later added
56. Hq.p., Hq.t.: "is" moved to after "this"
57. Sk.sh.: an open space;
    Sk.t.: typed in "on this earth";
    Sk.l.tr.: filled in, "on earth is accomplished"; (Sk.l.tr.)Gd.e.: "on earth is accomplished" replaced with "as a human being";
    Gd.hwr.: "as a human being";
    Hq.p., Hq.t., Hq.st.: "on earth is accomplished", but changed by Sk. in "Hq.t." to "on this earth";
    Sk.c.tp.: "on this earth"
58. (Sk.l.tr.)Gd.e.: added, "may be asked";
    Hq.p., Hq.t., Hq.st.: added "comes"
59. Sk.sh.: in sh. "self-discipline" and "self-disciplined" are written in the same way;
    Sk.t., Sk.c.tp.: ", self-discipline?";
    all other documents: "self-disciplined"
60. (Sk.l.tr.)Gd.e.: "that" replaced with "to say";
    Gd.hwr., Hq.p., Hq.t., Hq.st.: "that" omitted
61. Sk.t., Sk.l.tr., Sk.c.tp.: "cannot";
    (Sk.l.tr.)Gd.e., Gd.hwr., Hq.p., Hq.t., Hq.st.: "can't"

not[62] " man uses[63], which[64] he does not think is[65] wise, or is[66] just to do. In that case it is different. But when there is something of which he thinks that[67] it is just, it is[68] good, it is[68] right, and [69]that he thinks "I can not", it is there[70] that self-discipline lacks. When a person says, "I cannot[71] tolerate", "I cannot[72] endure", "I cannot[72] bear", "I cannot[72] forgive", all these are the signs of the lack of self-discipline. In order to see this question more clearly, one must picture oneself as two beings: one the king, and the other [73]as the servant[73]. When one wishes, it is the king who wishes, and the part that[74] says "I cannot"[75], it[76] is the

---

62. Sk.t., Sk.c.tp.: "cannot";
Sk.l.tr.: "cannot"; (Sk.l.tr.)Gd.e.: "can't";
Gd.hwr., Hq.st.: "can't"
Hq.t.: "can't" changed by Sk. into "cannot";
Hq.p.: "cannot" changed by Gd. to "can't"
63. (Sk.l.tr.)Gd.e.: "man uses" moved to before "the words"
64. (Sk.l.tr.)Gd.e.: "which" replaced with "of what";
Gd.hwr., Hq.p., Hq.t., Hq.st.: "of what" instead of "which"
65. (Sk.l.tr.)Gd.e.: "is" changed to "it";
Gd.hwr., Hq.p., Hq.t., Hq.st.: "it" instead of "is"
66. (Sk.l.tr.)Gd.e.: "is" crossed out;
Gd.hwr., Hq.p., Hq.t., Hq.st.: "is" omitted
67. (Sk.l.tr.)Gd.e.: "that" crossed out;
Gd.hwr., Hq.p., Hq.t., Hq.st.: "that" omitted
68. Sk.l.tr.: "or" instead of "it is"; (Sk.l.tr.)Gd.e.: "it is" restored
69. Sk.sh.: added by Sk. in sh. after "that", "it is then";
Sk.t., Sk.l.tr., Sk.c.tp.: "that it is then he thinks";
(Sk.l.tr.)Gd.e.: "that it is then he thinks" replaced with "he says";
Gd.hwr., Hq.p., Hq.t., Hq.st.: "he says" instead of "that he thinks", but in "Hq.t." changed by Sk. to "that it is then he thinks"
70. (Sk.l.tr.)Gd.e.: "there" changed into "then";
Gd.hwr., Hq.p., Hq.t., Hq.st.: "then", changed back by Sk. in "Hq.t." into "there"
71. (Sk.l.tr.)Gd.e.: "cannot" changed to "can't";
Gd.hwr., Hq.p., Hq.t., Hq.st.: "can't"
72. (Sk.l.tr.)Gd.e.: "cannot" changed to "can't"
73. Sk.t., Sk.c.tp.: "as" omitted;
Sk.l.tr.: "as the subject" instead of "as the servant"; (Sk.l.tr.)Gd.e.: "as the servant" changed into "his servant";
Gd.hwr., Hq.t., Hq.st.: "his servant", but changed back in "Hq.t." by Sk. into "the servant";
Hq.p.: "the servant", changed by Gd. into "his servant"
74. Gd.hwr.: "that" changed into "which";
Hq.p., Hq.t., Hq.st.: "which" instead of "that"
75. (Sk.l.tr.)Gd.e., Hq.st.: "cannot" changed into, "No, I can't";
Gd.hwr., Hq.p., Hq.t.: "No, I can't", but changed back by Sk. in "Hq.t." to "I cannot"
76. (Sk.l.tr.)Gd.e., Hq.p.: "it" crossed out;
Hq.t.: "it" omitted, but reinserted by Sk.;
Hq.st.: "it" omitted

servant who says "I cannot" [77]. If the servant has the [78] way, then the king is in [79] the place of the servant, and the more the servant has his way, the more the servant rules, and the king is servant . . . [80] Naturally, therefore, a conflict comes upward [81], and that reflects on the whole [82] life, [83]and the whole life becomes unlucky malheureuse [83]. If a person were [84] pious or good or religious, it makes no difference. If man does not realise the kingdom of God within himself, and realises [85] his spirit to be king, he does not accomplish the purpose of [86] life.

---

77. (Sk.l.tr.)Gd.e.: "who says 'I cannot'" crossed out;
Gd.hwr., "who says that" instead of "who says 'I cannot'";
Hq.p., Hq.t., Hq.st.: "who says 'I cannot'" omitted, but again added by Sk. in "Hq.t."
78. (Sk.l.tr.)Gd.e.: "the" changed to "his";
Gd.hwr., Hq.p., Hq.t., Hq.st.: "his", but in "Hq.t." Sk. changed "his" back to "the"
79. Gd.hwr.: "on", changed back by Gd. to "in"
80. Sk.sh.: an open space after "servant";
all other documents: "obeys." instead of "is servant"
81. Sk.sh.: "upward" seems to be what Pir-o-Murshid said, although "up" may have been meant. As the prepositions "up" and "in" are very similar signs in shorthand, later on "upward" was changed to "(inwardly)";
Sk.l.tr.: "inwardly" instead of "upward";
(Sk.l.tr.)Gd.e.: "comes inwardly" changed into "begins inwardly";
Gd.hwr., Hq.p., Hq.t., Hq.st.: "begins inwardly"
82. Sk.sh.: later "whole" changed into "outward" in sh.;
Sk.l.tr.: "outward";
Gd.hwr., Hq.p., Hq.t., Hq.st.: "outer";
Sk.c.tp.: "outward"
83. Sk.sh.: "malheureuse" (the French word for "unlucky") added in lh. by Sk. to make it clear that Pir-o-Murshid had said "unlucky";
all other documents: "malheureuse" omitted;
(Sk.l.tr.)Gd.e.: rewritten to read, "making the whole life a misery";
Gd.hwr., Hq.p., Hq.t., Hq.st.: "making the whole life a misery", but in "Hq.t." Sk. changed this back to "and the whole life becomes unlucky";
Hq.st.: "making the whole life misery"
84. (Sk.l.tr.)Gd.e.: "were" changed into "be";
Gd.hwr.: "was" instead of "were";
Hq.p., Hq.t., Hq.st.: "be"
85. (Sk.l.tr.)Gd.e.: "realises" changed into "realise";
Gd.hwr., Hq.p., Hq.t., Hq.st.: "realise"
86. (Sk.l.tr.)Gd.e.: "his" added;
Gd.hwr., Hq.p., Hq.t., Hq.st.: "his" added, but in "Hq.t." Sk. crossed out "his"

Sakina Furnée's shorthand reporting.

[1]December 1922

The Attitude [2]

[3]All affairs of life depend upon man's attitude. And the mechanical work that is psychologically done in everything[4], is such that before man ~~sets~~ steps

---

Documents:

Sk.sh. = Sakina Furnée's shorthand reporting.

Gd.h. = Sherifa Goodenough's early handwritten text with some editing and without the questions and answers.

Tp.c. = a typescript made from "Gd.h.", without the questions and answers.

Gd.t. = a later typescript made on Gd.'s typewriter with large letters, made from "tp.c." and without the questions and answers.

Sk.t. = a later typescript made under Sk.'s direction from "tp.c." and "Sk sh."

Hq.t. = a typescript made at Headquarters, Geneva from Sk.t. but without the questions and answers.

Hq.st. = a Headquarters stencil made in Geneva from Hq.t. and identical to it in its wording. Therefore it is not mentioned in the notes except in note 2.

Sk.c.tp. = Sk.'s later neatly typed copy, made from "Sk.sh." with the questions and answers included.

Sr.Sk. = an extensive errata list on which in later years Sakina Furnée and Sirdar van Tuyll exchanged comments on revisions made in the texts.

Notes:

1. Sk.sh.: although no date is mentioned in Sk.sh., 11 December 1922 may be assumed to be the day this lecture was given. The previous lecture taken down by Sk. in shorthand in the same notebook is known to have been from 11th December 1922, and the lecture which follows bears the date of 12th December 1922;
   tp.c.: in Sk.'s hwr., "11 Dec." added to "1922";
   Gd.t.: in Sk.'s hwr. added: "11 Dec." and the originally typed year, "1923", changed by Sk. to "1922"
2. Tp.c., Hq.t.: "Address to mureeds" added;
   Gd.t., Sk.t., Hq.st.: "ADDRESS to MUREEDS" added;
   Hq.t., Hq.st.: "GATHEKA" added above, followed by the Invocation
3. Sk.sh.: after the first paragraph in Sk.'s shorthand notebook follows a space: one open line;
   Sk.c.tp.: Sk. at a later date considered the first paragraph to be the beginning of an unfinished lecture, and therefore she left 3/4 page open, and went on with the remaining part of the lecture on a new page, separately dated "December 1922". The other documents, however, consider these two parts as one lecture
4. Tp.c.: "in everything" put in parentheses;
   Gd.t. Sk.t., Hq.t.: "in everything" omitted

forward to work, he sees his attitude being[5] reflected on his affair. For an[6] instance, a person starts to do something with doubt in his spirit[7]; in that affair he sees the shadow of doubt. When a person wants to do something which he knows is not quite just, before he begins the work, he sees the phantom of injustice before him.[3]

[8]Momentary loss and gain does not . . . . They all sum up in one.[8] The heart of man, as Sufis say, is a mirror; all that is reflected in this mirror is reflected on another[9]. When man has doubt in his heart, that doubt is reflected upon every ~~doubt~~ heart[10] with whom that man[11] comes in contact with[12]. When he has faith, that faith is reflected in everybody's[13] heart. Can there be [14]more interesting study and a greater wonder than to observe this keenly in life? As soon as man is able to watch this phenomena[15] in life, it is just like a magic lantern, that makes all clear to one[16]. How foolish in this light would appear to man the cleverness and the crookedness[17] of the (dishonest?)[18], who ~~could~~ for a moment thinks[19] that he profits[20] by it, and who for a moment may seem to profit[21] by it. Worldly gains, which are snatched from one hand to another[22], are

---

5. Gd.h.: first "being" omitted, then reinserted
6. Gd.h., tp.c., Gd.t., Sk.t., Hq.t.: "an" omitted
7. All other documents: "mind" instead of "spirit"
8. Gd.h.: instead of the incomplete passage, in parentheses added by Gd., "Momentary losses and gains don't matter much. They all sum up in one balance when the moment comes." Then this whole passage was crossed out by Gd.;
   all other documents: this passage omitted
9. Gd.h.: "projected upon other mirrors" instead of "reflected on another";
   tp.c., Gd.t., Sk.t., Hq.t.: "projected upon other mirrors"
10. Sk.c.tp.: "every heart" omitted
11. Gd.h., tp.c., Gd.t., Sk.t., Hq.t.: "which he" instead of "whom that man"
12. Ibid.: "with" omitted
13. Sk.sh.: afterwards Sk. changed "everybody's" into "every";
    all other documents: "every" instead of "everybody's"
14. Gd.h., tp.c., Gd.t., Sk.t., Hq.t.: "a" added
15. Gd.h.: "the phenomena";
    tp.c., Sk.c.tp.: "this phenomenon";
    Gd.t., Sk.t., Hq.t.: "that phenomenon"
16. Gd.h., tp.c., Gd.t., Sk.t., Hq.t.: "is making all so clear to him" instead of "makes all clear to one"
17. Gd.h., tp.c., Gd.t., Sk.t., Hq.t.: "crooked ways" instead of "crookedness"
18. Ibid.: "dishonest" without parentheses and question mark;
    Sk.c.tp.: an open space instead of "(dishonest?)"
19. Sk.c.tp.: "think" instead of "thinks"
20. Gd.h., tp.c., Gd.t., Sk.t., Hq.t.: "is profiting" instead of "profits"
21. Ibid.: "be benefited" instead of "profit"
22. Ibid.: "the other" instead of "another"

not worth making . . . [23] heart be reflected by the element which is foreign to it.

This life on earth upon which one [24] cannot depend even on the morrow, only that which is comforting or consoling through all this life of falsehood, is that feeling of purity in one's own life [25], when one feels that one's [26] attitude [27] is right and just. The one who experiences it will certainly say that it is greater than all the riches [28] of the world.

It is the knowledge of this philosophy which seems to be lost from the heart of humanity at the present time. It is therefore that all things go wrong. And if there is any preventive which can be used against it, it is to make one's own life as much as one can an example of one's idea [29], although to make it perfect [30] is most difficult. There is nothing like trying, and if once failed, another time one will succeed [31].

Question: . . . . [32]

---

23. Sk.sh., Sk.c.tp.: a space, indicating that Sk. missed one or more words;
    Sk.t.: "the" added by Sk. in the margin;
    the other documents: no space before "heart"
24. Gd.h.: "one" omitted;
    tp.c., Gd.t., Sk.t., Hq.t.: "we" instead of "one"
25. Gd.h., tp.c., Gd.t., Sk.t., Hq.t.: "heart" instead of "life"
26. Gd.h., tp.c., Gd.t., Sk.t., Hq.t.: "own" added;
    Sr.Sk.: "own" to be added
27. Gd.h., tp.c., Gd.t., Sk.t., Hq.t.: "in life" added, but put in parentheses by Sk. in "Gd.t.";
    Sr.Sk.: "in life" to be omitted
28. Gd.h., tp.c., Gd.t., Sk.t., Hq.t.: "wealth" instead of "riches"
29. Ibid.: "ideal" instead of "idea"
30. Ibid.: "perfectly" instead of "perfect"
31. Ibid.: "may be successful" instead of "will succeed"

Documents used for the questions and answers:

Sk.sh. = Sakina Furnée's shorthand reporting of three questions and answers, with the first question missing

Sk.lh. = Sk.'s hwr. transcription from her sh.r. (the last part). Sk. wrote above "Following after the address 'The Attitude', Dec. '22."

Sk.c.tp. = Sk.'s later neatly typed copy made from "Sk.sh." with the questions and answers included

Notes:

32. Sk.sh., Sk.lh., Sk.t., Sk.c.tp.: no question

Answer: There are some who will say, "Yes, for certain error[33] here[34], now a suffering has come; I shall bear it". No doubt he is brave and just, but I personally would prefer that man, who would resist against suffering by realising that his birthright as[35] a divine right, is happiness alone. And pain and suffering is foreign to his soul, it does not belong to it, he does not want it, he will not have it.

[36]*Question: Is suffering necessary for evolution?*

Answer: Suffering is helpful to evolution, not necessary. In addition therefore, we must not seek suffering in order to evolve. We must avoid suffering in order [37]to . . . . A little[38] failure to a wise person is a teaching, but it is better if he avoided learning in that way.

Question: Would it be possible to gain the same amount of[39] [40]*in life . . . .*[41]*?*

Answer: Certainly possible, but most difficult.

---

33. Sk.t.: "errors" instead of "error"
34. Sk.lh.: "here" omitted, but later added by Sk.;
    Sk.c.tp.: "here" omitted
35. Sk.lh.: "is", afterwards changed back by Sk. into "as"
36. Sk.sh.: this question has been added later by Sk. in sh. after the first sentence of the answer;
    Sk.lh.: the question written by Sk. after the first sentence of the answer;
    Sk.t., Sk.c.tp.: the question put before the answer
37. Sk.lh.: "to" omitted, and an open space after "order";
    Sk.t.: "to" omitted, and an open space after "order", but later "in order....." put in parentheses by Sk.
38. Sk.lh., Sk.t.: "Every" instead of "A little"
39. Sk.sh.: later Sk. wrote above in sh.: "degree of evolution";
    Sk.lh., Sk.t., Sk.c.tp.: "degree of evolution" instead of "amount of"
40. Sk.c.tp.: added "without pain" before "in life"
41. Sk.lh.: added by Sk.: ". . . (without suffering)";
    Sk.t.: later added in pencil by Sk.: "(without suffering)"

Sakina Furnée's shorthand reporting.

Paris, 12th December 1922

The Struggle of Life

No one can deny the fact[1] that life in the world is one[2] continual struggle. The one who does not know the struggle of life is either an unmatured[3] soul, or a soul who has risen above the life of this world. The object of [4]human being in this world is to attain to the perfection of humanity, and therefore it is necessary that man must go through this,[5] what we call [4]struggle of life.

Now there are two different attitudes that one shows while going through that[6] struggle of life. One struggles along bravely through life, the other becomes disappointed, heart-broken, before arriving at his destination. No sooner man

---

Documents:

Sk.sh. = Sakina Furnée's shorthand reporting.

Sk.hwr. = Sakina Furnée's handwritten transcription of her shorthand reporting, with some alterations, preserved by Headquarters on a microfiche;
(Sk.hwr.) Gd.e.: Sherifa Goodenough's editing, corr. and changes on this same document;
(Sk.hwr.) Sk.c.: some 30 years later, Sakina Furnée again went over her shorthand reporting of this lecture and restored several of the changes made by Gd. to what Sk. had taken down originally. In a few cases, however, Sk. did not interpret correctly some of the words in sh.; for instance, she transcribed "After" in the last paragraph as "Self", which are very similar signs in sh.

Sk.tp. = a typescript made from "Sk.sh." and "Sk.hwr." by Sakina or under her direction.

An edited version of this lecture has been published in *The Sufi Message of Hazrat Inayat Khan*, Volume VI (1962), on page 87, 1st paragraph, and page 89, 3rd paragraph to the end of the chapter. This version is so altered, however, that it could not be included in the notes.

Notes:

1. (Sk.hwr.) Gd.e.: "the fact" crossed out
2. Sk.hwr.: "a" instead of "one"
3. Sk.tp.: "unmatured" changed into "unmature";
(Sk.hwr.) Gd.e.: "immature"
4. (Sk.hwr.) Gd.e.: "the" added (or "The")
5. Ibid.: "this," crossed out
6. Sk.hwr.: "this" instead of "that";
Sk.tp.: "this"

gives up[7] his[8] courage to go through the struggle of life, [9]the burden of the whole world [10] falls upon his head. But the one who goes along struggling through it, he alone makes his way. The one whose patience is exhausted, the one who has fallen in that [11] struggle, he is trodden upon by those who walk through life. Even bravery and courage is not sufficient to go [12] through the struggle of life. There is something else which [13] must be studied and understood.

One must study the nature of life, one must understand the psychology of that[6] struggle. In order to understand this struggle, one must see how many sides there are to this struggle [14]. . There are three sides to this struggle [15]: [4]struggle with oneself, [4]struggle with the [16] others, and [4] struggle with circumstances. There is perhaps one [2] person who is capable of struggling with himself, but that [17] is not sufficient. There is another person, who is able to struggle with others, but even that is not sufficient. There is a third person who answers the demand of circumstances, but even that is not sufficient. The thing is that [18] all these [19] three things must be studied and known, and one must be able to manage the struggle in all these three directions.

And now the question is where should one begin, and where should one end? Generally one starts by struggling with others, and he [20] struggles along all his [21] life, and he [20] never comes to an end. And if the person is wise, he [22] struggles with conditions, and perhaps he accomplishes things a little better. But the one who struggles with himself first, is the wisest, because, once [23] he has struggled with himself, which is the most difficult struggle, the other struggle will become easy for him. [4]Struggling [24] with oneself is like singing without an

---

7. (Sk.hwr.) Gd.e.: "does man give up" instead of "man gives up"
8. Ibid.: "his" changed to "the"
9. Ibid.: "than" added
10. Sk.hwr.: "life" instead of "world"; (Sk.hwr.) Sk.c.: "world" restored
11. (Sk.hwr.) Gd.e.: "that" changed to "this";
    Sk.tp.: "this"
12. (Sk.hwr.) Gd.e.: "for going" instead of "to go"
13. Sk.hwr.: "that" instead of "which"
14. (Sk.hwr.) Gd.e.: "this struggle" replaced with "it"
15. Ibid.: "to this struggle" crossed out
16. Sk.hwr.: "the" omitted
17. Ibid. : "this" instead of "that"
18. (Sk.hwr.) Gd.e.: "The thing is that" crossed out
19. Ibid.: "these" crossed out
20. (Sk.hwr.) Gd.e.: "he" crossed out
21. Ibid.: "his" changed to "one's"
22. Sk.hwr.: "and" instead of "he"; (Sk.hwr.) Sk.c.: "he" restored
23. (Sk.hwr.) Gd.e.: "once" crossed out; (Sk.hwr.) Sk.c.: "once" restored
24. Sk.hwr.: "struggle"

accompaniment. [4]Struggling with others is the definition of war, struggle [25] with oneself is the . . . [26] of peace. It might seem in the beginning and in its outward appearance that it is cruel to have to struggle with oneself, especially when one is in the right. But the one who has reached [27] deeper into life, will find that the struggle with oneself is the most profitable in the end.

Now coming to the question, what is the nature of the struggle with oneself? There are three aspects: to make our thought, speech and action answer the demand of our own ideal, while at the same time to give expression to all the impulses and all desires which are there as one's natural being. The next aspect of the struggle with oneself is to fit in with others, with their various ideas and with their various demands. For in this one has to make oneself as narrow as the accommodation, and as wide as the accommodation [28] that [29] demands [30] one to be, which is a delicate matter, difficult for everybody, even [31] to comprehend; to practise it . . . [32]. And the third aspect of the struggle with self, is to give accommodation to others in one's own life, in one's own heart, large or small [33], as the demand may be.

When we consider the question of the struggle with the [16] others, there are three things to think about: how to control and govern people and activities which happen to be our duty, our responsibility. Another aspect is how to allow ourselves [34] to be used by the others under different situations and positions in life. To what extent or where comes the line of limit where one should allow others to make use of our time, our energy, our work or [35] patience, and where to draw a line. And the third aspect is to fit in with the different forms [36] of

---

25. Sk.tp.: "struggling"
26. Sk.sh.: an open space;
    Sk.hwr., Sk.tp.: "definition" filled in
27. Sk.hwr.: "reaches"; (Sk.hwr.) Sk.c.: "has reached" restored
28. Sk.tp.: "and as wide as the accommodation" omitted, but later reinserted
29. (Sk.hwr.) Gd.e.: "that" crossed out
30. Ibid.: "of" added
31. Sk.tp.: "even" omitted
32. Sk.sh.: here Sk. missed a few words;
    Sk.hwr.: "still more difficult" filled in;
    Sk.tp.: later added "is still more difficult"
33. Sk.hwr.: "larger or smaller";
    Sk.tp.: "larger or small"
34. Sk.hwr.: "ourselves" omitted; (Sk.hwr.) Sk.c.: "ourselves" restored
35. Sk.tp.: ", our" instead of "or"
36. Sk.sh.: the sh. sign is not very clear, but seems to be "forms";
    Sk.hwr.: "standards" instead of "forms";
    Sk.tp.: "standards"

conception that different personalities have, who are of[37] various stages of evolution.

Now coming to this[38] third aspect of that struggle, which is[39] conditions: there are conditions which can be helped, and there are conditions which cannot be helped, before which one is helpless. And again there are conditions that can be helped, and yet one does not find in oneself that capability, that power and that[40] means to . . .[41] the condition. If one studies and thinks about these questions of life, and meditates[42] for the inspiration and light to fall on them, that one may understand how to understand[43], how to struggle through life, one certainly will (find ~~a~~ all help.)[44] Certainly one can arrive to[45] a state where one would find life easier.

Now in conclusion to what I have said, I should like to say how a Sufi would look at it, and how a Sufi would set to work. The Sufi looks upon the struggle[46] as an unavoidable struggle, and a struggle which must be gone through. He sees from his mystical point of view that ~~if he will take good much notice~~ the more he will take notice of his[47] struggle, the more the struggle will expand. And the less[48] he will make of it, the better he will . . .[49] able to pass through it. When he looks at the world, what he sees?[50] He sees everybody, his hand[51] before his forehead, looking only at his own struggle[52], which are[53] as big as his

---

37. (Sk.hwr.) Gd.e.: "of" changed into "at"
38. Sk.hwr.: "the" instead of "this";
    Sk.tp.: "the"
39. Sk.hwr.: "with" added;
    Sk.tp.: "the" added before "conditions"
40. Sk.hwr.: "those", although "that" is clearly taken down in sh.
41. Sk.hwr.: a blank;
    Sk.hwr.: filled in, "change";
    Sk.tp.: "change"
42. Sk.tp.: "meditated", later changed by Sk. in ink to "meditates"
43. Sk.hwr.: "how to understand" omitted;
    Sk.tp.: "how to understand" crossed out
44. Sk.sh.: Sk. put these words in parentheses, thereby expressing some uncertainty;
    Sk.hwr.: "find help" instead of "(find ~~a~~ all help.)";
    Sk.tp.: "find help"
45. (Sk.hwr.) Gd.e.: "to" changed into "at"
46. Sk.hwr.: "of" added, then crossed out
47. Sk.tp.: "the" instead of "his"
48. Sk.hwr.: "little" instead of "less"; (Sk.hwr.) Sk.c.: "less" restored
49. Sk.hwr.: one word skipped by Sk.; (Sk.hwr.) Sk.c.: "be" added;
    Sk.tp.: "be"
50. (Sk.hwr.) Gd.e.: "What does he see?" instead of "What he sees?"
51. Sk.hwr.: "hands"
52. Sk.tp.: "struggles"

own palm. He thinks: "Shall I sit like that[54] also, and look at my struggles?" That will not answer the ~~purpose~~ question. His work, therefore, is to engage in the struggle of others, to console them, to strengthen them, to give them a hand, and through that his own struggle . . .[55] makes him free to go forward.

Now the question is, how does he struggle? He struggles with power, with understanding, with open eyes and patience. He does not look at the loss; that which is lost, is lost. He does not think of the pain of yesterday; yesterday is gone for him. Yes[56], if there is a pleasant remembrance, he keeps it before him, for it is helpful on his way. He takes [57]the admiration and the hatred coming from those[58] around him both[59], with smiles. He only thinks that these both[60] things form rhythm in the rhythm[61] of a certain time of music; there is one and two, strong accent and weak accent. Praise cannot be without blame, nor blame can[62] be without praise. He does not allow his power to penetrate . . .[63], but he keeps the torch of wisdom before him, because he believes that the present is the reecho of the past, and the future will be the reflection of the present. It will not do to only[64] think of that moment, but to think where it comes from and where it goes. Every thought[65] comes to his mind, every impulse, every word he speaks, to him it is like a seed, a seed which falls in this soil of life and takes root. And in this way he finds that nothing is lost; every little good deed, every little act of kindness, of love, done to anybody, it will some day rise as a plant and bear fruit.

The Sufi does not consider life any different from a business, but he sees in the best manner how the real business can be achieved.

---

53. Sk.hwr.: "is" instead of "are"
54. Sk.tp.: "this" instead of "that"
55. Sk.sh.: here Sk. missed a few words;
Sk.hwr.: an open space; (Sk.hwr.) Gd.e.: filled in "becomes easier and that";
Sk.tp.: later added, "becomes easier and that"
56. Sk.hwr.: "Then," instead of "Yes,"
57. (Sk.hwr.) Gd.e.: "both" added
58. Sk.tp.: "those" omitted, but reinserted by Sk. in ink
59. (Sk.hwr.) Gd.e.: "both" crossed out
60. Sk.sh.: afterwards Sk. changed the sequence into "both these";
(Sk.hwr.) Gd.e.: "both these";
Sk.t.: later corrected in ink to "both these"
61. Sk.hwr.: "in the rhythm" omitted; (Sk.hwr.) Sk.c.: "in the rhythm" restored
62. (Sk.hwr.) Gd.e.: "can blame" instead of "blame can"
63. (Sk.hwr.) Gd.e.: "(penetrate) lead him blindfold";
Sk.tp.: later "penetrate" crossed out and "lead him blindfold" filled in
64. (Sk.hwr.) Gd.e.: "only to" instead of "to only"
65. (Sk.hwr.) Gd.e.: "that" added;
Sk.tp.: "that" added

The symbol of the mystics of China was a branch of fruit in their hand. What does it mean? It means the purpose of life is to arrive to that stage when every moment of life becomes fruitful. And what does fruitful mean? Does it mean fruits [66] for oneself? [67] No, the trees do not bear fruit for themselves, but for others. ~~A~~ True profit is not that profit which one makes for oneself. [68] True profit is that which one makes for others. After attaining [69] to all that one wants to attain, either earthly or heavenly [70], what is the result of it all? The result is only this, that all that one has attained, [71]one has acquired, whether earthly or heavenly[70], that one can place before others. In the language of Vedanta, [72]*propkar*, which means working for the benefit of others is the only fruit of life.

---

66. Sk.hwr.: "It does not mean fruit" instead of "Does it mean fruits"
67. Ibid.: the question mark replaced with a full stop
68. Sk.hwr.: "The" added
69. Sk.hwr.: "Self attaining"; (Sk.hwr.) Gd.e.: "The attainment" instead of "Self attaining". Reading again her shorthand reporting of this lecture, some 30 years later, Sk. misread "Self" for "After", which are very similar signs in sh.
70. Sk.hwr.: "earth or heaven" instead of "earthly or heavenly"
71. Ibid.: "and" added
72. Ibid.: "there is a word" added

Sakina Furnée's shorthand reporting.

Paris [1,2]

Attainment [3]

There are many in this world who push along[4] the object of their

---

Documents:

Sk.sh. = Sakina Furnée's shorthand reporting, taken down in a small green copybook containing reportings of lectures given in November and December 1922 in Paris.

Hl. = a reporting by Mademoiselle C. Hulot of a simultaneous translation into French, sentence by sentence, of the lecture given in English. Only the main part of the first paragraph has been taken down, and this fragment has not been mentioned in the notes except in note 1.

Sk.t. = a typescript made from Sakina's transcription of her shorthand reporting at Headquarters, Geneva.

Sk.l.tr. = Sakina Furnée's later handwritten transcription of her shorthand reporting; (Sk.l.tr.) Gd.e.: this same document was used later by Sherifa Goodenough for making corrections and for editing, in light blue ink.

Gd.hwr. = a copy in Gd.'s handwriting, made from "Sk.l.tr." with most of "(Sk.l.tr.) Gd.e." incorporated.

Hq.p. = a second copy in Gd.'s handwriting, made as a preparation for the "Hq.st.".

Hq.t. = a typescript made from "Gd.hwr." at Headquarters, Geneva, on a copy of which Sk. later restored to "Sk.t." most of the changes made by Gd.

Hq.st. = a stencilled copy issued by Headquarters, Geneva, made from "Hq.p."

Sk.c.tp. = a neat typewritten copy made by Sk. in later years from "Sk.t."

Notes:

1. Sk.t., Sk.c.tp.: "December 1922" added;
   Gd.hwr.: "Dec. 13th" written above;
   Hl.: "13 Décembre 22" written above;
   Hq.t.: later Sk. added in hwr.: "December 1922."
2. Sk.sh.: afterwards Sk. added, "Hotel Britannique - métro Châtelet, Avenue Victoria 20."
3. Sk.sh.: later Sk. wrote in lh. above the lecture: "Attainment III", and after the lecture had been assigned to the series of Gitas, Sk. added in lh. after the title: "Sadhana II 6. (282)", indicating that it had been included in Series II as number 6, whereas "(282)" refers to the number Sk. had assigned to the series of Gitas on this subject;
   Sk.t: "SADHANA THE ATTAINMENT", and in Sk.'s hwr. later written above: "Githa Sadhana II, 6"
   Sk.l.tr.: "Sadhana III or the Attainment" as a title; (Sk.l.tr.) Gd.e.: "Sadhana III or The Path of Attainment". Later Gd. added above: "Series II. Githa. Number ~~3~~ ~~6~~ 7.";
   Gd.hwr.: "Sadhana" as a title, and added above: "Series II. Githa; Number ~~3~~ 6.";
   Hq.p.: "Series II. Githa. Number ~~3~~ 6." Sadhana. The Path of Attainment.";
   Hq.t.: "Sadhana. Series II. Number 6.";

attainment as a football of enthusiasm[5]. They mean to take it, but without attention[6] they push it on, and that[7] occurs when one is too enthusiastic to attain to[8] a certain thing for which he[9] has not made himself[10] ready. One must remember that[11] in the path of attainment, that one[12] must feel[13] first strong enough to bear the burden of that which one wishes to attain[14]. The wisdom which one sees working behind nature, has attended it and[15] arranged it so, that every being and every thing will bear the weight that it can sustain[16]. Very often man's ambition runs before his power or wisdom[17]. He, before thinking whether he is entitled to[18] a certain thing, tries[19] to attain it[20], and it is this which

---

Hq.st.: "Series II. Githa. Number 3" (later changed by hand to "6"). "SADHANA. THE PATH OF ATTAINMENT";

Sk.c.tp.: added as a title: "SADHANA, THE ATTAINMENT"

4. Hq.p., Hq.t., Hq.st.: "away" instead of "along", probably a misreading from "Gd.hwr." In Sk.sh. "along" was clearly taken down.
5. Sk.l.tr.: "out" inserted by Sk. before "of enthusiasm";
   (Sk.l.tr;)Gd.e.: "out of" replaced with "with their";
   Gd.hwr.: "of enthusiasm" first omitted, then "with their enthusiasm" inserted by Gd.;
   Hq.p., Hq.t., Hq.st.: "with their enthusiasm"
6. Sk.t., Sk.c.tp.: "intention" instead of "attention";
   Sk.l.tr.: "attention" changed by Sk. into "intention", then restored to "attention";
   Hq.t.: "attention" changed by Sk. into "intention"
7. Gd.hwr., Hq.p., Hq.t., Hq.st.: "this" instead of "that"
8. Hq.p., Hq.t., Hq.st.: "to" omitted
9. Sk.l.tr.: "he" changed by Sk. into "one";
   Hq.p.: "one", changed by Gd. to "he"
10. Sk.l.tr.: "himself" changed by Sk. into "oneself";
    Hq.p.: "oneself", changed back by Gd. to "himself"
11. (Sk.l.tr.) Gd.e.: "that" changed into "this";
    Gd.hwr., Hq.p., Hq.t., Hq.st.: "this" instead of "that"
12. Gd.hwr.: "one" omitted
13. Sk.l.tr., Hq.p., Hq.t., Hq.st.: "feel" moved to after "first"
14. (Sk.l.tr.) Gd.e.: "attain" changed into "lift";
    Gd.hwr., Hq.p., Hq.t., Hq.st.: "lift", but on a copy of "Hq.t." changed back by Sk. to "attain"
15. Sk.t.: "intended it and" instead of "attended it and";
    Sk.l.tr.: "attended" changed to "intended", and "it" first omitted, then reinserted by Sk.; (Sk.l.tr.) Gd.e.: "intended and has";
    Gd.hwr., Hq.p., Hq.t., Hq.st.: "intended and has"
16. (Sk.l.tr.) Gd.e.: "that it can sustain" changed into "it is intended to bear";
    Gd.hwr.: "it is intended to bear";
    Hq.t., Hq.st.: "that it is intended to bear", changed back by Sk. on a copy of "Hq.t." to "that it can sustain"
17. (Sk.l.tr.) Gd.e.: "or wisdom" changed into "of bearing";
    Gd.hwr., Hq.p., Hq.t., Hq.st.: "of bearing", but changed back by Sk. on a copy of "Hq.t." into "or wisdom"
18. Gd.hwr., Hq.p., Hq.t., Hq.st.: "attain" added

causes[21] very often failure. Man must become entitled first to have what he wishes to have. This makes it easy for him to gain what he wishes to gain, and it easy to attract[22] to him what he wishes to attract[23].

There is one thing which is desiring, and[24] there is another thing which is imagining. Lying in a grass hut, one can desire for[25] a solid wall around his hut, but one can imagine a palace before him[26]. Therefore it is not imagination which helps[27] in the[28] attainment, it is the earnest desire which helps to attain it[29].

There are things which are within one's reach, there are things which are beyond one's reach. One must first[30] prove to one's own self[31] the capability of attainment, what is[31] within one's reach. This gives one[32] sufficient[33] self-confidence in order[34] to attain that which seems[35] beyond his[36] reach. In the

---

19. (Sk.l.tr.) Gd.e.: "tries" changed into "strives";
Gd.hwr., Hq.p., Hq.t., Hq.st.: "strives", but changed back by Sk. on a copy of "Hq.t." to "tries"
20. Sk.l.tr.: "it" omitted; (Sk.l.tr.) Gd.e.: "it" reinserted
21. (Sk.l.tr.) Gd.e.: "causes" moved to after "very often"
22. Sk.sh.: "it is easy to attract" may have been said, but Sk. crossed out "it easy to", replaced it with "this" in sh. and added an 's' to "attract";
Sk.t., Sk.c.tp.: "that attracts";
Sk.l.tr.: "it easily attracts"; (Sk.l.tr.) Gd.e.: "this easily attracts";
Gd.hwr.: "this easily attracts";
Hq.p., Hq.t., Hq.st.: "it easily attracts", but changed by Sk. on a copy of "Hq.t." into "that attracts"
23. (Sk.l.tr.) Gd.e.: "what he wishes to attract" changed into "that which he wishes to gain";
Gd.hwr.: "that which he wishes to gain";
Hq.p., Hq.t., Hq.st.: "what he wishes to attain"
24. Gd.hwr.: "and" omitted
25. (Sk.l.tr.) Gd.e.: "for" crossed out;
Gd.hwr., Hq.p., Hq.t., Hq.st.: "for" omitted
26. Sk.l.tr.: "one" instead of "him"
27. (Sk.l.tr.) Gd.e.: "so much" added;
Gd.hwr., Hq.p., Hq.t., Hq.st.: "so much" added, but crossed out by Sk. on a copy of "Hq.t."
28. (Sk.l.tr.) Gd.e.: "the" crossed out
29. (Sk.l.tr.) Gd.e.: "which helps to attain it" replaced with, "that is needed for it";
Gd.hwr., Hq.p., Hq.t., Hq.st.: "that is needed for it", replaced by Sk. on a copy of "Hq.t." with "which helps to attain it"
30. Hq.t.: "first" omitted, later added by Sk.
31. Gd.hwr.: "one's capability of attaining things which is";
Hq.p., Hq.st.: "one's capacity of attaining things which are"
Hq.t.: "one's capacity of attaining things which are", changed by Sk. into: "one's capability of attainment what is"
32. Sk.l.tr.: "a" instead of "one"; (Sk.l.tr.) Gd.e.: "a" changed back to "one"
33. Gd.hwr.: "sufficient" crossed out
34. (Sk.l.tr.) Gd.e.: "in order" crossed out
35. Hq.p., Hq.t., Hq.st.: "is" instead of "seems", but on a copy of "Hq.t." changed back by Sk. to "seems"

path of attainment, one must keep the eye of justice open. One must be able to know what attainment is right for him [37] to attain [38], and which [39] attainment he does not deserve. There is no soul in this [40] world who is not striving after something. To one his object of striving [41] is distinct, for [42] another, perhaps, it is perplex . . . [43]. Yet no one is living and not striving after something. According to the extent that the object is clear to one [44], it is easy for him to attain [45].

In the process of attainment there are four stages. In the first place in mind the object must be concrete [46], which one wishes to attain. Next it must be reasoned out how the desire can be materialised. Third is [47] what material is to be used, and to be obtained for it. The fourth is [48]composing, forming or building of that [49] object.

The central theme of the whole creation is attainment. In the striving of all souls in the world, there is one impulse, and that is [50]divine impulse. Yet, [51]man who ignorantly strives after something, and wrongly goes to work about

---

36. Sk.l.tr.: "one's" instead of "his";
    Gd.hwr.: "his" changed into "one's";
    Hq.p., Hq.t., Hq.st.: "one's"
37. Sk.l.tr.: "one" instead of "him"
38. Hq.p., Hq.t., Hq.st.: "to attain" omitted, but added back in a copy of "Hq.t." by Sk.
39. Gd.hwr., Hq.p., Hq.t., Hq.st.: "what" instead of "which"
40. Hq.p., Hq.t., Hq.st.: "the" instead of "this"
41. (Sk.l.tr.) Gd.e.: "the object of his striving"
42. (Sk.l.tr.) Gd.e.: "for" changed into "to";
    Gd.hwr., Hq.p., Hq.t., Hq.st.: "to" instead of "for"
43. Sk.sh.: a small blank after "is perplex", where "is perplexing" may have been said;
    Sk.t., Sk.c.tp., Sk.l.tr.: "is perplex" without open space;
    (Sk.l.tr;)Gd.e.: "seems perplexed";
    Gd.hwr., Hq.p., Hq.t., Hq.st.: "seems perplexed"
44. Gd.hwr.: "him" instead of "one"
45. Sk.l.tr.: "for one to attain";
    (Sk.l.tr.) Gd.e.: "to attain it" instead of "for him to attain";
    Gd.hwr., Hq.p., Hq.t., Hq.st.: "to attain it", but changed on a copy of "Hq.t." by Sk. into "for him to attain"
46. (Sk.l.tr.) Gd.e.: "must be concrete" moved to after "wishes to attain";
    Hq.p.: "must be created", then "created" replaced with "concrete"
47. Sk.t.: "Third" instead of "Third is";
    all other documents: "The third is"
48. Sk.l.tr., Gd.hwr., Hq.p., Hq.p., Hq.st.: "the" added
49. (Sk.l.tr.) Gd.e.: "that" changed to "the";
    Gd.hwr., Hq.p., Hq.t., Hq.st.: "the", but changed back by Sk. in a copy of "Hq.t." to "that"
50. (Sk.l.tr.) Gd.e., Hq.p., Hq.t., Hq.st.: "the" added
51. (Sk.l.tr.) Gd.e., Gd.hwr., Hq.p., Hq.t., Hq.st.: "the" added

it[52], ends in disappointment, disappointment not only to himself, but even to God. The one who knows his affair, and who accomplishes it rightly, fulfils the mission of his life and the wish of God. No matter what man[53] accomplishes, it is only a step towards[54] something else. As one goes along accomplishing in the path of attainment, he[55] in the end arrives at the ~~fulfilment of~~ purpose of his life[56]. In the final attainment is the purpose[57] of all souls, although in the beginning they[58] seem different.

---

52. (Sk.l.tr.) Gd.e.: "wrongly goes to work about it" changed into "sets to work about it wrongly"
53. (Sk.l.tr.) Gd.e.: "man" changed into "one";
    Gd.hwr., Hq.p., Hq.t., Hq.st.: "one" instead of "man", but changed back by Sk. on a copy of "Hq.t." to "man"
54. (Sk.l.tr.) Gd.e.: "towards" changed to "toward";
    Gd.hwr., Hq.p.: "toward", but in "Hq.p." changed back by Gd. to "towards"
55. Sk.l.tr.: "one" instead of "he"
56. (Sk.l.tr.) Gd.e.: "aim of life" instead of "purpose of his life";
    Gd.hwr.: "aim of life", then replaced with "final attainment";
    Hq.p., Hq.t., Hq.st.: "aim of life"
57. Sk.l.tr.: "is the purpose" omitted;
    (Sk.l.tr.) Gd.e., Gd.hwr., Hq.p., Hq.t., Hq.st.: "aim" instead of "purpose"
58. Sk.l.tr., Gd.hwr., Hq.p., Hq.t., Hq.st.: "it" instead of "they", but on a copy of "Hq.t." changed back by Sk. into "they"

Sakina Furnée's shorthand reporting.

Paris [1]

[2]

The Manner of the Prayer

There are three kinds[3] among those who are in a habit to offer prayer.

Documents:

Sk.sh.	=	Sakina Furnée's shorthand reporting.
Sk.hwr.	=	Sakina Furnée's hwr. transcription of her shorthand reporting; (Sk.hwr.) Gd.e.: this same document was used later by Sherifa Goodenough for editing.
Gd.h.	=	a copy, hastily copied by Gd. in hwr. from "Sk.hwr.", with some editing; the further editing by Gd., "(Sk.hwr.) Gd.e.", must have taken place later.
O.t.	=	an old typescript made from "(Sk.hwr.) Gd.e.", and later used as a first book-preparation.
Hq.p.	=	a preparation for the Headquarters' stencil in the series of Religious Gathekas, made from the "o.t." but without the Invocation.
Hq.t.	=	a typescript made from "Hq.p.", to which Sk. added the first three words of the Invocation and the number "4" in hwr., to indicate its insertion in the Headquarters' series of Religious Gathekas.
Hq.st.	=	a stencilled copy made at Headquarters, Geneva, from the "Hq.t.", but sometimes going back in its wording to "Sk.hwr."
Bk.p.2	=	for this second book-preparation a copy of "Hq.p." was used.
Bk.	=	the book *The Unity of Religious Ideals* (1929), compiled by Sherifa Goodenough, Part I, chapter VI.

Notes:

1. Sk.sh.: although none of the documents bears a date, in Sakina Furnée's shorthand copybook this lecture follows after the lecture "Attainment" of 13th December 1922, and precedes the lecture "The Music of the Spheres", known to have been given in Paris on 15th December 1922. It may therefore be dated 14th December 1922.
2. Sk.sh.: later added by Sk.: "Religious Gatheka 4";
   Sk.hwr., Gd.h.: later written above "Religious Gatheka" in Gd.'s hwr.;
   all other documents: typewritten above, "Religious Gatheka", in a copy of "Hq.t." followed by the first three words of the Invocation in Sk.'s hwr., and in "Hq.st." by the Invocation. On copies of "o.t." and "Hq.p.", "Religious Gatheka" was crossed out when these documents were used as a first and second book-preparation (bk.p.1, bk.p.2)
3. (Sk.hwr.) Gd.e.: "of people" added, and later crossed out by Sk.
   o.t., Hq.p., Hq.t., bk.: "of people" added

There is one who by praying fulfils a certain duty which he considers[4] among all the[5] duties of life. He does not know to whom he is praying, he thinks, to[6] some God. If he is in the congregation, he of necessity, he[7] feels[8] obliged to do as the[9] others do. He is like one among the sheep who go[10] on, he[11] does not know where and why. Prayer to him is something that he must do, because he is put in a position[12] where he cannot[13] help it, in order to fall in with the custom of the family or community, and in order to (respect)[14] those around[15] him. He does it as everybody else. His prayer is mechanical, and if it makes any effect, it is very little.

And the second kind of person who offers his prayers is the one who offers the[16] prayers because he is told[17] to do so, and yet is[18] confused if there is any God, if his prayers are[19] heard. He may be praying and at the same time confusion is[20] in his mind, ~~is~~ [21]"Am I right or wrong?"[21] If he is a busy man,

---

4. (Sk.hwr.) Gd.e.: "as ~~being~~ one" added;
   o.t., Hq.p., Hq.t., Hq.st., bk.: "as one" added
5. (Sk.hwr.) Gd.e.: "other" added, and later crossed out by Sk.;
   o.t., Hq.p., Hq.t., bk.: "other" added, but on a copy of "Hq.t." put in parentheses by Sk.
6. O.t.: "of", afterwards changed in ink into "to"
7. All other documents: "he" omitted
8. (Sk.hwr.) Gd.e.: "feels of necessity" instead of "of necessity , he feels"
   o.t., Hq.p., Hq.t., bk.: "feels of necessity", but changed by Gd. in "bk.p.2" to "of necessity feels"
9. O.t.: "the" omitted
10. All other documents: "goes" instead of "go"
11. Gd.h.: "he" omitted
12. Gd.h.: "situation" instead of "position";
    (Sk.hwr.) Gd.e.: "position" changed into "situation";
    o.t., Hq.p., Hq.t., bk.: "situation" instead of "position"
13. Gd.h.: "can't" instead of "cannot"
14. Sk.sh.: "respect" put in parentheses by Sk. to indicate her uncertainty if this word has been said;
    Sk.hwr.: dots under "respect" indicating uncertainty;
    all the other documents: "respect"
15. Gd.h.: "round" instead of "around"
16. O.t.: "his" instead of "the"
17. Bk.: "taught" instead of "told"
18. Gd.h.: "is" omitted
19. Gd.h.: "really" omitted;
    (Sk.hwr.) Gd.e., o.t., Hq.p., Hq.t., Hq.st., bk.: "really" added
20. Gd.h.: "may be going on" instead of "is";
    (Sk.hwr.) Gd.e., Hq.p., Hq.t., Hq.st., bk.: "may be going on";
    o.t.: "going on" instead of "is"
21. Gd.h.: "whether I am doing right or I am doing wrong";
    (Sk.hwr.) Gd.e.: "~~whether he is doing right or is doing wrong~~? Am I doing right or doing wrong?";
    o.t., Hq.p., Hq.t., Hq.st., bk.: "Am I doing right or wrong?"

he might think: "Am I giving my time to something really profitable, or [22] wasting it? I see no one before me, I hear no answer to my prayers [23]". He does it because he was told by someone to do it, or because [24] it might do some good to him [25]. His prayer is a prayer in the dark. The heart, which must be open [26] to God, is covered by his own doubt [27], and if he prayed in this way for thousand years, it is never heard. It is this kind of a [28] soul who in the end loses his faith, especially when he meets with [29]disappointment, and he prays [30], and if [31] his prayer is not answered, that puts an end to his belief.

Then there is a third person who has imagination, which is [32] strengthened by faith. He does not only pray to God, but he prays before God, in the presence of God. Once the [33] imagination has helped man to bring the presence of God before him, God in his own heart is wakened. Then before he utters a word, it is heard by God. When he is praying in a room, he is not alone; he is there with

---

22. Sk.hwr.: "am I" added;
Gd.h., o.t., Hq.p., Hq.t., Hq.st., bk.: "am I" added
23. (Sk.hwr.) Gd.e.: "prayer" changed to "prayer";
all other documents: "prayer"
24. Gd.h.: "because" changed to "perhaps";
bk.p.2: "perhaps" added after "because";
bk.: "perhaps" after "because"
25. Gd.h.: "be doing him some good" instead of "do some good to him";
(Sk.hwr.) Gd.e.: "bring him some good";
o.t., Hq.p., Hq.t., Hq.st., bk.: "bring him some good"
26. Sk.hwr.: "opened"; in sh. the same sign is used for "open" and "opened";
Gd.h.: "opened";
(Sk.hwr.) Gd.e.: "open" changed to "opened";
Hq.p., Hq.t., Hq.st., bk.: "opened"
27. O.t., Hq.p., Hq.t.: "doubts" instead of "doubt";
bk.p.2: "doubts", changed to "doubt" by Gd.
28. Gd.h.: "a" omitted;
(Sk.hwr.) Gd.e.: "a" crossed out;
all other documents: "a" omitted
29. Gd.h.: "a" added;
(Sk.hwr.) Gd.e.: "a" added;
all other documents: "a" added
30. Sk.hwr.: "and he prays" omitted; (Sk.hwr.) Gd.e.: "and he prays" reinserted;
o.t., Hq.p., Hq.t.: "if he prays";
bk.p.2: "if he prays" changed to "and prays";
bk.: "He prays"
31. O.t., Hq.p., Hq.t.: "if" omitted, but reinserted by Gd. in "bk.p.2"
32. Gd.h.: "is" omitted
33. Gd.h.: "the" omitted;
bk.p.2: "the" crossed out by Gd.;
bk.: "the" omitted

God. Then God to him is not in the highest Heaven, but next to him, in him [34], before him. Then Heaven to him is a the [35] earth, and the [36] earth for [37] him is Heaven. No [38] one [39] is then so living as God, so intelligible as God, and all the names and forms before him, all are covered under that [40]. Then every word of prayer he says [41], it [42] is a living word. It does not only bring him [43]but blessings [43] to all those around him. It is this manner of prayer which is only [44] the right way of prayer [45], and by that [46] manner the object that is to be fulfilled by prayer is accomplished.

- - - - - - - - - -

Question: Il faut mesurer ses forces pour atteindre au but, mais combien peut on savoir les forces qu'on a? [47]

---

34. Gd.h.: "in him" moved to after "before him";
    (Sk.hwr.)Gd.e.: "in him" moved to after "before him";
    o.t., Hq.p., Hq.t., Hq.st., bk.: "before him, in him"
35. Gd.h.: "on" instead of "the";
    (Sk.hwr.)Gd.e.: "the" replaced with "on";
    all other documents: "on" instead of "the"
36. O.t.: "the" omitted
37. Ibid.: "to" instead of "for"
38. Sk.hwr.: "No" changed to "Not"
39. Gd.h.: "to him" added;
    (Sk.hwr.)Gd.e.: "to him" added
    all other documents: "to him" added
40. Gd.h.: "him" instead of "that", afterwards changed by Gd. to "Him";
    (Sk.hwr.)Gd.e.: "That" crossed out and "Him" added, but in parentheses
41. Bk.: "utters" instead of "says"
42. (Sk.hwr.)Gd.e.: "it" crossed out;
    all other documents: "it" omitted
43. Sk.hwr.: "but" moved to after "blessings,";
    Gd.h.: "blessing, but blessings" instead of "blessings, but";
    all other documents: "blessing, but blessings"
44. Sk.hwr.: "only" moved to after "the";
    (Sk.hwr.)Gd.e.: "only" moved to before "is";
    all other documents: "only is the"
45. Bk.p.1,2,: "prayer" changed to "praying" by Gd.;
    bk.: "praying" instead of "prayer"
46. Sk.hwr.: "this" instead of "that";
    all other documents: "this"
47. Sk.sh.: this question in French was written by Sk. in lh. after the reporting of the lecture, without the answer. It refers to the lecture "Attainment" of 13th December 1922, beginning on page 257

Sakina Furnée's shorthand reporting.

Paris, [1] December 1922

The Music of the Spheres

There are many in this world who look after wonders; if one only noticed how much there is in this world, which is all phenomena. The deeper one sees in life, the wider life opens itself to him, and every moment of his life then becomes full of wonders and full of splendour[2].

Coming to the subject of the music of the spheres, which I am to speak to you this evening, I should like to say that in everyday language what we call music is only a miniature of which is behind this all, and which has been the source and origin of this nature. It is therefore that the wise of all ages have considered music to be a sacred art, for in music the seer can see the picture of the whole universe. And the wise can interpret the secret and the nature of the working of the whole universe in the realm of music. This idea is not a new idea, and at the same time it is always new. Nothing is as old as the truth, and nothing is as new as the truth. Man's desire to search for something traditional,

---

Documents:

Sk.sh. = Sakina Furnée's shorthand reporting.

Lf. = a neatly hwr. copy made by M.lle Lefèbvre of a simultaneous translation of the lecture in French also taken down by M.lle Lefèbvre.

Sk.l.tp. = a typewritten copy of a new transcription of the shorthand reporting (Sk.sh.) made by Sakina Furnée some thirty years later.

L.M. = the lecture was first published in a French translation in a bimonthly French bulletin *Le Message* of July/August 1953.

A highly edited version of this lecture appears as two chapters with the same title, combined with parts of other lectures on music, in Volume II of *The Sufi Message of Hazrat Inayat Khan* (1960).

Notes:

1. Sk.sh.: the lecture appears in one of Sakina's shorthand notebooks of December 1922, but bears no date;
   Lf.: "15 Décembre 1922" written above
2. Sk.l.tp.: "splendours"

for something original, and man's desire to satisfy ...[3] for something new, all these tendencies can be satisfied in the knowledge of truth. In all the religions, for instance in the Vedas of Hindus, one reads *Nada Brahma*, sound being the Creator.

In the words[4] of the wise of the ancient India[5] . . . [6]which means: "first song, then Vedas or Wisdom". When you come to the ideas that we read in the Bible, we find "First was the Word, and the Word was God"[7]. When we come to Qur'an, we read, "*Kun, fa yakun*". The Word was pronounced, and all that is created was manifest. This shows that the origin of the whole creation is the sound. No doubt in the way that the Word is used in our everyday language, is a limitation of that sound which is suggested by these Scriptures. The language is made of comparative objects, and that which cannot be compared has no name. Truth is that which can never be spoken, and what the wise of all ages have spoken [8]is, several tried their best to express little, as they can[8]. There is a verse in Persian language, it is the verse of Hafiz, who says that there is a tradition in the Orient, that, "When God commanded the soul to enter the human body, which is made of clay, the soul refused, and then angels were asked to sing, and on hearing the angels sing, the soul entered the body, which it had feared to be a prison". It is a philosophy which is poetically expressed in this story, and the remark of Hafiz is that people say that on hearing the song, the soul entered the body, but in reality the soul itself was a song.

As far as the modern science can reach, those who have (probed)[9] the depth of [10]material science, they do not deny the fact that the origin of the whole creation is in the movement, in other words, in the vibrations. And it is this

---

3. Lf.: "son besoin de" (tr.: "his need of") after "satisfy";
   Sk.l.tp.: an open space in parentheses
4. Lf.: "écrits" (tr.: "writings");
   Sk.l.tp.: "works"
5. Lf.: "on lit aussi" after "India"
6. Sk.sh.: an open space;
   Lf.: no space left after "India" and "which means" not translated;
   Sk.l.tp.: an open space after "India"
7. See John i.1
8. Sk.sh.: "several" erroneously read as "they have" and an open space after "as they can";
   Lf.: "est le peu de chose qu'il a été donné d'exprimer en paroles" (tr.: "is the little that was given to express in words");
   L.M.: "est ce qu'ils ont réalisé, et ils ont essayé d'en exprimer un peu, de leur mieux, comme ils le pouvaient" (tr.: "is that which they have realized, and tried to express a little, as best they could")
9. Sk.sh.: "probed" in parentheses, showing Sk.'s uncertainty of having heard this word pronounced;
   Sk.l.tp.: "probed" without parentheses
10. Sk.l.tp.: "the" added

original state of the existence of life which is called in the traditions of the old: sound, or the Word. The first manifestation of this sound is therefore audible, the next manifestation visible. But that I mean in the form of expression of life, that life has expressed itself first as sound, next as light. And this argument is supported by the Bible, where it is said: "First was the Word, and then came light".[11] Again one finds in a Sura of Qur'an: "Allah . . . "[12], which means: "God is the Light of Heaven[13] and of the earth".

The nature of creation is ~~a~~ the doubling of one. And it is this doubling aspect which is the cause of all duality in life. And this double nature represents one part positive, the other negative, one expressive, the other responsive. And therefore spirirt and nature in this creation of duality stand face to face. And as there is the first aspect, which I have called sound, and the next which I have called light in these opposite nature aspects or their response . . . aspects[14], the[15] first, the light, only works, and still deeper if the creation goes, there is sound. In the nature, which is face to face with the spirit, what is first expressed is the light, or what man first responds to is the light, and what next man responds to, or what touches man deeper, is the sound.

Human body is a vehicle of the spirit, a finished vehicle which experiences all different aspects of creation, which does not mean that all other forms and names which exist in this world, some as objects, others as creatures, are not respondent to the expression of the spirit. Really speaking, every object is respondent to the spirit and the work of the spirit, which is active in all aspects, in all names and forms of this universe. One reads in the great work of a Persian poet and mystic, Moulana Rumi, that the earth, the water, the fire, and the air, before man they are objects, but before God they are as living beings. They work at His command, as man understands living beings, working under the command of his master. If the whole creation can be well explained, it is the different phases of the sound, or of vibration, which have manifested in their different grades in all their different forms in life. If the whole creation can be explained, the different objects, and different names and forms are but the

---

11. See Genesis i.3
12. Sk.sh.: "Allah" followed by some illegible words, which may refer to the words from Sura xxiv.35 in the Qur'an: *"Allahu nuru samati wa 'l ardi"*
13. Sk.l.tp.: "Heavens"
14. Sk.sh.: a small blank after "response", which could indicate that "responsive" was said instead of "response";
    Sk.l.tp.: "or their response . . . aspects" omitted
15. Sk.l.tp.: "the" omitted

expression of vibrations (explained)[16] in different aspects. Even all that what we call matter, or all that we call substantial, and all that does not seem to speak or sound, it is all in reality vibration. And the beauty of the whole creation is this, that the creation has worked in two ways: in one way it has expressed, and in the other way it has made itself a mould to respond. For instance, there is a substance, matter, to touch, and there is a sense to feel touch. There is a sound, and at the same time there is a hearing which can hear sound. There is [17]light, there is [18]form, there are colours, and at the same time there are eyes to see them. And what man calls beauty is the harmony of all one experiences. And what is, after all, music? What we call music is the harmony of the audible notes. In reality there is a music in the colour, there is a music in lines, there is a music in the forest where there is a variety in trees and plants, how they correspond[19] each other. The wider one observes nature, the more it appeals to one's soul. Why? Because there is a music there, and to the extent one sees deeper into life, and one observes wider into life, the more and more music one listens, the music which answers the whole universe. But to the one whose heart is open, he need not go as far as the forest. In the midst of the crowd he can find music, at this time, when human ideas are so changed owing to the ma. . .[20], that there is no distinction of personality. But if one only studies human nature, then a piano of a thousand octaves even cannot reproduce[21] the variety what human nature can represent; how the people agree with one another, how they disagree; some become friends after a contact of one moment, some in thousands of years cannot become friends. If one could only see to what pitch the different souls are tuned, what octave different people speak, what standard different people have . . . .[22] Sometimes there are two people who disagree, and there is a third people[23], and all unite together. It is not the nature of music? The more one studies with a[24] harmony of music, and then studies human nature, how they

---

16. Sk.l.tp.: a space instead of "(explained)";
    Lf.: "(explained)" not translated;
    L.M.: "manifestées" (tr.: "manifested")
17. Sk.l.tp.: "a", but later crossed out
18. Ibid.: "a" added
19. Ibid.: "with" added
20. Ibid.: "materialism" instead of "ma . . ."
21. Ibid.: "produce", later changed back by Sk.in ink to "reproduce"
22. Sk.sh.: an open space;
    Lf.: "on verrait que chacune représente une note différente" (tr.: "one would see that each one represents a different note");
    L.M.: "quelles différentes sortes d'idéal ils ont!" (tr.: "what different kinds of ideal they have!")
23. Sk.l.tp.: "person" instead of "people"
24. Ibid.: "the" instead of "a"

agree and how they disagree, how there is attraction and repulsion, the more one will see that all is music.

But now there is another question to be understood, that what generally man knows is the world that one sees around oneself. Very few in the world trouble to think that there is something besides what one realizes around oneself. To many it is a story when they hear that there are two worlds. But if one looked deep within oneself, it is not only two worlds, it is so many worlds that it is beyond expression. That part of one's being which is ~~open~~ receptive, is mostly closed ~~by~~ in the average man. What he knows is expressing outwardly and receiving from the same sphere [25]from which he can receive from himself [25]. For instance, the difference between a simple man and a thinking person who understands deeper is that when the simple person has received the word only in his ears, the thinking person has received the same word which he has heard, as far as his mind. Well, therefore, the same word has reached the ears of one and the heart of the other. And at the same time this man to whose ears the word touched, he has only seen the word; but to whose heart the word has touched, he has seen still deeper. If this simple example is true, and [26] reasonable, it can be that one person who lives only in this external world, another person lives in two worlds, [27]and a third lives in many worlds [27] ~~same~~ [28] at the time.

When a person says, "Where are those worlds, I do not know, are they above the sky or beneath [29] the earth?" All these worlds are in the same place. They are [30], as a poet has said, as [31] the heart of man. If once expanded, it becomes larger than all Heavens. Therefore the deep thinkers of all ages have taken one principle for [32] wakening to life, and that principle is: emptying the self. In other words, making oneself [33]accommodation, clearer and fuller, in order to accommodate all experiences more clearly and more fully, all the tragedy of life, all sorrows and pains of life, being mostly to the surface of the life in the world.

---

25. Sk.sh.: a dotted line under this phrase indicates that Sk. felt uncertain about how correctly she took it down;
    L.M.: "qu'il peut recevoir venant de lui-même" (tr.: "what he can receive coming from himself")
26. Sk.l.tp.: "and" omitted, then reinserted in ink by Sk. instead of the comma after "true"
27. Ibid.: this phrase first omitted, then added by Sk. in ink
28. Ibid.: "same" restored, but placed after "at the"
29. Sk.sh.: "beneath" may have been said, but the shorthand signs for "beneath" and "down" are not very different;
    Sk.l.tp.: "down" instead of "beneath"
30. Sk.sh.: "They are" as the beginning of another sentence;
    Sk.l.tp.: "we are" read for "They are", and added by Sk. to the previous sentence
31. Sk.l.tp.: "as" replaced with "that:"
32. Ibid.: "of" instead of "for"
33. Ibid.: "an" added

If one was fully awake to life, if one could respond to life, if one could perceive life, he does not need to look for wonder, he does not need to communicate with spirits, for every atom in this world is a wonder for him, and he sees with open eyes.

Now coming to the question, that who dive deep into life and who touch the depth within, what is their experience? For this there is a verse in Persian; Hafiz has said: [34]"It is not known that yet how far is the destination, but only so much I know, that music from far is coming to my ears"[34]. The music of the spheres, according to the point of view of the mystic, is like the lighthouse in the port that one sees in the sea, which promises him coming nearer to the destination. Now you may ask, "What music this may be?" If there was not harmony in the essence of life, the life would not have created harmony in this life of variety, and man would not have longed for something which was not in his spirit. And all in this world, which seems lacking harmony, is in reality the limitation of man's own vision. The wider the horizon of his observation becomes, the more harmony of life he enjoys. Therefore, in the very depth of man's being, the harmony of the working of the whole universe sums up in a perfect music. Therefore the music, which is the source of the creation, music which is found towards the goal of creation, is the music of the spheres, and heard and enjoyed by those who touch the very depth of their own lives.

---

34. Lf.: "Ma destination m'est encore inconnue; tout ce que je sais c'est que je commence à entendre la musique" (tr.: "My destination is yet unknown to me; all that I know is that I am beginning to hear the music");
Sk.I.tp.: "It is not known that . . . how far is the destination, but only so much I know, that music from far is coming to my ears";
L.M.: "Je ne sais pas à quel point la destination est éloignée, mais je sais que la musique lointaine vient à mes oreilles" (tr.: "I do not know how distant the destination is, but I do know that the music from afar is coming to my ears")

Sakina Furnée's shorthand reporting.

Paris, Rue St. Séverin, December 1922[1]

2

My subject of this evening will be the[3] art.

Documents:

Sk.sh. = Sakina Furnée's shorthand reporting.

Sk.lh.. = Sk.'s longhand transcription of her shorthand reporting; (Sk.lh.) Gd.e.: Sherifa Goodenough later used this same document for editing. The questions and answers after the lecture were not included in Sk.lh. In later years this same document was used for making the lecture into a Social Gatheka.

Lf. = a reporting by M.lle Lefèbvre of the simultaneous translation into French, not mentioned in the notes as it does not provide any further indication of what was said by Pir-o-Murshid Inayat Khan on this occasion.

Hq.t. = a typescript made from "(Sk.lh.) Gd.e." at Headquarters, Geneva.

Hq.st. = a stencilled copy made from "Hq.t." at Headquarters, Geneva.

Sk.l.tp. = a typescript make by Sk. or under her supervision, or her re-transcription of the shorthand reporting ("Sk.sh."), some 30 years later, as the text of the lecture in "(Sk.lh.) Gd.e.", "Hq.t." and "Hq.st." appeared to deviate considerably from the original reporting. In the upper right corner, after the date, Sk. added in tp.: "For a circle of friends."

The lecture has first been published in the magazine *Soufisme*, no. 2, of February 1926, in a French translation made from the reporting of the lecture in English, not following M.lle Lefèbvre's reporting of the simultaneous translation.

Much later this lecture has been designated as part of the Headquarters' series of "Social Gathekas", where it became item no. 41.

Notes:

1. Sk.sh.: no date appears in Sk.'s sh. notebook of December 1922. M.lle Lefèbvre, who took down a simultaneous translation of the lecture in French, dated it 16 December 1922, which would correspond with the sequence of the lectures in Sk.'s notebook;
   Sk.lh.: no date;
   (Sk.lh.) Gd.e.: later added by Gd. what seems to be the wrong date: "December 27? '22, rep. by S. Furnée."
   Sk.l.tp.: "Paris, December 1922"

2. Sk.sh.: in later years Sk. added "Art" in lh. above the lecture, together with her filing nr. "(410)", thereby indicating that even at that time the lecture had not yet been assigned to any of the Headquarters' series;
   Sk.lh.: "Beloved ones of God" written above. Although not taken down by Sk. in her sh.r., these words almost always were said by Pir-o-Murshid when addressing his audience;
   (Sk.lh.)Gd.e.: "Beloved ones of God, my subject of this evening will be the art" crossed out and

Many think that art is something different from nature. But if I were to say[4], that[5] art is the finishing of nature. And one may ask that[6] can man improve upon nature which is made by God?[6] But the fact is that God Himself through man finishes His creation in art. As all different elements are God's vehicles, as all the trees and plants are His instruments to create through, so the[7] art is the medium of God through whom[8] God Himself creates and finishes His creation. [9]No doubt, every so- called art is not necessarily art. By looking at the real art, man is able to say [10] that [11]Thy will is done on earth as in Heaven [11]. In this whole creation, from one thing to another, through evolution the Creator has worked. In man the Creator has finished, so to speak, the [7] nature. But at the same time the creative faculty is still working through man. Therefore art is the next step towards creation. In reality all creation, scientific or artistic, is the [7] art. But mainly the object which is produced with the sense of beauty, and which appeals to the sense of beauty in man, is principally the [7] art. [9]Besides being the creative power of God, it is the expression of the soul of the artist. [12]Artist cannot give what he has not collected, although man ignores the way how [13] the artist's soul conceives, only recognizing what the soul of the artist has produced. Once the artist [14] is understood that he [15] conceives also, not only produces, then it is not difficult for a man with awakened heart to see into the soul of an artist. For the[7] art in colour, in line, is nothing but the re-echo of his soul. If the soul of the artist is going through torture, his picture gives one the feeling of awe. If

---

"Art" written above instead. In later years "Social Gatheka nr. . . . " was written above, and at another time "41" was added;

Hq.t., Hq.st.: omitted "My subject of this evening will be the art", and added above "SOCIAL GATHEKA", followed by the Invocation and by the title "Art"

3. (Sk.lh.)Gd.e.: "the" crossed out
4. Ibid.: ", but I say" instead of "But if I were to say"
5. Sk.lh., Hq.t., Hq.st.: "that" omitted
6. (Sk.lh.)Gd.e.: "that" crossed out and the following question put in quotation marks; Hq.t., Hq.st.: "that" omitted and the question in quotation marks
7. (Sk.lh.)Gd.e.: "the" crossed out; Hq.t., Hq.st.: "the" omitted
8. (Sk.lh.)Gd.e: "whom" changed into "which"; Hq.t., Hq.st.: "which" instead of "whom"
9. (Sk.lh.)Gd.e.: a new paragraph
10. Sk.lh.: "see" instead of "say"
11. See Matt. vi.10, Luke xi.2; all other documents: quotation marks before "Thy" and after "Heaven"
12. Sk.lh.: "An" added
13. (Sk.lh.)Gd.e.: "how" replaced with "that", but then restored to "how"
14. (Sk.lh.)Gd.e.: "the artist" changed to "it"; Hq.t., Hq.st.: "it" instead of "the artist"
15. (Sk.lh.)Gd.e.: "he" changed into "the artist"; Hq.t., Hq.st.: "the artist" instead of "he"

the soul of the artist is enjoying harmony, you will see harmony in his colours, in the lines. What does it show? It shows that the soul works automatically through the brush of the artist. The deeper [16] the artist is touched by the beauty that his soul conceives from outside, the greater appeal it makes for [17] those who see his production.

Now coming to the question, what is it in line and colour which has such an influence on man's faculty? It is the vibrations which the colour produces which thrill the centres which are hidden in the body and which are the centres of [18] intuitive faculties. Sometimes [19] a person looks at a colour and immediately feels thrilled by it. The degrees [20] of vibration [21] that different colours produce are [22] different and therefore the influence is different. At the same time, one person is more open to the effect and influence. [23]Another person is so blocked that upon him colours make little impression. And the very [24] reason may be said to be the cause which makes woman respondent more [25] to colour and to line than man. For woman by nature is responsive, man by nature is expressive. Therefore, while woman receives the impression of the colour, man expels [26] them [27]. But at the same time, the difference between a man with fine feelings, with intuitive faculty awake [28], and a man whose faculties are not yet open [29], is

---

16. (Sk.lh.)Gd.e.: "deeper" changed into "more deeply";
    Hq.t., Hq.st..: "more deeply" instead of "deeper"
17. (Sk.lh.)Gd.e.: "for" changed into "to";
    Hq.t., Hq.st.: "to" instead of "for"
18. Sk.lh., Hq.t., Hq.st.: "the" added
19. Sk.lh.: "Sometimes" misread as "Say";
    (Sk.lh.)Gd.e.: "Say" changed into "So"
    Hq.t., Hq.st.: "So"
20. Sk.lh.: "The degrees" misread as "Each degree";
    Hq.t., Hq.st.: "Each degree"
21. Sk.lh.: "vibrations";
    Hq.t., Hq.st.: "vibrations"
22. Sk.lh., Hq.t., Hq.st.: "is" instead of "are"
23. (Sk.lh.)Gd.e.: ". Another" changed into ", another";
    Hq.t., Hq.st.: ", another"
24. (Sk.lh.)Gd.e: "very" changed into "same"
25. Sk.lh.: "more respond" instead of "respondent more";
    (Sk.lh.)Gd.e.: "responsive more";
    Hq.t., Hq.st.: "more responsive"
26. Sk.sh.: afterwards Sk. changed "expels" into "repels" in lh.;
    all other documents: "repels"
27. Sk.lh.: "them" replaced with "it";
    Hq.t., Hq.st.: "it" instead of "them"
28. Sk.lh.: "awake" changed to "awakened";
    Hq.t., Hq.st.: "awakened"

only this: that the former responds to the colour and the latter does not.

Now coming to the question of strong colours and of mild[30] colours. Strong colours make more distinct vibrations; their effect is more distinct than of the mild[31] colours, and therefore it is natural that the strong colours can make impression upon every soul. But at the same time to distinguish the impression made by [31]mild colours wants a[32] delicacy of sense. For an[33] instance the simple words of language of everyday life are understood by everyone. But the fine shades which follow the words are not understood by everybody. Therefore sometimes[34] the[35] colour which is only a colour to everybody, to a person with a fine sense it[36] has its value, its degree of influence. [9]The harmony of the[7] colour is based on the same foundation as the harmony of music. The reason is that music is audible vibrations, colour is[37] visible form of vibrations. But from [37]metaphysical point of view the[7] colour has a great significance in man's life. The first important thing that is to be understood in connection with colour[38] that all[39] different colours come from the essence of life[40]. All different colours are the different degrees of light. No doubt there are three aspects of light, and it is this which produces confusion in the mind of those who have not thought upon

---

29. Sk.lh., Hq.t., Hq.st.: "opened" instead of "open" (the same in sh.)
30. (Sk.lh)Gd.e.: "mild" changed to "soft";
Hq.t., Hq.st.: "soft" instead of "mild";
Sk.l.tp.: "milder" instead of "mild"
31. (Sk.lh.)Gd.e.: "mild" changed to "soft";
Hq.t., Hq.st.: "soft" instead of "mild"
Sk.l.tp.: goes back to "mild"
32. (Sk.lh.)Gd.e.: "a" crossed out, but then restored;
Hq.t., Hq.st.: "a" omitted
33. (Sk.lh.)Gd.e.: "an" crossed out;
Hq.t., Hq.st.: "an" omitted
34. Sk.lh.: "that light" read for "sometimes", then crossed out;
Hq.t., Hq.st.: "sometimes" omitted;
Sk.l.tp.: "sometimes" again added
35. Sk.lh.: "the" omitted, but later added in lh. by Sk.;
(Sk.lh.)Gd.e.: "the" crossed out;
Hq.t., Hq.st.: "the" omitted
36. (Sk.lh.)Gd.e.: "it" crossed out;
Hq.t., Hq.st.: "it" omitted
37. (Sk.lh.)Gd.e.: "the" added
Hq.t., Hq.st.: "the" added
38. All other documents: "is" added
39. Sk.lh.: "all" omitted;
Hq.t., Hq.st.: "all" omitted
40. (Sk.lh.)Gd.e.: "life" changed into "light";
Hq.t., Hq.st.: "light" instead of "life";
Sk.l.tp.: goes back to "life" as in the original sh.r.

the subject [41] if the colour can be called light. And [42] these three aspects of light are in this way: One aspect of light is [43] which manifests through the colour, the radiance of the colour itself. The other [44] aspect is the light of the sun or of something else, which throws its light upon the colour. The light of the colour responds to that light. The third light is the light of the eyes, which sees [45]. Therefore the same colour is not the same, nor its influence is [46] the same for everybody, not only for the reason that the degree of the sight [47] of [48] every person is different, and the difference of the light that falls on the subject is different, or ~~the light~~ that the degree of the colour is different, but also the element which that particular colour represents has a certain degree of response [49] in a certain (extent) individual [49].

According to the mystical idea there are four principal elements which can be distinguished, and one which is indistinct. The distinct elements are the[7] earth, the[7] water, the[7] fire, [50] the[7] air. Not according to the meaning that [51] a scientist would take from [52] it, but according to the meaning that the mystic has [53]. It will take perhaps time if I tried to explain the difference of [54] the mystical

---

41. Sk.lh.: a full stop after "subject";
Hq.t., Hq.st.: a full stop after "subject"
42. (Sk.lh.)Gd.e.: "And" changed to "then";
Hq.t., Hq.st.: "then" instead of "And"
43. Sk.lh.)Gd.e.: "is" crossed out;
Hq.t., Hq.st.: "is" omitted
44. (Sk.lh.)Gd.e.: "other" changed to "next";
Hq.t., Hq.st.: "next" instead of "other"
45. Hq.t.: "sees" later changed in ink by Sk. to "see"
46. (Sk.lh.)Gd.e.: "is" moved to before "its influence"
47. Sk.lh.: "light" instead of "sight";
Hq.t., Hq.st.: "light"
Sk.l.tp.: goes back to "sight" as in the original sh.r.
48. (Sk.lh.)Gd.e.: "of" changed to "in", but then restored to "of"
49. Sk.lh.: "in a certain extent, individual";
(Sk.lh.)Gd.e.: "to a certain extent in an individual";
Hq.t., Hq.st.: "to a certain extent in an individual"
50. Sk.lh. "and" instead of a comma;
Hq.t., Hq.st.: "and"
51. (Sk.lh.)Gd.e.: "meaning that" changed into "sense in which";
Hq.t., Hq.st.: "sense in which" instead of "meaning that"
52. (Sk.lh.)Gd.e.: "from" crossed out;
Hq.t., Hq.st.: "from" omitted
53. (Sk.lh.)Gd.e.: "~~it has for the mystic~~ the mystic sees" instead of "the mystic has";
Hq.t., Hq.st.: "the mystic sees"
54. (Sk.lh.)Gd.e.: "of" changed into "between";
Hq.t., Hq.st.: "between" instead of "of"

conception and that of the scientist. The indistinct element is the ether. Now [55] all these elements are in the body of man, in his mind and in his deeper self. The whole building of an individual existence is built by these five distinct elements, and it is not necessary that on every plane of existence a certain element is predominant, which continues to be [56] in every plane. I have meant [57] that it is not that a certain predominant [58] element which is in one plane, continues to be predominant in all planes. It is possible that there can be harmony in the elements which are predominant in the inner plane with those who are predominant in the outer plane. In short, it is according to the working of the different elements in one's being [59] one is respondent [60] to the different colours which represent the different elements. From the point of view of a mystic the yellow is the colour of the earth, the[7] green or the[7] white the colour [61] of [62] water element, ~~fire that~~ red that of the fire element and blue of the air element. If the colour of the ether element was asked, the mystic says [63]: grey. By grey you may think what [64] you like. It is most interesting for a student of colour to see that all colours are, so to speak, different shades of light. And what does it show? It shows that light itself has manifested in variety in the form of many colours.

Now coming on the question of line. Many of those [65] lovers or students of art feel a great influence, a great effect that a line makes. A straight [66] line, a horizontal line, a line with [67] curve, a circle, it makes such a difference in the

---

55. (Sk.lh.)Gd.e.: "Now" crossed out;
    Hq.t., Hq.st.: "Now" omitted
56. Sk.sh.: "predominant" added by Sk. in lh.:
    Sk.lh.: "predominant" added;
    Hq.t., Hq.st., Sk.l.tp.: "predominant" added
57. (Sk.lh.)Gd.e.: "have meant" changed to "mean";
    Hq.t., Hq.st.: "mean" instead of "have meant"
58. (Sk.lh.)Gd.e.: "predominant" moved to before "in one plane", then again restored
59. Sk.lh.: "that" added;
    Hq.t., Hq.st.: "that" added
60. (Sk.lh.)Gd.e.: "respondent" changed to "responsive"
61. Sk.lh., Sk.l.tp.: "colours" instead of "color"
62. Sk.lh., Hq.st., Hq.t.: "the" added
63. Sk.sh.: afterwards Sk. changed "says" to "answers";
    all other documents: "answers"
64. Sk.sh.: afterwards Sk. changed "what" into "anything";
    all other documents: "anything" instead of "what"
65. Sk.lh., Hq.t., Hq.st.: "of those" omitted
66. (Sk.lh.)Gd.e.: "straight" first replaced with "upright", then with "vertical";
    Hq.t., Hq.st.: "vertical" instead of "straight"
67. Sk.lh., Hq.t., Hq.st.: "a" added

form. And the more one studies to what extent line makes [67]difference, the more one will find that the secret of the whole beauty is in the line. And it is difficult to say what form, what line is the right line; and the man has to accept that [68] what one cannot learn by study, intuition teaches. The only reason that from the mystical point of view one can give about the secret of line, is that the effect of a certain line arranges the inner [69] planes of [37]human being in such a condition that for the moment one looks at the line, one is, so to speak, in a kind of spell by [70] that line. The secret of this can be found in the secret of concentration, that every object man thinks upon [71] may be [72], be it for a moment, has an effect upon his whole being, [73] and there is a harmony between lines. The harmony of the[7] lines is more difficult and more complex to understand than even the harmony of colour; and the harmony of line [74] touches deeper than the harmony of colour. A room [75] beautifully furnished with [76] costly furniture, but if the things are not kept in harmony according to the science of lines, you will find a kind of confusion in the room [77]. The same thing in the[7] dress. The dress may be very costly, beautiful in colour, and if it lacks line, it lacks a great thing [78] in beauty.

Therefore in the[7] art line is the principal thing. It is the secret of art and it is the secret of its charm. And that [79] artist who has conceived the beauty of

---

68. Sk.lh.: first "and the man has to accept that" changed into "except that", then restored to "and man has to accept that";
    Hq.t., Hq.st.: "and man has to accept that"
69. Sk.sh.: added by Sk. in sh. "and outer";
    all other documents: "and outer" included
70. (Sk.lh.)Gd.e.: "by" changed to "of";
    Sk.sh.: "by" changed to "of" in sh.;
    Hq.t., Hq.st., Sk.l.tp.: "of" instead of "by"
71. Sk.lh.: "about" instead of "upon";
    Hq.t., Hq.st.: "about"
72. Sk.lh.: "may be" crossed out;
    Hq.t., Hq.st.: "may be" omitted
73. Sk.sh.: the sentence seems to continue;
    (Sk.lh.)Gd.e.: a new sentence and a new paragraph indicated
74. Sk.lh.: "lines";
    (Sk.lh.)Gd.e.: the plural "s" first crossed out, then restored;
    Hq.t., Hq.st.: "lines"
75. (Sk.lh.)Gd.e.: "~~If a room is~~", "~~In a room~~" "If a room is" instead of "A room";
    Hq.t., Hq.st.: "If a room is"
76. Sk.l.tp.: "very" instead of "with"
77. (Sk.lh.)Gd.e.: first "the room" replaced with "it", then restored to "the room"
78. Sk.sh.: "thing" replaced in sh. with "part"; later "part" changed into "deal";
    Sk.lh.: "deal" instead of "thing";
    Hq.t., Hq.st., Sk.l.tp.: "deal" instead of thing"
79. (Sk.lh.)Gd.e.: "only the" instead of "that";
    Hq.t., Hq.st.: "only the"

line can only [80] express it in his art.

The[7] art has three aspects. One aspect is that the artist tries to copy exactly that which he sees. That artist is contemplative. And it is not a small thing to be able to copy exactly as the object is [81]. For the success of this artist is sure. With all man's craving for something new, what really he wants is something he has seen. Is it not something wonderful, is it not great to be able to copy the nature as it is, to produce the same in the soul of man as it [82] is in nature?

Another aspect of art is the improvement on nature, which the artist makes by exaggeration. And the benefit of this art is more attraction than impression. No doubt in this form of art the artist can fulfill his soul's (purpose) [83]. But at the same time the artist may go far away from nature. And the further he goes, the more he destroys the beauty of art. For nature and art both must go hand in hand.

Now coming to the third aspect of the[7] art, and [84] that aspect is a [85] symbolical art. Symbology [86] has not come from human intellect, for it is born of the intuition. The finer the soul, the more [87] equipped in some way [88] or the[7] other in the symbological [89] idea. A fine soul always dreams symbolical [90] dreams. And when the soul becomes finer still, it interprets the dream to itself, understanding the meaning of that symbology[86]. The artist who produces in his art a symbolical[90] idea has learned it from what he has seen in nature and has interpreted that in his art. Certainly, it is inspiration. The finer is [91] the artist, the

---

80. (Sk.lh.)Gd.e.: "only" crossed out;
Hq.t., Hq.st.: "only" omitted;
Sk.l.tp.: added after "only": "(also)"
81. (Sk.lh.)Gd.e.: "~~as is the object~~" "the object" instead of "as the object is";
Hq.t., Hq.st.: "the object"
82. (Sk.lh.)Gd.e.: "it" crossed out;
Hq.t., Hq.st.: "it" omitted
83. (Sk.lh.)Gd.e.: "purpose" without parentheses;
Hq.t., Hq.st.: parentheses omitted
84. (Sk.lh.)Gd.e.: "and" crossed out;
Hq.t., Hq.st.: "and" omitted
85. (Sk.lh.)Gd.e.: "a" crossed out;
Hq.t., Hq.st.: "a" omitted
86. (Sk.lh.)Gd.e.: "Symbology" changed to "Symbolism";
Hq.t., Hq.st.: "Symbolism"
87. (Sk.lh.)Gd.e.: "more" changed into "better"
Hq.t., Hq.st.: "better" instead of "more"
88. Hq.t.: "way" omitted, but added later by Sk. in ink
89. (Sk.lh.)Gd.e.: "symbological", which is an obsolete form, changed to "symbolical";
all other documents: "symbolical"
90. Sk.lh.: "symbological" although her sh.r. has "symbolical"
91. (Sk.lh.)Gd.e.: "is" moved to after "artist"

finer his symbolical way of producing. [9]In every piece[92] of art one can ~~see~~ observe three things: its surface, its length and width, and its depth. That[93] I do not say in the sense of ordinary words[94]. The surface means what the picture is, the length and width is the story that it tells, and the depth is the meaning that it reveals. Therefore[95] the best way of appreciating and studying the works of an artist, these three faculties must be developed. [96]Art is a very vast subject. One lecture[97] is not sufficient for this subject. [98]Therefore I will leave for this evening at this.[96, 98]

- - - - - - - - - -

[99]*Question: If a person has neither nor[100] painting nor music nor any of the recognized arts[101] in him, can he express art in another way?*

Answer: Every soul has a[102] faculty of art and one can use that faculty in all one does in life. It is not at all necessary that in order to use the faculty of art one must be an artist. The art can be employed to every action one does, to every word one speaks, through every movement one makes and through every sentiment one has. And it is the one who lives in art in this manner that I have explained, is the perfect artist. And what perfect artist means? That what the soul had longed to become, it has arrived at this stage.

Question: Is one nearer to art in copying nature or by symbolism?

---

92. (Sk.lh.)Gd.e.: "piece" changed into "work";
Hq.t., Hq.st.: "work" instead of "piece"
93. Sk.l.tp.: "This" instead of "That"
94. (Sk.lh.)Gd.e.: "sense of ordinary words" rewritten to read, "ordinary sense of the words";
Hq.t., Hq.st.: "ordinary sense of the words"
95. (Sk.lh.)Gd.e.: "for" added;
Hq.t., Hq.st.: "for" added
96. (Sk.lh.)Gd.e.: this last passage ("Art is . . . at this") crossed out
97. Sk.lh.: "One series of lectures" instead of "One lecture";
(Sk.lh.)Gd.e., Hq.t., Hq.st.: "A series of lectures"
98. (Sk.lh.)Gd.e., Hq.t., Hq.st.: this sentence omitted
99. The following questions and answers, taken down in shorthand by Sk., also appear in her later retranscription of her shorthand reporting, but were not added in the Hq.t. and Hq.st.
100. Sk.lt.tp.: "nor" omitted
101. Ibid.: "art" instead of "arts"
102. Sk.sh.: after "a" Sk. added a sh. sign which could well mean "its". Probably Sk. felt uncertain if "a" or "its" was said;
Sk.l.tp.: no word added after "a"

Answer: Symbolism is the inside of the nature, and copying is the outside of the nature. It is nature in both.

[103] The idea of beauty and ugliness: the more limited the object is, the more faults it shows. And the wider you observe, the less faults you will see. This shows that ugliness belongs to the limitedness of the observation, and beauty belongs to the expansion of observation. And this suggests that when one sees all before one, it is all in its place, and it is all harmonious and beautiful. And when one sees it by separating it from all else, but [104] part of it, then he sees the defect and the lack. Therefore this defect, though it seems that it belongs to that particular part, but in reality this lack is the separation of its whole. All that is in part is poor, and is [105] out of place. All that is whole, is rich and perfect. In this idea there is the explanation of the secret of art, and the secret of the whole life.

---

103. After the second question and answer follows a passage on the subject of art, which probably is an answer to a question not taken down by Sk. In Sk.sh. it belongs to the same lecture on art.

104. Sk.sh.: later Sk. added "a" in sh;
Sk.l.tp.: "a" added

105. Sk.l.tp.: "is" omitted

Sakina's shorthand reporting

[1]December 1922

[2]

[3]My subject of this afternoon is "The Poet and the Prophet".

Documents:

Sk.sh. = Sakina Furnée's shorthand reporting

Sk.lh. = a transcription in Sk. hwr. of her shorthand reporting used for editing in later years by Sherifa Goodenough as a preparation for an article published in magazine *The Sufi* of September 1935, into which the lecture "Poet and Prophet" of 3 April 1923 has been intercalated. In the notes Gd.'s editing has been indicated by "(Sk.lh.) Gd.e."

Lf. = a reporting by M.lle Lefèbvre of the simultaneously given translation into French, only mentioned in note 1 for the date

tp. = a typescript made from "(Sk.lh.) Gd.e." and from the lecture "Poet and Prophet", given on 3 April 1923. V. *Complete Works - Original Texts* 1923-I, where the document "Gd.a.p." indicates Gd.'s first preparation for the article of the two lectures combined

Km.tp. = a neatly typewritten copy on yellowish paper, made by Kismet Stam in later years from "tp." with the lecture of 3 April 1923 included

S. = *The Sufi*, a bi-annual "Journal of Mysticism", Vol. 1 no. 6 of September 1935, where the two lectures appear combined

Notes:

1. Sk.sh., Sk.lh.: no date mentioned by Sk. In Sk.'s copybook, marked "1922 Nov.Dec."; the last lecture is dated "18th December". From an old newspaper announcement it appears that Pir-o-Murshid gave a lecture in Paris entitled "The Poet and the Prophet" on 17th December 1922 and this lecture in Sk.'s copybook comes just before the one on 18th December;
   Lf.: the date of 17 December 1922 is written above;
   (Sk.lh.) Gd.e.: later Gd. added above Sk.lh.: "Paris, December 1922";
   tp.: "November 1922", replaced by Sk. with "December 1922"
2. Sk.lh.: "Beloved ones of God" written above, although in Sk.sh. this was omitted. These were the opening words which Pir-o-Murshid generally used.
3. Sk.sh.: afterwards Sk. wrote "The Poet and the Prophet" in lh. above the lecture, adding her filing number, "(212)", thereby indicating that the lecture was not included in one of the Headquarters' series;
   Sk.lh.: later Sk. wrote above as a title: "The Poet and the Prophet" and crossed out "Beloved ones of God" and the first sentence;
   tp., Km.tp., S.: "The Poet and the Prophet" as a title, and "Beloved ones of God" and the first sentence omitted

There exists a saying in [4]English language that a poet is a prophet, and in this saying there seems to be a great significance and hidden meaning. [5] There is no doubt that[6] poetry is not necessarily a prophecy, but[7] prophecy is born in poetry. If one were to say that poetry is the body which is adopted by the spirit of prophecy, it would not be wrong. I will[8] repeat the same in connection of[9] poetry what[10] Wagner has said, that[11] music is not necessarily knowledge[12], and[13] the same thing with poetry, that[14] true[15] poetry is not necessarily a verse written in lines[16]. Poetry is an art, is a[17] music expressed in beauty and harmony of words.[18] No doubt the verses, the poetry which one reads every day, [19]is

---

4. (Sk.lh.) Gd.e.: "the" added by Gd.;
all other documents: "the"
5. Sk.sh., Sk.lh.: a small space after "meaning";
tp., Km.tp., S.: added a passage from "Poet and Prophet" of 3 April 1923 ("The source of . . . certainly a poet.")
6. Sk.lh.: "that" omitted, "though" added;
(Sk.lh.) Gd.e.: "that" added, then crossed out;
tp., Km.tp., S.: "though" instead of "that"
7. (Sk.lh.) Gd.e.: "but" changed into "yet";
all other documents: "yet" instead of "but"
8. (Sk.lh.) Gd.e.: "I will" replaced by "To";
all other documents: "To" instead of "I will"
9. (Sk.lh.) Gd.e.: "of" replaced by "with";
all other documents: "with" instead of "of"
10. (Sk.lh.) Gd.e.: "what" changed to "that";
all other documents: "that" instead of "what"
11. (Sk.lh.) Gd.e.: a colon instead of "that";
all other documents: a colon instead of "that"
12. (Sk.lh.) Gd.e.: "knowledge" changed first to "notes", then to "noise";
all other documents: "noise", although in Sk.sh. "knowledge" is written clearly
13. (Sk.lh.) Gd.e.: "and" crossed out, "it is" added;
all other documents: "and" omitted, "it is" added
14. (Sk.lh.) Gd.e.: "that" crossed out;
all other documents: "that" omitted
15. Sk.lh.: "through" instead of "true";
(Sk.lh.) Gd.e.: "through" changed back to "true"
16. Sk.lh.: Sk. added "metre";
(Sk.lh.) Gd.e.: "lines" crossed out;
tp., Km.tp., S.: "metre" instead of "lines"
17. All other documents: "a" omitted
18. Tp., Km.tp., S.: a passage added at this point from the lecture "Poet and Prophet" of 3 April 1923 ("The reason for this. . .in divine essence.")
19. (Sk.lh.) Gd.e.: rewritten to read, "are sometimes a pastime"; Sk.lh.: later added again "for" after "sometimes", but crossed out by Gd;
all other documents: "are sometimes a pastime"

sometimes there for a pastime, at other times for[20] an amusement, but the real poetry[21] comes from the dancing of the soul, and no one[22] can the soul dance except[23] the soul itself would[24] be inclined to dance, and [25]no soul can dance which is not sane[26]. In the Bible there is a hint that no one will enter the Kingdom of God whose soul is not born again, and being born means being alive. It is not only a jolly disposition or an external inclination to merriment and pleasure that gives the sign of a living soul, for the external joy and amusement may come even by the[27] external being of man living[28]. Although in the outward joy and happiness also there is a glimpse of the joy and happiness which is in the depth of man. But when the soul becomes loving, that is the sign of the soul having been born again. What makes it ~~alive~~ living? It makes itself living when it strikes its[29] depth instead of striking the surface of life. And what makes the soul strike into the depth of one's being instead of striking outward[30]? The soul, after being[31] struck against the iron wall of this life of falsehood, when it goes backwards within itself, it[32] strikes itself, and by striking there it becomes living. [33]In order to make this idea more clear, I should like to give you an example. There is a man who goes[34] into the world, a man with thought, with[35] feeling, with energy, with desire, with ambition, with enthusiasm, to live and work in life.

---

20. Sk.lh.: "for" omitted, then reinserted by Sk.;
    (Sk.lh.) Gd.e.: "for" crossed out;
    all other documents: "for" omitted
21. Sk.lh.: ~~music~~ poetry"
22. Sk.sh.: "no one" later crossed out and changed to "how";
    all other documents: "how"
23. All other documents: "that" added
24. (Sk.lh.) Gd.e.: "would" crossed out;
    all other documents: "would" omitted
25. All other documents: "? And" instead of ", and"
26. Sk.sh.: afterwards Sk. crossed out "not";
    (Sk.lh.) Gd.e.: "not ~~sane~~, then written above "sane" "~~living~~ alive";
    all other documents: "not alive"
27. (Sk.lh.) Gd.e.: "life of the" added, then crossed out
28. (Sk.lh.) Gd.e.: "living" replaced with "being alive";
    all other documents: "being alive" instead of "living"
29. (Sk.lh.) Gd.e.: "its" changed to "the", then "its" restored
30. Sk.lh.: "outward" changed to "outwardly";
    all other documents: "outwardly"
31. (Sk.lh.) Gd.e.: "being" changed into "having";
    all other documents: "having"
32. (Sk.lh.) Gd.e.: "it" crossed out;
    all other documents: "it" omitted
33. (Sk.lh.) Gd.e.: rewritten to read, "An example will make this idea clearer";
    all other documents: "An example will make this idea clearer"
34. Sk.lh.: "out" added, then crossed out by Sk.
35. (Sk.lh.) Gd.e.: "with" crossed out;
    all other documents: "with" omitted

And as the actual nature of life is, his experience will show him constantly being[36] up against an iron wall, [37]every direction he strikes. And the nature of man is, when there is a struggle, then he struggles with it. He lives in the outward life, he goes along struggling in life, he knows not any other part of life, for he lives only ~~in the~~ on the surface. There is another one, sensitive, true, sympathetic, tenderhearted. Every blow coming from the outer world, instead of giving him an inclination of striking outwardly, he strikes[38] inwardly. And what is the consequence of it? The consequence of it[39] that the soul of man which, after being born on this earth seems to be living, but in a grave, becomes wakened by this action.[40] And once the soul is wakened in this way, it expresses itself outwardly, whether in music, in art, in poetry, [41]in action. In whatever way it expresses itself, it is a poet. [42]Poet has two lines of[43] life: one line imagination, the other line feeling, both things which are most essential in the spiritual path. Man, however learned and good, at the same time lacking these two qualities, can never arrive at a satisfactory result, especially in the spiritual path.[44]

In support to what I have said ~~that the spirit~~ the[45] poetry is the body and prophecy is the spirit behind it, I should like to point out that[46] the sacred scripture[47] of all ages, whether of the Hindus or of the [48], of the race of

---

36. Sk.lh.: "lead" instead of "being";
(Sk.lh.) Gd.e.: ~~lead that he is knocking his head knocking~~ ;
all other documents: "striking" instead of "being"
37. (Sk.lh.) Gd.e.: "in" added;
all other documents: "in" added
38. (Sk.lh.) Gd.e.: "~~causes him to strike~~ makes him strike" instead of "he strikes";
all other documents: "makes him strike"
39. Sk.lh.: "is" instead of "of it";
all other documents: "is" instead of "of it"
40. Tp., Km.tp., S.: a passage added from the lecture "Poet and Prophet" of 3 April 1923 ("In the life of many. . .can be expressed in your life.") added
41. (Sk.lh.) Gd.e.: "or" added;
all other documents: "or" added
42. Sk.lh.: "A" added;
all other documents: "A" added
43. (Sk.lh.) Gd.e.: "of" replaced with "in";
all other documents: "in" instead of "of"
44. Tp., Km.tp., S.: a passage added from the lecture "Poet and Prophet" of 3 April 1923 ("The poet who cannot express. . .and condition in all we do.") added
45. (Sk.lh.) Gd.e.: crossed out: "In support of what I have said, the";
all other documents:: "In support of what I have said, the" omitted
46. (Sk.lh.) Gd.e.: crossed out "I should like to point out that";
all other documents: "I should like to point out that" omitted
47. All other documents: "Scriptures"

Ben[49] Israel—all these scriptures—[50] was[51] given in poetry or in poetic prose. No spiritual person, however great, however pious and spiritually advanced, has ever been able to give to the world the[52] scripture except those blessed with the gift of poetry. One may ask: these days, when everything people wish to know[53] plainly spoken, "cut and dried"[54] as they say in English, is[55] this the [56] of the present time, have been so accustomed to learn all things, especially of[57] science, explained in clear words, and at the present time when sentiment takes a second place in life's affairs? But it must be understood that facts about the names and forms of this world may be scientifically explained in plain words. But when one wishes to interpret the sense that one gets when looking at life, we cannot explain it except in the way that the prophets have explained it: in poetry. In the first place, no one has ever explained nor can ever explain truth in words. To try to[58] explain truth in words is just like trying to put the ocean in a bottle. Language is only for the convenience of everyday affairs: even the deepest sentiments one cannot explain in words.

The Message that the prophets have given to the world from time to time is an interpretation of the idea of life that they have received, in their own words.

---

49. (Sk.lh.) Gd.e.: "Beni" instead of "Ben";
all other documents: "Beni"
50. (Sk.lh.) Gd.e.: "-all these scriptures-" crossed out;
all other documents: "-all these scriptures-" omitted
51. Sk.lh.: "were" instead of "was";
all other documents: "were"
52. Sk.lh.: "a" instead of "the";
all other documents: "a"
53. (Sk.lh.) Gd.e.: "people wish everything to hear" instead of "everything people wish to know";
all other documenls: "people wish to have everything"
54. Sk.sh.: Sakina wrote above the shorthand symbols, "cut" and "dry" in lh., indicating that she may have been unfamiliar with this American expression, taken from tobacco farming (properly, "cut and dried", but it would have been difficult to hear the "d" at the end);
all other documents: "dry" instead of "dried", indicating the idiom was not known to the editors
55. Sk.lh.: "and" instead of "is";
(Sk.lh.) Gd.e.: "and" crossed out and "is" restored
56. Sk.sh.,Sk.lh.: an open space;
(Sk.lh.) Gd.e.: filled in: "case, when the people";
all other documents: "case, when the people"
57. (Sk.lh.) Gd.e.: "of" crossed out and written above "~~concerning~~ in";
all other documents: "in" instead of "of"
58. (Sk.lh.) Gd.e.: "and" instead of "to";
tp., Km.tp.: "and" instead of "to"

Inspiration begins in poetry and culminates in prophecy. [59]And [60]the picture of the poet and the prophet is this, that when the soul has risen from its grave, so to speak, and is beginning to make graceful movements, it is the poet. But when the same soul begins to move and to dance to the north pole and to the south pole, the soul who can touch the[61] heaven and earth in its dances[62] and express all the beauty it sees, that is prophecy[63].

[64]Poet when he is developed reads the mind[65] of the universe, and very often it happens that the poet himself does not know the proper meaning of what he has said. Very often one sees that a poet has said something, and after many years a moment comes when he knows the real meaning of what he has said once. And what does it show? It shows that behind all these different activities there is the divine, which is[66] hidden, and very often a divine (being)[67] manifests through an individual, that individual not knowing that it's[68] divine[69].

In the words of the Oriental people, the prophet is called *peramba*[70], which means the messenger, the one who carries the word of someone to someone else. And the reason why?[71] No doubt, there are many who view that according to the spiritual idea, but there is another point of view to take, that in reality every individual in this world is a medium of an impulse which is hidden

---

59. Tp., Km.tp., S.: a passage added from the lecture "Poet and Prophet" of 3 April 1923 ("The tendency of receiving. . .brought to the world a scripture") added
60. (Sk.lh.) Gd.e.: "And" crossed out;
all other documents: "And" omitted
61. (Sk.lh.) Gd.e.: "the" crossed out;
all other documents: "the" omitted
62. (Sk.lh.) Gd.e.: "dance";
all other documents: "dance"
63. Sk.lh.: "the prophecy";
(Sk.lh.) Gd.e.: "the prophet";
all other documents: "the prophet"
64. Sk.lh.: "A" added;
all other documents: "A"
65. S.: "minds"
66. (Sk.lh.) Gd.e.: "~~life~~ Being" added, "which is" crossed out;
all other documents: "Being" added, "which is" omitted
67. (Sk.lh.) Gd.e.: "a divine (being)" changed into "the Divine Being";
all other documents: "the Divine Being"
68. Sk.lh.: "it is" instead of "it's";
all other documents: "it is"
69. (Sk.lh.) Gd.e.: "divine . . ." completed to "the divine impulse that manifests through him";
all other documents: "the divine impulse that manifests through him."
70. See Glossary: Payghambar
71. (Sk.lh.) Gd.e.: rewritten to read, "And what is the reason why?";
all other documents: "And what is the reason?"

behind him, and that impulse he gives out, only that he does not know it. It is not only living beings, but one can see even in the[72] objects. Every object has its purpose, and by fulfilling its purpose, that object is fulfilling the scheme of ~~its~~ nature. Therefore, whatever be the line of work of man, whether business, or[73] commerce, science, or music, or art, or poetry, he is a medium in some way. There are mediums who are the mediums[74] of the living beings; there are mediums of those who have passed to the other side, and there are mediums who represent their country, their nations[75], their race. Every individual in his own way is acting as a medium in some way or other. When the prophet dives deep, when the poet dives deep into self, what in the innermost being he finds[76]? He touches that perfection which is the source and goal of all things, and as by connecting an electric wire with the battery, it takes the force, the strength of the battery; the poet who has touched the innermost of his being, he[77] has touched the perfect being of God, and from there[78] he derives that wisdom and that beauty and that power which belongs to the perfect self of God. No doubt there is real and false, and there is raw and ripe in all things.[79]

Poetry comes from the tendency of contemplation. Man with imagination cannot retain the imagination, cannot mould it, cannot build it unless there was[80] contemplative tendency within him. The more one contemplates, the more one is able to conceive what one receives. Not only this, but after the contemplation one is able to know a certain idea more clearly than if that[81] idea had only passed through his[82] mind. The process of contemplation is like the work of camera.

---

72. Sk.lh.: "it in the" instead of "even in the";
    Tp., Km.tp., S.: "it in" instead of "even in the"
73. Sk.lh.: "or" omitted;
    all other documents: "or" omitted
74. Tp., Km.tp., S.: "medium"
75. Sk.lh.: "nation";
    all other documents: "nation"
76. (Sk.lh)Gd.e.: "he finds" replaced with "does he find" and moved to the beginning of the question, before "what";
    all other documents: "what does he find", as above
77. (Sk.lh.) Gd.e.: "he" crossed out;
    all other documents: "he" omitted
78. Sk.lh.: "that" instead of "there", then again changed by Sk. to "that";
    all other documents: "that"
79. Tp., Km.tp., S.: a passage added from the lecture "Poet and Prophet" of 3 April 1923 ("Now the question is. . .one could certainly find.") added
80. All other documents: "is the" instead of "was"
81. Sk.lh.: "this" instead of "that";
    all other documents: "this"
82. All other documents: "one's" instead of "his"

When the c.[83] is put before a certain object, and made[84] the focus right, then only that much object is taken in the camera. And therefore, necessarily, when the object before oneself is limited, then one can see through the object more clearly. The appeal that a poet makes to his readers is[85] because he tells them of something he has seen behind these ideas that everybody knows and sees.

[86] Prophet goes still further. He does not only contemplate on[87] one idea, but he can contemplate on any idea. There comes a time in the life of the ~~life~~ [88], or[89] the one who is contemplating, that[90] on whatever object he casts his glance upon[91], that object opens and reveals to him what it [92] in its heart. In the history of the world, you will find that with their great imagination, with their great dream, trance, and joy in the divine life, the prophets have been great reformers, the knowers of science, the knowers of medicine, even the knowers of the [93] of the state. That itself shows the balance, that it is not only one-sided development, only becoming a dreamer or going into the[94] trance, it is both sides: it is an example of God in man that the prophet manifests. You can see in the life of Joseph, in his story you see[95] he was as innocent, as simple as anybody, to go with his brothers, to yield to them, and to be led to his

---

83. Ibid.: "camera"
84. (Sk.lh.) Gd.e.: "is made" instead of "made", and moved to before "right"; all other documents: "made", moved to before "right"
85. (Sk.lh.) Gd.e.: "is" changed to "exists"; all other documents: "exists" instead of "is"
86. All other documents: "The" added
87. Sk.lh.: "upon" instead of "on"; all other documents: "upon" instead of "on"
88. Sk.lh.: "prophet" filled in; (Sk.lh.) Gd.e.: "prophet" replaced with "seer", then restored to "prophet"; all other documents: "prophet"
89. Sk.sh.: later Sk. added "of" in sh.
90. (Sk.lh.) Gd.e.: "that" replaced with "when "; all other documents: "when" instead of "that"
91. All other documents: "upon" omitted
92. Sk.sh.: a sh. word in faint pencil, which might be "carries"; Sk.lh.: illegible; (Sk.lh.) Gd.e.: "is hidden". Above this, Sk. wrote: "it contains", to which Gd. added "concealed", crossing out "is hidden", but then restoring "is hidden"; all other documents: "is hidden"
93. Sk.sh., Sk.lh.: a blank; (Sk.lh.) Gd.e.: filled in "~~management~~ administration"; all other documents: "administration" added
94. (Sk.lh.) Gd.e.: "the" changed into "a"; all other documents: "a" instead of "the"
95. (Sk.lh.) Gd.e.: "you see" replaced with "that"; all other documents: "that"

destruction. In this story with Zuleikha[96] you will see there is[97] human being, there is a tendency to[98] beauty, and at the same time there is the [99], "What am I doing, what shall I do?" For the later in his life[100] you will see the one who knows the secret of dreams, a mystic who interpreted the dreams of the king, and later in [101] life you will see that he became[102] the minister, and[103] the work of the administration in his hands, able to carry out the work of the state[104]. There is little known about the life of Muhammad[105], and whatever there[106] is known, it[107] is so little known and so[108] much misinterpreted. One can only study the life of the prophet[109] and see in the capacity of a child towards his parents, then in the capacity of a young man, proving to be a soldier[110]; as a contemplating[111] man, as a dreamer for years dreams[112] in the caves of the mountains, at the same time a prophet, who spoke[113] about the life which is hidden under the surface [114]

---

96. In Islamic sources, the name given to Potiphar's wife.
97. Sk.sh.: Sk. apparently heard "is" for "his";
    all other documents: "his"
98. (Sk.lh.) Gd.e.: added, "yield to";
    all other documents: "yield to"
99. Sk.sh.: a gap;
    (Sk.lh.) Gd.e.: "thought" filled in;
    all other documents: "thought"
100. Sk.lh.: "~~For the~~ ~~Later in his~~ Later" instead of "For the later in his life";
    (Sk.lh.) Gd.e.: "Later on in his life";
    all other documents: "Later on in his life"
101. Sk.lh.: afterwards "his" added;
    all other documents: "his" added
102. Sk.lh.: "becomes", then changed by Sk. to "became";
    all other documents: "becomes"
103. (Sk.lh.) Gd.e.: "and" replaced by "with";
    all other documents: "with" instead of "and"
104. Sk.sh.: later Sk. wrote "executive" in lh. in the margin
105. (Sk.lh.) Gd.e., Tp., Km.tp.: "Muhammed";
    S.: "Mohammed"
106. All other documents: "there" omitted
107. Ibid.: "it" omitted
108. Tp., Km.tp., S.: "is" instead of "so", probably a misreading
109. (Sk.lh.) Gd.e.: "prophet" changed to "Prophet";
    all other documents: "Prophet"
110. In the stories of the life of the Prophet Muhammad, there are none of his having been a soldier, though as a caravan trader he would undoubtedly have been trained in arms
111. (Sk.lh.) Gd.e.: "contemplating" changed to "contemplative";
    all other documents: "contemplative"
112. Sk.lh.: "dreaming" instead of "dreams";
    all other documents: "dreaming"
113. (Sk.lh.) Gd.e.: "speaks" instead of "spoke";
    all other documents: "spoke"

standing against all opposition, opposition so great that his own people, his own friends, who were once his loving friends, became bitter when they saw that he brought a new spirit in the old religion. He still continues, he continues to love humanity, continues[115] all that comes to meet[116] all the opposition as it came[117], and fulfilled[118] the message which was the mission of his life, not only giving the spiritual idea to the people, not only giving the religion, but giving a mould[119] of life in all its aspects.[120]

No doubt, people have removed spirituality far from materialism, also God is far removed from humanity, and therefore man cannot conceive the idea God[121] speaking through man, one like himself. Even a religious man who reads [122]Bible from day to day will[123] with great difficulty understand the verse, "Be perfect as your Father Who is in Heaven."

The Sufi Message and its mission in the world is to bring to the consciousness of the world this saying of the world[124], that[125] how man can dive so deep within himself that[126] he can touch the depths[127] where he is united with the whole life, with all souls. And how he can derive from that source harmony,

---

114. Sk.sh.: a space;
all other documents: the sentence continues without the space
115. (Sk.lh.) Gd.e.: "continues" changed into "~~meeting~~ continues to meet";
all other documents: "to meet" instead of "continues"
116. (Sk.lh.) Gd.e.: "to meet" crossed out;
all other documents: "to meet" omitted
117. (Sk.lh.) Gd.e.: "came" changed to "comes";
all other documents: "comes"
118. (Sk.lh.) Gd.e.: "fulfilled" changed into "fulfills";
all other documents: "fulfills"
119. (Sk.lh.) Gd.e.: "mould" changed to "model";
all other documents: "model" instead of "mould"
120. Tp., Km.tp., S.: a passage added from the lecture "Poet and Prophet" of 3 April 1923 ("Yes, there are two distinct works. . .towards perfection.") added
121. (Sk.lh.) Gd.e.: "of God's" instead of "God";
all other documents: "of God's"
122. All other documents: "the" added
123. Sk.lh.: "can" instead of "will";
all other documents: "can"
124. Sk.lh.: "saying of the world" crossed out by Sk.;
all other documents: "saying of the world" omitted and a colon added after "this"
125. (Sk.lh.) Gd.e.: "that" crossed out;
all other documents: "that" omitted
126. (Sk.lh.) Gd.e.: "that" crossed out and replaced with "? Yet", but then the question mark after "himself" crossed out, "Yet" crossed out and "that" restored
127. Sk.lh.: "depth" instead of "depths";
all other documents: "depth"

beauty, peace, and power, and that[128] time when the world seems to have moved far from spiritual idea and when it is most necessary that the spiritual idea may unite humanity, divided by sects and creeds. The Sufi movement is not forming a special community or a special sect; on the other hand, it is bringing that message of love and simplicity[129] and uniting beyond the differences of sects and creeds in the one wisdom[130].

---

128. (Sk.lh.) Gd.e.: "and that" changed to "at this"; all other documents: "at this"
129. Tp.: "simplicity", later crossed out by Sk. and replaced with "sympathy" in ink
130. Sk.lh.: "the one   of wisdom", with "of" crossed out later by Sk.; (Sk.lh.) Gd.e.: "bond" filled in gap and "of" restored; all other documents: "the one bond of wisdom"; Sk.sh., Sk.lh.: dots placed under "the one wisdom" , indicating Sk.'s uncertainty whether "the one bond of wisdom" was said, or "the one wisdom"

Sakina's shorthand reporting

Paris, 18th December 1922,
Rue St. Séverin[1]

Poetry

In the[2] poetry it is the rhythm of the poet's soul which is expressed. There are moments in the time[3] of every soul, at ~~those~~ these moments[4] the

---

Documents:

Sk.sh. = Sakina Furnée's shorthand reporting of the lecture, with questions and answers (the last portion of which, however, appears to have been lost).

Km.t. = A typescript prepared by Kismet Stam, very close to Sk.sh., including the questions and answers

Hq.t. = a typescript prepared at Headquarters, Geneva, showing considerable editing (probably by Sherifa Goodenough), and not including the questions and answers. This typescript divides the lecture into two parts and contains the apparatus and designations to indicate it had become two sequential numbers (21 and 22) in the series "Social Gathekas", a series designed for reading at meetings of the World Brotherhood.

Hq.st. = a stencilled (cyclostyled) text prepared for distribution to Sufi Centres by Headquarters, Geneva, and showing the same editing as the Hq.t. Here the lecture is divided and designated as in Hq.t.

S.Q. = an article in the Sufi Quarterly, a publication issued by Headquarters, Geneva, in Vol. I, No. 2, pages 70-73 ((September, 1925). For this publication, the text of Hq.t. or Hq.st. was used, but further edited by Mumtaz Armstrong, the editor.

o.t. = and old typewritten copy of undetermined provenance, reflecting the text of Hq.t., but with yet further editing and several mistakes

Sk.l.t. = a new transcription from her shorthand made in later years by Sakina Furnée.

Notes:

1. Rue St. Séverin is an address in Paris where one of the French mureeds lived;
   o.t., Sk.l.tr.: "reported by Sakina";
   Hq.t., Hq.st.: "Social Gatheka. Number 21." followed by the Invocation; later "Social Gatheka. Number 22." (this lecture was divided into two parts);
   Sk.l.tr.: "For a circle of friends."
2. Hq.t., Hq.st., S.Q., o.t.: "the" omitted
3. Hq.t., Hq.st., S.Q., o.t.: "life" in place of "time"

soul feels itself ~~pregnant~~ rhythmic[5]; and the children, who are beyond the conventionalities of life, begin to dance at these moments, or begin to speak by[6] themselves words which rhyme, or[7] repeat phrases which are alike and which[8] harmonize together. It is a moment of [9]soul's awakening. [10]Somebody's[11] soul wakens oftener than another person's soul.[10] But in the life of every soul there are times when such [12]awakening comes. And the soul who is gifted with[13] the expression[14] of thought and idea[15], shows his gift in poetry.

Among all things of[16] this[17] world ~~that~~ which are valuable, the ~~world is~~ word is most precious, for in the word you can find [18]light which[19] gems and jewels do not possess. In a word you can find[18] an intoxication which[20] no wine can give. In a word you can[21] find ~~all~~ a life that could heal the wounds of the heart. Therefore poetry in which [22]soul is expressed is as living as a human being. If I were to say that [23]if God bestows the greatest reward on man, it is[22] eloquence, poetry, it would not be an exaggeration. For, as I have said, that[24] it is the gift of the poet which culminates in time to[25] the gift of prophecy. There is a Hindu idea which explains this better[26], and that[27] idea

---

4. Hq.t., Hq.st., S.Q., o.t.: "when" instead of "at these moments"
5. Hq.t., Hq.st., S.Q., o.t.: "rhythmical"
6. Hq.t., Hq.st., S.Q., o.t.: "to" in place of "by"
7. Hq.t., Hq.st., S.Q., o.t.: "to" added
8. Hq.t., Hq.st., S.Q., o.t.: "which" omitted
9. All other documents: "the" added
10. Hq.t., Hq.st.: "And the soul of some persons awake oftener than the soul of others."; S.Q.: "And the souls of some persons awake oftener than the souls of others."
11. Km.t., Sk.l.t.: "One person's" instead of "Somebody's"
12. Hq.t., Hq.st., S.Q., o.t.: "an" added
13. Ibid.: "has the gift of" instead of "is gifted with"
14. Km.t., Sk.l.t.: "expressions"
15. Hq.t., Hq.st., S.Q., o.t.: "ideas"
16. Ibid.: "in" instead of "of"
17. O.t.: "the" instead of "this"
18. Ibid.: these parts of the sentences omitted, probably inadvertently
19. Hq.st., S.Q.: "that" instead of "which"
20. Km.t.: "you" inserted, but crossed out
21. O.t.: "could" instead of "can"
22. Km.t.: "the" inserted, but crossed out;
    Hq.t., Hq.st., S.Q., o.t.: "the"
23. Hq.t., Hq.st.: "the greatest beauty that God bestows on man is";
    S.Q.: "the greatest beauty God bestows on man is";
    o.t.: "the greatest bounty that God bestows on man is"
24. Hq.t., Hq.st., S.Q., o.t.: "that" omitted
25. Ibid.: "in" instead of "to"
26. Ibid.: "very well" instead of "better"

is that the vehicle of the goddess of learning is eloquence.

Many live, and few think. [28]Among the few who think, there are fewer still who can express. [29]Those who think and cannot express, their[30] soul's impulse is repressed. And[31] it is in the expression of the soul that the divine purpose is fulfilled. And in poetry it is the divine impulse to express something which is fulfilled.

Yes, there is a true poetry and there is a false poetry, just like[32] there is a true music and a false music. A person knowing many words, knowing[33] syllables, [34]if he fits them in, he mechanically will arrange something, but it[33] is not poetry. Be it[35] poetry, art, or music, it[36] must suggest life, and it can only suggest life if it is[37] the deepest impulse of the soul. But if it does not, then it is dead. There exist verses of great masters, [38]whatever period they have existed, whose verses[37] have resisted the sweeping wind of destruction; [39](they pass) every movement of all ages[38]. And what is in their verse that[40] has resisted against[41] the ever-destroying influence of time? That resistive[42] power in their words was the life that was put into it[43]. The trees that live long have their[44] roots deep-set, and so are[45] the living verses. We only read them as we see the trees. If we only saw where the root of these verses is, we shall[46] find them[47] in the soul, in the spirit.

Now coming to the question, what wakens the soul to this rhythm

---

27. Ibid.: "this"
28. Ibid.: "And" added
29. Ibid.: "In" added
30. Ibid.: "the" instead of "their"
31. O.t.: "And" omitted
32. Hq.t., Hq.st., S.Q., o.t.: "as" instead of "like"
33. Ibid.: "many" added
34. Ibid.: "can fit them together and arrange something mechanically, but that"
35. Ibid.: "Whether it be" instead of "Be it"
36. Km.t., Sk.l.t.: "they" instead of "it"
37. Sk.sh.: Sk. later changed "is" to "comes from";
    All other documents: "comes from"
38. Hq.t., Hq.st., S.Q., o.t.: "of whatever period that"
39. Ibid.: "which blows at every moment, always"
40. O.t.: "which" instead of "that"
41. Hq.t., Hq.st., S.Q., o.t.: "against" omitted
42. Ibid.: "resisting"
43. Ibid.: "them" instead of "it"
44. Km.t.: "the" instead of "their"
45. Hq.t., Hq.st., S.Q., o.t.: "it is with" instead of "are"
46. Ibid.: "should"
47. Ibid.: "it"

which brings about poetry? It is something that touches in the poet that predisposition[48] which is called love. For with love harmony comes, beauty comes, [49]rhythm comes, light comes, life comes[49]. It seems[50] all that is good and beautiful and worth[51] attaining is centered in that one spark that is hidden in the heart of man. When the heart speaks of its joy, of its sorrow, it is all interesting, it is all appealing. The heart does not tell a lie; it always tells the truth, for by love it becomes sincere, and it is through the sincere heart that true love manifests. One may live in a company where there is[52] always amusement[53], [54]merriment, and beauty[55]. And one may live that life for twenty years. But the moment one realizes the movement[56] in the depth of one's heart, one feels that the whole twenty years'[57] life was nothing. One moment of living[58] with a living heart is more[59] worth while than a hundred years' long life[60] with a heart[61] dead. Many[62] we see in this world with all their comfort and fortune[63], and[64] all that they need in life, and yet [65] leading an empty life. There is nothing; their life is more unhappy than perhaps the person who is starving through life for days and days[65]. He is to be more[66] pitied whose soul is starving than the one whose body is starving only[67]. For

---

48. Ibid.: "of the soul" added
49. Ibid.: "rhythm, light and life come" instead of "rhythm comes, light comes, life comes"
50. Ibid..: "that" added
51. Km.t.: "worthwhile"
52. S.Q.: "are" instead of "is"
53. Hq.t., Hq.st., S.Q., o.t.: "amusements" instead of "amusement";
    o.t.: ", always a good time," added after "amusement"
54. Sk.sh: "past-time" added by Sk. in lh.;
    Km.t.: "pass time" added
    Hq.t., Hq.st., S.Q., o.t.: "pastimes" added;

55. Hq.t., Hq.st., S.Q., o.t.: "mirth and merriment" instead of "merriment and beauty"
56. O.t.: "love" instead of "movement"
57. Km.t.: "life" omitted (later added in ink);
    Hq.t., Hq.st., S.Q., o.t.: "years of" instead of "years'"

58. O.t.: "life"
59. Hq.t., Hq.st., S.Q., o.t.: "better" instead of "more"
60. Ibid..: "a hundred years of life" instead of "a hundred years' long life"
61. Ibid.: "that is" added
62. Ibid.: "do" added
63. Ibid.: "fortune and every comfort" instead of "all their comfort and fortune"
64. Ibid.: "and" omitted
65. Ibid.: "yet living a shallow life, with nothing in their lives; more unhappy, perhaps, than one who is starving for days together"
66. Ibid.: "more" moved to before "to be"
67. Ibid.: "only" moved to before "is starving"

the one whose body is starving, he[68] is yet alive, but [69] whose soul is starved, he[69] is dead.

Those who have shown great inspiration, and who have given to the world precious words of wisdom, they were the farmers who were ploughing on[70] the soil of their[71] heart.

That is the reason why there are few poets in this world, for the path of the poet is contrary to the path of a worldly man. The real poet, although he exists on this earth, but he[72] dreams of different worlds[73], where he gets his ideas from[74]. The true poet is a seer at the same time, or else he could not bring[75] the subtle ideas that touch the heart[76] of the listener (reader?)[77]. The true poet is a lover and [78]admirer of beauty. If his soul was[79] not impressed by beauty, he could not bring it out[80] in his poetry.

[81]But now, to tell you what does stimulate[82] the gift in the one who is born with the gift of poetry? Is it pleasure or is it pain? Not at all[83] pleasure. The[84] pleasure makes the gift frozen[85]. It is the pain that the sensitive poet's soul has to go through in this life. One may ask that[86], would it be a wise[87] thing to seek pain if one wants to be a good poet? It would be just like if one thought[88] crying was[89] a virtue, [92] if one hurt[90] oneself, and

---

68. Ibid.: "he" omitted
69. Ibid.: "he" moved to before "whose"
70. Ibid.: "plowed furrows in" instead of "were plowing on"
71. Ibid.: "the" instead of "their"
72. Ibid.: "yet" instead of "but he"
73. Ibid.: "a different world" in place of "different worlds"
74. Hq.t., Hq.st.: "from where he gets his ideas" instead of "where he gets his ideas from"; S.Q.: "from which he gets his ideas"
75. S.Q.: "out" added
76. Hq.t., Hq.st., S.Q., o.t.: "hearts"
77. Km.t.: "readers", with "listeners" typed above and a "?" in ink next to the two words; Hq.t., Hq.st., S.Q., o.t.: "reader" instead of "listener (reader?)"; Sk.l.t.: "readers (listeners)"
78. Hq.t., Hq.st., S.Q., o.t.: "an" added
79. O.t.: "were" instead of "was" ("were" is the correct conditional in English)
80. Hq.t., Hq.st., S.Q., o.t.: "out beauty" in place of "it out"
81. Hq.t., Hq.st.: a second "Gatheka", no. 22, begins here
82. Hq.t., Hq.st., S.Q., o.t.: "stimulates" instead of "does stimulate"
83. Ibid.: "at all" moved to after "pleasure"
84. Ibid.: "The" omitted
85. Ibid.: "freezes the gift" instead of "makes the gift frozen"
86. Ibid.: ", Then" in place of "that,"
87. Ibid.: "good" instead of "wise"
88. Ibid.: "thinking" instead of "if one thought"
89. Ibid.: "is" in place of "was"

cried a little[91]. Who with a living heart can live in this world as it is and not suffer, and not experience pain? Who with any tendency to feel, to sympathize, to love, and[92] would not go through pain? Who with any sincerity in his nature could go[93] from morning till evening through [94]insincerity and falsehood and. . .[95] of human nature? In short, [96]man with tender feelings[97], [96]man with open heart cannot avoid suffering. At every step he takes, suffering meets[98].

A poet begins with the admiration of beauty, and his gift becomes mature[99] in shedding tears over[100] the disappointments that he meets with in life. When he has passed that phase, then comes another interesting[101] phase: when he begins to laugh at the world. He rises beyond tears after having shed[102] enough. This does not mean that he becomes critical, that he sneers at life. No, he sees the funny[103] side of things, and he sees the whole life, which was once a tragedy, in the form of comedy. This stage is like a[104] consolation ~~after~~ for[105] him from above after his moments of great pain and suffering in[106] life.

And there comes another stage, when he rises beyond that[107] stage, when[108] he sees the divine element working in all forms, in all ~~ways~~ names, when he begins to see his Beloved in all forms, in all names. That[109] comes in the life of a poet as the[110] joy in the life of a young lover. It brings in his

---

90. Km.t., Sk.l.t.: "hurted" (incorrect English) instead of "hurt"
91. Hq.t., Hq.st., S.Q., o.t.: changed to "to hurt oneself a little and cry"
92. Ibid.: "and" omitted
93. S.Q.: "without pain" added
94. Hq.t., Hq.st., S.Q., o.t.: "the" added
95. Sk.sh.: an illegible sign; later Sk. wrote in "crudity", but this cannot have been the sh.; all other documents: "crudity"
96. Hq.t., Hq.st., S.Q., o.t.: "a" added
97. Ibid.: "feeling" instead of "feelings"
98. Ibid.: "him" added
99. Ibid.: "matures"
100. O.t., Sk.l.t.: "to" instead of "over"
101. Km.t., Sk.l.t.: "interesting" left out
102. Km.t.: "them" added after "shed", but then crossed out; Hq.st., S.Q.: "shedding" instead of "having shed"
103. S.Q.: "humerous" [sic] instead of "funny"
104. Hq.t., Hq.st., S.Q., o.t.: "a" omitted
105. Ibid.: "to" instead of "for"
106. Ibid.: "through" instead of "in"
107. Km.t., Sk.l.t.: "this" instead of "that"
108. Km.t., Hq.st., S.Q., Sk.l.t.: "where" instead of "when"
109. All other documents: "This" in place of "that"
110. Hq.t., Hq.st., S.Q., o.t.: "a" instead of "the"

life another period. Whatever be his condition in life, rich or poor, in comfort or without, he is never without his Beloved. His divine Beloved is always in his presence. When he arrives to that[111] period, he pities that lover who has only a limited beloved to admire, to love. For he has now arrived to[112] a stage that when[113] alone, when[113] in a[114] crowd, when[113] in the North or South or[115] West or [116]East, on earth or in Heaven, always he is in the presence of his Beloved.

And if one step further he reached[117], then it becomes difficult for him to express his emotion, his impulse in poetry. For then he himself becomes a[118] poetry. What he feels, what he thinks, what he says, what he does, all is poetry. At this stage he comes to touch that [119]unity which unites all things in one. But in order enjoy this stage, the soul must become so mature[120] as to enjoy it. An infant soul would not be able to enjoy this[121] particular consciousness of all-oneness.

From that[122] time in the poetry of that poet one will find glimpses of prophetic expressions[123]. It is not only the beauty of words and meanings, but his words become illuminative[124], and his verses become life-giving. There are in this world souls who are pious, who are wise, who are spiritual, but among them the one who is capable of expressing his realization of life, of truth, is not only a poet but a prophet.[125]

----

111. Km.t., Sk.l.t.: "this" instead of "that";
Hq.t., Hq.st., S.Q., o.t.: "at this" instead of "to that"
112. Hq.t., Hq.st., S.Q., o.t.: "at" instead of "to"
113. Hq.t.: "whether" instead of "when"
114. Hq.t., Hq.st., S.Q., o.t.: "the" in place of "a"
115. Ibid.: "in the" instead of "or"
116. Ibid.: "in the" added
117. Hq.t., S.Q., o.t.: "he reaches", moved to before "one step further";
Hq.st.: "he reached", moved to before "one step further"
118. S.Q.: "a" omitted
119. Sk.sh.: Sk. later added "ideal of"
all other documents: "ideal of" added
120. Hq.t., Hq.st., S.Q., o.t.: "matured" instead of "mature"
121. Ibid.: "the" instead of "this"
122. Ibid.: "this" instead of "that"
123. Ibid.: "expression" instead of "expressions"
124. Ibid.: "illuminating" instead of "illuminative"(an established but less usual English usage)
125. Ibid.: these documents end here;
Hq.t., Hq.st.: added at end: "To be read at meetings of the World Brotherhood."

Question: *Does the gift prophecy include the foretelling [126]the future?*

Answer: Yes. That is why[127] in the English word there is also a meaning of foretelling. But in the East there is a word, *Pakhambar*, which means only a Messenger. But this must be understood, that a prophet is not in the sense of the word the future teller, or the fortune teller, because the deeper he sees in life, the more he closes his lips. In the first place the one who realizes perhaps a little more than his fellow man[128], he out of modesty will not let his fellow man[128] know that, "I know more than you", and if [129]told the future, the whole world will walk after him, because everybody is anxious, "What will come to me?" But in the word seer it is plain that he sees not only [130]the present, but in the past and in the future. But one who speaks of what he knows, there is always a doubt whether he knows. It is always against the principle of a true mystic to claim any knowledge, inspiration or power, more than his fellow man[128]. Besides that, it is not fair to God, the Source from where he receives his knowledge. For an instance, if a friend trusts you with a secret, your first duty is to guard the secret of the friend, perhaps more carefully than your own secret. The prophet is trusted with the revelation, with the ~~secret~~ revelation of God, and his fulfilment of the mission of his life is in carefully guarding the trust given to him. Once he has proved himself untrustworthy[131] to the trust that is given to him, he no longer can be a prophet. It is just like it happens among friends. It is a great moral to keep the secret of a friend. There true religion begins. To give up a friend's secret with all one's love and sympathy, and yet to hand over the secret to someone else, is . . . .

Question: *That[132] gift of prophecy exists in the fine specimen of poetic art, and therefore, is it within the possibility of those who gather it*

---

126. Km.t., Sk.l.t.: "of" added
127. Ibid.: "why" omitted
128. Ibid.: "fellowmen" instead of "fellow man"
129. Ibid.: "he" added
130. Ibid.: "in" added
131. Sk.l.t.: "unworthy" rather than "untrustworthy"
132. Km.t., Sk.l.t.: "This" instead of "that"

themselves?

Answer: Yes. There exists all; only one has to find it.

Question: To ~~see~~ look at the world laughing, does that not mean to attach less importance to all other[133] things?

Answer: Yes. There is a point of view; when one sees from that[132] point of view life, one cannot help smiling. And the further and further you go, the more life presents to you something that gives you sufficient appearance to enjoy and amuse yourself. For an instance, the first thing that will make you smile is how everybody is running after his interest, and how he finds his ways through different roads and valleys, and different paths, and how one knocks the other down to go further, and how one pushes another behind, and how one closes his mouth and ~~goes~~ puts him down and goes forward. Is there anything that[134] you do not see in human nature, biting or kicking[135] or fighting? It is all there. There is nothing of the animal nature that is not in human. But man excels the animal. But that is only a smile; the laughter comes afterwards, the laughter[136] when one can see where it all ends. If one is capable[137] seeing all these various ends, in the end there is the laughter.

Question: [138]Often ends in something very dramatic. Then where is sympathy?

Answer: In this period of a poet's advancement, that pity which he had, that sentiment, that sympathy which he had already, it has in some way turned into smiles and laughter. It is something which is turned inside out. What was first outside, the pity and shedding of the tears, has now come inside, and outside is the smile and

---

133. Ibid.: "earthly" added
134. Km.t.: "that" omitted
135. Ibid.: "quicking" instead of "kicking"
136. Km.t.: "comes" added later in ink; Sk.l.t.: "comes" added
137. Km.t., Sk.l.t.: "of" added
138. Km.t., Sk.l.t.: "It" added

laughter. And therefore both exist at the same time, laughter on the lips, smile on the lips, and pity in the heart at the same time. When the poet is laughing, his heart is crying at the same time. It is natural.

Question: *Is it necessary for a poet to pass by that phase?*

Answer: Yes, if he was passing. If he were standing, it were not necessary.

Question: *Cannot happiness be a. . .?*

Answer: Happiness: you suggest to me a word on which I would lecture all day. But at the same time, if one really experiences and realizes happiness, the smiles,[139] the laughter, the tears, all would become nothing but illusion. Neither smiles[140] would express happiness nor tears. For an instance, why does one enjoy the dramatic[141] plays ~~of plays~~ more than comedy? If the soul is seeking always for happiness, why is the soul more touched by tragedy than comedy? Therefore, can anybody say happiness is only an outward thing, or from outward things comes happiness? If anyone with some authority can find out a source of happiness, he can only find it out in pain. But at the same time a question comes to my mind without your asking . . .[142]

---

139. Km.t.: "~~and~~" instead of ","
140. Km.t., Sk.l.t.: "smile" instead of "smiles"
141. Ibid.: "tragic" in place of "dramatic"
142. Ibid.: typed at the end: "Unfortunately the continuation of this is not to be found."

Sakina Furnée's shorthand reporting.

[1]Rue St. Séverin, 18 December 1922[2]

3

Music

It is music only which has beauty, which has power, charm, and at the same time can raise the soul beyond form. It is therefore that in the ancient times the greatest of the prophets have been great musicians. For an[4]

Documents:

Sk.sh. = Sakina Furnée's shorthand reporting. In the margin Sk. added in Dutch: "begin 2 blz.eerder", meaning "beginning 2 pages back", thereby indicating that this was the continuation, two weeks later, of the lecture on music of 5th December 1922, for some reason interrupted.

Lf. = a later hwr. copy made by M.lle Lefèbvre from her reporting of a lecture of 18/19 December 1922, in a simultaneous French translation, sentence by sentence, combined with the simultaneous French translation of the lecture on music of 5th December 1922. Differences between "Lf." and Sakina's shorthand reporting are not mentioned in the notes except in note 42.

Hq.st.1 = a stencilled copy made from "Sk.sh." at Headquarters, Geneva, in the form of a Social Gatheka, of the combined texts of the lectures on music of 5th and 18/19th December. It became nr. 23 in the series of "Social Gathekas".

Gd.t. = a later copy of Gd.'s edited text of "Sk.sh." of 5th and 18/19th December 1922, typed after 1927 on Gd.'s typewriter with large letters as one lecture.

Hq.t. = a later typescript copied from an earlier "Hq.t." with some editing, made at Headquarters, Geneva, in the form of a Social Gatheka, from "Hq.st.1" and "Gd.t.", in which the lectures of 5th and 18/19th December 1922 appear as one lecture.

Hq.st.2 = a second stencilled copy, made from "Gd.t." at Headquarters, Geneva, in the form of a Social Gatheka. It became nr. 37, probably erroneously added to this series a second time. This document also shows the texts of 5th and 18/19th December 1922 on music as one lecture.

Notes:

1. Sk.sh.: a question mark in parentheses added after the date of 18 December 1922;
   Lf., Gd.t.: "19th December 1922", which seems more likely than 18th December, as on that day a long lecture with questions and answers had already been given at the same place: Rue St. Séverin 16, Paris. Moreover, 19th December was a Tuesday, the day on which a fortnight earlier the beginning of this lecture had been given.
2. Gd.t.: above the combined texts of 5th and 18/19th December 1922 "Rue St.Séverin" was replaced with "Paris"
3. Gd.t.: "PUBLIC LECTURE" added above the combined texts of 5th and 19th December 1922;
   Hq.st.1, Hq.t.: "SOCIAL GATHEKA. Number 23" added, followed by the Invocation;
   Hq.st.2: "SOCIAL GATHEKA. Number 37" added, followed by the Invocation
4. All other documents: "an" omitted

instance in the life[5] of the Hindu prophets one finds Narada, the great prophet of the Hindus, a great musician at the same time. And Shiva, a God-like prophet of [6] Hindus, who was the inventor of their[7] sacred vina. Krishna is always pictured with a flute. There is a well-known[8] of the life of Moses, a legend which says[9] how [10] Moses heard a command [11] at the [12] Mount Sinai in words "Musake" [13], "Moses heard" or "Moses pondered" [14], and in [15] this revelation that came to him was of tone and rhythm, and he called it by the same name of a man [16], "Musake" [17]. And the words such as "music" or [18] "musake" [19] have come from that word. David, whose [20] song and whose voice [21] have [22] been known for ages, that [23] his message was given to the world [24] in the form of music. Orpheus of the Greek legends, the knower of the mystery of tone [25] and of [26] rhythm, and who [27] had, by the knowledge of

---

5. Hq.st.1, Hq.t.: "life" changed to "lives"
6. Ibid.: "the" added
7. Ibid.: "the" instead of "their"
8. Sk.sh.: "legend" added later by Sk. in lh.;
   all other documents: "legend"
9. Hq.st.1, Hq.t.: "tells" instead of "says"
10. Gd.t., Hq.st.2: "that" instead of "says"
11. Sk.sh.: written in lh. above "a command": "a divine command"
    Hq.st.1, Hq.st.2: "a divine comment" instead of "a command";
    Hq.st.1, Hq.t.: "a divine command"
12. All other documents: "on" instead of "at the"
13. Gd.t.: "Muse, ke"
14. Hq.st.1, Hq.t.: "'Moses Hear' or 'Moses Ponder'";
    Gd.t., Hq.st.2: "'Moses heard' or 'Moses Pondered'" replaced with "'Moses hark'"
15. Hq.st.1, Hq.t.: "on instead" of "in"
16. All other documents: "of a man" omitted
17. Gd.t., Hq.st.2: "Musik" instead of "Musake"
18. Ibid.: "and" instead of "or"
19. Hq.st.1, Hq.t.: "Musiki";
    Gd.t., Hq.st.2: "musike"
20. Gd.t.: "David whose" later changed to " David's";
    Hq.st.2: "David's"
21. Sk.sh.: clearly written: "voice";
    Gd.t., Hq.st.2: "verse" instead of "voice";
    Hq.t.: "voice"
22. Gd.t., Hq.st.2: "has" instead of "have"
23. Hq.st.1, Hq.t.: "that" omitted
24. Gd.t., Hq.st.2: "to the world" omitted
25. Hq.st.1, Hq.t.: "tune" instead of "tone"
26. Hq.st.1, Hq.t.: "of" omitted
27. Hq.st.1: "and who" omitted
    Gd.t.: "and who" later crossed out by Gd.;
    Hq.st.2: "and who" omitted

time [28] and rhythm, power over the hidden forces of nature. The goddess of learning [29], of knowledge among Hindus, whose name is Saraswati, is always pictured with [30] vina, and what does it suggest? It suggests [31] that all learning [32] has its essence in music. And besides ~~the charm~~ a [33] natural charm that music has, music has a magic power [34], a power which [35] can be experienced even now. It seems that [30] human race has lost a great deal of [30] ancient science of magic, but if there exists [36] any magic, it is in [37] music. Music, besides power, is intoxication. When it intoxicates those who hear, how much more it must intoxicate those who play or sing themselves, and how much more it must intoxicate those who have touched the [38] perfection in it [39], and those who [40] have contemplated upon it for years and years. It gives them a greater joy and exaltation even than a king feels when [41] sitting on his throne. [42]

According to the thinkers of the East, there are four [43] different intoxications: [44] the intoxication ~~is~~ of beauty and youth and of [45] strength, then the intoxication of wealth, and the intoxication of power, command of the power of ruling [46], and there is the fourth intoxication which is the

---

28. Sk.sh.: clearly "time" reported;
    Gd.t., Hq.st.2: "tone" instead of "time"
    Hq.t.: "time" later changed to "tone" in ink by Sk.
29. Gd.t., Hq.st.2: "learning" changed to "beauty"
30. All other documents: "the" added
31. Hq.st.1, Hq.t.: "It suggests" omitted
32. Gd.t., Hq.st.2: "learning" changed to "harmony"
33. All other documents: "the" instead of "a"
34. Gd.t., Hq.st.2: "power" changed into "charm"
35. Ibid.: "a power which" changed into "that"
36. All other documents: "exists" changed into "remains"
37. Ibid.: "in" omitted
38. Hq.st.1, Hq.t.: "the" omitted
39. Gd.t., Hq.st.2: "in it" replaced with "of music"
40. Ibid.: "those who" omitted
41. Ibid.: "when" omitted
42. Lf.: here was added "Histoire Farabi", an indication that Pir-o-Murshid at this point of the lecture told the story of Farabi; see Volume 1923 II in this series: "Art and Religion" of 18 December 1923, page 910
43. Gd.t., Hq.t., Hq.st.2: "five" instead of "four"
44. Gd.t.: "first" added by Gd. in hwr. before "intoxication", and "is" restored;
    Hq.st.2: "the first intoxication is"
45. Gd.t., Hq.st.2: "of" omitted
46. Hq.st.1, Hq.t.: "third is of power, command, the power of ruling" instead of "intoxication of power, command of the power of ruling";
    Gd.t., Hq.st.2: "intoxication of power, command, rule, the power of ruling"

intoxication of learning, of knowledge [47]. But all these four intoxications fade away just like stars before the sun in the presence of the intoxication of music. The reason is that it touches the deepest part of man's being. Music reaches further than any other impression one gets from the external world can reach. And then the beauty about [48] music is that music is the source of creation, and the means of [49] absorbing it. In other words, by music the world was created and it is again music with which it is withdrawn in the source which has created [50]. In support to this argument, you will read in the Bible that first was the Word and the Word was God [51]. That "Word" means sound, and from sound you can grasp the idea of music. Then there is an Eastern legend that comes [52] from centuries [53], the legend that when God made man out of clay, and asked the soul to enter, the soul refused to enter in that [54] prison house, and then God commanded the angels to sing. And as the angels sang ~~life~~ the soul entered [55], being intoxicated by the song.

But now in this scientific and material [56] world also we see an example of this kind. Before a machine, a mechanism must [57] run, it must first make [58] noise. It first becomes audible and then [59] shows its life. You [60] can see that [54] in a ship, in a aeroplane, in an automobile. [61]Of course I cannot explain this idea just now, because this idea belongs to the mysticism of sound. Just now I wish to deal with the subject of music [61]. Before an infant is capable of admiring a colour or form, it enjoys [62] sound. If there is

---

47. Gd.t., Hq.st.2: "of knowledge, learning" instead of "learning, of knowledge"
48. Ibid.: "about" changed to "also of"
49. Ibid.: "absorption" instead of "absorbing it"
50. Hq.st.1, Hq.t.: "it" added;
    Gd.t., Hq.st.2: "from which it was created" instead of "which has created"
51. John i.1
52. Hq.st.1, Hq.t.: "has come" instead of "comes"
53. All other documents: "ago" added
54. Hq.st.1, Hq.t.: "this" instead of "that"
55. Gd.t., Hq.st.2: "the body" added
56. Ibid.: "material and scientific"
57. All other documents: "will" instead of "must"
58. Hq.st.1, Hq.t.: "a" added
59. Hq.t.: added "(that)" after "then";
    Gd.t., Hq.st.2: "then" replaced with "that"
60. All other documents: "You" replaced by "We"
61. Hq.st.1, Hq.t.: this passage ("Of course...of music") shortened to read, "This idea belongs to the mysticism of sound."
    Gd.t.: this passage crossed out by Gd.;
    Hq.st.2: this passage omitted
62. Gd.t., Hq.st.2: "admires" instead of "enjoys"

any art that can please the aged most, it is music. If there is any [63] which can charge youths [64] to life and to enthusiasm, to emotion and to passion, it is music. If there is any art in which a person can fully express his feeling, his emotion, it is music which is best suited [65] for it. At the same time, it is something that gives man that force and that power of activity which makes [66] the soldiers march with the beats of the drum and [67] the sound of the trumpet.

In the traditions of the past it [68] was [69] said [70], "On the Last Day there will be the sound of the trumpets [71] before the end of the world". This shows that music is connected with [30] beginning of creation, with its continuity [72], and with its end. The mystics of all ages have loved music most. In almost all the circles of the inner cult, [73]whatever part of the world they are, music seems [74] to be the central part of their ritual [75]. And with [76] those who attain to that perfect peace which is called *nirvana*, or in the language of the Hindus it is called *samadhi*, it is more easily done by music [77]. Therefore [78] Sufis, especially those of the Chishtia [79] School of the ancient times, have taken music as a source of their meditation, and by so meditating ~~they have arrived~~ they derive much more benefit than those who meditate without the [80] help of music. The effect that they experience is the unfoldment of the soul, opening of the intuitive faculties; and their heart, so to speak, opens to all the beauty which is within and without, uplifting them and at the same time bringing

---

63. All documents: "art" added
64. Gd.t., Hq.st.2: "youth"
65. Gd.t., Hq.st.2: "most fitted" instead of "best suited";
    Hq.t.: "best fitted"
66. Hq.st.1, Hq.t.: "make"
67. Gd.t., Hq.st.2: "on" instead of "and"
68. Hq.t.: "it" omitted, but later again added in ink by Sk.
69. Gd.t., Hq.t., Hq.st.2: "is" instead of "was"
70. All other documents: the comma and quotation marks replaced with "that"
71. Gd.t., Hq.st.2: "trumpet"
72. Ibid.: "continuity" changed to "culmination"
73. Gd.t., Hq.t., Hq.st.2: "in" added
74. Gd.t., Hq.st.2: "happens" instead of "seems"
75. Hq.st.1: rewritten to read, "the centre of their cult or their ceremony or ritual";
    Gd.t.: "the centre of their cult or their ceremony"
    Hq.t.: "the centre of their cult or their ceremony (or ritual)"
    Hq.st.2: "the centre of their cult or their ceremony"
76. Gd.t., Hq.t., Hq.st.2: "with" omitted
77. Gd.t.: rewritten to read, "do it more easily by music";
    Hq.t., Hq.st.2: "do it more easily by music"
78. Hq.st.1, Hq.t.: "the" added
79. See *Chishtiyya* in Glossary.
80. Hq.t.: "the" omitted

them that perfection for which every soul yearns.

- - - - - - - - - -

[81]

Question: [82] *The meaning of Chishtia*[79]*?*

Answer: There are two meanings which come to my mind of this word. This, or as far as I remember, comes from the Caucasian part of the world, and in the language of Russians [83] means: pure, clear, and therefore the work of the inner cult that the Sufi does is purifying himself from the element that is foreign to his soul. That is why the word "Sufi" is adopted, which means pure. Well, the other meaning which occurs to me is it has come from the word Christia, for it is an Order which has retained not only the teaching of Christ as a tradition or a scripture, but as a practice of life. And their principle has been that whatever religion may be in the country where they live, they live the life that Christ lived. In other words the imitation of Christ is the moral principle of Chishtis.

Documents for question and answer:

Sk.sh. = Sakina Furnée's shorthand reporting of one question and answer.

Sk.tp. = a typewritten copy made in later years from a transcription of "Sk.sh."

Notes:

81. Sk.tp.: added on top of a new page: "Question and answer after Social Gatheka 23 on 'Music'. December 1922."
82. Sk.tp.: "What is" added in sh.
83. Ibid. : "it" added

Sakina's shorthand reporting

Paris, at Baronne d'Eichthal[1]

[2]

[3] I would like to speak on the subject of harmony this afternoon, that[3] it seems that ~~the cause which makes beauty~~ that which makes beauty is harmony[4]. Beauty in itself has no meaning. A certain object which is called beautiful at a certain place and time is not beautiful at another place or[5] another time. And so it is with thought, speech, and action. That which is

---

Documents:

Sk.sh. = Sakina Furnée's shorthand reporting

Lf. = Mlle. Lefèbvre's reporting of the simultaneous French translation of the lecture, given sentence by sentence as Pir-o-Murshid Inayat Khan spoke. It is mentioned only in footnotes 34 and 75, and is not included when "all other documents" are mentioned

Sk.l.tp. = Sakina Furnée's transcription of her shorthand made in later years, incorporating alterations made mainly by Sirdar van Tuyll

Hq.st. = a Headquarters' stencil, edited probably by Sherifa Goodenough, not including the questions and answers

Hq.t.1 = a Headquarters' typescript, mainly following Hq.st.

Hq.t.2 = a later Headquarters' typescript, showing some departures from Hq.st.

Notes:

1. Sk.sh.: The lecture in Sk.'s copybook "Summer 1922, Winter 1923" taken down just before this one, shows the date "18 Dec.(?)", so this lecture must have been given soon after that date, in any case in the second half of December 1922.
2. Hq.st.: "Social Gatheka. Harmony." added above the lecture. Later added in hwr.: "No. 4"; Hq.t.1,2: "Social Gatheka. Harmony. Number 4" added; Sk.sh.: Sk. later added "Social Gatheka 4" in pencil above the lecture and she added "Harmony" above it in ink. In the margin Sk. wrote: "sent to Hq."
3. Hq.st., Hq.t.1: "(Beloved ones of God. I should like to speak on the subject of harmony, this afternoon.)" instead of "I would like to speak on the subject of h. this afternoon, that. . ." This was crossed out by Sk. in the Hq.t., where she substituted the first three words of the Sufi Invocation: "Toward the One, ..." Hq.t.2: omitted "I would like to speak on the subject of h. this afternoon, that..."
4. Sk.sh.: here and for the rest of the lecture, Sakina abbreviated "harmony" as "h." and "inharmony" as "inh."
5. All other documents: "at" added

called beautiful is only[6] at a certain time and condition, which makes it beautiful. Therefore, if one could give a true definition of beauty, it is harmony. Harmony is combination of colours, harmony is[7] drawing of [8]design or [8]line, that is called beauty. At the same time, a word, a thought, a feeling, an action that creates harmony is productive of beauty.

Now the question is[9] where comes the tendency to harmony and from where comes a tendency to disharmony? The natural tendency of every soul is towards harmony, and the tendency towards inharmony is an unnatural state of mind or affair. And the very fact that it is not natural, it is [10] void of beauty. The psychology of man is [11] that man responds to harmony or inharmony both [12]. He cannot help it because naturally he is made so; mentally and physically he responds to all that comes to him [13], harmonious or inharmonious. And the teaching of Christ that [14] "resist not evil" is a hint not to respond to inharmony. For an [15] instance, a word of kindness, a [16] sympathy, an action of love and affection has a [17] response, but at the same time a word of insult, an action of revolt or hatred, that creates a[14] response too and this [18] response creates more inharmony in the world. By giving a[14] way to inharmony, one allows inharmony to multiply.

At this time, when one sees in the world the greatest unrest and discomfort all over [19] pervading, where does it come from? It seems that it is [9] the ignorance of this fact that inharmony will create [20] inharmony and will multiply into [21] inharmony. A person has a [22] natural tendency: [23] if he sees he is insulted, he thinks the proper way of answering is to insult the [24] person

6. Ibid.: "so" added
7. Ibid.: "the" added
8. Ibid.: "a" added
9. Ibid.: "from" added
10. Ibid.: "makes it" instead of "it is"
11. Ibid.: "such" added
12. Ibid.: "both" placed after "responds"
13. Ibid.: "be it" added
14. Ibid.: a comma in place of "that"
15. Ibid.: "an" (or "a") omitted
16. Ibid.: "of" instead of "a"
17. Ibid.: "finds" instead of "has a"
18. Ibid.: "that" instead of "this"
19. Ibid.: "allover" placed after "pervading"
20. Ibid.: "creates" instead of "will create"
21. Ibid.: "into" omitted
22. Ibid.: "the" instead of "a"
23. Ibid.: "that" added
24. Ibid.: "other" added

still more. By this he gets a momentary satisfaction to have given a good answer, but he does not know that[25] by his good answer, what he has done[25]. He has given to that power which was given by one[26], a response[27], and these two powers, being negative and positive, create by them[28] more inharmony.

"Resist not evil" does not mean receive evil unto[29] yourself. "Resist not evil" only means this: do not send[30] the inharmony that comes to you, just like[31] a person playing tennis would throw[32] back the ball with his racket. But at the same time it does not suggest that you[33] receive the ball with open hands. The tendency towards inharmony[34] must be like[35] a rock ~~being~~ in the sea; through the wind, through the storm, the rock stands in the sea and the waves come[36] with all their[37] force and yet the rock is still, stands[38], bears[39] it all, the waves behind[40].

By fighting with inharmony one increases[41]; by not fighting it, one does not give fuel to that[42] fire which would rise for destruction and would cause destruction. But, no doubt, the wiser you become, the more difficulty[43] you have to face in life, because every kind of inharmony will be directed to you for the very reason that you will not fight it. But at the same time, one must know that with all that difficulty you have helped that inharmony, which

---

25. Ibid.: "that" omitted, and "what he has done" placed after "know"
26. Ibid.: "came from the other" instead of "was given by one"
27. Ibid.: "response" instead of "a response", placed at the beginning of the sentence, after "He has given"
28. Ibid.: "by them" omitted
29. Ibid.: "into" instead of "unto"
30. Ibid.: "back" added
31. Ibid.: "as" in place of "like"
32. Ibid.: "send" in place of "throw"
33. Ibid.: "should" added
34. Ibid.: "harmony" instead of "inharmony";
    Lf.: "inharmonie"
35. Ibid.: "may be likened to" instead of "must be like"
36. Ibid.: "each wave comes"
37. Ibid.: "their" omitted
38. Sk.sh.: Later Sk. added "it all" in sh.
39. Hq.st , Hq.t.1: "bear", but in the Hq.t.1, Sk. changed it back to "bears"
40. Sk.sh.: here follows a sh.-sign, which could mean "however", but it is uncertain. Then follows a blank;
    All other documents: "letting the waves beat against it" instead of "however ? the waves behind"
41. All other documents: "it" added
42. Ibid: "the" instead of "that"
43. Sk.sh.: the 's' of the plural is often omitted in sh., especially in obvious cases.

would have otherwise multiplied, to be destroyed. It is not without advantage, for every time you stand against inharmony, you increase your strength, although outwardly it may seem a defeat. But one conscious of the increase of one's [44] power will never admit that it is a defeat. [45]And no sooner the time is passed, the person against whom it seems defeat will realize the same as his defeat. [45] After [46] the time has [47] passed, the person against whom one has stood firm will realize that it was his defeat.

Life in the world has a constantly jarring effect, and the finer you become, the more trying it becomes to you. And time comes that when a person is sincere and good-willing, kind and sympathetic, the worst [48] life becomes for him. But if he is discouraged in it, he goes under. If he kept his courage, then you find that it was not disadvantage [49] in the end, because his power will someday increase to that stage, to that degree, that his presence, his word, his action will control the thoughts and feelings and activities [50] of all. For he will get that heavy rhythm, the rhythm that will make the rhythm of everybody else follow it. This is the attribute which is called in the East the quality of the master-mind. But in order to stand firm against the inharmony that comes from without, one must first practise to stand firm against all that comes from within, from one's own self. For our soul [51] [52]self is more difficult to control than the others. And when one is not able and ~~when~~ one has failed to control oneself, it is most difficult to stand against the inharmony without.

Now the question is, what is it that causes inharmony in oneself? It is weakness, physical weakness or mental weakness, but it is weakness. Very often, therefore, one finds that it is bodily illness that causes inharmony and causes inharmonious tendencies. Besides there are many diseases of the mind which the scientist of today has not yet found. Today in the world there are

---

44. All other documents: "his" instead of "one's"
45. Ibid.: This sentence ("And no sooner. . .as his defeat") was omitted. As Pir-o-Murshid repeated the sentence a little differently, it may have been his intention that the first sentence be crossed out.
46. Ibid.: "And as soon as" instead of "After"
47. Hq.st.: "he", changed back to "has" by Sk.
48. All other documents: "worse" instead of "worst"
49. Sk.sh.: Above the word in sh. Sk. repeated "disadvantage" in lh.; All other documents: "disadvantageous" instead of "disadvantage"
50. All other documents: "actions" instead of "activities"
51. Perhaps "sole" (meaning "own") was intended
52. All other documents: "it" added

two things: one thing is[23] a person is considered [53], who is too ill perhaps, as an insane person. Well, [54] then there are all other illnesses, which are not counted at all. These people are counted among the sane people, and as a[15] notice is not taken of the defects which are of the diseases of mind, and as they are not noticed, [55] man has [56] never a chance to notice them within himself; he is continually finding faults [57] with others. If he is in an office, if he is in a good position, if he is at home, everywhere he causes inharmony. Nobody knows, for ~~today~~ to be called [58] insane, he must first be called insane.

The health of [7] mind is a question so little thought [59] about [60] these days. In the point of [61] fact as there become [62] more solicitors, more lawyers, more barristers, more courts, and more judges, so there come more cases. Constantly [63] prisons increase, and what is the out [64]? After a person has gone to prison, [65]comes back, he has forgotten where he was, he goes again in the same path. For the disease is not found out. At the [66] court a person is judged, but it is not found out psychologically [67] what is the matter, what caused him to do [68] this. One can find in these prisons thousands of people. [69]There is something the matter with their minds. [69] And if [70] a thousand years they were kept in prison, they would not improve. Nothing but injustice given [71] to them by putting them in prison. It is just like putting a person in prison because his body is ill.

---

53. Ibid.: "is considered" placed after "perhaps"
54. Ibid.: "And" instead of "Well,"
55. Sk.sh.: "noticed" was written in parentheses;
    All other documents: "and as they are not noticed" was omitted
56. All other documents: "has" placed after "never"
57. Hq.t.1,2: Sk. crossed out the 's' of the plural
58. All other documents: "treated as" instead of "called"
59. Ibid.: "talked" instead of "thought"
60. Ibid.: "in" added
61. Ibid.: "the point of" omitted
62. Ibid.: "come" instead of "become"
63. Sk.sh.: later Sk. wrote "consequently" in lh. above the word in sh., "constantly";
    all other documents: "consequently"
64. Sk.sh.: a small blank;
    all other documents: "come" added
65. All other documents: "and" added
66. All other documents: "In" instead of "At the"
67. Ibid.: "psychologically" placed after "matter"
68. Sk.sh.: Sk. wrote "to" for "do"
69. All other documents: reordered to read, "with whose minds there is something the matter,..."
70. Ibid.: "for" added
71. Ibid.: "is awarded" instead of "given"

The cause of every discomfort and of every failure is inharmony. And what would be the most useful thing at the present moment in education?[72] To give the sense of harmony, to develop it in children. It will not be[6] difficult as it appears to be[73] to bring to their notice the inharmony.[74] What is necessary is to point out to the youths the different aspects of inharmony[75] in different aspects of life's affairs.

The work of the Sufi Message, a message which is of love, harmony, and beauty, is to waken the consciousness in humanity of the true nature of love, harmony, and beauty. And the training which is given to those who become initiated in the inner cult, is to cultivate these three principal[76] things, which are principal[77] factors in human life.

- - - - - - - - - -

Question: *At what age would you begin to develop in a child*[78]*?*

Answer: At the very beginning of a child's growth.

Question: *By which means do you develop in children this sense of harmony?*

Answer: I would develop in a child in his manner, in his action, in his speech first, believing that naturally he has got love for harmony, and inharmony that he shows is not in his nature. And therefore it is not difficult to put out which is not in his nature. But if personally you ask me this question to answer, with my experience, not only with children, but in persons of all ages of a great deal of variety, I should like to say: I never for one moment think that anything wrong belongs to anyone's nature. I only think that it is something outside, which has got hold of him, and which can be taken off some day or other, and therefore I believe that there is hope for every person. And if a person was accused to

72. Ibid.: "is to" instead of "?To"
73. Ibid.: "to be" omitted
74. Ibid.: "harmony to their notice" instead of "to their notice the inh."
75. Ibid.: "harmony" instead of "inh.". A simultaneous translation into French, written down by M-lle. Lefèbvre, has "inharmonie"
76. Ibid.: "principal" omitted
77. Ibid.: "principle", changed by Sk. in Hq.t.1,2 to "principal"
78. Sk.l.tp.: "the feeling of harmony" added

have been the very worst person yesterday, today I would look at him with hope, and think it has all gone from yesterday. Another thing I consider: that to accuse a person from [79] a fault or to think [80] a person with a thought that a person is wrong or inharmonious, that thought [81] creates in that person that which one is thinking of. But I must tell you that it is a difficult thing even for me. It is denying something which is before you, and it is not only standstill [82], but [83] activity [84]. It is just telling a person who is cross by nature, and ~~tells you hell~~ who is cross, [85] to say: "No, he is not cross."

Question: *That will change it?*

Answer: Surely. It is the same thing which the Christian Science says for the physical [86] It is in the mental [87] Of course a person who practises Christian Science, he wants to put his science so much into words that he makes persons [88] revolt against him [87] But as far as the idea goes, it is a most splendid idea [87] Denying a thing is destroying a thing, and to admit a certain thing is giving it a root [87] Even if a person says, "I have that enemy, and he is so bad to me" is really giving that enemy a strength from one's own spirit. But when you forget it from your mind: "Well, I have a good wish for everyone, I do not wish to look at anything that is disagreeable," it does not give that strength.

Question: *How does Murshid propose [89] deal with criminals?*

---

79. Ibid.: Sk. changed "from" to "of"
80. Ibid.: "of" added
81. Ibid.: "that" instead of "thought" (the sh.-signs for these two words are very similar)
82. Ibid.: "standing" instead of "stand"
83. Ibid.: Sk. inserted "being"
84. Ibid.: "active" instead of "activity"
85. Sk.sh.: Sk. added "with you" in sh.;
    Sk.l.tp.: "with you"
86. Sk.sh.: a blank;
    Sk.l.tp.: a semicolon in place of the empty space
87. Sk.sh.: a blank;
    Sk.l.tp.: a full stop in place of the empty space
88. Sk.l.tp.: "people" instead of "persons"
89. Sk.sh.: later Sk. added "to"

Answer: I would suggest those accused[90] a certain fault ~~to be brought~~ before being brought to a judge, those[91] should be brought to a jury of psychologists to see what is the matter with him first. And if a person is judged, they he must again be taken to the jury [92]in what way can they be cured of the fault they have in themselves [93] Then, instead of being sent in a[94] prison, I[95] should think they should be sent to a school which is intended for criminals [96]accounted to the credit of these professors[97] would have learned[98] with a better sense to be in the world.

Question: But[99] could you give us a more definite idea, [100]way of development of children in speech and action?

Answer: For an[101] instance, in the[102] speech there are two faults that a child commits[103] without knowing of the fault. One fault is that it wants to speak sometimes in the way that a child must not speak[104], where there is [105]no consideration of manner of the time [105] And in that way it creates inharmony. When it has spoken

---

90. Sk.sh.: Sk. added "of"; Sk.l.tp.: "of"
91. Sk.l.tp.: "they" instead of "those"
92. Sk.sh.: a blank; Sk.l.tp.: a comma in place of the empty space
93. Sk.sh.: a blank; Sk.l.tp.: a question mark in place of the empty space
94. Sk.l.tp.: Sk. changed "in a" to "into"
95. Sk.sh.: Sk. changed "a" to "I" in sh.; Sk.l.tp.: "one", changed back by Sk. to "I"
96. Sk.sh.: a small blank, which could also mean that a new sentence begins here
97. Sk.sh.: Apparently Sk. did not succeed in later years in reading her sh. of this sentence correctly. She may also have missed some words in sh. Sk.l.tp.: "criminals. I should be ~~accounted~~ committed to the critic of this professor". What Sk. read as "I should be" could also be read as "as to be".
98. Sk.sh.: Later Sk. added "and understood" in sh.; Sk.l.tp.: "and understood"
99. Sk.l.tp.: "But" omitted
100. Ibid.: "a" added in Sk.hwr.
101. Ibid.: "an" crossed out by Sk.
102. Ibid.: "the" crossed out by Sk.
103. Ibid.: Sk. crossed out "commits" and wrote "makes" in the margin
104. Ibid.: "in" added
105. Ibid.: ~~more~~ (no ~~more?~~) conside~~red~~ation of manner. ~~of the time.~~

something ~~what~~ in the form that ought to be [106] not spoken [104]. [107]Well, the unknown fault [108]that from childhood children [109] get [110] into a habit of speaking [111] something which is psychologically not right, without good results. Of course, this idea is very much considered in the East. But it is an idea that [112] must be considered wherever humanity exists. For an instance, there are many words which have their power behind it [113], there are many words which cause bad effects [114], psychologically. And [115] child in play does not consider what it says. It simply says; it does not feel backward to speak about death or somebody's illness, which perhaps is psychologically wrong. Besides, it is suggestive. If one child says to another: "I shall cut your head," another perhaps takes the knife and does it. Now in action: the child is full of activity and one child in a room is like hundred children. He is always active; he does not know what to do. Therefore, he is destructive; he may spoil things. If you stop him from one thing, he goes to another, and [116] to awake [117] in him that [118] what is destructive, what would make things wrong, one will waken in him that desire of [119] harmony. Besides, for a child to consider others, the comfort of others, the importance of the work of others, these are all necessary things. There is a saying in the East that a good manner in the child means good luck; bad manner means bad luck. And one can easily see the reason of it: that good manner attracts love, affection, and good will from all sides, and it helps the child to grow. Whenever a grown-up person sees a child with good manner, his first impulse is: may he be blessed, may he succeed in life. And that good will that

---

106. Ibid.: Sk. placed "to be" after "not"
107. Sk.sh.: a small blank;
Sk.l.tp.: a full stop in place of the empty space
108. Sk.l.tp.: "is" added
109. Ibid.: "they" instead of "children"
110. Ibid.: "will get" instead of "get"
111. Ibid.: "saying" instead of "speaking", in Sk.hwr.
112. Ibid.: "it", changed back by Sk. to "that"
113. Ibid.: Sk. crossed out "it" and wrote "them" instead
114. Ibid.: "a bad effect" instead of "bad effects"
115. Ibid.: "a" added
116. Ibid.: Sk. added "in order" in parentheses
117. Ibid.: "to awaken"
118. Ibid.: Sk. added "sense of" in the margin in parentheses
119. Ibid.: "for" instead of "of"

comes from the grown-up people is not taken by a child he[120] disturbs them. He is deprived of that blessing. And to me it seems that the first lesson of religion is to teach them [123]the mother, the father, the elderly people in the house, to consider[121] them[122]. And if the children are not trained in that, then, when they grow up, they cannot understand religion. Religion I mean in the sense of the word, not a special form of religion ~~but the~~. And what is really wanted in this world today is the bettering of the soul. A good time will only come when the coming generation will try and strive after the improvement of the soul.

Question: What must one do before an invading[123] army of Germans and Bolshevists?

Answer: I think that this saying must be blown in a trumpet through all the parts of the world. I say ~~that struggle with~~, "The[124] fight with another is war, and struggle with oneself is peace."

---

120. Ibid.: "who" instead of "he"
121. Ibid.: "to consider" placed by Sk. before "the mother"
122. Ibid.: "them" crossed out by Sk.
123. Ibid.: "advancing" instead of "invading"
124. Ibid.: "the" omitted

A handwritten copy by Sherifa Goodenough
from an unknown reporting.

1

2

In the East, and especially in India, the composition has been considered as a picture.

[3]If a painter makes a picture of the forest, in ten minutes all will be changed, the light, the[4] shade will be altered, the fruits will be different from time to time. If a photograph is taken, and the camera is moved around a person in ten different positions, there will be ten different pictures. If the

---

Documents:

Gd.h. = a handwritten copy of an earlier ms. made by Sherifa Goodenough for the purpose of editing , showing corr., changes and add. Several paragraphs later were taken by her to be inserted in one of her compilations on music. Gd.'s editing in this ms. is indicated by "Gd.e." in the notes.

Ng.t. = a typewritten copy made by Nargis Dowland of "Gd.h.", incorporating the editorial and other changes made by Sherifa Goodenough in "Gd.h.". Further editing and corr. by Gd. were handwritten on this typescript and are indicated by "Gd.e." in the notes.

Ng.t.2 = another typewritten copy made by Nargis Dowland, made from "Ng.t.1" and incorporating Gd.'s further editing ("Gd.e.") in "Ng.t.1." Sirdar van Tuyll, to whom Miss Dowland handed on her typescripts, made some further corr. written in by his secretary, An Spirlet, and indicated by "Sr.c." in the notes.

Sk.t. = a typewritten copy of "Ng.t.2" including Sirdar's corr. ("Sr.c."), made by Sakina Furnée or under her supervision.

Notes:

1. Although undated, this lecture is very similar in subject matter to other lectures on music given in November and December 1922. It could have been given in Paris or in England in December 1922.
2. Gd.h.: the title, "The Oriental Composers and their Works", does not seem to have been given by Pir-o-Murshid, but probably was added later by Gd. and intended for a more extensive treatment;
   all other documents: this title written above
3. (Ng.t.1) Gd.e.: this paragraph joined to the previous paragraph;
   Ng.t.2, Sk.t.: continues the previous paragraph
4. (Gd.h.) Gd.e.: ", the" changed into ". The"

picture of the material object varies so much, how much more various must be the picture of the imagination, of the thought? [3]

[5] Therefore, in the song very[6] little is given by the composer, the outline only, and the rest is the expression of the singer, of his feeling at the time of singing. [5]

[7] From[8] the beginning the pupil is [9] taught to improvise as much as to play,[9] expected not to play only, but to produce. First he listens to the *raga*s, and the picture of the *raga* is impressed upon his soul. Then he is given the outline of the composition and he improvises upon that. [10] When he has mastered this, he may improvise without any outline. [11] as the ~~drawing~~ design is given to the embroiderer, and the embroiderer chooses whether to [12] fill it in with silk or with gold, and [13] how to fill it in. [14] He listens to what his soul tells him and he produces that. [7,11]

[15] There is very little written music in the East. There are many reasons for this. There is a system of notation in the Sanskrit manuscripts,

---

5. (Ng.t.1) Gd.e.: this paragraph joined to the previous paragraph;
   Ng.t.2, Sk.t.: continues the previous paragraph
6. (Ng.t.1): "way" read for "very";
   Ng.t.2: "way";
   Sr.c.: "way" changed into "very"
7. (Ng.t.1) Gd.e.: this paragraph joined to the previous paragraph Ng.t.2, Sk.t.: continues the previous paragraph
8. Ng.t.1,2, Sk.t.: "In" instead of "From"
9. (Gd.h.) Gd.e.: this part of the sentence crossed out;
   Ng.t.1,2, Sk.t.: this part of the sentence omitted
10. (Gd.h.) Gd.e.: by small crosses, Gd. indicated that the passage in note 11 was to be inserted here, although it may have been said as an elaboration after the following sentence.
11. (Ng.t.1) Gd.e.: joined to the previous paragraph;
    Ng.t.2: continues previous paragraph;
    Sr.c.: moved, as in note 10;
    Sk.t.: as in note 10
12. (Gd.h.) Gd.e.: these three words first crossed out, then restored;
    Ng.t.1: "must" instead of "chooses whether to";
    Ng.t.2: "must";
    Sr.c.: "must" changed back to "chooses whether to"
13. Gd.h., Ng.t.1: a small space;
    Ng.t.2: "knows" typed in;
    Sr.c.: "knows" crossed out;
    Sk.t.: no space left open
14. Gd.h., Ng.t.1: an open space;
    Ng.t.2, Sk.t.: no space left open
15. (Ng.t.1) Gd.e.: a mark in the margin to indicate a new paragraph;
    Ng.t.2, Sk.t.: a new paragraph

but there are very few who read it. The system must needs [16] be a very complicated one; still, that is not the hindrance. The notation would hamper the musician, and not leave him free to sing and play what his soul speaks.

[17] I have seen myself that in playing and singing the *raga Jogia* [18] in the early morning, when people were [19] going to the temple and to the mosque, sometimes they would stop to listen and be rapt in the music. At other times, with the same *raga*, I did [20] not even impress myself. [21]According as the mood was.[17] [22]A musician may take one [23] *raga* and play that for hours, or he may go from one *raga* to another. But the more he plays one *raga*, the more he indulges [24] in that, the more he impresses his soul with it, ~~the~~ [25] more he will find in that.

Indian music gained very much by its contact with the Persian music. It learned the grace and expression of the Persian music. And it gained much from the beauty of the Arabic rhythm. After the Mogul Empire it was far more beautiful than it had been before.

[26]Having studied the music of East and West as a musician, I see [27] that there are many things that could [28] be introduced from the West to the Eastern music, and many things that could be introduced from the East to the West.

---

16. Ng.t.1: Nargis unable to read this word, a small space left open;
    Gd.e.: "needs" filled in
17. (Ng.t.1) Gd.e.: this paragraph joined to the previous paragraph;
    Ng.t.2, Sk.t.: continues the previous paragraph
18. Ng.t.1: Nargis unable to read this word, a small space left open;
    Gd.e.: "*Jogia*" filled in
19. All other documents: "are" instead of "were"
20. (Gd.h.) Gd.e.: "did" changed into "could"
21. (Ng.t.1) Gd.e.: ". According" changed into ", according"
22. Ng.t.1: a new paragraph for "A musician... find in that";Gd.e. :this paragraph joined to the previous paragraph;
    Ng.t.2, Sk.t.: continues the previous paragraph
23. Ng.t.2: "a" instead of "one";
    Sr.c.: restored "one"
24. Ng.t.1: "and more he indulge" instead of "the more he indulges";
    Ng.t.2: "and more he indulges";
    Sr.c.: back to "the more he indulges"
25. All other documents: "the" restored
26. (Ng.t.1) Gd.e.: a mark in the margin to indicate a new para graph
27. Ng.t.1: "saw";
    Gd.e.: back to "see"
28. (Gd.h.) Gd.e.: added "with advantage";
    All other documents: "with advantage"

Now the circumstances and [29] are drawing the East and West nearer together, it is most desirable that they should draw near together also in understanding and sympathy. For this people may say that [30]this is needed or that is needed.[30] I should say that what is needed is wisdom, philosophy, sympathy, consideration for another, feeling for another.[31] For[32] learning this it is [33] to learn this music where the soul is made the musician, where the soul[34] . In this a person learns what word is in tune, what[35] is not in tune, what action is harmonious, what action is not in harmony, what feeling is false, what feeling is ~~right~~ in the tone,[36] what thought is harmonious and what is not. [37]He learns meekness, gentleness, sympathy, consideration for another, all good manners.[37]

---

29. (Gd.h.) Gd.e.: "and" crossed out, no open space;
    Ng.t.1: an open space after "and" Ng.t.2, Sk.t.: "and" omitted and no space left open
30. Ng.t.1: "this is needed and that is needed" omitted;
    Gd.e.: this part of the sentence re-inserted
31. (Gd.h.) Gd.e.: added "to be human", and, having no more space, continued lower on the page with "Humanity is wisdom, is sympathy" after the next two sentences;
    Ng.t.1: "to be human", and "Humanity is wisdom, is sympathy" lower on the page;
    Gd.e.: "Humanity is wisdom, is sympathy" moved to after "to be human";
    Ng.t.2, Sk.t.: "to be human;
    humanity is wisdom, is sympathy" added
32. Ng.t.1,2, Sk.t.: "by" instead of "for"
33. Gd.h.: a small space;
    Ng.t.1: space omitted;
    Gd.e.: space restored;
    Ng.t.2, Sk.t.: no space left open
34. Ng.t.1: "where the soul" omitted;
    Gd.e.: "where the soul" restored;
    all other documents: "where the soul ."
35. (Gd.h.) Gd.e.: "speech" added;
    All other documents: "speech"
36. Ng.t.1: "tune";
    Gd.e.: changed back to "tone";
    Ng.t.2, Sk.t.: "tone"
37. Ng.t.1: a new paragraph;
    Gd.e.: joined this last sentence to the previous paragraph;
    Ng.t.2, Sk.t.: this last sentence joined to the previous paragraph

A text in the handwriting of SherifaGoodenough, from her own or someone e se's reporting.

[1]

Music

[2] In the old legends we find that in ancient times music had effect, not upon men or upon animals only, but upon[3] objects, upon the elements. The flames of fire burst out or the waters stopped running when music was sung or played. In the poem of Tansen, which you may have heard read and recited here many times, you will have heard that this was so. A person may ask, "Is this an exaggeration, or is music different now from then, or have we lost this art?" I will say that such singers as I heard sing in India when I was a boy, I never ~~not~~ heard since, in the next generation.

Documents:

Gd.h. = a handwritten copy of an earlier ms., made by Sherifa Goodenough, with some corr. and changes in her hwr., indicated by "Gd.c." in the notes. A few add. by Sirdar van Tuyll, written by his secretary, An Spirlet, are from a later date and copied from "(Ng.t.) Sr.c." and therefore not included in the notes.

Ng.t. = a typewritten copy made by Nargis Dowland of "Gd.h." in which the first paragraph of the lecture has been omitted, as Gd. crossed it out in "Gd.h." and inserted it in one of her compilations on music. A few add. and corr. made by Sirdar van Tuyll in this typescript are indicated by "Sr.c." in the notes.

Sk.t. = a typewritten copy of "Ng.t." with "Gd.c." and "Sr.c." incorporated, made by Sakina Furnée or under her supervision.

Notes:

1. Although undated, this lecture is very similar in subject matter to previous lectures on music during November and December 1922. As in the first paragraph Pir-o-Murshid refers to the poem "Tansen", published in the *Diwan of Inayat Khan*, Southampton, 1915, and to the place where this poem could have been "heard many times", which can only refer to the place in London where Pir-o-Murshid and a group of his disciples had gathered many times, and where he now found himself again with his followers, although by this time he was living in Suresnes, France. It may well have been in the second half of December 1922 that this visit to London took place, and that these words were said as an introduction to a performance of singing, accompanied by the vina, given by Pir-o-Murshid Inayat Khan.
2. Gd.h.: this paragraph crossed out with an annotation in Gd.'s hwr.: "already mentioned", which shows that she was using this ms. to make one of her compilations on music;
   Ng.t., Sk.t.: this paragraph omitted
3. (Gd.h.) Gd.c.: "things, upon" added

The singers of ancient times sang the same *rag*,[4] the same song, hundreds[5] of times, thousands of times, a million times. I have seen myself that, when I was given one song, I sang it over and over again, hundreds of times, thousands of times, and each time I found in it a new beauty. [6]When my turn came as a teacher, I found that, among my pupils, there was none[7] who had this patience. In the Parsi community alone I had at least five hundred pupils. None had the patience to repeat the same song over and over again so many hundred times. Each wanted a new song, a change. Really one song was enough for three years.

There was a great singer, [8] the last of the great classical singers. He lived at the court of the Maharajah . All day and night he practised and sang. He received a great patronage from the Maharajah, and there was no need for an artist to advertise himself, to see[9] managers and agents, to have his photograph taken. So he sang[10] all day and when he felt[11] the mood he went and sang before the Maharajah. My ~~grand~~father went to see him, and said to him, "It is a great enjoyment for me[12] to hear such a great singer [13] said,[14] "~~It is~~ I am nothing. I can do nothing. In thirty years' practice I have learned four notes." Orientals are very modest. They speak very modestly, saying, "It is nothing, I am nothing". My father thought, "Perhaps he is speaking in this way". But when he heard [15] singing, he

---

4. Gd.h., Sk.t.: "r"
5. Ng.t.:"hundred"; Sr.c.: plur."s" added
6. (Gd.h.) Gd.c.: "Then" added;
   Ng.t., Sk.t.: "Then"
7. Ng.t.: "one" instead of "none";
   Sk.t.: "one"
8. Cf. the second paragraph of the lecture "Music" (following on page 326), also of December 1922, which could refer to the same story, but told differently;
   Sk.t.: no space left open
9. Ng.t., Sk.t.: "many" added
10. (Gd.h.) Gd.c.: "sang" changed into "practised";
    Ng.t., Sk.t.: "practised"
11. Gd.h.: an illegible sign added after "felt";
    Ng., Sk.t.: "in" added
12. Ng.t., Sk.t.: "us" instead of "me"
13. All documents: an open space
14. (Ng.t.) Sr.c.: "said" replaced with "But he answered";
    Sk.t.: "but he answered"
15. Gd.h.: a small open space;
    (Ng.t.) Sr.c.: "him" filled in;
    Sk.t.: "him"

saw[16] that when those four notes,[17] the [18] mastered notes, were sung, a ~~miraculous~~[19] effect was produced.

It is by repetition of one thing, by association, that we can produce in ourselves the creative power. To have acquired a great store of knowledge, so many songs, so many [20] is nothing. It is the power of producing from within oneself, of creating, that is great.

Association is a great thing.[21] There is a Marathi poem in which the poet says: "I found on the road a piece of earth that smelt as sweet as amber. I asked it why it smelled so sweet, though it was only earth. It said, 'I am only earth, but I have been in contact with amber.'"

By the association of holy persons, of sages, we are ourselves helped. That is why, if we have this association, we should never leave[22] it.

In the practice of *samadhi*, which in the Sufi words is called *amal*, a certain degree of liberation of the spirit can be attained[23] in three or four hours. Every organ of the body holds the consciousness as in clutches, and the mind holds the consciousness. Sound ~~intoxicates~~ breaks down this hold. [24] It intoxicates and then frees. This practice, which can be done by the spiritually perfected person in three or four hours, can be done by music, by playing and especially by singing, in half an hour, or a quarter of an hour. [25]

---

16. (Gd.h.) Gd.c.: "found" written above "saw", then crossed out
17. (Gd.h.) Gd.c.: added "of which he spoke";
    Ng.t., Sk.t.: "of which he spoke"
18. Gd.h.: a small open space;
    Ng.t.: "the" overlooked by Nargis when copying "Gd.h.";
    Sr. "the four" filled in; Sk.t.: "four" added
19. (Gd.h.) Gd.c.: afterwards "wonderful" added;
    Sk.t.: "wonderful"
20. (Gd.h.) Gd.c.: filled in "*raga*s" in the open space;
    Ng.t., Sk.t.:"ragas"
21. Ng.t.: This sentence left out;
    Sr.c.: this sentence re-inserted
22. Ng.t.: misread as "more learn";
    Sr.c.: put back to "never leave"
23. (Gd.h.) Gd.c.: added "by a perfect person";
    Ng.t., Sk.t.: "by a perfect person"
24. (Gd.h.) Gd.c.: added "Man comes out of his coverings"; apparently this sentence was forgotten in copying the text;
    Ng.t., Sk.t.: "Man comes out of his coverings"
25. Ng.t., Sk.t.: a paragraph added on Yogis and Sufis using music in their meditation, taken from a lecture given in an earlier year.

A handwritten ms. by Sherifa Goodenough,
probably made from her own longhand reporting.

Music [1]

In ancient times there was in India a great difference between the professional musicians and the amateurs. Firstly because the music had reached such a point of development that unless a person devoted his whole life to it, his whole energy, his whole effort, he could not excel. Unless he practised nine or ten hours a day, he could not play or sing perfectly. [2]
I remember that my grandfather, Moula Bakhsh, in his sixtieth year, when a great name had been made and all the learning accomplished, used to practise nine hours a day.

There were at the court of the Maharajah Sindia of Gwalior [3] years ago, two singers [4] who were accounted very great singers. It was

---

Documents:

Gd.h. = a handwritten copy by Sherifa Goodenough, probably made from her own lh. reporting of the lecture, with some add. and corr. by her, indicated by "Gd.c." in the notes.

Ng.t. = a typewritten copy made by Nargis Dowland of "Gd.h.", with corr. and add. incorporated. A few further corr. in this typescript were added by Sirdar van Tuyll, indicated by "Sr.c." in the notes.

Sk.t. = a typescript made of "Ng.t." by Sakina Furnée or under her supervision, including Sirdar's corr. ("Sr.c.")

Notes:

1. Although undated, this lecture is very similar in subject matter to the lectures on music given in Geneva, Switzerland, in November 1922. It could well have been given in Paris, in December 1922, to introduce a musical performance on the vina by Pir-o-Murshid Inayat Khan.
2. Gd.h.: an open space, indicating that something more was said;
Ng.t., Sk.t.: no space left open
3. Gd.h., Ng.t.: an open space;
(Ng.t.)Sr.c., Sk.t.: no space left open
4. Gd.h.: an open space where the two names of the singers may have been mentioned;
Gd.c.: "Abdul Siskhan" pencilled in, but this probably should be "Natthan-Pirbux", the coupled name of two well-known singers at the court of Maharajah Sindhia of Gwalior, who reigned from 1761 to 1794; the name Abdul Siskhan may have been mistakenly taken

said that they used to practise (they practised mostly at night)[5] having tied their hair with a rope, so that if sleep came upon them, the rope ~~might~~ should awaken them.[6] By this practice, with a great patronage of the Maharajah, they became very great and very renowned[7] singers.

[8] They were the last great singers of that time. [2] After that, ~~from~~ music fell into the hands of the amateurs, who made a great effect upon the public, because the general public could not appreciate the more perfect music.[9]

[2] the classical music declined. At the present time the classical music in India is heard only ~~at~~ in the ~~court~~ homes of some old Maharajahs and in the houses, I mean [10]cottages, of the musicians.

In India, a singer, when he begins to sing, sings first the keynote. This he repeats over and over, so as to put himself so much in union with his instrument that his voice and ~~the sound~~ the tone of the instrument may be one. Then he goes a little farther and returns to the keynote. Then he goes a little farther still, but always returns to the keynote.

This reminds him,[11] the keynote is God, to Whom all things return, from Whom all has come, Who is always present[12], and always the same.

---

down instead of "Abdul Aziz Khan", but no musician with such a name is known to have been associated with Sindhia court of Gwalior;
Ng.t.: "Abdul Siskhan(?)";
Sk.t.: no space left open

5. (Ng.t.)Sr.c., Sk.t.: parentheses omitted
6. Prof. R. C. Mehta has offered an annotation to this story: "The story of keeping awake through the night hours by tying one's tuft of hair (on head) to a ceiling, and practicing music (or doing other studies in the context of other arts or crafts) with great vigilance in such trying conditions is told of many musicians (which may be true in some cases). Such stories are told to pupils to persuade them to practice harder and harder through self endurance and sacrifice. The persuasion is that the path to excellence or glory is self discipline, endurance and devotion."
7. Ng.t.: an open space, as apparently Ng. was unable to read the handwritten word;
   Sr.c.: "renowned" filled in
8. Gd.h.: a space of almost two lines left open
9. (Gd.h.)Gd.c.: added, probably by Gd. herself, "good music is now neither patronised by the princes and potentates of the land, nor by the public";
   Ng.t., Sk.t.: this sentence added
10. (Gd.h.)Gd.c.: "the" added;
    Ng.t., Sk.t.: "the"
11. (Gd.h.)Gd.c.: "that" instead of a comma;
    Ng.t., Sk.t.: "that"
12. (Gd.h.)Gd.c.: first Gd. wrote "there" above "present", then crossed it out

[1] Paris, December 1922[2]

Beloved ones of God,

It is my great happiness to take part in the meeting of the members of the movement[3] and of our friends, which is held here to welcome our friend Mr. Zanetti, to congratulate him on his being the Executive Supervisor of our movement, and for welcoming him among us here in Paris.

Taking the opportunity of this occasion I should like to explain in a few words our aim, our object, our work.

The Message is the answer to the problem of the day. We do not desire to form a creed, to make a community by our efforts in this Sufi movement. On the other hand, we wish to try and raise our ideas above these boundaries of creeds and distinctions which keep humanity divided, by the means of spreading the divine truth, the spiritual ideal, in absence of which the[4] humanity is suffering, and at the present time suffering the most. When we see at[5] the condition of the world, business, commerce . . . [6] and all different aspects of life, it seems there is confusion, disturbance everywhere. And what is it caused by? It is caused by the absence of the realization of reality. And what is needed just now is to bring humanity to the consciousness of reality. And we in our efforts do not think that one particular method is the only method, but we take all methods to bring about, to waken in humanity the reality.

Documents:

Sk.sh. = Sakina Furnée's shorthand reporting.

Km.t. = Kismet Stam's typescript, made from Sk.sh.

Sk.t. = A typescript made in later years by Sakina Furnée or under her supervision.

Notes:

1. Sk.sh.: later Sk. wrote above the lecture, "To welcome our friend Mr. Zanetti"
2. Km.t.: "Winter, 1922"; added later, in another type: "at Baronne d'Eichthal's. Paris."; Sk.t.: "Winter, 1922, at Baronne d'Eichthal's. Paris."
3. At this time, the official name for all activities was "The Sufi Order", although Pir-o-Murshid was increasingly using the word "movement", which became the official name for the umbrella organization in October of 1923.
4. Km.t., Sk.t.: "the" omitted
5. Km.t., Sk.t.: "at" omitted
6. Sk.sh., Km.t., Sk.t.: a blank space

Our three distinct activities, such as the esoteric activity is to strengthen the ideas and the feelings of those who already have some philosophy of life. ~~They underst~~ The suffering in life has brought them some understanding, they want a hand: "What life has taught you,[7] at this moment you are looking at a different point of view, and yet you are right". This gives such a great strength. Besides the training or exercises, this is the main thing, for every soul has the truth in his depth. And when the soul awakens the first thing it wants is a helping hand. And yet it is something which comes from within. And when this is strengthened this person becomes firm in his life's progress, in his path.[8]

The other activity is the activity of Brotherhood. Of what the world is starving today is the lack of brotherhood, which is the main ideal of all religions which all prophets and teachers brought to the world, that main ideal that unites man in love and sympathy, and prompts man to do good towards one another. Among nations, among races, in every country you will find in all its different activities divisions, parties, one working against the other. Therefore there is unrest everywhere. Our work, therefore, is to waken that ideal of brotherhood which is the first and last lesson that mankind has to learn and live.

Our third activity and the most important is the activity in the religious line. Is it a new religion? No, there is nothing new under the sun, as Solomon says. It is only wakening in the heart of those who are following a particular religion the truth of their own religion, making man tolerant towards one another by understanding the other's religion. The one who looks with prejudice [9]does not only lack to understand the other, but his own faith . . . [10]The one who knows the depth of his own faith, he has touched the truth. He can tolerate the faith of another. When one cannot tolerate another, then the misunderstanding is in himself. Not only that, but the absence of religion that one sees just now, and the increasing wave of materialism and commercialism, that man does not see before him but the attainment of matter. All the unrest, all unharmony[11], the whole tragedy of the life is caused by man's whole concentration centred in the attainment of material gains. And the

---

7. Km.t., Sk.t.: "?" instead of ","
8. Sk.sh.: Sk. indicated by numbers that this should read "in his path, in his life's progress"; Km.t., Sk.t.: "in his path, in his life's progress"
9. Sk.sh.: a blank; Km.t., Sk.t.: no space
10. Sk.sh.: an open space, indicating a few words missed; Km.t., Sk.t.: no space
11. Sk.sh.: Sk. wrote out "unharmony" in lh.; Km.t., Sk.t.: "inharmony"

consequence is that the life is heavy for the poor and rich, for those in good ~~positions~~ . . . [12] for everyone life is difficult. Every day the life is becoming a burden, whatever his position, in domestic, in factory, in politics, he feels that there is a burden. It is the burden of the whole humanity, something which must evolve upward[13], towards the nobility of soul, the realization of reality. When this is pulled down, there will be constant fights; it will end in destruction.

Our work, therefore, is to do all in our power through every channel to bring before humanity the importance of the knowledge of reality. Therefore many who are drifting along here and there, no religion, no church, nor with any particular idea to hold on [14] very necessary that they may be provided with religious ideas which respect all religions, respecting truth in all its aspects. In order to work we have formed the group of the sympathetic friends. This is called Sufi Movement, to call humanity to unite in wisdom, whatever be their faith.

The movement has been working in the Western world now for ten years. The years of the war may be considered as gone in those anxious times; at that time not much work has been done. After the war, groups have been formed in France, Switzerland, Belgium, Holland. A group has existed in San Francisco first, then in England. As the work of the Order became more increased in its progress, it became necessary to organize the work in all these groups. And with the increase of this work, it was the help of God that our sympathetic help, Mr. Zanetti, who has now come with us, and has taken in his hand the reins[15] of the organization which [16] hope will be kept intact. [16] wish him most heartily success and God's blessing upon the post.
[17]

---

12. Sk.sh.: a blank;
    Km.t.,Sk.t.: "position", followed by a blank
13. Km.t., Sk.t.: "upwards" instead of "upward"
14. Sk.sh.: a small blank;
    Km.t.,Sk.t.: "to, it is" instead of the blank
15. Km.t.: "rein:;
    Sk.t.: "reign"
16. Sk.sh.: a small blank;
    Km.t., Sk.t.: "we"
17. Km.t.: continues with the following: (incomplete report) Mr. Zanetti: My Friends, Although Executive Supervisors are not supposed to make use of words but of actions, I should say a few words to you after all Murshid has said to you about the work. I can bring you no assurances of success, save the trust he has put on me. We all feel . . . I am very glad to have been here, to have seen you all, and that sympathy . . . .

Sherifa Goodenough's handwritten
manuscript, evidently a compilation

[1]

TRANQUILLITY

This evening's subject is tranquillity, which is the thing most essential to be developed, because all merits and all virtues are produced[2] by it.

If a person moves his arms continually, the muscles will increase and become strong. If he is always lying on a couch and does not move, they will shrink, and very soon he will look like a skeleton. ~~Many times people have got such disorders as dyspepsia only from the lack of activity.~~ If you are a business person and you go to see ten people a day, and talk with ten people and discuss the affairs, you will become rich[3]. If you are a business person and lie upon the couch and let the business be done by others, and let

---

Documents:

Gd.h. = A manuscript in the handwriting of Sherifa Goodenough, showing many corr. and insertions. This seems to be one of many compilations of the teaching of Pir-o-Murshid Inayat Khan made by Sherifa Goodenough in her function as editor of his work to prepare it for publication and/or distribution to Sufi centres.

Hq.t. = A typescript, seemingly prepared from Gd.h. at Headquarters, Geneva. It incorporates many of the editorial changes in Gd.h., and shows some further editing.

Sk.t. = A typescript prepared by Sakina Furnée or under her supervision, probably prepared from both Hq.t. and Gd.h., as it shows editorial changes made in both documents.

Notes:

1. No indication appears on the document (Gd.h.) of a time or place for the original lecture or lectures on which this ms. is based. The subject matter indicates the general period of the latter part of 1922. This document has never been published or circulated, and is printed here to preserve these teachings, undoubtedly originating with Pir-o-Murshid Inayat Khan, with the caution that no assumptions should be made with regard to the integrity of the language in this compilation
2. Gd.h.: "due to" written above "produced", then crossed out;
   Hq.t.: "(due to)" following "produced"
3. Gd.h.: "become rich" crossed out, "prosper" written above;
   Hq.t., Sk.t.: "prosper" instead of "become rich"

the servant bring you even dinner where you are lying, then your business will not prosper. This shows that activity has the tendency to form, and repose ~~has is the tendency to hold, to seize, to stop all things~~[4] annihilation, the ruination[5] of all things. All this manifestation of the world has been made[6] by the activity of an unseen power that we call God. That means, all the men and women and everything that we see around us, all the forms and those things that we do not see but yet perceive, such as thoughts and feelings, and kindness and goodness, and bravery have been produced[7] by the activity[8]. ~~If that invisible power that~~ [three illegible words] ~~that one being.~~ If I were to speak of this, it would take me into another subject; but briefly, that invisible power, that immortal life, that one being has produced all by his activity, and repose holds, seizes, stops all things.

There are two things, the poison, and the sugar which we eat every day and are very happy to have. If we were to drink the poison, tomorrow we should not even be alive to ask for it. This makes us say, the poison is of no use. And yet the doctors and the chemists make a great many things from the poison, to cure different diseases. In some illnesses sugar is very harmful, and the doctors have to prevent their patients from eating it for months and months. So we see that the merit is not in the sugar nor in the poison, but in the person who knows how to use each at the right time. [9]Much can be done by speech, but often silence can do still more.

By always moving all day, and always working we may become ill and ~~may even~~ have a fever. [10]Some diseases, such as dyspepsia are often caused by inactivity. The person did not want the disease, but by the[11]

---

4. Gd.h.: apparently Gd. first wrote "has", then crossed that out and wrote "is the" and continued the sentence with "annihilation, the ruination of all things"; then she added the passage "tendency to . . . all things" and indicated it should be inserted before "annihilation"; then she crossed out the passage "tendency to . . . all things", then restored part of it, then crossed it out again;
   Hq.t.: "is the" instead of the crossed out passage;
   Sk.t.: "has the tendency to stop all things, is the" instead of the crossed out passage
5. Gd.h.: beneath the word "ruination" Gd. wrote "success", then crossed it out
6. Gd.h.: above "made" Gd. wrote "produced", then crossed it out;
   Hq.t.: "(produced)" after "made"
7. Gd.h.: above "produced" Gd. wrote "manifested", then crossed it out;
   Hq.t.: "manifested" instead of "produced"
8. Sk.t.: "of that invisible power" added
9. Gd.h.: This sentence is written on a small separate piece of paper, with an indication to insert it at this point
10. Gd.h.: Later Gd. wrote "On the other hand" before "Some diseases . . .";
   Hq.t., Sk.t.: "On the other hand" added at the beginning of this sentence
11. Sk.t.: "the" omitted

inactivity it has come.

To come now to my subject, which is tranquillity, all our failures and our mistakes are caused by activity.

A person who always walks very fast will always stumble; there is always a chance of his falling down. [12] If there is a hole, he will put his foot in it, because he sees only the aim to which he is going, he does not see the road.[12] A person who speaks very quickly does not give himself time to think of what he is going to say and he often says what he did not mean to say. Then, afterwards, he repents and thinks, ~~He says~~ I ought not to have said that. If someone asks him a question he says Yes or No before he has heard the end of the sentence. [13] Too much activity makes a person extremely sad or extremely joyful. If he has a feeling against someone, just a spark of feeling, by his activity it increases, and at once it becomes a fire. If he has a little joy, by the activity, in a moment it becomes so great that he does not know what he is doing. A little sorrow at once becomes a mountain of sorrow.

You will[14] always find that those who are very quick in their actions, in their decisions, who ~~decide~~ at once decide and at once do, have many failures in life. Those who take time to consider, to understand what should be done, [15] succeed.

Our condition is such that we do not wait to hear the other half of the sentence before we ~~answer~~ speak. The end of the sentence may be tragedy and the beginning comedy. We have heard only the comedy and we laugh. Then we have shown ourselves foolish. Or the beginning is tragedy. At once we make such a face. We do not wait for the end. If we do not hear the end of the sentence, how can we keep the rein of tranquillity in our hand? [16] ~~The~~ This is the cause of all the troubles that we are now in. Activity has increased so much that we see only the object, only what we want to do. There is no balance.[16]

---

12. Gd.h.: this sentence appears on a separate piece of paper, with an indication to insert it at this point;
    Sk.t.: this sentence omitted
13. Hq.t.: "That is why sometimes in the place of No he says Yes, and in the place of Yes he says No." added
14. Gd.h.: "You will" crossed out, "We" substituted;
    Hq.t., Sk.t.: "We" instead of "You will"
15. Gd.h.: "those" inserted;
    Hq.t., Sk.t.: "those"
16. Gd.h.: These three sentences written on a separate piece of paper, with an indication to insert them at this point

In our actions, so many times [17] do a thing quickly, and then repent. We should consider every night ~~all that~~ what we have done, what we have said all[18] day. [19] At whatever age and stage of life we are, however young you may be, we should do this. You should not think, I am young. I will do all the undesirable things I want to now. When I am old I shall be very wise. You should think that the time of life is very short in comparison with what has to be learnt. There is much to be learned and the days of life are too short.[fx,20] Then, if you do not repent, you are a saint, you are perfect as your Father in heaven is perfect. But if you do repent, then the thought comes, At such a time I ought not to have thought that, it was not right, At such an hour I ought not to have acted[21] so, at such and such a time I ought not to have felt so. Then if our intelligence is [22] enough to tell us this afterwards, it must be great enough to tell us so beforehand.

There are five degrees of intelligence distinguished in Sufism.

The first is *Nafsi Amarra*[23], the ego[24] of the ordinary person, who does what he feels inclined to do and does not care about the result. If he hits[25] a dog in the street and feels inclined to hit it, he hits it and does not care what the result it[26]. If there is an old lady walking [27] in the street, [28] he pushes against her, and if she falls down he does not care. He sits in the cafés and among the[29] undesirable people[30], and only cares that he may have

---

17. Hq.t., Sk.t.: "we" inserted
18. Gd.h.: "all" crossed out and "in the" substituted;
    Hq.t., Sk.t.: "in the" instead of "all"
19. Gd.h.: These sentences written on the following page with an indication to insert them at this point;
    Sk.t.: this passage follows the rest of the paragraph (after ". . . beforehand.")
20. Gd.h.: Later, Gd. added "Every foolish action leads to a still greater foolishness [then altered to 'foolish action'], and every wise attempt leads to a greater wisdom.";
    Hq.t.: this sentence also inserted, with "foolishness" but no "and";
    Sk.t.: this passage also inserted, with "foolishness"
21. Sk.t.: "asked" instead of "acted" (probably a typographical error)
22. Gd.h., Hq.t., Sk.t.: "developed" added
23. Hq.t.: "*Umara*";
    Sk.t.: "*Ammara*"; see *nafs-i ammarah* in Glossary
24. Gd.h.: "ego" crossed out, and "intelligence" substituted
25. Gd.h.: "hits" crossed out, and "sees" substituted;
    Hq.t., Sk.t.: "sees"
26. Gd.h.: although "it" is clearly written, "is" must have been intended;
    Hq.t., Sk.t.: "is"
27. Hq.t.: "with her basket" added
28. Hq.t.: "~~and feels i~~"
29. Gd.h.: "among the" crossed out, and "does all" substituted, but the "does all" crossed out and "among the" restored

money enough to do the same thing tomorrow. If he is brought before the judge and ~~given a trial~~ sent to prison, he only cares about the prison; he does not think, what action has brought me here?

Just like the cats and dogs. If two dogs fight and one bites the other, the one who is bitten goes home sorry about his hurt, and the winner goes away pleased at having bitten the other[31]. He does not repent of having bitten the other[32]. He does not think, what made me fight?

This is the ordinary person.

The second sort of intelligence is *Nafsi Lauwama*[33]. This is the intelligence of the person who does the foolish action but then repents. Afterwards he thinks, I spoke inconsiderately to my friend. I did not show respect to this venerable person, to my father, to my mother. But at the moment when he was disrespectful he had no thought. To repent afterwards cannot change what is done. What we do is done for ages. At the time of his anger he is blinded—he cannot help it, but afterwards he recognizes that this was not right for him.

[34] Hafiz says: "If your shield is not ready at the time when the attack is made, what is the use?" The shield is tranquillity, which preserves us from all ills. If it is not ready, if it is not in your hand until the attack is past, what is the use? If the arms are not in your hand until afterwards, what is the use? If our intelligence does not tell us until afterwards what is right, ~~what~~ that is of no use. It must tell us beforehand.[34]

The third kind of intelligence is *Nafsi Mutmaina*. This is the intelligence of the person who feels the inclination to do ~~the~~ an undesirable thing, but then the will[35] comes and says, do not do it. It is not right for you. You will repent later. He has the desire, but the voice within, the voice of God comes and says, this is not right. And to whom does this come? It comes to those who believe, who lean upon God, who depend upon Him, who

---

30. Gd.h.: "people" crossed out and "actions" substituted, but then "actions" crossed out and "people" restored;
Hq.t.: "and does all undesirable actions" instead of "and among the undesirable people";
Sk.t.: "among undesirable people" instead of "and among the undesirable people"
31. Hq.t.: "dog" added
32. Hq.t., Sk.t.: "dog" added
33. Hq.t.: a blank instead of "*Lauwama*"; see *nafs-i lawwama* in Glossary
34. Gd.h.: This passage was written on a separate piece of paper with an indication to insert it at this point
35. Gd.h.: above "the will" Gd. wrote "the strength comes";
Hq.t.: "(the strength comes)" added after "the will";
Sk.t.: "the strength comes, the will comes"

trust in the truth. It does not come to those who trust in[36] their intellect, their own mind, their own wisdom. So many writers there have been, such great minds, writers of books upon philosophy and history and such subjects, and in their own lives they have made great mistakes. Because they trusted in their intellect, in their own ——[37] strength. This is the cause of all the troubles in which we are now, that we do[38] ~~not~~ trust in our own mind, in our own intellect,[39] in our sword, in our strength. [40] We do not say to God, save us from these difficulties and these troubles, because You[41] only are our defence and our preserver. Guide our path and lead us aright, because You are[42] our saviour. We do not[43] lean upon God[44]. You may say, can I not reason? Can I not think? I know what is better for me and what is worse for me. Why should my mother tell me? Because if you do not listen to your father and mother, how can you listen to ~~your~~ that voice? Listen to your [45] father here to prepare yourself to [46] that mother and father [47] that are[48] in heaven.

The fourth sort is *Nafsi Alima*[49]. This is the intelligence of ———— ————[50] no thought comes of what is not right, that thinks and does[51] only

---

36. Gd.h.: "trust in" crossed out, and "depend upon" substituted;
    Hq.t., Sk.t.: "depend upon"
37. Gd.h.: an illegible word, crossed out
38. Hq.t.: "do" omitted
39. Hq.t., Sk.t.: "in our experience," inserted
40. Sk.t.: "If we leaned upon God, we should not be in these troubles." inserted
41. Hq.t., Sk.t.: "Thou" instead of "You"
42. Hq.t., Sk.t.: "Thou art" instead of "You are"
43. Gd.h.: "We do not" crossed out, and "if we" substituted, also changing "lean" to "leaned"
44. Gd.h.: "we should not be in these troubles" added;
    Hq.t.: "If we lean[sic] upon God we should not be in these troubles" instead of "We do not lean upon God.";
    Sk.t.: this sentence omitted here (v. n. 40 above)
45. Gd.h.: "mother and" added;
    Hq.t., Sk.t.: "mother and father"
46. Hq.t.: "listen to" added
47. Hq.t.: "also" added
48. Gd.h.: "are" crossed out, and "is" substituted;
    Hq.t., Sk.t.: "is"
49. Gd.h.: the word *Alima* looks to have been written in later, perhaps in another hand
50. Gd.h.: two illegible words crossed out, then "the righteous and saintly persons to whom" added;
    Hq.t.: "the righteous and saintly persons to whom";
    Sk.t.: "the saintly persons to whom"
51. Gd.h.: "that thinks and does" later altered to "who think and do";
    Hq.t., Sk.t.: "who think and do" instead of "that thinks and does"

what is right. You will say, can a human being be like this? They must be very different from us. I will say, ask a musician. When someone plays or sings, he knows ~~at once~~ what note it is, C or D or G or F. To another ~~who is not so much occupied with music~~ it is a sound, but he does not know what note it is. The musician at once plays any note he wishes to play, or sings it. Another, who is not so much occupied with music, may take ten minutes or half an hour finding which string [52] produces F. It is like a person who, without looking, puts out his hand and puts it in the right place. These[53] are the saints. It is not for ordinary people.

The fifth ~~his~~ sort of intelligence is *Nafsi Lamina*[54] , the intelligence of the prophet. Whatever he does is right, and if it is wrong, if he does it, it becomes right. What is wrong for the world is right for him. Just as here, if a man goes into a room full of people, he must take off his hat. It would not be right for him to have his hat on. In the East he must have his turban, or his [55] on his head. To be bareheaded is to insult people. It is just the opposite. Just as what was right for Christ was wrong to the Jews. Therefore the world cannot understand him.

It is tranquillity only that can develop us to these five degrees of intelligence.

However great the intelligence is, however great the skill, by the lack of tranquillity, repose, ~~loses~~[56] it is all lost.

You will see great actors and actresses, however great they are, when they come on the stage they become so nervous ~~that they couldn't do anything~~, their activity increases so much, that[57] all that they have learnt is lost. The same thing is with speakers. However well they speak, however wise they may be, when they begin to speak, they want to say it all at once, to have done it. Because the activity has taken hold of them, that activity which has brought out this whole manifestation. And there is no way to stop it but the practice of tranquillity.

---

52. Gd.h.: "produces" altered to "can produce";
Hq.t.: "and thread can produce" instead of "produces";
Sk.t.: "can produce"
53. Hq.t.: above the first "e" of "These" is written an "o", indicating that the word might be "Those"
54. Hq.t.: a blank;
Sk.t.: "*Salima*"; see *nafs-i salima* in Glossary
55. Gd.h., Hq.t: a blank;
Sk.t.: ", or his " omitted
56. Gd.h.: above "loses", "spoils" written, then crossed out
57. Hq.t.: "and" instead of "that"

TRANQUILLITY[58]

I will say a few words in explanation of the point that the outer self should be kept tranquil though the mind be angry or excited. At first sight this[59] may seem to be falsehood in this in showing oneself calm when the feelings are not calm.

The true self is always tranquil and enjoying perfect rest and perfect peace. Why, then, is the external self agitated? It is agitated because of the picture of the world that is thrown upon it. The picture of the world is itself an exciting picture. And the picture that is most important to the self is the picture of the self. If the whole world is well-dressed, and the self is badly dressed, the self says, "Why am I not well-dressed?" If all the world has food and the self has no food, it does not matter to the self that all the world has food; it says, "Why am I not fed?" So the picture of the self is the most important. We always see that if someone has put on a soldier's uniform, even if he be a weak person, he will try to hold himself straight, to walk stiffly in the street. As soon as someone has put on a priest's dress, though [60] young, he will try to be meek and gentle.

The picture of the self should be tranquil and calm. To keep it calm, great strength of body as well as mind in needed. A strong person is calm, whatever tricks you play upon him, whatever difficulties come. I have seen that the wrestlers, who are very strong, are calm people. [61] (~~There was a wrestler, ——~~[62], ~~the greatest wrestler of India, who made the tour of the West. He was a very calm man, because of his strength.~~)

Weakness of body produces lack of calm. This is why an old person is usually excited by a word, by the smallest thing. A person who is ill, also, is easily excited. Sometimes a person who usually is quiet, if he has a fever, or a headache, or some little indisposition, wants to quarrel, to fight, to bite.

---

58. Gd.h., Hq.t.: This passage appears on a separate page with this title; Sk.t.: only a line separates this passage from the rest, with no title
59. Gd.h.: "this" altered to "there"; Hq.t., Sk.t.: "there"
60. Gd.h., Hq.t., Sk.t.: "he may be very" added
61. Hq.t.: This passage is neither crossed out nor put in parentheses; Sk.t.: this passage omitted
62. Hq.t.: "Hulam" inserted in the blank; properly Ghulam

A stencilled typescript from Headquarters, Geneva

[1]

Series 2 GATHEKA Number 2[2]

Toward the One, the Perfection of Love, Harmony and Beauty, the Only Being, united with All the Illuminated Souls, who form the Embodiment of the Master, the Spirit of Guidance.[3]

SUFISM NOT PASSIVISM[4]

Very often the Sufi Message, in its form of beneficence, is taken to be what they call in these days passivism[5], and those who are unfavorable to the idea of passivism[5] explain it as being[6] "Peace at any price."[7] Sufism does

Documents:

Hq.st.1 = a stencilled (then called cyclostyled) typescript prepared at Headquarters, Geneva, for distribution to Sufi Centres, probably by Sherifa Goodenough

Hq.t. = a typed version made at Headquarters, Geneva, perhaps as a preparation for the following document

Hq.st.2 = a later stencilled version prepared at Headquarters, Geneva, for distribution to Sufi Centres

S. = An article published in *The Sufi*, Vol. IV, No. 1 (January, 1938) on pp. 3-5. This article was based on Hq.st.2, but further edited

Gd.h. = a document in the handwriting of Sherifa Goodenough, perhaps a highly edited version of a part of the present lecture (see note 7, below)

Notes:

1. No location or date for this lecture is known
2. Hq.t., Hq.st.2: Instead of "Series 2. Gatheka. Number 2", " Social Gatheka. Number 1"
3. S.: Neither the classification nor the Invocation included
4. Hq.t., Hq.st.2, S.: "PACIFISM" instead of "PASSIVISM";
   S.: below the title, "by Inayat Khan":
   Gd.h.: on a small, separate piece of paper, Gd. wrote: "Please note that it should be: Sufism not Pacifism. Gatheka 2."
5. Hq.t., Hq.st.2, S.: "pacifism" instead of "passivism"
6. S.: "being" omitted

not teach that. Sufism does not mean goodness, kindness, or piety; Sufism means wisdom. All things in life are materials for wisdom to work with, and wisdom cannot be restricted to any principles. Among Sufis there have been great souls who were kings, or else[8] in the position of a beggar; saints and[9] workmen, commanders, generals, businessmen, statesmen, prophets; in all different walks of life, the Sufis of different ages have practised Sufism. This shows that no one can point out with the[10] finger, "This particular belief, or tenet, is a Sufi doctrine." There are two things, sound and notes. Notes point out the degree of the sound, but sound is all notes, not any note in particular. So is Sufism; it[11] is all beliefs and no belief in particular. There is no action which the Sufi calls right, or wrong; for every action can become right and can become wrong. It depends upon the use or abuse of the action, its fitness or unfitness. Right or wrong depends upon the attitude and situation, not on the action. This [12]naturally gives the Sufi tolerance towards another, and makes him ready to forgive another and unwilling to form an opinion about the action of another person.

This attitude keeps the Sufi far removed from saying that peace is good or war is good. The Sufi will say, "War is good at the time of war, peace is good at the time of peace."

But then you will say that if all things are right in their proper place, then Sufism has nothing to do in life. In answer to this I will say that there is one principal mission of Sufism, that is to dig the ground under which the

---

7. Gd.h.: In the hwr. of Sherifa Goodenough appears the following passage: "Passivism. Miscellaneous. Magazine. Some people who are narrow and bigoted on the question of nationalism put every idea which helps souls to evolve and unite under the heading of passivism, which they define as peace at any cost. Most of them are national fanatics and some, who are not fanatics, think it is to the interest of the nation to have the majority in it ignorant of high ideals. They think quietness, a friendly attitude toward mankind, and love of peace ~~make~~ unfits them for being truly patriotic. Often clever people keep others from enlightenment in order to use them as their tools in any way they like. This spirit of obscurantism is stronger now than before, and by this attitude they sacrifice the world for the nation, men for land, love for wealth, and God for religion, and truth for living, and peace for possession." No context is known for this passage, though it relates to the subject matter in the present lecture, and could be an answer to a question following the lecture (though it is not entirely in the usual language of Pir-o-Murshid Inayat Khan). Rather than omit the passage entirely from the *Complete Works*, it was decided to present it here in a footnote.
8. S.: "so others" instead of "or else"
9. S.: "," instead of "and"
10. S.: "a" instead of "the"
11. S.: "Sufism" instead of "So is Sufism; it"
12. S.: "conviction" added

light of the soul becomes buried. The same is [13]teaching of Christ, who has said, that no one shall cover his light under a bushel; also, "Raise your light on high."

The condition of the world today[14] is such that humanity has become abnormal in these days[15]. Man is not only frightened at badness, but also at goodness; man does not only dread war, but also peace; man is not only tired of enmity but also of friendship;[16] man does not suspect[17] his adversary today but even his own brother. It seems as if the mind of the world were not only tired but ill; it seems as if humanity had had a nervous breakdown. Man, individually or collectively, does not know his life's purpose or goal. The Sufi Message warns humanity to know life better and to achieve freedom in life; it warns man to[18] accomplish what he considers good, just, and desirable; and[19] before every action to note its consequences by studying the situation, by judging his own attitude, by studying beforehand the method which one adopts to act in life.

It is true that Sufism does not only guide[20] those who are religious, mystical, or visionary, but the Sufi Message gives to the world the religion of the day, and that is to make one's life a religion,[21] to turn one's occupation, one's profession into religion, to make one's ideal a religious ideal. Sufism has as its object the uniting of life and religion[22], which so far seem to have been kept apart. Think, when once a week a person will go to church and all the other days of the week he will devote to his business, how can he benefit by [23]religion? Therefore the teaching of Sufism is to make everyday life into a religion, that every action in life may have some spiritual fruit.

The method for world reform which different institutions have adopted today is not the method of the Sufi movement. We think that if ill is contagious, good must be more so. The depth of every soul is good; every soul is searching for good, and by the effort of individuals who wish to do good in the world much can be done, even more than what a materialistic

---

13. Hq.t., Hq.st.2, S.: "the" added
14. S.: "today" omitted
15. S.: "in these days" omitted
16. S.: "man is not only tired of enmity, but also of friendship;" omitted
17. S.: "only" added
18. S.: "that he should" instead of "to"
19. S.: "and" omitted
20. S.: "not only guides" instead of "does not only guide"
21. S.: "to make one's life a religion," omitted
22. S.: "religion and life" instead of "life and religion"
23. S.: "his" added

institution can do. No doubt for the general good there are political and commercial problems to be solved and little can be done in that direction before several difficult problems have been solved; but that must not debar individuals from progress, for it is the individualistic progress through the spiritual path which alone can bring about the desired condition in the world.[24]

---

24. Hq.t., Hq.st.2: "To be read at the Meetings of WORLD BROTHERHOOD." added

An old typescript (original unknown)

1

Eteqad Rasm o Rivaj[2]

Among the Hindus there has been an old belief, which is now taken to be a superstition, even in India. Every Brahman avoided, in other words took great care to keep away himself, his shrine of worship, his food, woman during m.[3] period, and [4]newborn child from the shadow of Shudra, or outcaste.[5]

Now, the times being different, naturally that belief is seemingly meaningless. But in point of fact there was an occult meaning hidden behind it. Shadow is caused by the wall of a personality[6] standing against the sun, the sun which is life-giving to plants and human beings, to animals and to all, and the direct rays of which give all things new life. Places which are hidden

---

Documents:

O.t. = an old typescript, probably made from a longhand reporting, not in the Archives. It shows corr. in Sherifa Goodenough's handwriting, which are indicated in the notes as "(O.t.)Gd.c."

Hq.t. = a typescript made from "O.t." (with Gd.'s corr. incorporated) at Headquarters, Geneva

Hq.st. = a stencilled copy, nearly identical to "Hq.t.", made at Headquarters, Geneva.

Notes

1. No date or location for this lecture is known;
   O.t.: later added by Gd., "II. 10";
   Hq.t., Hq.st.: added, "Series II. GATHA. Number 10.", followed by the Invocation
2. Hq.t.: "SUPERSTITIONS, CUSTOMS AND BELIEFS" added before 'ETEQAD, RASM u RAVAJ";
   Hq.st.: "SUPERSTITIONS, CUSTOMS AND BELIEFS" added after 'ETEQAD, RASM u RAVAJ"
3. All other documents: "maternity"; however, it seems possible that some form of "menstrual" may have been said
4. (O.t.)Gd.corr.: "the" added;
   Hq.t. Hq.st.: "the" added
5. Shudra refers to the lowest caste, not the same as outcaste
6. (O.t.)Gd.corr.: "personality" changed into "person";
   Hq.t., Hq.st.: "person" instead of "personality"

from the sun, flat or mountainous, become the centre of all diseases. Personality that stands in the light of any person, causing thereby hindrance in the life of that person, is an example of this analogy[7].

The difference between the true teacher and the false, both of whom have always existed in the world, has been distinct. The false one stood in the light of his pupil; the true one showed him the way by standing on the side.

The psychology of the shadow is very complex. The shadow of an unholy person falling upon food will certainly take away the living substance from it; if it fell upon a person in a negative state, a woman sitting aside, or[8] a child, it would produce exhaustion and lifelessness, also in the souls who are going through a process of recuperation or growth. Very often a tree standing above a plant, keeping from it the light, hinders the growth of the plant; so is the shadow of the unholy. It can for the moment darken the soul of those passive and receptive of spirit. No doubt the power of darkness and illusion itself, as shadow, has no existence in reality. However, it is evident; so is the influence of immature souls.

The spiritual souls have a contrary influence to this. Their presence is a stimulus to intelligence; their influence is comfort-giving and inspiring. The phenomena[9] of a spiritual personality is that in his presence the memory becomes keen, the waves of inspiration rise, the clouds of depression clear away, hope springs from the depth of the heart, and the soul within begins to feel living. Love manifests through thought and feeling, and all that was once dead lives again.

This shows that personality is a mystery. It gives life and causes death; it raises one to heaven, and throws another back to the depths of earth. The influence of personality may change one's life, environment, and all affairs. Its influence can turn the wheel of life to the right or wrong side, turning thereby the trend of all the affairs of life.

Very often most innocent, good and pure-minded souls, owing to the lack of positiveness in their natures, become the victims of undesirable personalities, personalities that stand in their lives, obscuring the light for which they crave. And this may continue for a long period of time. Once a person is accustomed to being in the shade, then he is afraid to come out

---

7. (O.t.)Gd.corr.: "analogy" crossed out;
Hq.t., Hq.st.: "analogy" omitted
8. Hq.st.: "of" instead of "or"
9. The singular, "phenomenon", was meant;
Hq.t., Hq.st.: "phenomenon"

in the sunlight, though inwardly he may be drawn to it.

The more dense[10] a person is, the grosser is his shadow; in other words, the more material a person is, the heavier is his influence.?[11]

The whole idea of life is to live freely; with freedom to gaze over the open spaces, to look through[12], having nothing to hide or conceal; the light of truth to shine from within and the light of the sun from[13] without; light all around, no shadow of any kind hindering the light which is the soul of every being.

---

10. (O.t.)Gd.c.: "denser" instead of "more dense";
    Hq.t., Hq.st.: "denser"
11. (O.t.)Gd.corr.: this part of the sentence crossed out;
    Hq.t., Hq.st.: this part of the sentence omitted
12. (O.t.)Gd.corr.: omitted the semicolon after "through", and added, "space freely,"
13. (O.t.)Gd.corr.: "from" crossed out; Hq.t., Hq.st.: "from" omitted

SUPPLEMENT

1923

A copy in the handwriting of Sherifa Goodenough,
from a reporting not in the archives

1 11 February 1923

Pasi Anfas

It is said of[2] the large[3] cobras, [4]which are enormously big animals which live in the thick forests or in the mountains,[4] that they[5] attract animals or birds by the power of the breath. When the large[3] cobra is hungry, which it feels[6] after[7] three months or six months, he[8] by inhaling the breath[9]

Documents:

Gd.h.1 = a copy in Sherifa Goodenough's handwriting, from a reporting which is not in the archives

Gd.h.2 = a copy in Sherifa Goodenough's handwriting, made from Gd.h.1, but edited extensively

Hq.t. = a typewritten copy of "Gd.h.2" made at Headquarters, Geneva, with no changes in wording, and therefore not mentioned in the notes (except notes 1 and 29)

Hq.st. = a stencilled copy made from "Hq.t." at Headquarters, Geneva, with no changes in wording, and therefore not mentioned in the notes (except notes 1 and 29)

Notes:

1. Gd.h.1: Gd. wrote "II.7." (indicating the series and number);
   Gd.h.2: Gd. wrote "Series II Gatha Number 7" across the top, and below that "Pasi Anfas. Breath.";
   Hq.t.: across the top: "Series II. GATHA. Number 7." followed by the Invocation, and then "BREATH. PASI ANFAS.";
   Hq.st.: across the top "Series II. GATHA. Number 7." followed by the Invocation, and then "PASI ANFAS. BREATH."
2. Gd.h.2: "that" instead of "of"
3. Gd.h.2: "large" omitted
4. Gd.h.2: "enormous animals living in dense forests or in the mountains," instead of "which are enormously big animals which live in the thick forests or in the mountains,"
5. Gd.h.2: "that they" omitted
6. Gd.h.2: "is" instead of "it feels"
7. Gd.h.1: "after" later crossed out, "once" substituted;
   Gd.h.2: "once in"
8. Gd.h.2: "he" omitted
9. Gd.h.2: "it" added

draws animals of[10] its prey near. In its exhaling there is magnetism, power, and influence, in its inhaling there is attraction.[11] Mystics of the[12] ancient times have learned much from cobras. Mahadeva, the Lord of Yogis, has the cobra as his necklace. The peace and stillness of this animal, the contentment with which it waits for its sustenance is[13] wonderful and most instructive for an adept on the spiritual path. One who masters breath becomes ~~as~~ invigorated and strengthened in his mind, becomes quiet and peaceful and achieves self-control. In the cobra there is[14] far-reaching breath, so it[15] is the breath of the mystic. The mystic[16] breath is not what they call[17] deep breathing. His is the inmost reaching breath[18], which touches every plane of his being. Every movement robs[19] a great portion of breath, every excitement takes[20] a great amount[21] of life force from a person[22]. Therefore those who master breathing first learn control not only on[23] every passion or[24] condition but on[23] every movement. By first[25] trying to make the body still one can practise[14] breath better. Therefore, among the Yogis different postures are taught. Every posture allows the breath to take a certain direction, for every direction the breath takes has a different result. It is posture and thought, both together,[26] help to direct ~~both~~ the breath in a certain direction.[27] Breath, being[28] a life power, in whichever direction[29], whatever centre it is directed to, it brings it[30] to a new life.

---

10. Gd.h.2: "animals of" omitted
11. Gd.h.2: "The" added
12. Gd.h.2: "the" omitted
13. Gd.h.2: "are" in place of "is"
14. Gd.h.2: "the" added
15. Gd.h.2: "it" omitted
16. Gd.h.2: "mystic's" in place of "mystic"
17. Gd.h.2: "is called" instead of "they call"
18. Gd.h.2: "breath reaching inmost" instead of "inmost reaching breath"
19. Gd.h.2: "one of" added
20. Gd.h.2: "away" added
21. Gd.h.2: "deal" instead of "amount"
22. Gd.h.2: "from a person" omitted
23. Gd.h.2: "over" instead of "on"
24. Gd.h.2: "and" in place of "or"
25. Gd.h.2: "first" moved to after "trying"
26. Gd.h.2: "that" added
27. Gd.h.2: "As" added
28. Gd.h.2: "is" instead of "being"
29. Gd.h.2: originally, Gd. wrote "in whichever direction", then crossed it out; Hq.t., Hq.st.: "in whichever direction" omitted
30. Gd.h.2: "it" omitted

A copy in the handwriting of Sherifa Goodenough,
made from an original not in the archives

1

February 13, 1923[2]

Pasi Anfas

Different conditions and the changes that take place in the world have their effect upon [3]mind, as[4] the different conditions of the mind have their effect upon the body. As bodily illness makes man irritable, confused and exhausted in mind, so different conditions of mind cause health[5] illnesses[6] in the body. The link between the body and the mind is the breath, a link by[7] which[8] the influence[9]

Documents:

Gd.h.1 = a manuscript in the handwriting of Sherifa Goodenough, with some editing, made from an unknown original

Gd.h.2 = another manuscript in the handwriting of Sherifa Goodenough, made from "Gd.h.1" and showing further editing in the preparation of the lecture for inclusion in the Gatha series

Hq.t. = a typescript made for Headquarters, Geneva, from Gd.h.2, showing the same editing

Hq.st. = a stencilled copy distributed by Headquarters, Geneva, and identical in wording to "Hq.t." (and therefore not mentioned in the notes after note 1).

Notes:

1. Gd.h.1: "II.8." added, indicating the series and number of this Gatha;
   Gd.h.2: "Series II. Gatha. Number 8." added, and below that "Pasi Anfas. Breath.";
   Hq.t.: across the top "Series II. GATHA. Number 8.", followed by the Invocation, and below that "BREATH. PASI ANFAS.";
   Hq.st.: as in "Hq.t.", except "PASI ANFAS" before "BREATH"
2. This lecture was given in Paris or Suresnes.
3. Gd.h.2: "the" added;
   Hq.t.: "the"
4. Gd.h.2: "and" instead of "as";
   Hq.t.: "and"
5. Gd.h.1: later "or" was written in the margin in a different hwr. (Gr.?);
   Gd.h.2: first "and" written, later changed to "or";
   Hq.t.: "or"
6. Gd.h.1: later "illnesses" changed to "illness";
   all other documents: "illness"
7. Gd.h.1: later "by" changed to "through";
   all other documents: "through"
8. Gd.h.2: "the exchange of" added, but then crossed out
9. Gd.h.1: later an "s" added to make "influence" plural;
   all other documents: "influences"

of the body and the mind [10] are exchanged, and work one upon the other [11]. By the use of breath in physical culture the health and vigour of the body [12] is projected, so to speak, upon the mind. By the use of concentration through the breath the light of the mind is thrown upon the body, which takes away from the body all heaviness and stiffness, making it light and exhilarated. Breath in this way acts like a ball in tennis, thrown from one side to the other, and the force of its movement ~~is~~ comes from the side[13] it is directed. Therefore when from the body[14] it is directed to the mind, the mind becomes subject to the influence of the body, but when from the side of the mind it is directed toward the body, in this case the body becomes subject to the mind. Very often dervishes and fakirs in the East who[15] live upon alms and go several days fasting[16] and have several sleepless nights of [17] vigil, often[18] do things which are difficult for a wrestler, [19] boxer, or for a[20] ~~strong~~ muscular person to do[21]. [22] There are some among dervishes who exercise jumping into the[23] fire, standing [24] hours in the water,

---

10. Gd.h.2: "is made, and they" added, but then crossed out
11. Gd.h.2: "one upon the other" rewritten to read: "upon one another";
    Hq.t.: "upon one another"
12. Gd.h.2: "breath" instead of "body";
    Hq.t.: "breath"
13. Gd.h.1.: "from which" added;
    all other documents: "from which"
14. Gd.h.2: "from the body" moved to after "it is directed";
    Hq.t.: as in Gd.h.2
15. Gd.h.1: "many of" added, and "who" changed to "whom";
    Hq.t.: "many of whom"
16. Gd.h.2: "without food" instead of "fasting";
    Hq.t.: "without food"
17. Gd.h.2: "spend many nights in sleepless" instead of "have several sleepless nights of";
    Hq.t.: "spend many nights in sleepless"
18. Gd.h.2: "often" omitted;
    Hq.t.: "often" omitted
19. Gd.h.2: "a" added;
    Hq.t.: "a"
20. Gd.h.2: "any other" in place of "for a";
    Hq.t.: "any other"
21. Gd.h.2: "to do" omitted;
    Hq.t.: "to do" omitted
22. Gd.h.2: "Some dervishes practise" instead of "There are some among dervishes who exercise";
    Hq.t.: "Some dervishes practise"
23. Gd.h.2: "the" omitted;
    Hq.t.: "the" omitted
24. Gd.h.2: "for" added;
    Hq.t.: "for"

sitting or lying on iron pricks, thrashing one's[25] bare arms and limbs[26], cutting oneself[27] with knives and swords, [28]all these[29] things belong[30] beyond the power of a physically strong man. In many cases[31] a physically strong man suffers to the extent of [32] his strength when he is exposed to pain or torture. This explains that, though the power of breath is the main source of physical development, yet breath is the principal thing in the development of mind in which the work[33] of the breath is much[34] more valuable.

---

25. Gd.h.2: "their" instead of "one's";
Hq.t.: "their"
26. Gd.h.2: "legs" instead of "limbs";
Hq.t.: "legs"
27. Gd.h.2: "themselves" in place of "oneself";
Hq.t.: "themselves"
28. Gd.h.2: later "and" added;
Hq.t.: "and"
29. Gd.h.1: "these" replaced by "such";
all other documents: "such"
30. Gd.h.1: "belon", apparently for "belong"; later crossed out and "are" added;
all other documents: "belong" replaced with a comma
31. Gd.h.2: "Often" instead of "In many cases";
Hq.t.: "Often"
32. Gd.h.2: "in proportion to" instead of "to the extent of";
Hq.t.: "in proportion to"
33. Gd.h.1: later "work" replaced with "influence";
all other documents: "influence"
34. Gd.h.2: "much" omitted;
Hq.t.: "much" omitted

A copied text in the handwriting of Sherifa Goodenough, possibly made from her own lh. reporting of the lecture

1 2

The Scandinavian myth of Balder[3] tells that Balder, the god of youth, beauty, kindness and gentleness, was pursued by enemies, who sought[4] to kill him. [5] his (friend), to protect him, cast a spell[5] upon all the trees of the forest, and every plant that has root in the ground and grows upward to heaven, that no weapon ~~and~~ wrought from any of them should have power to harm Balder[6]. But, [7] in his[8] uttering the words with which he charmed the [9] plants,

Documents:

Gd.h.1 = a copy in Sherifa Goodenough's handwriting, probably made from a reporting

Gd.h.2 = a second copy in Sherifa Goodenough's handwriting, made from "Gd.h.1", but corrected and further edited by Gd.

Hq.t. = a typescript made from "Gd.h.2" at Headquarters, Geneva

Hq.st. = a stencilled copy made from "Hq.t." at Headquarters, Geneva, and identical in wording to it. Therefore, it is not mentioned in the notes after note 1.

Notes:

1. Gd.h.1: afterwards added "II.8" and the title "The Myth of Balder", then added "Nakshi Bandi"; Gd.h.2: afterwards added "Series II. Gatha. Number 8." and "Nakshi Bandi. Symbology." and the title, "The Myth of Balder"; Hq.t.: "Series II. GATHA. Number 8.", followed by the Invocation, then "SYMBOLOGY. NAKSHI BANDI." and the title "The Myth of Balder."; Hq.st.:"Series II. GATHA. Number 8.", followed by the Invocation, then "NAKSHI BANDI. SYMBOLOGY." and the title "The Myth of Balder."
2. Gd.h.1: later added the date, "February 1923", which must have been in the first half of the month, as after that Pir-o-Murshid left by ship for the United States. The lecture must have been given in Paris or Suresnes.
3. Gd.h.2, Hq.t.: "of Balder" omitted
4. Gd.h.2, Hq.t.: "wanted" instead of "sought"
5. Gd.h.1: an open space to indicate that in the reporting some word or words were either missed or illegible; in some versions of the myth it is Frigg, Balder's mother, who seeks to protect him; Gd.h.2, Hq.t.: no space, and "his (friend), to protect him, cast a spell" replaced with "For his protection a spell had been cast"
6. Gd.h.2, Hq.t.: "him" instead of "Balder"
7. Gd.h.2: rewritten to read, "~~when~~ in this charm ~~was uttered~~ the mistletoe had been forgotten"; Hq.t.: "in this charm, the mistletoe had been forgotten"
8. Gd.h.1: later "his" crossed out
9. Ibid.: "trees and" added

had forgotten that mistletoe[7, 10], which has no root in the ground, [11]the mistletoe [12] made an arrow ([13]spear) from the mistletoe, shot at Balder and wounded him to death.[11]

Its[14] interpretation is an answer to the question which often arises in our[15] intelligent mind[16]. [17]Why god-like people were[18] treated cruelly continually through all periods of the world's history, and how could any person in the world think of causing harm to that[19] who attracted the sympathy of almost every soul they met on the earth.[17] Their adherents spread their teachings and the beauty of their life and character among all, wise and foolish, kind and cruel. They[20] all became more or less ~~of~~ impressed by what they learn[21] of the godly soul[22]. Even those whose soul has[23] not yet risen to human evolution, but[24] who only live like trees and plants, living, and yet dreaming, unaware of life, except their own activity. But the one who could not be impressed by this spell, [25]to whom even if the spell was cast,[25] it could not have reached, and [26]if it were reached with a great difficulty, it[26] is the godless, who is like the mistletoe, who lives[27] without any root. The mourning for which[28] is continued in the[29] memory of the death of that god. In reality it is celebrating the birth of what was born of[30] him, it was divine knowledge.

---

10. Ibid.: later "mistletoe" crossed out
11. Gd.h.2, Hq.t.: rewritten to read, "and from its wood an arrow was made, with which Balder was hit and wounded to death."
12. Gd.h.1: an open space; in the myth it is Höd, the blind god, who kills Balder
13. Gd.h.1: an undecipherable word, replaced with "from", then crossed out, before "spear"
14. Gd.h.2: "The" instead of "Its", then restored to "Its"
15. Gd.h.1: the hwr. looks like "our", although it could be read as "and"; all other documents: "and"
16. Gd.h.2, Hq.t.: a comma instead of a full stop
17. Ibid.: this passage put between quotation marks, with a question mark at the end, after "earth"
18. Ibid.: "were" moved to beginning of sentence, after "Why"
19. Ibid.: "those" instead of "that"
20. Gd.h.2: "They" first omitted, then restored
21. Gd.h.2, Hq.t.: "learned" instead of "learn"
22. Hq.t.: "souls" instead of "soul"
23. Gd.h.2, Hq.t.: "had" instead of "has"
24. Ibid.: "but" omitted
25. Gd.h.2: rewritten to read: "whom, even had the spell been cast upon him,"; Hq.t.: as in Gd.h.2
26. Gd.h.2: first rewritten to read: "if it had reached, with great difficulty," then changed to "had it reached, only with great difficulty,"; Hq.t.: "had it reached, only with great difficulty,"
27. Gd.h.2, Hq.t.: "living" instead of "who lives"
28. Ibid.: "this" instead of "which"
29. Ibid.: "the" omitted
30. Ibid.: "from" instead of "of"

A copy in the handwriting of Sherifa Goodenough,
made from an original not in the archive

September 25, 1923[1]

Etekad, Rasm u Ravaj[2]

There are superstitions and customs connected with the wedding observed in Europe, such as throwing an old shoe after the newly married couple as they go away, and throwing rice. The rice signifies flourishing, multiplication, prosperity, and providence, whereas old shoes are the old times passed in life and new life begun. The ring[3] that a[4] bridegroom ~~puts on the finger of the~~ and bride put on each other's finger is the sign of bond, which is the real meaning of marriage. The hands that the priest joins[5] of the two[5] is the possession of one another, suggesting that each holds the other. The custom of the Greek church

---

Documents:

Gd.h. = a copy in the handwriting of Sherifa Goodenough, made from an unknown original

Hq.st. = a stencilled copy, made from "Gd.h." with a few editorial changes, and circulated by Headquarters, Geneva

Hq.t. = a typed copy made by Headquarters, Geneva, based on "Hq.st.", showing minor editorial changes

Gd.t. = a later typescript on Sherifa Goodenough's large-lettered typewriter

Notes:

1. This talk must have been given in Suresnes, where the Summer School was nearing its end for 1923
2. Gd.h.: later added "III.2." indicating the series and number of this Gatha;
   Hq.st.: "Series III GATHA Number 2" added, followed by the Invocation, followed by "ETEKAD RASM U RAVAJ SUPERSTITIONS, CUSTOMS AND BELIEFS." and then, as a title, "WEDDING CUSTOMS";
   Hq.t.: "Series III. GATHA. Number 2." added, followed by the Invocation, followed by "SUPERSTITIONS, CUSTOMS AND BELIEFS. ETEKAD, RASM U RAVAJ." and then "Wedding Customs."
   Gd.t.: "Series III. GATHA. Number 3." added, then "ETEKAD RASM U RAVAJ. SUPERSTITIONS, CUSTOMS AND BELIEFS." and then "WEDDING CUSTOMS.";
   —see *'itiqad, rasm o rawaj* in Glossary.
3. All other documents: "rings" instead of "ring"
4. Gd.h.: later "a" crossed out, "the" added;
   all other documents: "a" omitted
5. All other documents: "that the priest joins" changed to "joined by the priest" and moved to after "of the two"

where wreaths are put on the heads[6] of bride and bridegroom is the exchange of thoughts and feelings and walking three times round the altar is suggestive of God between them, uniting them both one with the other[7] in [8]divine link, the link which is [9]everlasting as God Himself. And the custom of the bride[10] kissing the hand of the bridegroom, which is still continued at the time when[11] the rhythm of the world is quite changed, it[12] only explains the response from the side of the bride [13]which is the secret of nature's harmony, although what generally happens[14] is ~~the other way~~ just the opposite, but that brings about the happy medium.

---

6. All other documents: "head" instead of "heads"
7. Hq.t.: "one with the other" left out in the typing, later added
8. Hq.t.: "a" added
9. Gd.h.: "as" added, then crossed out
10. Hq.st., Hq.t.: "bride's" in place of "bride";
    Gd.t.: "'s" added in hwr.
11. Hq.t.: "when" omitted
12. Gd.h.: "it" later crossed out;
    all other documents: "it" omitted
13. Gd.h.: "in" added;
    all other documents: "in"
14. Gd.h.: "later" added;
    all other documents: "later"

A copy in the handwriting of Sherifa Goodenough, the origin of which is not known

[1]

[2]

Breath

Mind is creative and thought is living, but out of what does mind create a thought? Out of the atoms of the mental sphere.[3] But the current which attracts the desired atoms to complete a thought is the breath. Not that breath which is outwardly manifest, that part of breath the action of which is incomprehensible to[4] every man. The more length[5] breath has, the more scope it gives[6] for the creation of thought. It is therefore that the thoughts of the sages and mystics who have gained mastery over breath are more ~~complete~~ substantial

---

Documents:

Gd.h. = a copy in the handwriting of Sherifa Goodenough, the origin of which is not known

Hq.t. = a typewritten copy made at Headquarters, Geneva, showing a few editorial changes

Hq.st. = a stencilled copy, circulated by Headquarters, Geneva, made from "Hq.t." and identical to it in wording. Therefore, it is mentioned only in notes 2 and 3

Gd.t. = a later typescript made on Sherifa Goodenough's large-lettered typewriter, made from "Hq.st." and identical to it in wording. Therefore, it is mentioned only in notes 2 and 3.

Notes:

1. At a later time, Gd. wrote "Sept. 25, '23" on the ms., at which time the Summer School in Suresnes was nearing its end
2. Gd.h.: Gd. later added "III.1." indicating the series and number of this Gatha;
   Hq.t.: across the top: "Series III. GATHA. Number 1.", followed by the Invocation, and then "BREATH. PASI ANFAS.";
   Hq.st.: across the top: "Series III. GATHA. Number 1.", followed by the Invocation, and then "PASI ANFAS. BREATH.";
   Gd.t.: "Series III. GATHA. Number I", then "PASI ANFAS. BREATH.", without the Invocation
3. Hq.st., Gd.t.: a question mark (?) instead of a full stop (.)
4. Gd.h.: later "incomprehensible to" crossed out and "not felt by" written instead;
   Hq.t.: "not felt by"
5. Gd.h.: "and breadth" added later;
   Hq.t.: "and breadth"
6. Gd.h.: later "gives" was crossed out and "produces" written instead, but then "produces" was crossed out and "gives" restored

and complete in themselves [7] besides [8] more expressive and impressive their thoughts prove to be[9]. The breadth of the breath is in its volume. This comes by the facility one has of breathing through wide ~~and~~ nostrils and open lungs. The secret of the power of voice is also to be found in this. A[10] commander of an army whose voice[11] carries through the army and impresses the soldiers, thus encouraging them to fight, has breath as its secret behind it. 'Ali, by his invocation of the sacred word which he sometimes used to cry aloud on the battlefield, used to cause the enemies to tremble.

The length of the breath shows the length of life; lengthy breath is the sign of long life. This comes not only by wide nostrils and open lungs, but also by the accommodation that the body has for the breath, not only the nose and the chest, but also the head and the abdomen. There are some whose breath has a[12] volume, or breadth, but not [13] length, and there are others who have length and no breadth[14]. But it is the balance of the length and breadth of the breath which gives balance to the mind.

---

7. Hq.t.: "and" added
8. Hq.t.: "they prove to be" added
9. Gd.h.: later "their thoughts prove to be" changed to "they prove to be";
   Hq.t.: "their thoughts prove to be" omitted
10. Hq.t.: "The voice of a" instead of "A"
11. Ibid.: "which" instead of "whose voice"
12. Ibid.: "a" omitted
13. Gd.h.: "much" added later;
    Hq.t.: "much"
14. Gd.h.: Gd. accidentally wrote "breath", but clearly "breadth" is intended

A copy in the handwriting of Sherifa Goodenough,
the origin of which is not known

[1]

[2]

The real purity is experienced, not by[3] the outer ablutions, not by keeping away evil thoughts, but by keeping the heart pure from feelings, feelings[4] which disturb the rhythm of the mind and thus upset the whole spirit. Feelings have a greater power than thoughts. If evil thoughts are as monsters, evil[5] feelings are as demons. Such feelings as [6]robbing [7]one of his rights or of[8] his belongings have a great[9] disturbing effect upon the spirit; before such a feeling is put into action the effect is less[10], while putting it [11] into action it is less, but afterwards

---

Documents:

Gd.h.	=	a copy in the handwriting of Sherifa Goodenough, the origin of which is not known
Hq.t.	=	a typewritten copy made from Gd.h. at Headquarters, Geneva, showing a few editorial changes
Hq.st.	=	a stencilled copy, circulated by Headquarters, Geneva, made from "Hq.t." and identical to it in wording. Therefore, it is mentioned only in note 2
Gd.t.	=	a later typescript made on Sherifa Goodenough's large-lettered typewriter, made from "Hq.st." and identical to it in wording. Therefore, it is mentioned only in note 2

Notes:

1. Gd.h.: Gd. wrote the date, "Sept. 25, 1923", in the upper right-hand corner
2. Gd.h.: Gd. later added "Takua Taharat III.1." above the text;
   Hq.t.: "Series III. GATHA. Number 1.", followed by the Invocation, followed by "EVERYDAY LIFE. TAKUA TAHARAT.";
   Hq.st.: as in "Hq.t." except that "TAKUA TAHARAT" comes before "EVERYDAY LIFE";
   Gd.t.: as in "Hq.st.", but without the Invocation
3. Hq.t.: "means of" added
4. Gd.h.: second "feelings" later crossed out;
   Hq.t.: "feelings" omitted
5. Gd.h.: "evil" later replaced with "the ill"
6. Hq.t.: "the desire of" added
7. Hq.t.: "one" changed to "someone"
8. Hq.t.: "of" omitted
9. Gd.h.: "great" later changed to "very";
   Hq.t.: "very"
10. Gd.h.: "less" later changed to "more";
    Hq.t.: "more"
11. Hq.t.: "it is being put" instead of "putting it"

the effect reaches its utmost[12]. The[13] life rightly and honestly lived has inner struggles, but when[14] by ~~the lack of~~ adding to it feelings that disturb life's tranquillity one only adds to one's troubles in life, which then become endless. Purity of heart must not be considered a virtue, but a necessity, a necessity not only to be considered for the good of the[15] others, but for one's own life. The feelings which produce that weakness in the heart which[16] take away strength from the eyelids; the glance drops instead of the eyes standing[17] gazing straight. Nothing in the world, however valuable or rare, can supply[18] this loss. The main thing that must be remembered is that the soul is pure and the lack of purity it cannot ~~with~~ bear without feeling restless. The spirit has a tune and [19]rhythm. When it is out of ~~rhythm~~ tune and out of rhythm, if the riches of the whole world would be given to it, it is worth nothing. It is the[20] purity and peace which is the soul's constant seeking.

---

12. Gd.h.: "its utmost" later changed to "is most", but without crossing out "reaches"; Hq.t.: "is most" in place of "reaches its utmost"
13. Hq.t.: "The" omitted
14. Hq.t.: "when" omitted
15. Hq.t.: "the" omitted
16. Hq.t.: "which" omitted
17. Hq.t.: "firmly" instead of "standing"
18. Gd.h.: "make up for" later replaced "supply"; Hq.t.: "make up for"
19. Hq.t.: "a" added
20. Hq.t.: "the" omitted

A copy in the handwriting of Sherifa Goodenough,
the origin of which is not known

Sept. 26, '23

Takua Taharat III.2 [1]

As the rust is natural to the iron and as the[2] milk turns sour, so is the heart that becomes rusted and its feeling, which by nature is as pure as milk, turns sour. Then nothing in the world is tasteful to that person and life with all its beauty becomes worthless. It is this condition which must be avoided. The[3] adept must keep his mind pure from the[4] rust. [5]The rust comes from allowing the heart to bear spite and malice[6] against anyone, by having hatred and prejudice against anyone, by having spite,[7] by wanting to take revenge, by looking down upon another with contempt, and by the feeling of jealousy, rivalry,

---

Documents:

Gd.h. = a copy in the handwriting of Sherifa Goodenough, possibly made from her own longhand reporting, showing a few editorial changes

Gd.t. = a typewritten copy made on Gd.'s large-lettered typewriter, reflecting the changes made in Gd.h.

Hq.t. = a typescript made at International Headquarters, Geneva, for distribution to a limited number of Sufi centres

Hq.st. = a stencilled copy made at International Headquarters, Geneva, for distribution to a wider circle of Sufi centres

Notes:

1. Gd.t.: across top, "Series III. GATHA. Number 2." and then below, "TAKUA TAHARAT. EVERYDAY LIFE.";
   Hq.t.: same as Gd.t., except the Invocation added and "EVERYDAY LIFE" before "TAKUA TAHARAT";
   Hq.st.: same as Gd.t., but with Invocation added
2. Gd.h.: Gd. later crossed out "the"
3. Gd.h.: Gd. later crossed out "The" and wrote "An" instead;
   all other documents: "An"
4. Gd.h.: Gd. later crossed out "the", also omitted in all other documents
5. All other documents initiate a new paragraph here
6. Ibid.: "malice and spite"
7. Ibid.: "by having spite," omitted

or envy. [8]Heart wants a constant care to keep it from getting rusted, for the nature of this life of illusion is such that some little unimportant things, which are not of the least value, the[4] coming from the outer life, the heart may be affected by and the rust may be produced [9]like mere [10] the touch[9] of water can produce rust upon the iron. Once the feelings [11] become soured it is as difficult, if not impossible, [12]to turn [13] the sour milk sweet.

A soul has brought from heaven [14] its love for sweet. It may after coming on earth develop a taste for salt, sour and bitter, but his [15] innate longing is always for the sweet and [16]the most his life needs[16] is not sugar, which is required in some degree for his [17] physical health, but the sweet which is the original property of his heart and which is needed the [18] most for his true happiness and real well being.

---

8. Gd.h.: Gd. later added "The" in the margin;
all other documents: "The"
9. All other documents: "as the mere touch"
10. Gd.h.: Gd. later wrote "ly" above the line to make the word "merely"
11. All other documents: "feeling has" instead of "feelings"
12. Gd.h.: Gd. later added "as" before "to"
13. Gd.h.: Gd. later crossed out "turn" and substituted "make";
all other documents: "it sweet again as to turn" added
14. All other documents: "Heaven"
15. Gd.t.: "its" typed over "his";
Hq.t., Hq.st.: "its"
16. Gd.h.: Gd. later revised this passage to read, "what his life needs most";
all other documents: "what his life needs most"
17. All other documents: "his" omitted
18. Gd. later crossed out "the", which is also omitted in all other documents

A copy in the handwriting of Sherifa Goodenough,
the origin of which is not known

Sept. 26, 1923

Pasi Anfas III.2 [1]

The [2] inspiration comes from the light thrown upon a certain ideal [3]. This comes from the light of the soul breath [4] falling upon the mind. There are two shadows, one that falls [5] upon the sky and the other [6] which falls upon the ground, the former known to the mystic and the latter to everyone. When the breath which is developed is thrown outwardly [7], its radiance produces light, and it is the different shades and grades of this light which ~~appear~~ manifest in ~~dif.~~ various

Documents:

Gd.h. = a copy in the handwriting of Sherifa Goodenough, possibly made from her own longhand reporting, showing a few editorial changes

Gd.t. = a typewritten copy made on Gd.'s large-lettered typewriter, reflecting the changes made in Gd.h.

Hq.t. = a typescript made at International Headquarters, Geneva, for distribution to a limited number of Sufi centres

Hq.st. = a stencilled copy made at International Headquarters, Geneva, for distribution to a wider circle of Sufi centres

Notes:

1. Gd.t.: across top, Series III. <u>GATHA</u>. Number 2. Then below, "PASI ANFAS. BREATH."; Hq.t, Hq.t.: same as Gd.t., except the Invocation added and in Hq.t., and "BREATH" before "PASI ANFAS"
2. Gd.h.: Gd. later crossed out "The"; all other documents: "The" omitted
3. Gd.h.: Gd. later changed "ideal" to "idea"; all other documents: "idea"
4. Gd.h.: "light of the soul breath" became "radiance of the breath"; all other documents: "radiance of the breath"
5. Gd.h.: "falls" crossed out and "is projected" inserted; all other documents: "is projected"
6. Gd.h.: "the other" rewritten as "another"; all other documents: "another"
7. Gd.h.: "outwardly" replaced with "outward" and the comma omitted; all other documents: "outward" and no comma

colours, suggesting to the mystic the different elements of[8] which the [9]colours ~~are expres~~ denote. The same breath has its [10] different action when it is thrown within. It falls upon [11] mind like a searchlight and shows to the intelligence the object of its search as things seen in a [12] daylight. Thus man knows, without making [13] any effort on the part of the brain, all he wishes to know and expresses in the way the person [14] is ~~accustomed~~ qualified to express. Inspiration, therefore, is one thing, qualification another thing. The inspiration is perfect when expressed by the qualified souls. Nevertheless inspiration does not depend upon [15] the qualification. The light that the breath throws upon [16] is every case different in its radiance. When far-reaching it illuminates the deepest corners of the heart, where the light has never reached, and if breath reaches further the light is thrown upon the mind of God, the store of all the knowledge there is.

---

8. Gd.h.: "of" later crossed out;
   all other documents: "of" omitted
9. Gd.h.: "particular" added;
   all other documents: "particular"
10. Gd.h.: "its" later crossed out and "a" inserted;
    all other documents: "a"
11. Gd.h. "the" inserted;
    all other documents: "the"
12. Gd.h.: "a" crossed out;
    all other documents: "a" omitted
13. Gd.h.: "making" later crossed out and "made" inserted after "effort";
    all other documents: "making" omitted
14. Gd.h.: "the person" crossed out and replaced by "each individual";
    all other documents: "each individual"
15. Gd.h.: "does not depend upon the" is rewritten to read "is independent of";
    all other documents: "is independent of"
16. Gd.h.: "the mind" added;
    all other documents: "the mind" added

Sherifa Goodenough's longhand reporting.[1]

Florence, 31 October 1923[2]

[3]

The Interdependence of Life Within and Without

This subject can be considered from three different points of view: In the first place to consider this[4] our physical body, how this expresses all that it partakes[5] as a[6] food, as a[6] drink, as a[6] medicine. If a person has a grosser food [7]it is expressed outwardly,[7] [8]if one has a finer food [7]it is expressed outwardly,[7] if one has a purer food it is manifested outwardly, [8]if one has not the consideration of this, it is also manifested outwardly. The body shows the same

---

Documents:

Gd.lh.r. = Sherifa Goodenough's longhand reporting of a lecture given in Florence, Italy, on Pir-o-Murshid's first lecture tour in that country. No simultaneous translation in Italian has been found, and the Pir-o-Murshid must have spoken very slowly, often repeating his words, in order to enable his audience to understand the lecture. On this same document the lecture was edited by Gd., which is indicated in the notes by "(Gd.lh.r.)Gd.e."

Hq.st.1 = a stencilled copy of the lecture, made at Headquarters, Geneva from "(Gd.lh.r.)Gd.e." and included by Gd. in the Headquarters' series of Gathekas. The first half of the lecture (up to ". . .to discriminate between right and wrong and between good or bad") was made into Gatheka nr. 5; the second half (from "And now coming to the point of religion. . .") became Gatheka nr. 6

Hq.t. = a typescript made at Headquarters, Geneva from "Hq.st.1", also divided into Gatheka 5 and Gatheka 6

Hq.st.2 = a slightly revised copy of "Hq.st.1", used to preserve the lecture on a microfiche, also made into Gatheka 5 and Gatheka 6. If in the notes a change refers to both "Hq.st.1" and "Hq.st.2", only "Hq.st." is mentioned

Notes:

1. See "Gd.lh.r." under "Documents" above
2. Gd.lh.r.: added "Filosofica", the hall where the lecture was given in Florence
3. Ibid: later added by Gd. in hwr.: "Gatheka" and in another hwr.: "No.5 - 6"; Hq.st., Hq.t.: first half of the lecture, added "GATHEKA Number 5.", followed by the Invocation; Hq.st., Hq.t.: second half of the lecture, added "GATHEKA Number 6.", followed by the Invocation. Under the title is added: "(Continuation)"
4. Hq.st.2: "this" omitted
5. Ibid.: "of" added
6. (Gd.lh.r.)Gd.e.: "a" crossed out; Hq.st., Hq.t.: "a" omitted
7. (Gd.lh.r.)Gd.e.: "it is expressed outwardly" crossed out; Hq.st., Hq.t.: "it is expressed outwardly", "the nature", "it takes the seed", and "it produces" omitted
8. Ibid.: "or" added

nature, [7]the nature[7] which it has inherited from the earth, to which it belongs; for the nature of this earth is such that when it takes the seed of flowers it produces flowers, and when [7]it takes the seed[7] of fruits, [7]it produces[7] fruits, and when it takes the seed of poison it produces poison. All different things are produced, but it is what it has taken; that is[9] the [10]. There is nothing that one eats or drinks or that this body takes which will be so assimilated altogether that this body will not manifest it outside. And in this way we can see the meaning of the subject that I am going to take today in the consideration of our physical body.

And when we think still further[11] we shall find ~~that~~ the action of the body on the mind and the action of the mind on the body. And that must be understood first by considering how intoxicants have a reaction on the mind, something which is quite material, something[12] which is physical, and[13] when that is taken, how it affects the mind, which is not material. The mind in point of fact is much greater than what the scientist today considers[14], the brain.

The word "mind" comes from the Sanskrit word *mana*[15], and from this word the English word "man" comes. Therefore, really speaking, what is man? What is his mind? [16]The words of Jesus Christ, that[17] man is as he thinks, man is his thought, man is his mind. Therefore it is not always the body, to which man attributes himself so much, that is his identification; his true identification is his mind.

All that one partakes[5] even physically in the form of[18] ~~outward~~ either[19] food or intoxicant, all that[20] has not only an[21] effect upon the body, but has

---

9. (Gd.lh.r.)Gd.e.: first "that is" changed into "these are", then restored to "that is"
10. Gd.lh.r.: an open space; (Gd.lh.r.)Gd.e.: "result" filled in;
    Hq.st., Hq.t.: "result" added
11. All other documents: "farther"
12. (Gd.lh.r.)Gd.e.: "something" crossed out;
    Hq.st., Hq.t.: "something" omitted
13. (Gd.lh.r.)Gd.e.: "and" crossed out;
    Hq.st., Hq.t.: "and" omitted
14. Ibid.: "it" added
15. Hq.t.: "manas": see glossary
16. (Gd.lh.r.)Gd.e.: "In" added;
    Hq.st., Hq.t.: "In" added
17. (Gd.lh.r)Gd.e.: "that" crossed out;
    Hq.st., Hq.t.: "that" omitted
18. (Gd.lh.r.)Gd.e.: "of" crossed out;
    Hq.st., Hq.t.: "of" omitted
19. Ibid.: "of" added
20. (Gd.lh.r.)Gd.e.: "all that" crossed out;
    Hq.st., Hq.t.: "all that" omitted

effect[22] upon the mind, and not only what the body partakes, but also what the mind partakes through the senses, that[17] has also[23] its influence on the body. For instance, all that one sees, it[24] is impressed upon the mind. One cannot help it, it is mechanically done, that impression is recorded. All that one hears, all that one[25] smells, all that one[25] tastes or touches, it is not that its effect is only upon the body, but its effect is upon the mind. That means that man's contact with the outer world is such that there is a continual mechanical interchange that is[26] going on; every moment of his life he is partaking all that his senses allow him to take in. [27]And therefore very often [28]man who is looking for the faults of the[29] others—when man[30] is looking at the evil—[31]he may not be a wicked person, but[32] he is partaking, without knowing it, all that is evil. And then the result is this: for instance, a person is impressed by a deceitful person. Now the [10] of that impression is that even when upon the honest person he will cast his glance[33], he will have the impression of deceit. And it is from this that all the pessimistic attitude comes. A person once deceived always is on the lookout; even with the honest person, he looks for deceit; he holds that impression within himself. For instance, a hunter who has come from the forest with a slap given to him by the lion, when he comes home, even the caress of his kind mother frightens him, that the lion has come[34]. When we consider how many impressions, agreeable and disagreeable, without knowing the consequence of it, we partake from morning till evening, and in this way, without a person's meaning to become wicked, he turns to become[35] wicked.

---

21. (Gd.lh.r.)Gd.e.: "an" crossed out;
    Hq.st., Hq.t.: "an" omitted
22. (Gd.lh.r.)Gd.e.: "has effect" crossed out;
    Hq.st., Hq.t.: "has effect" omitted
23. Hq.t.: "also" omitted
24. (Gd.lh.r.)Gd.e.: "it" crossed out;
    Hq.st., Hq.t.: "it" omitted
25. (Gd.lh.r.)Gd.e.: "all that one" crossed out;
    Hq.st., Hq.t.: "all that one" omitted
26. (Gd.lh.r.)Gd.e.: "that is" crossed out;
    Hq.st., Hq.t.: "that is" omitted
27. (Gd.lh.r.)Gd.e.: a new paragraph indicated
28. (Gd.lh.r.)Gd.e.: "the" added;
    Hq.st., Hq.t.: "the" added
29. (Gd.lh.r.)Gd.e.: "the" crossed out;
    Hq.st., Hq.t.: "the" omitted
30. (Gd.lh.r.)Gd.e.: "when man" replaced with "who"
    Hq.st., Hq.t.: "who" instead of "when man"
31. Ibid.: "though" added
32. Ibid.: "yet" added
33. Ibid.: "he will cast his glance" moved to before "upon the honest person"
34. Ibid.: "that the lion has come" rewritten to read, "he thinks the lion came"
35. (Gd.lh.r.)Gd.e.: "to become" crossed out
    Hq.st., Hq.t.: "to become" omitted

[36]For in point of fact nobody is born wicked. For although the body belongs to the earth, yet the soul belongs to God. And from above nothing man [37] has got except goodness. The most wicked [38] person in the world, when you can touch the deepest depth of his being it is nothing but goodness. Therefore, if there is such a thing as wickedness, or badness, it is only that he has acquired it, and acquired it not willingly, but only by being open to all impressions, as it is natural that every man is open to impressions.

No doubt the secret of what may be called [39]superstition, which exists in the East and sometimes also in the West, the superstition of the omen is in this, in the impression. For instance, there have been beliefs that if you hear the sound of a certain bell there will be [40], or if you see such a person, good luck or bad luck will come to your family. People have sometimes believed blindly, and went [41] on believing for many, many years. Then other intellectual ones thought there was nothing in those superstitions, and have ignored them. But at the end of the study one will find that the secret of all those superstitions is nothing but the impressions, that it is only that what the mind has taken through the senses has its effect [42] upon the body alone, but also upon his [43] affairs.

There is the science of physiognomy or phrenology which goes as far as saying that [44] one acquires [45] helps [46] the different muscles of the features and head, according to what one has taken in his mind. And it is written in the *Qur'an* that every part of man's being will bear witness of his action. I should

---

36. (Gd.lh.r.)Gd.e.: indicated that no new paragraph should begin here
37. (Gd.lh.r.)Gd.e.: "man" moved to after "has"
    Hq.st., Hq.t.: "man" after "has"
38. (Gd.lh.r.)Gd.e.: "The most wicked" changed into "With the wickedest";
    Hq.st., Hq.t.: "With the wickedest"
39. Ibid.: "a" added
40. Gd.lh.r.: an open space;
    (Gd.lh.r.)Gd.e.: later filled in "a death in your surroundings,";
    Hq.st., Hq.t.: "a death in your surroundings,"
41. (Gd.lh.r.)Gd.e.: "went" changed to "gone";
    Hq.st., Hq.t.: "gone" instead of "went"
42. Ibid: added "not"
43. (Gd.lh.r.)Gd.e.: "his" changed into "man's"
    Hq.st., Hq.t.: "man's" instead of "his"
44. Ibid.: "what" added
45. Gd.lh.r.: a small space;
    Hq.st., Hq.t.: no space left open
46. Gd.lh.r.: an open space;
    (Gd.lh.r.)Gd.e.: later filled in"to form";
    Hq.st., Hq.t.: "to form"

say that it does not need to bear [47] witness in the hereafter, it bears [47] it every hour of the day. [48] If one will examine life, one will find that the mind and body are formed from what one takes from the outer world. As there are the words of Christ, "Where your treasure is there will your heart be also." [49] All that one values, it is that which he makes in [50] himself; he creates in himself all that he values. No doubt when a person is an admirer of beauty, he will always partake all that he sees as beauty, beauty of form, of color, of line, and beyond that beauty of manner, of attitude, which is a greater beauty still. No doubt, at this time of the condition of the world man ignores very much the beauty of culture and fineness. No doubt, it gives a warning that the world, instead of going forward, is going backward, for the reason that civilisation is not only an industrial development or a material culture, and if that is called civilisation it is not the right word for the right thing. And the explanation of civilisation is not very difficult to give. It is progress toward harmony, beauty, and love. And when one goes back from these three great principles of life, one may be very creative, but at the same time, it is not civilisation.

No doubt every race and every creed has its principles of right and wrong, but there is one [51] principle of religion, and one in which all creeds and all peoples can meet. And that principle is to see in action, [52] in thought and feeling, beauty. There is no action upon which there is a stamp that this is wrong or right. But what can be wrong, what can be [53] wicked, is what our mind is accustomed to see as wrong or wicked, because it is void of beauty. The one who, therefore, seeks beauty in all its forms, in action, in feeling, in manner, he will impress his heart with beauty.

[36]All the great ones who have come in the world from time to time to waken humanity to a greater truth, what did they teach, what did they bring to the world [54]? They brought beauty. It is not what they taught, it is what they

---

47. (Gd.lh.r.)Gd.e.: first changed "bear" and "bears" into "give" and "gives", then restored to "bear" and "bears"
48. Hq.st.2: "Now" added
49. See the New Testament, Matthew 6.21
50. Hq.t.: "in" omitted, but later Sk. again added "in" in ink
51. Gd.lh.r.: an open space; (Gd.lh.r.)Gd.e.: later filled in: "fundamental"; Hq.st., Hq.t.: "fundamental" added
52. Ibid.: added "in attitude,"
53. (Gd.lh.r.)Gd.e.: "what can be" replaced with "or"; Hq.st., Hq.t.: "or" instead of "what can be"
54. Hq.st., Hq.t.: "to the world" omitted

were themselves. The intellectual understanding of[55] beauty, or the talking about beauty: one cannot talk, one cannot speak enough about it; words are too inadequate to express either goodness or beauty. One can say in a thousand words, and yet one will never be able to express it. For it is something which is beyond words, and the soul alone can understand it.

And the one who will always follow in his life, in every little thing he does, the rule of beauty, he will always succeed, and he will always be able to discriminate between right and wrong and between good and bad[56].

[57]And now coming to the point of religion, looking at the subject from the spiritual point of view, there is a story told in India of the magic lantern which Aladdin saw. And what is this magic lantern? This is a magic lantern which is hidden in the heart of every soul. Only for the time being its light becomes covered, and all the tragedy of life comes from this covering of light. Why does man seek for happiness? Because happiness is his own being. It is not because he loves happiness or he would like to be happy, but he is happiness himself. And why does he seek for it? He seeks for it because he is happiness, and yet when he finds the happiness closed, he wants to look for it.

[36]Only the mistake that he makes, and that perhaps every man makes, is that he looks for[58] that happiness which could be found inside, he looks for it[24] outside.

The most powerful words that Christ has spoken are, "I am the truth and I am the way".[59] Now to consider this ~~phenom~~ sentence, "I am the truth and I am the way." This shows there are two things; there is truth, one thing, and there is the way, another thing. And when people confuse these two things, then they become perplexed and cannot find the way.

For the idea is this, that in the first place man always makes a wrong use of the word "truth". For he always calls fact "truth", but truth is something which uproots altogether the fact. But then what is fact? Fact is the illusion of truth, but fact is not the truth. [27]But now you may ask me, "What is truth?" That is the one thing you cannot speak in words. During my travelling very often I was asked, "But tell the Truth, tell us something about the Truth." When very much

---

55. (Gd.lh.r.) Gd.e.: "of" changed to "about";
    Hq.st., Hq.t.: "about" instead of "of"
56. Gd.lh.r.: added in hwr. by Sk.: "(to be continued.)"
57. (Gd.lh.r.)Gd.e.: at this point Gd. divided the lecture in two parts and indicated that here should begin the part made by her into Gatheka nr. 6; in Sk.'s hwr. added: "(Continued)"
58. (Gd.lh.r.)Gd.e.: "he looks for" crossed out;
    Hq.st., Hq.t.: "he looks for" omitted
59. See The New Testament, John 14:6: "I am the way, the truth, and the life."

urged by people I sometimes thought that [17] if I could have some bricks and I could write upon them, "Truth", and say, "Now hold it fast, for this is the Truth." For if Truth were so small that our human words could speak about it, or could contain it, then it could not be Truth.

[36] Therefore the Sufis have always named Truth by the word *Haqq*, which in other words means God Himself. It is that Truth which is the seeking of us all. And it is the most wonderful thing that one can see, that in the world, however false a person, he does not want another person to deceive him, or to be false to him. A man whose profession may be lying, from morning till evening he may be lying, but he does not want his wife to lie to him [60] when he comes home.

But what we do is that we satisfy [61]our craving for truth by[61] facts, supposing that they are truth. And it is by this contentment that so many creeds exist in this world and so many beliefs [62], and so [63] many so many beliefs, and they fight with one another. But nothing can satisfy the craving of our soul, which is continually in search of the Truth which no words can speak.

But now coming to the other part, "I am the way", it is a great problem to consider. The one who wants to find it at the first step, he very often [64]mistakes. He may find it, but it is not always so. But it is very strange how man ~~will~~ gives years and years in [65] the study of grammar, music, or science, but when it comes to the Truth, then he wants from you a direct answer. And if it were the lack of patience on his part, he [66] would be excusable; but it is not often so, he considers the Truth so little. [27] If he was [67] too eager, if he were too impatient, it were [68] possible that in one step he might reach the Truth; for there is every reason to be hopeful. For it is difficult to get gold, it is not so difficult if one really wants [45] the Truth. For gold is something which is outside; the Truth is something which is within ourselves. But how man wanders about all

---

60. (Gd.lh.r.)Gd.e.: "to him" crossed out;
    Hq.st., Hq.t.: "to him" omitted
61. (Gd.lh.r.)Gd.e.: rewritten to read: "ourselves and are contented with";
    Hq.st., Hq.t.: "ourselves and are contented with"
62. (Gd.lh.r.)Gd.e.: "beliefs" changed into "faiths";
    Hq.st., Hq.t.: "faiths" instead of "beliefs"
63. (Gd.lh.r.)Gd.e.: "so" crossed out;
    Hq.st., Hq.t.: "so" omitted
64. Hq.t.: Sk. added "makes" in ink in the margin
65. (Gd.lh.r.)Gd.e.: "in" changed into "to";
    Hq.st., Hq.t.: "to" instead of "in"
66. Hq.t.: Sk. changed "he" to "it" in ink
67. (Gd.lh.r.)Gd.e.: "was" changed to "were";
    Hq.st., Hq.t.: "were"
68. Hq.t.: Sk. changed "were" to "would be"

his life in search of something which can only be found within himself!

Only there is one consideration, the way. Why is there a way? The reason is: It is not because there is not already a way made between man and God. There was a way between man and God, but man has gone astray from the way; therefore, man is shown the way by his elder brother. For instance, if there was not a way, it would certainly be unjust to the birds and insects and all creatures if there was a bliss which is only given to man. God, Who [69] is the perfection of justice, in Whom [70] no injustice to be found, and He has not excluded any soul, however small, from this bliss.

And now coming to man, it seems that even the birds and beasts have their times when they concentrate, they meditate in their own way and they offer their prayer to God. There is no being on the earth, however small, who does not contemplate for a moment. And if man's sight were keen, he would also see in the mountains and in the trees, by sitting in the solitary woods, by sitting in the caves of the mountains, that they all have their prayer and they all have their at-one-ment with God. Why did [71] the great ones, the souls who did [71] not find rest and peace in the midst of the world, go to the wilderness? It was [72] in order to breathe the breath of peace, of calm that comes to them in the heart of the wilderness. And man, who is the most intelligent of all, is the most astray and has lost the way, in spite of all the pride that he has, that he has created an artificial world as an improvement upon nature. But in creating this artificial world he has lost his way. And in this artificial world that he has made, [73] is he happy? Does he not cause bloodshed every time more and more, and every time even worse than before? Is he not unjust to his fellow man? Is he not deceitful toward his fellow man? A world which can give him that intoxication and that can absorb all his mind and time and effort in that intoxication, how can that give him that happiness which is the craving of his soul?

It is therefore that the way has from time to time been shown to him who [74] and will be shown to him who for a time lifts his head up from this world and asks for the way to be shown. And although the way seems to be very far, yet the distances cannot be compared with the distances of this earth. The way

---

69. (Gd.lh.r.)Gd.e.: "Who" crossed out;
Hq.st., Hq.t.:"Who" omitted
70. Ibid.: "there is" added
71. (Gd.lh.r.)Gd.e.: "did" changed to "do";
Hq.st., Hq.t.: "do" instead of "did"
72. (Gd.lh.r.)Gd.e.: "was" changed to "is";
Hq.st., Hq.t.: "is" instead of "was"
73. Ibid.: "as a paradise" added
74. (Gd.lh.r.)Gd.e.: "to him who" crossed out;
Hq.st., Hq.t.: "to him who" omitted

is as [75] short, and even shorter than an inch, and it can be as long and as distant as thousands of such worlds as that where we are. This way contracts and stretches according to the attitude of the soul. However, there is one hope, and that is as God says in the scripture, "The one who comes to me one step, I go forward to him one hundred steps." [76]

Although there are many different opinions how the condition of the world should be bettered— [77] some think [78] by religious reform, some think by educational reform, some think by social reform the world can be bettered—and every reform made with the idea of doing some good is worthwhile. But the reform which is most needed today is the spiritual reform. Today the hour has come when narrowness should be abandoned, and that one may rise above those differences and distinctions which divide mankind [79]. And it is this rising which will raise our fellow men. For the Lord is not pleased when some children of His are considered one's brothers and sisters, and other children of His are considered as separate. For no father is pleased at seeing some children of his favoured and others neglected.

[36] What we need today is to train ourselves to tolerance to one another.

By spiritual reform I do not mean looking for wonder working or talking about metaphysical ~~and~~ problems. For the problem which is to be solved is solved by itself. We have only to wish and it is solved. What problem we have to solve today is the problem of reconciliation and reconstructions [80]. [81]

The way to spirituality is the expansion of the heart, the widening of the heart, in [82] order to accommodate the divine Truth [83]. Truth it is the heart which must be expanded, and it is with the expansion of the heart that the divine bliss is poured out. The true spirituality is the raising of the consciousness to that

---

75. Hq.st., Hq.t.: "so" instead of "as"
76. Actually from a *hadith* (saying) of the Prophet Muhammad.
77. (Gd.lh.r.)Gd.e.: "-" replaced with "and";
    Hq.st., Hq.t.: "and" added
78. Ibid.: "that" added
79. (Gd.lh.r.)Gd.e.: "mankind" changed to "men";
    Hq.st., Hq.t.: "men" instead of "mankind"
80. (Gd.lh.r.)Gd.e.: plural 's' of "reconstruction" crossed out;
    Hq.st., Hq.t.: "reconstruction"
81. (Gd.lh.r.)Gd.e.: later added, "which neither the politicians nor the statesmen have been able to solve, but it can only be solved by spiritual awakening.";
    Hq.st., Hq.t.: added the same passage, but ending with "by a spiritual awakening";
82. (Gd.lh.r.)Gd.e.: "in" changed to ". In";
    Hq.st., Hq.t.: ". In"
83. Ibid.: "Truth." omitted and the sentence continues with the following word "Truth"

plane which is the [84] of the Divine Being.

---

84. Gd.lh.r.: a small blank; (Gd.lh.r.)Gd.e.: later filled in "abode"; Hq.st., Hq.t.: "abode"

Appendix A

In the left-hand column appears the title of the lecture as originally given (or, in the absence of a title, a few words from the first sentence), followed by the date and the page on which the lecture begins in the present volume. In the far right-hand column appears the chapter number for the material published in book form, or the classification by series and number for the material privately circulated to Sufi centres. In general, the Gathekas, Social Gathekas, and Religious Gathekas were intended for use in meetings open to the public. The Gathas and Githas were used in classes in the centres for the training of initiates.

The Book: *The Inner Life*

Title of Lecture:	Date:	Page:	Designation:
The Preparation for the Journey	1 Sept.	3	Chapter I
The Object of the Journey	2 Sept.	17	Chapter II
Fulfilment of the Obligations of Human Life	4 Sept.	31	Chapter III
The Realization of the Inner Life	5 Sept.	39	Chapter IV
Freedom of Action	6 Sept.	47	Chapter V
The Law of the Inner Life	7 Sept.	55	Chapter VI
The Object of the Inner Life	8 Sept.	62	Chapter VII
The Attainment of the Inner Life	9 Sept.	71	Chapter VIII
The Angel-Man	11 Sept.	93	Chapter IX
Five Different Kinds of the Spiritual Souls	12 Sept.	99	Chapter X

Gathekas

"...the Sufi's aim in life..."	25 Nov.	185	Social Gatheka
"...on music..."	6 Dec.	221	Social Gatheka. Number 23.
"In the prayer of the Christian Church..."	6 Dec.	228	Religious Gatheka. Number 6.
The Attitude	11 Dec.	247	Gatheka
The Manner of the Prayer	14 Dec.	262	Religious Gatheka. Number 4.
"...art..."	16 Dec.	272	Social Gatheka. Number 41.
Poetry	18 Dec.	293	Social Gatheka. Number 21.
Music	18 Dec.	303	Social Gatheka. Number 23.
"...harmony..."	after 18 Dec.	309	Social Gatheka. Number 4.
Sufism Not Passivism	?	339	Social Gatheka. Number 1.

Gatha 1922

"Among the Hindus..."	Dec.?	343	*Eteqad Rasm o Rivaj*. Series II. Number 10.

Gathas 1923

"...the large cobras..."	11 Feb.	349	*Pasi Anfas*. Series II. Number 7.
"Different conditions..."	13 Feb.	351	*Pasi Anfas*. Series II. Number 8.

"The...myth of Balder..."	Feb.	354	*Nakshi Bandi*. Series II. Number 8.
"There are superstitions..."	25 Sept.	356	*Etekad, Rasm u Ravaj*. Series III. Number 2.
Breath	25 Sept.	358	*Pasi Anfas*. Series III. Number 1.
"The real purity..."	25 Sept.	360	*Takua Taharat*. Series III. Number 1.
"As the rust..."	26 Sept.	362	*Takua Taharat*. Series III. Number 2.
"The inspiration comes..."	26 Sept.	364	*Pasi Anfas*. Series III. Number 2.

Githas

"The secret of the working of the whole universe..."	6 Dec.	223	*Sadhana*. Series II. Number 4.
"For worldly attainment..."	11 Dec.	240	*Sadhana*. Series II. Number 5.
"There are many in this world..."	13 Dec.	257	*Sadhana*. Series II. Number 6.

Glossary of Foreign Words

The language in which the word is used is indicated after each word:

Arabic = A
French = F
Greek = G
Hebrew = Hb
Hindustani, Hindi = H
Italian = I
Latin = L
Persian = P
Sanskrit = S
Urdu = U

The usual meaning of the word, if any, is given first; if the word has a special use in Sufi terminology, this meaning is given second, indicated by (Suf); if the word seems to be used in some special sense by Pīr-o-Murshid 'Ināyat Khān, this is indicated by (IK); the number(s) at the end indicate(s) the page number(s) where the word appears.

Transliterations were made according to the following systems:

for Arabic: *The Encyclopedia of Islam* (New edition, Leiden, 1960-), except "k" and "dj" which have been replaced by "q" and "j".

for Persian: F. Steingass, *Comprehensive Persian-English Dictionary*, (8th edition, London, 1977).

for Sanskrit: M. Monier-Williams, *Sanskrit-English Dictionary*, (New Delhi, 1976; originally published in 1899).

anānda (S) - pleasure, joy, bliss;
- (Suf) the soul's existence, happiness, 214

anuvādī (S) - the "assonant" tone in a *rāga*, 138

artha (S) (*arth*) - aim, purpose; cause, motive, reason; advantage, use, utility; desire for riches, second motive in life according to Hinduism, along with *kama* (wish, desire) and *dharma* (q.v.); used in wishing well to another, 187

astāī (H) (***sthāī***) - the first section of a Hindustani melody;
- (IK) a new way of singing *khayāl*, the Mughal technique applied to Indian *rāgas*, 141, 147f.

aṭa-chautāla (H)- crooked four-beat time in Northern Indian music
- (IK) a rhythm of *dhrupad*, 145

ātman (S) - breath, soul;
- (Suf) soul, the real being of a person, 130

bāhya (S) - a small drum, the smaller of the two drums of a *tābla* set, 143

bānī (S) - a musical style, of which four or five are traditional;
- (IK) used in a more general sense for a school of vocal culture, 150

bhairavī (H) - one of the principal *rāgas*, meaning "ascetic", 139

bhajana (S) - worship; a religious song or recital, in which a choir may join the soloist, with instrumental accompaniment, 142

but (F) - end in the sense of goal, purpose, 219

chakra (H) - circular wooden castinets;
- (IK) a form of folk song, with strong rhythm, 149

chanda (S) - metre, one of the bases on which *prabandhas* (q.v.) are classified, 140, 144

chishtiyya (A,P) - one of the principal orders of Ṣūfīs, mainly on the Indian subcontinent, named after the city of Chisht in Khorāsān, 307-8

dādarā (H) - a semi-classical form of singing, and the syncopated rhythm associated with such singing;
- (IK) a folklore style of poetry set to music, with an odd rhythm, 150

deva (S) - heavenly, shining, divine; a deity, god; light, divine spark;
- (Suf) an angel, 94;
- (IK) an ancient style of singing, 150

dha (H) - the sixth note in the octave of the Indian musical scale (*grama*), 137

dharma (S) - morality; duty, any given social group's particular caste obligations; religious law, set of ethical principles, 186

dhāru (H) - an old form of singing;
- (IK) martial music in Prakrit period, 140, 145, 152

dhovā (S) - an old form of singing;
- (IK) a song in praise of a king, 145

dhrupada (S) (*dhurpada*) - an highly specialised and prized style of classical singing of ancient origin, 140, 145, 152

dim (H) - a syllable without meaning or "drum word" used in *tarānā* (q.v.) to turn vocal recital into "absolute" music, 201

etekad, eteqad - see *'itiqād*, etc.

farīstha khāslat (P/U)- angelic nature or disposition, 93

ga (H) - the third note in the octave of the Indian musical scale (*grama*), 137

gāndharva (S) - singers in the Hindu paradise of the god Indra, 150

gāthā (S) - verse, song, metre; part of the scripture of the Parsis
- (Suf) the name Pīr-o-Murshid 'Ināyat Khān gave to a series of his teachings, including several categories, 343 n. 1, 349 n. 1, 351 n. 1, 354 n. 1, 356 n. 1, 358 n. 2, 360 n. 2, 362 n. 1, 364 n. 1

gāthaka (S) - chanting of a sacred poem
- (Suf) the name Pīr-o-Murshid 'Ināyat Khān gave to a series of his teachings, including several categories, spelled *gatheka*, 185 n. 3,5, 222 n. 3, 228 n. 1, 247 n.2, 262 n. 2, 273 n. 2, 293 n. 1, 303 n. 3, 309 n. 2, 339 + n. 2

gāyātri (S) - singing; heavenly chants; a metre of Sanskrit poetry, 150

gīta (S) - song, hymn; a style of Indian singing, said to have ended in the 12th century, 145

gītha (S) - a variation of the word *gīta*
- (Suf) the name Pīr-o-Murshid 'Ināyat Khān gave to a series of his teachings, including several categories, 223 n. 1, 3, 231 n. 2, 240 n. 3, 257 n. 3

'itiqād, rasm o riwāj- (A, P/U) - beliefs (superstitions), habits and customs
- (Suf) used as the title of a series of lectures (*gāthās*); with a change of sequence, Pīr-o-Murshid 'Ināyat Khān called it "Superstitions, customs and beliefs", 343, 356

jhaptāla (H) - a rhythm (time measure) in Indian music, based on a combination of two and three beats, 145

jinn (A, P/U) - a spirit, inhabitant of an intermediary world between the angelic and the human, 94

jogiyā (H) - a *rāga* of the *bhairavī* (q.v.) group, 321

kaharvā (H) - a rhythm (*tāla*) of eight counts used in *ṭhumṛī* (q.v.);
- (IK) a *ṭhumṛī* used by dancers who sing while dancing, 149

kālaṅgaḍā (H) - a very popular *rāga*, especially for devotional songs, 139

kānhaḍā (H) - an important *rāga*, the name of which refers to the Karnatic music of south India, 139

kavitta (H) - a musical composition with a high density of words per line;
- (IK) an ancient song in Sanskrit, 144

khyāla (H) - a major vocal form in Hindustani music, 141

kīrtana (H) - a Carnatic, i.e. south Indian, form of melody, 140, 151

kṛiti (H) - a Carnatic, i.e. south Indian, form of melody, 140, 151

la (H) - a syllable without meaning or "drum word" used in *tarānā* (q.v.) to turn vocal recital into "absolute" music, 201

lavani (H) - (IK) a folk song composed by an amateur poet, 149

ma (H) - the fourth note in the octave of the Indian musical scale (*grama*), 137

malhāra (H) - a *rāga* associated with Tān Sen (q.v. in List of Persons etc.), said to be capable of producing rainfall, 139

mālkos (H) - a *rāga* of the *bhairavī* (q.v.) group, sometimes called *mālakauṅśa*, 139

mantra (S) - sacred text, prayer, 150

māṭhā (H) - an old style of singing;
- (IK) folk songs of the street, 140, 145, 146, 152

māyā (S) - subject to change, illusion, 38, 113

mīrāsī (H) - a category and caste of Muslim musicians in north India, with rural roots;
- (IK) a musician's interpretation of folklore, 150

mṛdaṅga (H) - the drum most used in Karnatic (south Indian) music, 145, 152

mukhya (H) - an outline or basic set of phrases of a *rāga*;
- (IK) keynote of a *rāga*, 138

Nada Brahma (S)- literally "sound God", meaning: God, the Creator, 198, 205, 267

nafs (A, P/U) - self, ego; essence, (see following entries)

nafs-i alimah (A,P) - the knowing self;
- (Suf) the fourth stage of the development of the self, where it knows the reasons for acting as it does, and always does right, 336-7

nafs-i ammarah (A,P)- the refractory self;
- (Suf) the lowest state of the self, characterized by ignorance and sensuality, 334-5

nafs-i lawwāma (A,P)- the repentant self;
- (Suf) the second stage of the development of the self (or ego), where intelligence begins to control, 335

nafs-i mutmāina (A,P)- the benevolent self;
- (Suf) the third stage in the development of the of self, in which the intelligence (as the voice of God) keeps the self from doing wrong, 335-6

nafs-i salima (A,P)- the perfected self;
- (Suf) the highest, perfected state of the self, exemplefied by a prophet, 337

naqsh-i kul (P)- meaning "throne of God" in medieval Persian; a *qalbāna* associated with Amir Khusrau (q.v. in List of Persons, Places, and Works), 142

ni (H) - the seventh note in the octave of the Indian musical scale (*grama*), 137

nirvāṇa (S) - extinguishment, annihilation;
- (IK) perfect peace, the equivalent of *samādhi* (q.v.), 307

pa (H) - the fifth note in the octave of Indian musical scale (*grama*), 137

Pagliacci (I) - see *I Pagliacci* in List of Persons, Places, and Works.

pakhawāj (H) - a drum similar to a *mṛdaṅga* (q.v.), used in northern India, 152

pallavi (H) - the first section of the melody in south Indian *rāga*s, corresponding to *astāï* (q.v.), 151

pasī anfās (A, P)- literally "watching breath";
- (Suf) the name Pīr-o-Murshid ʻInāyat K͟han gave to a category of his teachings, translated as "Breath", 349, 358 n. 2, 364

payg͟hambar (P)- message-bearer, prophet, 300

pilu (H) - a well-known *rāga* from the *kāphī* group, 139

prabandha (S) - a ancient form of singing, primarily Sanskrit;
- (IK) a metre rendered to music, 144-5

propkar (S) - charity, benevolence, 256

purana (S) - ancient lore; collections of myth and legend, 151

qalbāna (P) - a kind of song (see also *naqsh-i kul*), 142

rāga (S) - root meaning: to colour; that which creates feeling; a theme or a mode in Indian music; a fixed arrangement of notes, around which a musician improvises, 137, 138, 139, 320 f., 324

re (S) - the second note in the octave of the Indian musical scale (*grama*), 137

riāzat (U) - abstinence, discipline; asceticism;
(*riyādat*, A) - (IK) Sufi word for meditation, 74

sa (S) - the first note in the octave of the Indian musical scale (*grama*), 137

sādhanā (S) - subduing, mastering, accomplishing; leading straight to a goal;
- (Suf) the name Pīr-o-Murshid 'Ināyat Khan gave to a category of his teachings, translated as "The Path of Attainment", 223, 240, 257 n. 3

sāhitya (S) - a text, especially one set to music, 145

samādhi (S) - a state of consciousness in which absolute peace is experienced, 199, 307, 325

saṃvādi (S) - the "consonant" note in a *rāga*, which is the musical fifth of the *vādī* (q.v.), 138

saṅgīta (S) - general word for the arts of singing, playing musical instruments, and dancing, 145

sitār (S,H) - Indian musical instrument, mostly found in Northern India. The principles of the sitar are similar to those of the *vīṇā* (q.v.), but it is smaller and has no curved neck. The number of strings varies from three to seven. Its

the *vīṇā* (q.v.), but it is smaller and has no curved neck. The number of strings varies from three to seven. Its body is usually of gourd, cut in half, 152

sophia (G) - wisdom;
- (IK) often mentioned as related to the word *ṣūfī*

śruti (S) - in musical use, an interval smaller than a semi-tone, of which there are twenty-two to the octave, 137

ṣūfī (A) - usually derived from *ṣūf* (A), wool (woollen garments were worn by certain groups of ascetics as a sign of renunciation); applied to individuals and groups devoting their lives to inwardness and ascetism, eventually applied to the mystics generally, with the term *taṣawwuf* becoming the technical term for mysticism as such. An initiate does not traditionally refer to him- or herself as "a *ṣūfī*", but rather *mutaṣawwif*, one who is searching, or reaching out toward Sufism.

sūlaphā (H) - an irregular rhythm, meaning "zig-zag", properly *sūlaphākatā*, 145

svara (S) - diatonic interval, note; the seven notes of the scale, 152

tablā (S) - a small pair of drums used in northern Indian music, 143, 149, 152

takua - see *taqwā*

ṭappā (H) - a type of melody used in northern Indian singing, and the style of singing using those melodies;
- (IK) Persian vocal culture wedded to the Indian *rāga*, 148

taqwā ṭahārat (A)- piety is purity, God-consciousness as the means of purifying the self;
- (IK) the name Pīr-o-Murshid 'Ināyat Khan gave to a category of his teachings, translated as "Everyday Life",

		360 n. 2
tāranā (H)	-	a kind of Persian-influenced singing, where the text consists of the syllables for the rhythm (drum) notes, designed to render vocal music fully "absolute" by freeing it from verbal associations, 142, 201
tevrā (H)	-	a rhythm in north Indian music based on three and two beats, 145
ṭhumṛī (H)	-	a semi-classical style of singing in north India, 148-9
tītāla (H)	-	a rhythm in north Indian music based on three and two beats, also called *tīntāl* or *trītāla*, 145
tum (H)	-	a syllable without meaning or "drum word" used in *tarānā* (q.v.), 201
vādī (S)	-	the principal or "sonant" tone of a *rāga*, 138
vairāgya (S)	-	change or loss of colour; disgust, aversion; freedom from all worldly desires, indifference to life, asceticism; a *vairāgi* is a person with this quality;
	-	(Suf) indifference, independence, 95 f.
vīṇā (S)	-	Indian musical instrument;
(*bīn*) (H)	-	the *vīṇā*, the *bīn* of Northern India, also called *mahati vīṇā*, or *rudra vīṇā*, differs from the *sarasvati vīṇā* of Southern India. It is a stringed instrument, with seven strings and twenty-four frets, played with the fingernails or with a plectrum. The Northern *vīṇā* has two large gourd resonators, while the Southern one has a pear-shaped body and one gourd. Both instruments, often used for meditative purposes, were played with great mastery by Pīr-o-Murshid ‘Ināyat Khān
vivādī (S)	-	the "dissonant" tone of a *rāga*, opposed to the *vādī* (q.v.), 138 n. 2

List of Persons, Places, and Works

Akbar : (1542-1605) generally regarded as the greatest of the Mogul emperors of India, a patron of music (for a fuller entry, please see 1922 I), 152

Amīr Khusrau : (1253-1325) poet and musician, who decisively influenced the northern (Hindustani) style (for a fuller entry, please see 1922 I), 152

Arabian Nights : known as *The Arabian Nights' Entertainment* or *The Thousand and One Nights*, this extensive collection of stories in Arabic contains layers of text, the earliest from the 8th century extending up to the 16th century. There are many versions and various translations of different versions, but many stories incorporate alchemical elements, 132

Aurangzeb : (1618-1707) sixth of the "Great" Mogul emperors of India, known for his use of the religion of Islam as an opportune political ideology. He came to the throne through opposition to his liberal older brother Dārā Shūkoh, who had been influenced by the unusual figure, Sarmād (q.v.). They were both executed as heretics while Aurangzeb made his way to the throne. He also placed his father, Shāh Jāhan, under house arrest for the last years of his reign, 48

Baijū Bāvarā, Nāyaka : celebrated Indian composer of the 14/15th century, about whom little factual is known. His title Nāyaka indicates a master musician, whereas Bāvarā means "madman," apparently a reference to his unconventional life as a wandering mendicant. He is said to have invented a new style of singing, *hori-gāyakī*, and several important *rāga*s, including *gūjarī* *todī*. He was the teacher of Gopala (q.v.), 151

Balder : in Norse mythology, the beautiful and just son of the chief god Odin and his wife Frigg. He was killed when the blind god Höd, deceived by the evil Loki, hurled mistletoe at him, 354

Banda Nawāz : (1320-1422), full name Sayyed Muḥammad Gesū Darāz Banda Nawāz, Indian Ṣūfī saint and healer of the Chishtī Order, author of many books. His dargāh (tomb) near Gulbarga (Deccan) is a pilgrimage site, visited by Pīr-o-Murshid 'Ināyat Khān, whose grandfather was named after this saint, 198

Basel : industrial city and canton in northern Switzerland, on the Rhine river, near where Switzerland, France (Alsace), and Germany meet, 153

Beethoven, Ludwig van : (1770-1827) German composer, predominant in Western music in the early 19th century, 199

Bible, the : from the Greek *biblos*, title given to the combined collection of the Jewish Hebrew scriptures, known to Christians as the *Old Testament*, and the Greek Christian scriptures, the *New Testament*, 56

Bolshevists : a variation of Bolsheviks, meaning "majority" party, the Russian political faction led by Lenin which became predominant in the revolution of 1917, and became, in 1918, the Russian Communist Party, 318

Brahmins : Sanskrit *brāhmaṇa*, the highest social class in Hindu India, including the priests, philosophers, and scholars, 11

Christian Science : a church established by Mary Baker Eddy in 1879, with an emphasis on healing. Family history holds that Pīr-o-Murshid 'Ināyat Khān's third wife, an American whose maiden name was Ora Ray Baker, was related to Mrs. Eddy, 315

Clarens : a village in Switzerland near the east end of Lake Geneva, 169

Confucianism : a way of life founded in China by Confucius in the 6/5th century BCE, containing elements of religion and social philosophy and ethics, 78

Cushing, Marya : American woman who became a *mureed* at the Summer School in 1922, often called by her Sufi name, Khushi. She knew shorthand and sometimes assisted in taking down Pīr-o-Murshid 'Ināyat Khān's lectures. In the later years, she kept all the shorthand minutes at the International Headquarters of the Sufi Movement in Geneva from 1927-30. She died in 1948. (For more information, please see 1923 II or the *Biography*, 495), 1

David : (c. 1030-962 BCE), second king of Israel, who established Jerusalem as the capital and greatly extended the borders. He was also a musician and poet; more than half of the *Book of Psalms* in the Hebrew Scriptures is attributed to him, 304

Delibes, Léo : French composer (1836-1891) of operas and ballets, 148

Dīkshitar, Muttuswāmi : (1775-1835) south Indian composer of *kriti*s, a major genre of Karnatic classical music (stemming from the earlier *kīrtana*s), but strongly influenced by Hindustānī style. His Sanskrit texts are technically complex and full of mythological references; his musical style is dignified, with a slow tempo and heavily ornamented, 151

Dowland, Jessie Eliza : (18??-1953), English woman who became a *mureed* in 1919, known by her Sufi name Nargis. She managed a hotel in Southampton, England, and played a significant role in the publication of Pīr-o-Murshid 'Ināyat Khān's books, as well as writing three books herself. She remained active in the Sufi work all her life.

Egeling-Grol, Nelly : (1861-1939) Dutchwoman who became a *mureed* in 1921, and later a Murshida in the Sufi Order, known by her Sufi name Fazal Mai; she became a member of Pīr-o-Murshid 'Ināyat Khān's household in Suresnes, France, from 1922 on. (For further information, please see 1923 II), 17

Furnée, J. E. D. : (1896-1973) Dutchwoman who became a *mureed* in 1921, known by her Sufi name, Sakina (later Nekbakht). She became one of Pīr-o-Murshid 'Ināyat Khān's secretaries, and learned shorthand specifically to take down his lectures and other dictations, which she did most expertly. She became the keeper of the Biographical Department archives in Suresnes, and, through her creation of the Nekbakht Stichting, laid the foundations for these *Complete Works*, 1 and *passim*

Gaṇeśa (Ganesha) : elephant-headed god, son of Śiva (q.v.) and Pārvatī. As a giver of good fortune and remover of obstacles, Gaṇeśa is a very popular god in India, and his image is often seen at the entrance to temples or houses. As he symbolized devotion to parents and affectionate family life, his celebrations were often joined by Muslims, 143

Geneva : historic city and canton in southwestern Switzerland. After World War I it became the headquarters of the League of Nations, and was also adopted as the seat of the Sufi Order (from October 1923 on, the International Headquarters of the Sufi Movement) in the same period, 104

Genoa	: city on the northwestern shore of Italy (in Italian, Genova), 104
Goodenough, Lucy	: (1876-1937) Englishwoman who became a *mureed* in London during the First World War, and was known by her Sufi name, Sherifa. She became one of Pīr-o-Murshid 'Ināyat Khān's secretaries and the principal editor of his work for publication, and was initiated as a Murshida in 1923, 3
Gopāla, Nāyaka	: (15/16th century) a contemporary and perhaps student of Baijū (q.v.), also known as Gopāla Lāla, 152
Green--see Saintsbury Green	
Gruner, Dr. O. C.	: (1877-1972), English physician and medical researcher who was an early *mureed* in Leeds, England. He was probably the first person to take down Pīr-o-Murshid 'Ināyat Khān's lectures in shorthand, and he edited the early book *In an Eastern Rose Garden* (1921) and worked on a sequel, never published. In 1933 he moved to Montreal, Canada, where he lived and worked for the rest of his long life.
Ḥāfiẓ, Shams-ud-Dīn	: (1325?-1389), widely-known Persian poet, whose proverbial verses are quoted throughout the Muslim East (for a fuller entry, please see 1922 I), 20, 267, 271
Hogendorp, Jonkvrouwe Lakmé baronesse van	: daughter of Baron and Baroness (Mahtab) van Hogendorp van Notten. Her parents were among the first mureeds in Switzerland, and Pīr-o-Murshid 'Ināyat Khān often stayed at their home while visiting that country. She was still in her teens when Pīr-o-Murshid 'Ināyat Khān's dictated two series of musical lessons to

her.

Holland : properly an area on the west central coast of the Netherlands, including Haarlem and The Hague, but normally used as a name for the whole country, 104

I Pagliacci : opera composed by Ruggero Leoncavallo (q.v.) in 1892, 150

Jalāl-ud-Dīn Rūmī : (1207-1273) widely considered the greatest poet of the Persian language (for a fuller entry, please see 1922 I), 20, 209

Jāmī, Nūr-ud-Dīn : (1414-1492) Persian Sufi scholar and poet, often regarded as the last great mystical poet of Iran (for a fuller entry, please see 1923 I), 20

Jesus Christ : (4 BCE?-29 CE?) founder and central figure in the Christian religion, believed by Christians (and Muslims) to have been the Messiah, 6

Katwijk : seaside village in west central Netherlands, west of Leiden, divided into Katwijk-aan-Zee and Katwijk-aan-de-Rijn, where Pīr-o-Murshid ‘Ināyat Khān lectured in 1922, and where a Sufi congregational hall known as the Universel was later built (1975), 1 and *passim* through 103

Kerdijk, Kafia : a Dutchwoman who became a *mureed* in 1921, and who helped publish two Sufi booklets. She sometimes took down Pīr-o-Murshid ‘Ināyat Khān’s lectures in the Netherlands, 66

Khwāja Moīnuddīn Chishtī : see Moīnuddīn Chishtī, Khwāja

Koran : see *Qur‘ān*

Kṛṣṇa (Krishna) : widely-worshipped god in India, considered the eighth incarnation of Vishṇu. He appears in art often carrying or playing a flute, 82, 304

Lakmé : opera composed by Léo Delibes (q.v.) in 1883, the title of which is derived from the Hindu goddess of good fortune, Lakṣmī, 148

Lausanne : city in western Switzerland, on the north shore of Lake Geneva, 163

League of Nations : international organization founded by the victorious Allies after World War I to solve political problems and foster cooperation; its headquarters were in Geneva; after World War II, it was replaced by the United Nations, many agencies of which still operate from that site, 104

Leoncavallo, Ruggero : Italian opera composer (1858-1919), 150

LLoyd, Gladys I. : Englishwoman on whose initiative the Healing Activity of the Sufi Movement was set up as a separate activity, of which she became the first secretary; she was known mainly by her title, Kefayat. She sometimes took down lectures by Pīr-o-Murshid 'Ināyat K̲h̲ān, 112

Mahābhārata : one of the two major epics of India, describing at length the struggle for supremacy between two related families; the most known section is the *Bhagavad Gītā*, where the god Kṛṣṇa (Krishna) appears as a charioteer. The work is traditionally attributed to Vyāsa, 82, 151

Mary, the Virgin : the mother of Jesus Christ, an object of veneration in Christian tradition. She is often depicted in art standing on a crescent moon, 92

Mas̄navī : fully *Mas̄navī-ye ma'navī* (The Spiritual Couplets), major poetical work of Jalāl-ud-Dīn Rūmī (q.v.), a vast compendium of Sufi lore conveyed in fables and anecdotes, 209

Mitchell, Edgar A. : (1877-1939) Englishman who became a *mureed* of Pīr-o-Murshid 'Ināyat Khān during the First World War in London, known by his Sufi name Shabaz. He worked as a journalist in Southampton, England. He sometimes wrote down the lectures of Pīr-o-Murshid 'Ināyat Khān in shorthand, 25, 35, 44, 50, 58, 68, 85

Mogul Empire : those large parts of India which were ruled by a Muslim dynasty from the early 16th to the mid-18th centuries, and continuing in a much reduced form to the mid-19th century (sometimes transliterated as "Mughal"), 321

Mo'īnuddīn Chishtī, Khwāja : (1135-1229) founding figure of the Chishtī Order in India, whose *dargah* (tomb shrine) in Ajmer remains an object of pilgrimage. The Chishtīs make much use of devotional music in their spiritual practise (for a fuller entry, please see 1923 I), 198

Montreux : a series of resort communities on the eastern end of Lake Geneva in western Switzerland, 173

Morges : village on the north shore of Lake Geneva in western Switzerland, between Geneva and Lausanne, 185

Moses : (13th century BCE) Hebrew prophet who received the Torah on Mount Sinai (for a fuller entry, please see 1922 I), 304

Muḥammad, the Prophet : (570-632 CE) Arab prophet whose messages from God constitute the scriptures of Islam, the *Qur'ān* (q.v.; for a fuller entry, please see 1922 I), 10

Muḥammad Shah : (1701-1748) Mogul emperor in India from 1719-1748. He is regarded as an exceptionally ineffective ruler, although he was a great patron of the arts, especially music, 152

Nārada : a legendary musical figure in India, said to be one of the ten mind-born sons of Brahma, and inventor of the vina. Another later figure also called Nārada wrote a musical treatise in the 6/7th century BCE, 151, 199

Nayak Bhaiji Bhawer : see Baijū Bāvarā, Nāyaka

Nayak Gopal : see Gopāla, Nāyaka

Orpheus : ancient legendary Greek hero with extraordinary skill in music and song. Many stories about Orpheus emphasize his ability to control situations through his music, 304

Paderewski, Ignacy : Polish composer, pianist, and statesman, who became the first Prime Minister of Poland in 1919. Pīr-o-Murshid 'Ināyat Khān met Paderewski and his family in Switzerland in the autumn of 1923, 199

Pagliacci : see *I Pagliacci*

Paul, St : a younger contemporary of Jesus Christ (q.v.), who at first bitterly opposed Christianity, but after a dramatic conversion became its most ardent missionary. His letters written to various Christian communities have become a substantial part of the New Testament, the Christian scriptures, 69, 82

Qur'ān : the sacred scripture of Islām, the record of the revelations received by the Prophet Muḥammad (q.v.), 55

Rāma : one of the most widely worshipped gods in India, considered the seventh incarnation of Vishnu, whose story is related in the epic poem *Rāmāyaṇa*, 82, 210

Rāmāyaṇa : epic poem, believed to have been composed around 300 BCE by Vālmīki, relating the life story of Rāma, 82, 115, 151

Rumi : see Jalāl-ud-Dīn Rūmī

Sadarang : a singer in the court of the Mogul Emperor Muḥammad Shah, 152

Saintsbury Green, Sophia : (d. 1939) one of the most important English *mureeds*, who was the first Cheraga ordained to perform the Universal Worship (in 1921) as well as the first secretary of that activity; she was initiated as a Murshida in 1923. She sometimes took down lectures of Pīr-o-Murshid 'Ināyat Khān, 3

Saraswatī : Hindu goddess of wisdom and art, consort of Brahma, venerated as the goddess of eloquence, 305

Sarmād : a curious figure associated with Dārā Shūkoh, eldest son and designated successor of Shāh Jāhan. He was a wandering ecstatic, said to be of Jewish origin, who became a tutor to the prince, and who was accused of heresy and executed by Aurangzeb (q.v.), younger brother of Dārā Shūkoh, who eventually displaced and executed Dārā Shūkoh as well, thus becoming emperor. No association with Gwalior is known for Sarmād; he died and was buried in Delhi, 48

Shori, Miyan : a hereditary musician in the court of Afsul Daula of Oudh in the late eighteenth century, who developed the use of *tāna* (q.v.) in *khayāl* (q.v.), 142

Sindhia Mahādāji : (reigned 1761-94) ruler in northern India, whose capital was the rock fortress of Gwalior, 326

Sītā : Hindu goddess, consort of Rāma and embodiment of wifely devotion and self-surrender, 210

Śiva (Shiva)	: one of the principal Hindu deities, a complex figure associated with both asceticism and sensuality; he is sometimes depicted dancing, and is associated in legend with the origins of the vina, 304
Śūdra (Shudra)	: lowest caste, the "once-born" servants, 343
Solomon	: (fl. mid-10th century BCE) third king of Israel, known for his building of the Temple in Jerusalem, and renowned for his wisdom and therefore considered the author of Proverbs and Ecclesiastes, 329
Southampton	: port on the English Channel, where Pīr-o-Murshid 'Ināyat Khān had a number of followers, and where he often lectured when he was in England, 3, 130
Tān Sen (Tansen, Tānasena)	: (d. 1586 or 1589) famous singer and composer in the court of the Emperor Akbar (q.v.). Pīr-o-Murshid 'Ināyat Khān received the title Tansen-uz-Zamān from the Nizam of Hyderabad, 152, 199
Tūmbara	: legendary musician; like Nārada (q.v.) he was called *ṛishi* (sage), and was thought of as belonging to the community of musicians called *gandharva* in the court of the god Indra, 151, 199
Tuyll, Sirdar and Saida van	: Dutch mureeds of Pīr-o-Murshid 'Ināyat Khān at whose seaside villa in Katwijk-aan-Zee the Dutch summer school of September 1922 was held, 1
Tyāgarāja	: (1767-1817) well-known Karnatic (south Indian) musician of Tanjore, revered as a saint (his name means "he who renounced the kings and courts"). He composed a large number of *kritis*, many based on his devotion to Rāma, and greatly influenced later developments in singing, 151
Vālmīki	: ancient sage who is believed to have been the author of the *Rāmāyaṇa* (q.v.) about 300 BCE, 151

Vedānta : the orthodox system of Hindu philosophy, based on the interpretation of the *Upanishads*, themselves elaborations on the most ancient scriptures, the *Vedas*, 37, 56

Vevey : small city on the northern shore of Lake Geneva in western Switzerland, between Lausanne and Montreux, 178

Wiseman, Salima : an early English *mureed* of Pīr-o-Murshid ‘Ināyat Khān who sometimes took down his lectures and who assisted Nargis Dowland in the publishing work in Southampton, 128

Zanetti, E. de Cruzat : (1875-194?) born in Cuba, he grew up in the United States and was graduated from Harvard, later taking a law degree from Harvard as well, having studied also in Geneva. He met Pīr-o-Murshid ‘Ināyat Khān in Geneva in 1922, became a *mureed*, and was asked to assume the position of Executive Supervisor of the Sufi organization, which he did, serving in that capacity until the mid-1930s. He died during the Second World War, 328

Zürich : largest city in Switzerland, located in the north central part of the country, 157

INDEX